Reviews of the Original Dutch Version of
Davai! The Russians and Their Vodka

All of the phenomena associated with Russian drinking that I know of appear in this book. Holding your breath, draining your glass in one swig, beer as a chaser, and usually a bite of something or other, pickle or smoked herring... All aspects of vodka and its consumption are discussed at length. Trommelen sets the tone, and literature completes the story... The entirety of Russian literature makes an appearance. Pushkin, Gogol, Turgenev, Dostoyevsky, Tolstoy, Babel, Blok, and Bunin – they have all written about vodka, and how! *Davai!* will stimulate your thirst like few other books.

Guus Luijters, *Het Parool*

Amid all the boozy quotes, Trommelen tells us about Russia, the land of alcohol, how the Russians drink, and why... *Davai!* "is not intended to be merely an ode to this representative of 'the green serpent,'" the author tells us. But his work does indeed become something of an ode – and a terrific one at that.

Olaf Tempelman, *Volkskrant*

A pleasant, easy-to-read, illustrated book in which Russians themselves remark on their drinking behavior, specifically in their literature across the centuries, from Dostoyevsky to Solzhenitsyn... But *Davai! The Russians and Their Vodka* is anything but a melancholy book. You can enjoy it in sips. You don't have to finish the bottle in one evening, and you don't have to drain the glass in one gulp. The book whets your appetite. You just keep reading. It seems to be just as addictive as that crystal-clear beverage.

Albert Megens, *Brabants Dagblad*

There has never before been such a comprehensive examination of that "drink that would give you strength when you are weak..." The book is full of examples of these sayings, and the literary quotes especially... make you crave more.

Fransiska Kleijer, *Tijdschrift voor Slavische Literatuur*

The Russians

DAVAI!

and Their Vodka

The Russians

DAVAI!

and Their Vodka

Edwin Trommelen

Translated by David Stephenson

Russian Life
BOOKS

Translation of this book was made possible through generous financial support from

N ederlands
letterenfonds
dutch foundation
for literature

Edited by Nora Seligman Favorov

Cover: *The Kissing Ceremony*, Vladimir Makovsky (1895)
Back cover author photo: Wim Salis

This book is an original translation of
Davaj! De Russen en hun wodka (Mets & Mets) © 2010, Edwin Trommelen
English translation copyright © 2012, Russian Information Services.
All rights reserved.

ISBN 978-1-880100-72-1

Library of Congress Control Number: 2012920079

Russian Information Services, Inc.
PO Box 567
Montpelier, VT 05601-0567
www.russianlife.com
orders@russianlife.com
phone 802-234-1956

Есть люди, умеющие пить водку, и есть люди, не умеющие пить водку, но все же пьющие ее. И вот первые получают удовольствие от горя и от радости, а вторые страдают за всех тех, кто пьет водку, не умея пить ее.

There are people who know how to drink vodka, and there are people who don't know how to drink vodka but drink it all the same. And the first lot, you see, get satisfaction from joy and from sorrow, and the second lot suffer for all those who drink vodka without knowing how to.[1]

Isaac Babel, *Odessa Tales:*
"How It Was Done in Odessa" (1923-25)

Зачем нужна свобода русскому человеку, если нет ему воли погулять да повеселиться всласть, на погибель души, на страх врагам, так, чтобы перед смертью, которая никого не минует, было что вспомнить?

Не любят русские люди мелочничать по углам, в одиночку, кустарным способом, в час по чайной ложке. Пускай так пьют алкоголики: американцы в Америке, французы во Франции. Они пьют, чтобы напиться – для затуманивания мозгов. Напьются, как свиньи, и – спать. А мы употребляем вино для усиления жизни и душевного разогрева, мы только жить начинаем, когда выпьем, и рвемся душою ввысь и возвышаемся над неподвижной материей, и нам для этих движений улица необходима, корявая провинциальная улица, загибающаяся черным горбом к белому небу.

What's the use of freedom to a Russian if he can't go a little wild and enjoy himself to the damnation of his soul, the terror of his enemies, and to have something to look back on before death, which spares no man?

We Russians are not fond of tippling behind closed doors, in solitude, on the sly, one teaspoon per hour. Let the alcoholics drink this way: the Americans in America, the French in France. They drink to get drunk, to cloud their brains. They drink like pigs then go to sleep. We drink to intensify life and to fire our souls. Only when we start drinking do we come to life, our spirit rising above all inert matter. And to achieve this we need a street, a crooked, provincial street that inclines toward the white sky in the form of a black hump.[2]

Abram Tertz, *The Makepeace Experiment* (1963)

– Так, значит, богу угодно. От судьбы не уйдешь. Сейчас вот мы икрой закусываем, а завтра, гляди, – тюрьма, сума, а то и смерть. Всякое бывает. Теперь взять к примеру хоть Петра Семеныча...

"So it is God's will, it seems. There is no escaping your fate. Here today we are eating caviar and tomorrow, for all we know, it will be prison, beggary, or maybe death. Anything may happen. Take Pyotr Semyonich, for instance. . . ."[3]

Anton Chekhov, "In Trouble" (1887)

Contents

Preface

И чего она все сердится! – жаловался он поминутно, как ребенок. – Tous les hommes de génie et de progrès en Russie étaient, sont et seront toujours des картежники et des пьяницы, qui boivent en zapoy... а я еще вовсе не такой картежник и не такой пьяница...

"But why is she always so angry!" he complained incessantly, like a child. "All men of genius and progress in Russia were, are and ever will be gamblers and drunkards who drink themselves into a stupor ... but I'm not yet such a gambler or such a drunkard, by no means."[1]

Fyodor Dostoyevsky, *Demons* (1871)

A BOOK ABOUT VODKA – hasn't there already been plenty written about that? This is a question I hear often. And yes, all sorts of things have been written about vodka, but most of those books talk about how the colorless beverage is made, then present a short history, a few cocktails and recipes, and a list of the best-known brands. These books do not say much about how people – in this case, Russians – relate to vodka, nor, especially, how it has been reflected in their literature.

When you say vodka, you're talking about Russia. Some nationalities – the Poles especially – might take umbrage at such a statement. Well, they can fight that out among themselves. It is no accident that Russia is the focus of my attention and love, though certainly not love alone. I began studying Russian in 1983 and lived there for six months. Since then I have traveled across the country many times. Most of my work has to do with Russia.

In all those years, the Russians have never disappointed me. They're a fascinating people – a people full of contrasts, to be sure, as this book will show – and the frequent visitor also discovers those contrasts in himself. By nature, I am a level-headed person, but in Russia I routinely lose my temper. Usually it's about some trivial matter that can't be helped. But the fits of dismay alternate with moments of bliss, because something you dared not dream of works out perfectly. You're unable to make a simple repair to your Lada, and just then a helicopter arrives to whisk you away. When I was a student in Moscow in 1986, I was treated like a prince, but now I sometimes get pitying looks when I say that I don't own a Mercedes and that I ride my bike or take the train everywhere. In short, it's a wonderful and unpredictable country, where the tears are bitterer and the laughter is heartier.

And of course, vodka is unavoidable there. You inevitably come across it sooner or later, usually sooner. In 1986, Gorbachev's prohibition campaign was underway. It was in the midst of this campaign that I had my first experience getting drunk on vodka. The ten different mini-bottles of vodka that I had bought in the hard currency store left a gruesome effect in their wake. My head remained crystal-clear, but my stomach was in tatters for two days. A lot more vodka followed in subsequent years: at the *kolkhoz* at ten in the morning with pickles and a little salt; at the prison camp in the middle of the day to stay on good terms with the officers; or in the evening – indeed, mostly in the evening – with friends sitting around the kitchen table.

Once, when I was moving, I had to throw away empty vodka bottles that had been gathering dust on my balcony. But I soon regretted it. I realized that those bottles carried memories, and so I deliberately began collecting bottles. But that's not a sustainable hobby, nor is it particularly interesting. So then I started collecting stories, or, better yet, quotes. But quotes without a story behind them are pointless. When I reflected on it further (over a glass of vodka), it occurred to me that, taken together, all those quotes could tell a story. A story about Russia.

My good fortune – "Russia's good fortune" – is that the country has one dominant drink: vodka. Other alcoholic beverages may be enjoyed, but none of them are woven into the fabric of Russian life the way (home-distilled) vodka is. But of course, it goes deeper than that. As a painter friend of mine put it: "Vodka has accompanied Russians on life's journey, it accompanies them here and now, and it will accompany them in the future." It is impossible to imagine life in Russia without vodka. At the same time, vodka is "Russia's sorrow." It claims many victims, and alcoholism has taken a devastating toll on rural Russia. The rate of alcohol-attributable mortality rises and falls in Russia, but consistently ranks among the highest in the world. Although this somber aspect is not an emphasis of my book, it is addressed. The book is not intended to be merely an ode to this representative of "the green serpent."

But the greatest good fortune for this book is Russia's unsurpassed literature, a literature that has produced heartbreaking vodka tableaux, full of euphoric moments of intoxication and binge drinkers gone astray, from pitiful village priests to fatalistic intellectuals. These vodka drinkers are what *Davai! The Russians and Their Vodka* is about. Of course, this book is also about vodka itself: an omnipresent and constant factor in Russian history, a drink for the great and the lowly, in times of happiness and in times of calamity. I hope that *Davai!* has become what I set out to create: a bittersweet book written with love and compassion for the Russian drinker and based on great respect for Russian culture. I also hope that the reader will gain as much enjoyment from reading it as I did from writing it, that it will be like a pick-me-up, something to warm the Western soul. And, finally, that the reader will gain a better understanding of Russians and what drives them.

NOTES FOR READERS

To promote legibility, I have not given years of birth and death for the quoted authors. I have indeed indicated the year in which the respective book was published, or in some cases – if the work was not published until much later – the year in which it was written, even if that is sometimes hard to know for sure. The same is true of the paintings and posters that are reproduced. In the "history" chapters, I did consider it important to provide the years of birth and death for the tsars and party leaders. To keep readers from losing their way in the obscurity of Russian history, I have provided these dates in parenthesis upon initial reference to the respective dignitary.

Finally, I would note that the number of vodka citations in Russian literature is so large that nothing close to all of them could be included in this book. Moreover, the Russians are still writing. I intend to post the most captivating and revealing of them on my website (edwintrommelen.nl) in due course.

–E.T.

Portrait of Dmitry Mendeleev, Ivan Kramskoy (1878). Mendeleev, a chemist, famously "invented" vodka by devising a better way to distill and purify it.

What is Vodka?

VODKA (Russ., = little water), a clear, colorless, strong alcoholic beverage, distilled, mostly made from grain such as rye or barley, but sometimes from potatoes in combination with grain. The grains are germinated, and in that way the starch yields fermentable sugar, which is fermented with water into a light alcoholic liquid, after which the liquid is distilled. The alcohol content of vodka varies widely. In Russian rural areas, vodka is distilled that is approximately 60% alcohol; commercial vodka is mostly 40 to 45% alcohol. Vodka does not undergo maturation, like most other distilled products; instead, it comes directly out of the distilling vessel and into bottles for the market. Vodka is the national alcoholic beverage of not only Russia, but also Poland and Finland. It is also produced in many other countries, including the Netherlands and Belgium.

Grote Winkler Prins[1]

The standard of identity for vodka was promulgated in 1949 [and] provided that it was neutral spirits distilled from any material at or above 190 proof, reduced to not more than 110 proof and not less than 80 proof and, after such reduction in proof, so treated as to be without distinctive character, aroma, or taste. Although no explicit definition of the term "distinctive" could be found in the hearing record, the testimony indicates that vodka is to be as tasteless and odorless as possible.

U.S. Bureau of Tobacco and Firearms[2]

Водка, крепкий алкогольный напиток; смесь ректифицированного этилового спирта с водой. Выработка В. (хлебного вина) в России началась в конце 14 в. В. делалась из ржи, пшеницы и ячменя. Для приготовления В. смесь спирта с водой (сортировку) пропускают через активированный уголь, затем фильтруют. Выпускаются В., содержащие 40, 50 и 56 объемного % спирта. Добавляя в В. настои на травах, семенах, кореньях и пряностях, приготовляют различные настойки. Другие виды В. получают перегонкой перебродивших сладких жидкостей. Так, из виноградного сока делают виноградную В., из вишневого – вишневую и др.

Vodka, a strong alcoholic drink, a mixture of rectified ethyl spirits and water. In Russia, the production of V. (grain wine) began in the late 14th c. V. was made from rye, wheat and barley. In order to prepare V., a mixture of spirits and water is passed through activated charcoal, then filtered. V. is produced with an alcohol content of 40, 50 and 56%. Various liqueurs are made by infusing vodka with herbs, seeds, roots and spices. Other sorts of V. are made from the fermentation and distillation of sweet liquids. For example, the juice of grapes is made into grape vodka, of cherries – cherry vodka, etc.

Great Soviet Encyclopedia (1969-1978)

Vodka is derived from the Russian word for "water," *voda* (pronounced: *vadá*). It is a diminutive and means literally "little water." Russians are big on euphemisms. And on creating diminutives of diminutives, because "vodka" can yield a further diminutive: *vódochka*. This can create problems for students of Russian, because plain water also has a diminutive that's spelled almost the same: *vodíchka*. So if a Russian asks you if you want another "(little) little water" – and I assure you that this is not hypothetical; both terms are widely used – you will have to determine from the stress whether he wants to get you drunk or keep you sober.

Edwin Trommelen (2011)

Good grain vodka [*khlebnaya vodka*] should be as clear as spring water; it should have a strong, sharp smell and should not have a burnt or excessively tart flavor. When shaken, bubbles should appear that rapidly burst. When lit, it should burn with a blue flame, leaving pure, flavorless water. When drunk by healthy individuals, such vodka should have no unpleasant side-effects. There should be no giddiness or headaches, no excessive acidity in the stomach, and no sense of lassitude, depression, anger, or rage.[3]

Dr. G. A. Blosfeld (1798-1884, professor of forensic medicine in Kazan, 1846)

– Какой-водки-то? Какой! А такой, чтобы, как следует, все нутро воротила, чтобы всю душеньку охватила и примерно, как огнем, значит...

– Ну, у нас такой водки нет! А водка – настоящая... Жидкая, как есть... Хошь стакашком ее пей, хошь рюмочкой – все одно... сама в рот льется.

"What sort of vodka, you ask? You ask! The kind that really turns your insides topsy-turvy, that takes total hold of your soul, and just right, like you're on fire, that's the kind...."

"Well, we don't have any vodka like that! But our vodka is the real thing... Liquid, as it should be... You can drink it from a tumbler, you can drink it from a shot glass – makes no difference... it'll go down just right."[4]

Pavel Zasodimsky, *Each According to His Ability* (1878)

1

Vodka on Life's Journey

Нет, этого уже невозможно выгнать: он говорит, что в детстве мамка его ушибла, и с тех пор от него отдает немного водкою.

No, there's no cure for it. He says his nurse dropped him when he was a child, and ever since he has smelt of vodka.[1]

Nikolai Gogol, *The Inspector-General* (1836)

AT EVERY STAGE OF the journey that constitutes their lives, at each traditional milestone of birth, marriage, and death, at every manner of official and personal celebration, vodka is the Russian's constant companion. One of the participants in a temperance congress early in the twentieth century put it this way:

When the Russian is born, when he marries or dies, when he goes to court or is reconciled, when he makes a new acquaintance or parts from an old friend, when he negotiates a purchase or a sale, realizes a profit or suffers a loss – every activity is copiously baptized with vodka. But there is more to it than that. At any holiday or at the end of the working day, the Russian is drawn to the street, to other people; a company gathers, vodka is bought: conversation runs smoother and livelier over a drink. And so, vodka, vodka, vodka... an ocean of alcohol. The Russian spends his entire life, from cradle to grave, bathing and swimming in this drunken sea.[2]

BIRTH

Russians first encounter vodka immediately after birth. Even as the infant is being wrapped in swaddling clothes, relatives raise a glass to him. Another opportunity presents itself shortly thereafter: the baptism. An opportunity taken not only by family, friends, and acquaintances...

Правда, что при определении Савки явилось было и еще одно маленькое препятствие, которое состояло в том, что никак не могли найти его записанным в метрические книги перегудинской церкви, но это ужасное обстоятельство для школ гражданских – в духовных училищах принимается несколько мягче. В духовных училищах знают, что духовенство часто позабывает вписывать своих детей в метрики. Окрестивши, хорошенько подвыпьют – боятся писать, что руки трясутся; назавтра похмеляются; на третий день ходят без памяти, а потом так и забудут вписать.

However, another little obstacle cropped up during Savka's admissions process, namely that no record of him could be found in the Peregudy church registry. This circumstance, which would have been dreadful if he was applying to a secular school, was treated more leniently by religious schools. Religious schools know that the clergy often forgets to inscribe their children into the registry. After the christening, they have a few drinks and are afraid to write with an unsteady hand. The next day they are a bit hungover; on the third day they don't remember a thing. And then they simply forget to make the entry.[3]

Nikolai Leskov, *The Priest Who Was Never Baptized* (1877)

If the child's parents are Jewish, they can take the opportunity of their son's circumcision ("may God give us a boy...") to have a glass. Although alcohol plays a smaller role in the lives of Russian Jews as compared with their Orthodox compatriots, they are certainly not averse to drinking. The scene described below takes place in Odessa, a city in Ukraine where a large number of Jews have lived since time immemorial. It is not clear whether the participants in the ceremony are also drinking, but Isaac Babel leaves no doubt about the mohel himself.

Нафтула был в Одессе такое же городское имущество, как памятник дюку де Ришелье. Он проходил мимо наших окон на Дальницкой с трепаной, засаленной акушерской сумкой в руках. В этой сумке хранились немудрящие его инструменты. Он вытаскивал оттуда то ножик, то бутылку водки с медовым пряником. Он нюхал пряник, прежде чем выпить, и, выпив, затягивал молитвы. Он был рыж, Нафтула, как первый рыжий человек на земле. Отрезая то, что ему причиталось, он не отцеживал кровь через стеклянную трубочку, а высасывал ее вывороченными своими губами. Кровь размазывалась по всклокоченной его бороде. Он выходил к гостям захмелевший. Медвежьи глазки его сияли весельем. Рыжий, как первый рыжий человек на земле, он гнусавил благословение над вином. Одной рукой Нафтула опрокидывал в заросшую кривую, огнедышащую яму своего рта водку, в другой руке у него была тарелка. На ней лежал ножик, обагренный младенческой кровью, и кусок марли. Собирая деньги, Нафтула обходил с этой тарелкой гостей, он толкался между женщинами, валился на них, хватал за груди и орал на всю улицу.

– Толстые мамы, – орал старик, сверкая коралловыми глазками, – печатайте мальчиков для Нафтулы, молотите пшеницу на ваших животах, старайтесь для Нафтулы... Печатайте мальчиков, толстые мамы...

Мужья бросали деньги в его тарелку. Жены вытирали салфетками кровь с его бороды. Дворы Глухой и Госпитальной не оскудевали. Они кишели детьми, как устья рек икрой. Нафтула плелся со своим мешком, как сборщик подати.

In Odessa, Naftula was just as much a part of the town as the Duc de Richelieu's statue. Often he would pass our windows on Dalnitskaya carrying the worn and greasy midwife's bag in which he kept his simple appliances. Now he would pull from it a little knife, now a bottle of vodka and a piece of gingerbread. He would sniff the gingerbread before drinking, and when he had drunk he would start moaning prayers. He was redheaded, Naftula was, like the first redheaded man on Earth. When he was doing his snipping, he didn't drain the blood off through a little glass tube but sucked it away with his splayed lips, and his tangled beard got all blood-smeared. When he went out to the assembled guests he would be tipsy, his bear-eyes shining with merriment. Redheaded, like the first redheaded man on Earth, he would nasally intone a blessing over the wine. With one hand he would tip the vodka into the hirsute, crooked, and fire-breathing pit of his mouth; in his other would be a plate. On it lay the little knife crimson with infant gore, and a piece of lint. When he was collecting his fee, Naftula would present this plate to all the guests, bump about among the womenfolk, roll on them, grab them by the bosoms, and yell so that the whole street could hear.

"Fat mommas," the old man would yell, his coral eyes gleaming, "bud little boys for Naftula, thresh wheat on your bellies, do your best for Naftula. Bud little boys, you fat mommas."

The husbands would cast coins on his plate; the wives would wipe the blood from his beard with napkins. The courtyards of Glukhaya and Hospital Streets knew no lack of children: they seethed with them like river mouths with fish-roe. Naftula used to toddle about with his little bag just like a tax-collector.[4]

Isaac Babel, "Karl-Yankel" (1931)

MARRIAGE

A Russian grows up and becomes a young man. Tradition dictates that he must drink and smoke, that he not lag behind his friends in that regard, that he must know how to party. It is a rite of passage; drinking is an element of manliness. A young man who does not drink is often called a "red maiden," a "wet chicken" or a *baba* (peasant woman).

The next phase comes when he is man enough to think about marriage. The bottle is uncapped when he pairs off, and the actual agreement is also celebrated with vodka, as is the "showing of the bride." In keeping with tradition, the prospective groom's acquaintances take advantage of this occasion to have a drink. And of course, the groom himself has certain obligations toward his future father-in-law...

— Ну, Солопий, вот, как видишь, я и дочка твоя полюбили друг друга так, что хоть бы и навеки жить вместе.

— Что ж, Параска, — сказал Черевик, оборотившись и смеясь к своей дочери, — может, и в самом деле, чтобы уже, как говорят, вместе и того... чтобы и паслись на одной траве! Что? по рукам? А ну-ка, новобранный зять, давай магарычу!

И все трое очутились в известной ярмарочной ресторации — под яткою у жидовки, усеянною многочисленной флотилией сулей, бутылей, фляжек всех родов и возрастов.

— Эх, хват! за это люблю! — говорил Черевик, немного подгулявши и видя, как нареченный зять его налил кружку величиною с полкварты и, нимало не поморщившись, выпил до дна, хватив потом ее вдребезги. — Что скажешь, Параска? Какого я жениха тебе достал! Смотри, смотри, как он молодецки тянет пенную!..

"Well, Solopy, what can I say, your daughter and I love each other so much that we could spend the rest of our lives together."

"Alright, Paraska," said Cherevik, laughing and turning to his daughter. "Maybe you really should, as they say, the two of you... you might as well graze on the same grass! So, are we shaking hands on it? And now, my new son-in-law, how about a toast?"

And all three found themselves at the market's famous watering hole, a tent owned by a Jewish woman that was crammed with a vast array of bottles, jars and flasks of every age and pedigree.

"Atta boy! I like you already," said Cherevik, a little sloshed, as he watched how the newly-betrothed filled a pint mug and without so much as a flinch, downed it to the bottom and smashed it to bits.

The Wedding, Leonid Solomatkin (1872)

"What do you say to that, Paraska? See what a husband I found for you? Just look how he pulls in the foam!"[5]

Nikolai Gogol, "The Fair at Sorochintsy" (1831)

When the wedding day arrives, the guests drink as they escort the young couple. At every step of the way, the bride and groom encounter different rituals that involve drinking. Sometimes people (who call themselves friends) spell out the bride's name in glasses of vodka, and the groom is obligated to keep drinking throughout. Or they might come across a table bedecked with food and vodka, another obstacle the couple must surmount. Thus, the first days of their married life turn into an orgy of drinking, full of licentious song, brawling, and uncouth pranks.

С теткой покойного деда, которая сама была на этой свадьбе, случилась забавная история: была она одета тогда в татарское широкое платье и с чаркою в руках угощала собрание. Вот одного дернул лукавый окатить ее сзади водкою; другой, тоже, видно, не промах, высек в ту же минуту огня, да и поджег... пламя вспыхнуло, бедная тетка, перепугавшись, давай сбрасывать с себя, при всех, платье... Шум, хохот, ералаш поднялся, как на ярмарке. Словом, старики не запомнили никогда еще такой веселой свадьбы.

An amusing incident happened to my grandfather's aunt who was at that wedding herself; in a flowing Tartar dress, she was walking around with a goblet in her hand treating the company. The devil prompted someone to splash vodka over her from behind; another one, it seems, was just as clever: at the same moment he struck a light and set fire to her... The flame flared up; the poor aunt, terrified, began flinging off all her clothes before everybody... The din, the laughter, the hubbub that arose – it was like a fair. In fact, the old people had never remembered such a merry wedding.[6]

Nikolai Gogol, *Evenings Near the Village of Dikanka:* "St. John's Eve" (1831)

Everyone, young and old, is expected to drink until they fall down. The more the guests drink, the greater the honor for the newlyweds and their family. The last of the guests left standing is awarded the honorary title of "vodka tsar."

In earlier times, country weddings were not only celebrations for the couple in question – the entire village went on a binge. There were two days of partying in the home of the bride and groom, and the third day was reserved for the hangover.

DEATH

Russians are of course sad when someone dies, but at the same time they are more resigned by nature than is the average Westerner. Death is part of life; everyone's turn comes eventually, and there's no getting around it. Life goes on, and sometimes Russians wonder whether celebrating might be the best thing to do. As in the eighteenth century in the village of Goryukhino:

Обряд похорон происходил следующим образом. В самый день смерти покойника относили на кладбище – дабы мертвый в избе не занимал напрасно лишнего места. От сего случалось, что к неописанной радости родственников мертвец чихал или зевал в ту самую минуту, как его выносили в гробе за околицу. Жены оплакивали мужьев, воя и приговаривая: "Свет-моя удалая головушка! на кого ты меня покинул? чем-то мне тебя поминати?" При возвращении с кладбища начиналась тризна в честь покойника, и родственники и друзья бывали пьяны два-три дня или даже целую неделю, смотря по усердию и привязанности к его памяти. Сии древние обряды сохранилися и поныне.

Funeral ceremonies were performed in the following way. On the day of death the deceased was taken directly to the cemetery so that his corpse should not unnecessarily take up space in his cottage. As a result, it often happened that the corpse, to the indescribable joy of the relatives, would sneeze or yawn just as it was being conveyed out of the village in its coffin. Wives would bewail their husbands, howling and muttering, "Light of my life, my brave darling! Whom have you left me to? How shall I keep your memory sacred?" After the return from the cemetery a wake in honor of the deceased would commence, and relatives and friends would be intoxicated for two or three days, even for an entire week, depending on their zeal and degree of attachment to his memory. These ancient rites have been preserved to this day.[7]

Alexander Pushkin, "The History of the Village of Goryukhino" (1830)

At the gravesite, most Russians drink a single glass and eat nothing more than a pickle. For the deceased, a glassful is sprinkled on the grave. The *pominki* (funeral banquet) takes place at home. A special place is set for the deceased at the table, under the icons, and the first spoonful of a meal is for him, as is the first glass of vodka. The *pominki* takes place on the third, ninth, and fortieth days after the death. On the ninth and fortieth days, when the soul of the deceased goes to heaven, the men stand at the grave holding lit candles, and they have a glass of vodka; the women have a glass of wine. Russians sometimes commemorate their dead on the sixth and twentieth days after the death as well, and after six months and one year. They also commemorate the deceased on his name day and birthday and on so-called ancestors' day.

There is often a table with a bench at a gravesite, so that relatives can eat a snack or have a drink close to the deceased. They leave flowers, cakes, cigarettes, and candy on the grave, and sometimes crosses kneaded from well-cooked rice, or eggs bearing images of Russian Orthodox crosses. The deceased receives a glass of vodka that stays at the grave, in keeping with an old custom whereby nothing can be taken home from the cemetery. At the end of the day, ravens and crows circle the cemetery looking for scraps and broken eggs – until they are chased off by children hunting for candy, or by local drunks who down the vodka on behalf of the deceased.

Initially, Orthodox Russians were not allowed to drink vodka during *pominki*, so they drank red wine instead. Once they started drinking vodka on those occasions, they were not supposed to clink glasses and instead had to look at the glass and make the sign of the cross with their eyes. That remained the case in the Soviet era. There has been a death in the village described below, and the protagonist realizes that he has to visit the bereaved.

На столе стояла следующая еда: селедка с луком и маслом, студень, яйца, крупнорубленные, облитые сметаной, открытые консервные банки с сайрой, консервы в томате, печенье и мед. Без меда не бывает ни одних поминок.

Усевшись, мы прежде всего съели по ложке меда – полагается по обычаю.

– Ну что же, мужики, теперь вроде бы все собрались, помянем...

– Не чокаться, мужики, не чокаться. На поминках не полагается.

Если бы кто-нибудь не видел происходящего, а только слышал, то он по этому возгласу: «Не чокаться, мужики, не полагается» – точно подсчитал бы, сколько раз поднимались от стола тяжелые граненые стаканы.

Велик ли обычай – не чокаться, – но сразу все как-то притихли, сразу все поняли важность происходящего. Не чокнувшись, выпили и закусили.

– А ведь как помер-то, – доносилось с женского стола. Это значит, вновь пришедшей рассказывают все подробности, как именно Иван Дмитриевич помирал. – Голова, говорит, разламывается. Я говорю, полежи, Ваня. Приляг, пройдет. Сразу, сразу послушался, прилег. Потом как крикнет: «Баба!» Я к нему. А он уж только глядит.

– Как помер-то, а? Такую смерть за деньги не купишь.

– Не купишь, милочка, не купишь.

– Кабы такую смерть бог послал...

– Не говори, милочка, не говори.

У нас за столом тянулась своя ниточка.

– А ведь очередь-то, мужики, была не его.

– Нет, не его.

– Она, брат, очередь не признает. Бывает, вроде и молодой и на вид и так, а смотришь, и нет.

– Известно, скрипучее дерево дольше стоит.

– Вон хоть теперь соседа твоего возьми. Алкоголик? Алкоголик...

– Ну, давайте, мужики. Не чокаться, не чокаться, не полагается.

The table was spread with the following foods: herring with onion in oil, aspic, coarsely chopped eggs smothered in sour cream, open tins of saury and tins of fish in tomato sauce, as well as cookies, and honey. No *pominki* is complete without honey.

After we sat down, the first thing we did was eat a spoonful of honey each, such is the custom.

"Here we are, muzhiks. Everyone seems to be present, so it's time to pay tribute to the departed..."

"Don't clink glasses, muzhiks. You're not supposed to at *pominki*."

If someone could listen in on what was happening, but not see anything, they would still know just how many times the faceted glass tumblers were raised in tribute by the number of times the phrase "Don't clink glasses, muzhiks. You're not supposed to at *pominki*" was pronounced.

It's a small thing, the custom of not clinking glasses, but everyone immediately falls silent, everyone immediately recognizes the importance of what is taking place. Without clinking glasses, we down our vodka and take a bite of food.

"Oh, and how he died," could be heard from the women's table. This meant that someone new had shown up and was being given a detailed account of how Ivan Dmitriyevich breathed his last. "His head was killing him, he said. 'Lie down for a bit, Vanya' I told him. 'Once you lie down, it'll pass.' Right away, right away, he followed my advice and lay down. And suddenly he's screaming, 'Woman!' I'm there like a shot. And he just lay there, staring."

"What a way to go, eh? You can't buy a death like that."

"No you can't, dearie, you just can't."

"If only God would send such a death..."

"You can say that again."

Our table had its own strand of conversation.

"But you know, it wasn't supposed to be his turn, muzhiks."

"Nope. Sure enough."

"Death doesn't care whose turn it is, brother. You've got people who seem to be young and look just fine and the next thing you know, they're gone."

"It's well known that the creaking tree lasts longer."

"Take the case of that neighbor of yours. An alcoholic? You bet..."

"Well, let's drink, muzhiks. Don't clink your glasses. You're not supposed to."[8]

Vladimir Soloukhin, "The Funeral Banquet" (1973)

Of course, the priest officiating over the funeral is entitled to a glass of vodka, as are the members of the band playing the dirges. The family of the deceased cannot forget the gravediggers either; that would be unseemly. If you get a job at a cemetery, you have to know how to dig a grave and how to construct a coffin, as well as cemetery etiquette...

Наливали по-кладбищенски: каждый себе. Испокон веков так: на кладбище сивуха рекой течет, особенно в сезон, ноздря в ноздрю никто не гоняется, всем под самый жвак хватает. [...]

Одно запомни и другое: выпить не отказывайся никогда. Ты че? У людей горе, а тебе выпить с ними лень... Сам вот не проси, некрасиво, а помянуть нальют – не отказывайся. Это нам можно. Ни Петрович, никто еще ругать не будут. Горе разделил, по-русски... Летом одного захоранивали, нам наливают. А тут Носенко идет, из треста, заместитель управляющего. Мы стаканы прятать... Раевский сунул в штаны, а у него там дыра... Стакан пролетел, а он стоит, как обоссанный. И стакан котится...

THE WORD "VODKA"

Тайна имени «водка» заключена в ее воздействии на народные массы, в той смеси желания и стыда, которая имеет сходную с эротикой стихию. Алкоголик превращает водку в свою невесту; он боится открыть все свои чувства к ней и одновременно не в состоянии сдерживать их. «Водка» – одно из самых сильных русских слов. Русские смущаются от произнесения этого слова. Провинциальные девушки до сих пор стараются его не произносить. Упоминание о водке порождает атмосферу заговора, мистическую экзальтацию. В русском сознании возникают архаическое брожение, языческое оцепенение, боязнь, как при встрече с медведем, ворожба, заклинания. Вокруг бога-водки образуется слабое поле человеческого сопротивления. По своей сути водка – беспардонная, наглая вещь.

The secret of the word "vodka" consists in its effect on the masses, in that blend of desire and shame that bears an elemental resemblance to the erotic. The alcoholic sees vodka as a woman. He is afraid to reveal his feelings for her but at the same time is incapable of containing them. "Vodka" is one of the most powerful words in the Russian language. Russians feel uncomfortable saying it. To this day, provincial girls try to avoid pronouncing it. Any mention of vodka arouses in the Russian consciousness an atmosphere of conspiracy, of mystical exaltation. It stirs primitive rumblings, a pagan torpor, sorcery, incantation, and fear of the sort prompted by an encounter with a bear. A weak field of human resistance forms around the Vodka God. In its essence, vodka is a shameless, insolent thing.[9]

Victor Erofeyev, "The Russian God" (2002)

THE FIRST TIME that "vodka" appeared in writing in Russia was in 1533, in a yearbook of the city of Novgorod. The word refers to a medicinal beverage. After that, the term appears in Russia only occasionally – for example, in 1666, in a petition from archimandrite Bartholomeus concerning the old ascetic Yephrem, who lived in a cell in isolation, but who secretly received "beverages, wine and votka" from his children. And in a 1695 letter, Peter the Great declares his intention to drink "beer, Rhine wine, and votka" to the health of the addressee. "Votka" here refers to flavored vodka. Thus, when Pushkin uses the term "vodka" in his 1833 epic poem, *Yevgeny Onegin* and in the 1836 novella, *The Captain's Daughter,* he is talking about vodka with flavoring. To refer to flavorless liquor, the Russians used terms such as tsar's wine, grain wine, green wine, white wine, table wine, or simply *vino* (wine). Cognac was called "French vodka."

Beginning in the early eighteenth century, vodka was mentioned in legal instruments, and *ukases* were literally dedicated to vodka. The *ukase* by Tsaritsa Elizabeth dated June 8, 1751, "Who may have casks for the production of vodka," is the best-known one, but not the first. The word "vodka" then disappeared from official documents, only to reemerge in 1906.

According to the renowned Russian dictionary by Vladimir Dal, as of 1860 Russians frequently used the term "vodka" to refer to the alcoholic drink as we know it today. All in all, it can be concluded that the term "vodka" as referring to pure Russian liquor took root in the nineteenth century. And it was not until 1936 that the Soviet government officially banned the term "grain wine" and standardized the term "vodka."

Some Slavic peoples have other words for referring to vodka or vodka-like beverages: in Bulgaria *rakiya*, in Serbia *voda* or *vodica*, in Ukraine *gorilka*, and the Poles use *wódka* as well as the old-fashioned *gorzalka* (related to the Czech *kořalka*, meaning drink or spirits). In southern Russia, the term *okovita* is sometimes used.

Чего, думаем, Носенко скажет. Ни слова не сказал. А в обед всем велел в контору. Когда, говорит, официально предлагают помянуть, это не возбраняется, только не слишком. [...]

– А если, говорит, кого увижу – по углам распивают, пеняйте на себя... Его слова, Носенки. А ты раз не пьешь – отпей для вида, а остальное, скажи, в бутылочке мне оставьте. Понял?

They were each pouring their own; that's how it's done at the cemetery. From time immemorial that's how it's been: the *sivukha* [raw vodka] flows in rivers, especially in season. Nobody's jostling to get some; there's enough to clean your teeth with. [...]

There's a thing or two you've got to remember: never turn down a drink. What kinda thing is that? People are grieving and you can't be bothered to drink with them?... Now don't go asking for one yourself, it's not nice, but when they pour one in remembrance, don't say no. We're allowed that. Petrovich isn't gonna call you out, and neither is anybody else. You were just sharing in their grief, the Russian way... We buried a guy last summer and they were pouring a round. And here comes Nosenko from the office, the deputy director. We hid our glasses... Rayevsky stuck his in his pants, but he had a hole... The glass went right through, and he's standing there like he wet his pants. And the glass is rolling...

"What'll Nosenko say?" we're thinking. He didn't say a word. And he called everyone into the office at lunchtime. "When you're invited to officially remember the dead," he says, "there's no rule against that, but don't overdo it." [...] "But if," he says, "I see someone off drinking on the sly, he'd better say his prayers..." Nosenko's very words. And since you don't drink, take a sip for appearance's sake, and as for the rest, tell them to leave it in the bottle for me. Got it?[10]

Sergei Kaledin, "The Humble Cemetery" (1987)

This is how it was when ordinary people died. When an important party member or statesman died, the entire Soviet Union went into mourning. State television would broadcast a ballet, and radio aired solemn music. All party leaders, with the exception of Khrushchev, were interred in the wall of the Kremlin, whereas Lenin and (initially) Stalin were given places in the special mausoleum on Red Square. That mausoleum, from which party leaders viewed parades, looks more spartan than it actually is. British historian Simon Sebag Montefiore described what it was like: "There were chairs hidden there for those of weak disposition to take a rest, and even better, there was a room behind with a bar for those who needed Dutch courage. The first Bolshevik Head of State, Yakov Sverdlov, died in 1919 after a freezing parade; the Politburo member Alexander Shcherbakov died after attending the 1945 victory parade; the Czech President Klement Gottwald died after enduring the icy hours of

Stalin's funeral on the Mausoleum."[11] A glass of vodka does not always bring deliverance.

BIRTHDAYS AND NAME DAYS

Я-то ведь ничего не жалел. Я ведь в России такие пиры закатывал своим гостям, будучи бедным человеком, господа! Празднуя день рождения, к примеру, я шел с приятелями на базар и покупал полмешка мяса, господа, и звал сорок человек, и покупал алкоголь, чтоб на каждого человека приходилось по русскому расчету: на мальчика – бутылка водки, на девочку – бутылка вина. Я тратил все деньги, все до копейки, еще и занимал порой, и никаких счетов в банке у меня не было, меня мало интересовало, что будет завтра. "Бог даст день, Бог даст пищу", – как говорила моя бабушка Вера.

I, after all, begrudged nothing, gentlemen. Such feasts I put on for my guests in Russia, even though a poor man! To celebrate my birthday, for instance, I went to the bazaar with friends and bought fifty pounds of meat, gentlemen, and invited forty people, and bought liquor the Russian way, allowing a bottle of vodka per boy, a bottle of wine per girl. I spent all my money, to my last kopek, and at times I also borrowed. I had no bank accounts, I cared little what the morrow would bring. "God will give the day, God will give us food," as my grandma Vera used to say.[12]

Edward Limonov, *It's Me, Eddie* (1979)

Russians celebrate not only their birthday, but also their name day, in honor of the saint for whom they are named. In other words, someone named Nikolai celebrates his name day on December 19 (according to the Russian Orthodox calendar; on December 6 according to the Gregorian calendar); Pavel, the Russian variant of Paul, celebrates his name day on July 12 (June 29). If he is named for the Apostle Paul, that is; if he's named for Paul the Hermit, then he celebrates it on January 15 (January 2). Natalya's name day is September 8 (August 26).

И о душе своей заботился солидно, по-барски, и добрые дела творил не просто, а с важностью. А какие добрые дела? Лечил мужиков от всех болезней содой и касторкой и в день своих именин служил среди деревни благодарственный молебен, а потом ставил полведра, думал, что так нужно. Ах, эти ужасные полведра! Сегодня толстый помещик тащит мужиков к земскому начальнику за потраву, а завтра, в торжественный день, ставит им полведра, а они пьют и кричат ура, и пьяные кланяются ему в ноги. Перемена жизни к лучшему, сытость, праздность развивают в русском человеке самомнение, самое наглое.

And he concerned himself with the salvation of his soul in a substantial, gentlemanly manner, and performed deeds of charity, not simply, but with an air of consequence. And what deeds of charity! He treated the peasants for every sort of disease with soda and castor oil, and on his name day had a thanksgiving service in the middle of the village, and then treated the peasants to a gallon of vodka – he thought that was the thing to do. Oh, those horrible gallons of vodka! One day the fat landowner hauls the peasants up before the district captain for trespass, and next day, in honor of a holiday, treats them to a gallon of vodka, and they drink and shout "Hurrah!" and when they are drunk bow down to his feet. A change of life for the better, and being well-fed and idle develop in a Russian the most insolent self-conceit.[13]

Anton Chekhov, "Gooseberries" (1898)

RELIGIOUS HOLIDAYS

Church holidays have traditionally been the most important pretext for celebration. You could tell whether it was a major or minor holiday from the amount of beer that the celebrants brewed or the number of cases of vodka they bought. In earlier days, "beer fests" were held for certain saints. On those occasions, villagers were granted special permission to brew beer. Any leftover beverage was sealed up. On other holidays, Russians typically drank vodka and went on a rampage, as the notes from a seventeenth-century traveler illustrate:

For the greater the feast, the larger is the measure of their potations. It is quite ludicrous to see old men and boys mixed up together, delighted with the same sports and jests and games, and with the constant motion of beams, on which they sometimes stand and sometimes sit, celebrating their chief festivals with this lazy agitation of their bodies. The livelong day the air is filled with the ringing of church bells on every side, though there be no devotion in the churches, as if it were enough to mark the solemn festival of the day by the mere beating of the inanimate air. Hardly any great festival of the year passes without being followed by a conflagration. These fires are all the more disastrous because they mostly break out in the nighttime; and sometimes they utterly consume to ashes some hundreds of wooden houses.[14]

Johann Georg Korb, *Diary of an Austrian Secretary of Legation at the Court of Tsar Peter the Great* (1700)

One of the most important festivals is *Maslenitsa* (Butter Week), the week prior to the great fasting, comparable to Mardi Gras for Catholics. Russians bid farewell to winter by burning a doll, after which spring arrives to revive nature. This is celebrated with vodka and pancakes. During *Maslenitsa* each day of the week has a different theme; Tuesday, for example, is the happy day, and Wednesday is the feast day. But Thursday is the real party, because that's when the vodka flows most freely. In the Smolensk region, it used to be the custom that on Thursday women would go into the fields, drink vodka, and pull the scarves off of each other's heads. Over the course of this week, Russians go on sleigh rides, build snow cities, go to carnivals, and have fistfights. Sunday is the Day of Forgiveness, when people ask one another to forgive them their trespasses. After that, they fast until Easter.

> All during Holy Easter, not only did good friends visit [each other] in private homes, but everyone – lay and ecclesiastical people, men and women – avidly patronized simple *kabaki*, that is beer, mead, and vodka houses. They drank so much that frequently people were seen lying here and there in the streets, and some of them had to be thrown onto wagons or sleighs by their relatives and taken home. Under the circumstances, it may be understood why many people, murdered and stripped of their clothing, were found in the morning lying in the streets. Now, thanks to the Patriarch, these great excesses from visits to taverns or pothouses have abated somewhat.[15]
>
> Adam Olearius, *The Travels of Olearius in Seventeenth-Century Russia* (1656)

Easter is the most important holiday in the Russian Orthodox Church. That was true in Olearius's day, around 1640, and it is still true today. Even after the revolution, Russians did not forget the big holidays, and occasionally serious disturbances erupted. In 1928, 21 people in Moscow lost their lives

The Easter Procession, Vasily Perov (1861)

during Easter, "fifteen of them because of vodka." According to an Associated Press dispatch dated April 18, the first-aid posts were overwhelmed: "With their heads clouded by vodka, people fell under the wheels of cars, buses, and streetcars, while some even drank gasoline and hurled themselves into Easter celebrations with fists, knives, and other weapons. Window panes were smashed, but the troops quickly put an end to the violence." The police arrested 1,500 revelers.

At midnight on Dmitry's Day, the night of October 26, the "tribute to the granary" takes place, a ritual that concludes the harvest festivities. The owner takes a bottle and a glass from his pocket and goes to the front left corner of the granary. He faces the corner, pours himself a glass of vodka, drinks it down, and says, "This one is for me." Then he pours a second glass and sprinkles it in the corner, saying, "This one is for you, Father, to keep you from burning down. Just as vodka burns but does not burn down, so too will you not burn down. Amen." He repeats the ritual in all four corners. When he has done that, he stands in the middle of the granary, pours the last glass, and drinks it down, saying, "Thank you, Father, and may you guard my grain." After that, the owner pours the rest of the vodka on the ground, breaks the bottle, and throws its neck outside.

Many festivals for local saints took place in October and November. Each village celebrated its name day and thus had its own festival. Many peasants would travel from one village to the next, turning the season into a continuous junket of boozing. Drinking was one of the few releases available to them. Religion served as a mask for the festivals, even though that was hardly necessary; the people felt no shame and simply saw the church festivals as a good excuse to drink. In his book, *Living Water*, David Christian quotes a description by the author Zablotsky-Desiatovsky:

> In one village we found all the peasants in a delirium of drink and debauchery because of the holiday. "What are you celebrating and why are you so drunk?" we asked.
>
> "What do you mean, why? Today is the Assumption of the Mother of God. Do you know her, master, eh?"
>
> "But the day of the Assumption was yesterday!"
>
> "So what! You've got to drink for three days."
>
> "Why three days? Do you think the Mother of God commanded that?"
>
> "Everyone knows that! Yes, she ordered it. Our Lady knows that we like to drink!"[16]

Other renowned holidays are the feast day of St. George on April 23 (old-style), the day when serfs had the right (until the end of the sixteenth century) to switch to a different lord, and *Nikolin Den*, the feast day of St. Nicholas. The latter is observed on two days: December 19 (December 6) for St. Nicholas of Myra and May 22 (May 9) in honor of Nicholas the Miracle Worker.

Russia also has a huge number of days of fasting – some two hundred single- or multiple-day fasts. This includes almost every Wednesday and Friday, as well as the St. Peter's fast (from the first week after Pentecost to July 12, which means that it varies in length), the fast for the assumption of Mary (two weeks in August), the Christmas fast (fourteen days before Christmas), and the most important one: the seven weeks before Easter, known as the Great Fast (*Veliky Post*). The list of foods forbidden during the Great Fast included meat, milk, eggs and butter, and also fish during the first and fourth weeks. In general, Russians followed the rules. Vodka was of course completely forbidden. Well… completely? There are some people who drink special "Lenten vodka."

OTHER HOLIDAYS

Church and personal holidays are not the only occasions that Russians celebrate. There are others: New Year's, of course, and before the revolution there were also various imperial holidays, in honor of the tsar and the fatherland. Even prisoners and their guards observed these holidays.

Жандармам дают всякий царский день чарку водки. Вахмистр дозволял Филимонову отказываться раз пять-шесть от своей порции и получать разом все пять-шесть; Филимонов метил на деревянную бирку, сколько стаканчиков пропущено, и в самые большие праздники отправлялся за ними. Водку эту он выливал в миску, крошил в нее хлеб и ел ложкой. После такой закуски он закуривал большую трубку на крошечном чубучке, табак у него был крепости невероятной, он его сам крошил и вследствие этого остроумно называл "сан-краше". Куря, он укладывался на небольшом окне, – стула в солдатской комнате не было, – согнувшись в три погибели, и пел песню.

On every Imperial holiday the gendarmes are given a glass of vodka. The sergeant allowed Filimonov to refuse his share five or six times and then to receive them all at once. Filimonov scored on a wooden tally-stick how many glasses he had missed, and on the most important holidays he would go for them. He would pour this vodka into a bowl, crumble bread into it and eat it with a spoon. After this dish he would light a big pipe with a tiny mouthpiece, filled with tobacco of incredible strength that he used to cut up himself, and therefore rather wittily called "*sans-cracher*." As he smoked he would fold himself up on a little window-seat, bent double – there were no chairs in the soldiers' rooms – and sing his song.[17]

Alexander Herzen, *My Past and Thoughts* (1854)

The abundance of feast and fast days in old Russia and compliance with the associated regimens meant that whenever a Russian was allowed to drink, he did so to excess. It was no holds barred, and let tomorrow bring what it may. This basic attitude was apparently grafted onto Russian DNA. To this day, Russians tend to binge-drink, and leaving a half-full bottle is taboo.

Holidays – to say nothing of the annual fair (*yarmarka*) – used to be tied to the seasons and adjusted to the rhythm of the village, and thus planting and harvest times largely coincided with periods of fasting. Work could not be stopped. Anyone who did drink during busy times quickly lost his social status. Which is to say that people in rural areas could handle drinking, and true alcoholism was rare prior to World War II.

That was not so much the case with urban workers, in part because working in factories involved fewer peak periods. In any event, in the nineteenth century "modern" drinking culture slowly gained the upper hand over the traditional culture rooted in the peasantry. The latter tended toward drinking collectively, in large amounts, and only on holidays, whereas urbanization and the development of a money-based economy made modern drinking culture increasingly individualistic. In the traditional world, drinking was a social and ritual activity that arose more from conventions than from individual impulses. As the countryside increasingly forgot its traditions, the control mechanisms that defined the rhythm and patterns of drinking also disappeared. The decision about whether or not to drink reflected the need of the individual, not that of the community. Even though the tendency to go all out when it came to drinking survived, there was no consideration of tomorrow. Thus, urban workers became famous for their frequent drunkenness. After World War II, and even more so after the collapse of the Soviet Union, the focus shifted back to rural Russia, but without the traditional social control mechanisms.

Thus, with growing industrialization and the associated urbanization, Russians, who from time immemorial had never drunk on working days, began increasingly to drink alone – and, moreover, whenever they felt like it. In this way, the 1917 revolution, with its emphasis on the urban proletariat, indirectly and inadvertently encouraged individual drinking behavior, despite the fact that in the first years after the revolution drinking was not even allowed. The older generation clung to its religious celebrations, especially in the countryside, whereas younger Russians – whether or not they were churchgoers – were happy to take advantage of feast days in order to get drunk.

The communists were also fond of holidays. The Day of the October Revolution (November 7), Labor Day (May 1), and International Women's Day (March 8) were all intended to replace religious holidays, to legitimize the Soviet regime, and to provide it with symbols. But the average Russian

The Kissing Ceremony, Konstantin Makovsky (1895)

simply added the growing number of Soviet holidays to the list of traditional celebrations and decided that he should also mark the new holidays by getting drunk.

In fact, a Russian can find all sorts of reasons to celebrate. The Five-Year Plan is fulfilled: celebrate! A cosmonaut launches into space: celebrate! The harvest is in: celebrate! Most occupational groups had a holiday; miners, educators, policemen, and border troops all had their own day, and most of them still exist. President Vladimir Putin has always been a fervent advocate of establishing a ranking of holidays, declaring May 9, the Day of Victory over Nazi Germany, the most important one.

И получается, что Девятое мая – всем праздникам праздник. Нужно лезть в воду, ловить карасей и покупать в магазине водку. Ничего, что владимирского производства, на фронте и не такую пивали, а эта – очень даже гожа.– Федорыч, ты мимо пойдешь, зайди к Володе Солоухину, позови, скажи, нельзя – День Победы. [...]

У зовущих теперь меня к столу не может уложиться в сознании, что человек не хочет выпить. А если он говорит, что не хочет, значит, не хочет выпить именно с ними, гнушается их компанией, пренебрегает, зазнался, отрывается от масс и вообще много о себе понимает. [...] Выпьем за тех, кто воевал, за тех, кто в тылу и на фронте ковал победу! После речи, во время чоканья стакан о стакан, слышались отрывочные реплики: – Да, надо.

– Нельзя, такой день.

– Никак нельзя.

– Тут уж что говорить.

– Такой день раз в жизни.

– За всю историю.

– Ну, мужики, будем здоровы.

– С праздничком!

– Никак нельзя...

Я слегка удивился сути реплик. Получалось, что собравшиеся вроде бы и не хотят выпивать, и не стали бы, и не любят, но вот ничего не поделаешь: «надо», «никак нельзя».

По-моему, тонким стаканом водки можно наказывать провинившихся. Мы же должны были пить добровольно, мало того, желая друг другу самого лучшего и драгоценного – здоровья.

It turns out that May 9 is the holiday to end all holidays. You have to get in the water, catch carp, and buy vodka in the store. No matter if it's the local stuff. At the front they would have been lucky to get even that. In fact, it's exactly what the occasion calls for.

"Fyodorych, you'll be passing his place. Stop in and invite Volodya Soloukhin. Tell him he's gotta' come – it's Victory Day, after all." [...]

The people summoning me to the table could not get it through their heads that someone might not want to drink. And if he says he doesn't want to, it's as if he's saying he doesn't want to drink with them, that he finds their company distasteful, that he looks down on them, that he's putting on airs and is trying to set himself apart from the masses, and in general has a big head. [...]

"Let's drink to those who fought, to those who forged victory both on the front lines and at the home front!"

After the speech, during the clinking of glasses, you could hear fragments of conversation:

"You've just gotta."

"What are you gonna do? A day like today."

"No getting around it."

"No question."

"It's a once in a lifetime thing."

"Throughout history."

"Well, muzhiks, to our health."

"To the holiday!"

"No getting around it..."

I was somewhat taken aback by the essence of this talk. It was as if those assembled didn't really want to drink, and they wouldn't have, and didn't like it, but what can you do? "You gotta." "No getting around it."

It seems to me that a little glass of vodka can be used to punish offenders. But we were supposed to be drinking voluntarily, and on top of that, wishing each other the best and most valuable thing – health.[18]

Vladimir Soloukhin, The Ponds of Olepino (1973)

One of the most popular holidays in Russia is International Women's Day, on March 8. Children make drawings for their mothers and men give flowers to female colleagues, friends, and wives. Flower sales on that day are off the chart. But after the usual ceremonies, many men give their own twist to the holiday.

В канун Восьмого марта заходим в типографский буфет и видим картину, как говорят, достойную кисти. В том промежутке между столами, где в обеденное время выстраивается очередь, стоит на коленях мастер-цинкограф и преданными глазами смотрит на Валентину Васильевну, женщину уже не молодую, но молодящуюся и гладкую.

– Вот это сцена! – восклицает, останавливаясь у двери. – Вот это действительно поздравление с Женским днем.

– Не скажите. Бывает и по три человека вот так стоят.

– И все на коленях?

– Ну! На водку просят.

The day before March 8 we walk into the publishing house's lunchroom and see a picture worthy of the canvas, as they say. In the space between tables where people stand in line at lunchtime, the zincography foreman is on his knees with a look of devotion on his face gazing up at Valentina Vasilyevna – a woman past her prime but made up to look younger than her years.

"Now that's a sight!" he exclaims, stopping in the doorway. "That's what I call a Woman's Day tribute."

"That's nothing. Sometimes you'll see three at a time standing like that."

"All on their knees?"

"Sure! They're asking for vodka money."[19]

Igor Vinogradov, "Modern Knights" (1999)

In the Soviet Union, paydays were also cause for celebration, and for purely practical reasons: money in one's pocket. Sometimes, a Russian would drink up his entire monthly wage in one day. As a result, the Supreme Soviet occasionally

A Soviet era advertisement stating that "Wine, vodka, cordials, liqueurs, preserves, fish, confections, matches, cigarettes, salt, sugar. Can be bought in Consumer Union stores."

heard proposals to the effect that paydays should occur twice a month. Did the delegates not realize that this could simply double the problem?

A proposal to introduce a Day of Sobriety has not yet been adopted. Not counting that day, present-day Russia already has 266 (!) holidays. A small sampling of the ones that have not already been mentioned:

January 25	Tatyana's Day (academic holiday)
February 18	Day of Russian Science
March 18	Day of the Tax Inspector
April 12	Day of the Cosmonaut
May 19	Day of the Pioneer
June 12	Day of Sovereignty
July 31	Day of the Navy
August 22	Day of the State Flag
September 25	Day of Machine-Building
October 30	Day of Victims of Political Repression
November 10	Day of the Police
December 12	Day of the Constitution

The idealist Levin, in Lev Tolstoy's *Anna Karenina*, is a typical intellectual whose sympathies lie with the ordinary people, the peasants (*muzhiks*). Levin wonders who drinks more: "We go around saying that the people drink; I don't know who drinks more, the people or our own class; the people at least drink on feast days, but…"[20] It is clear. Even on holidays dedicated to study and development, the intelligentsia hits the bottle.

Казалось бы, что люди, стоящие на двух крайних пределах просвещения, – дикие мужики и образованнейшие люди России, мужики, празднующие введение или казанскую, и образованные люди, празднующие праздник именно просвещения, – должны бы праздновать свои праздники совершенно различно. А между тем оказывается, что праздник самых просвещенных людей не отличается ничем, кроме внешней формы, от праздника самых диких людей. Мужики придираются к знамению или казанской без всякого отношения к значению праздника, чтобы есть и пить; просвещенные придираются ко дню св. Татьяны, чтобы наесться, напиться без всякого отношения к св. Татьяне. Мужики едят студень и лапшу, просвещенные – омары, сыры, потажи, филеи и т. п.; мужики пьют водку и пиво, просвещенные – напитки разных сортов: и вина, и водки, ликеры, сухие, и крепкие, и слабые, и горькие и сладкие, и белые и красные, и шампанские. Угощение мужиков обходится от 20 коп. до 1 руб.; угощение просвещенных обходится от 6 до 20 руб. с человека. Мужики говорят о своей любви к кумовьям и поют русские песни; просвещенные говорят о том, что они любят "alma mater" и заплетающимися языками поют бессмысленные латинские песни. Мужики падают в грязь, а просвещенные – на бархатные диваны. Мужиков разносят и растаскивают по местам жены и сыновья, а просвещенных – посмеивающиеся трезвые лакеи.

Нет, в самом деле – это ужасно! Ужасно то, что люди, стоящие по своему мнению на высшей ступени человеческого образования, не умеют ничем иным ознаменовать праздник просвещения, как только тем, чтобы в продолжение нескольких часов сряду есть, пить, курить и кричать всякую бессмыслицу; ужасно то, что старые люди, руководители молодых людей, содействуют отравлению их алкоголем, – такому отравлению, которое, подобно отравлению ртутью, никогда не проходит совершенно и оставляет следы на всю жизнь.

One would think that men who stand at the two extreme ends of enlightenment, the wild peasants and the most cultured of Russian men – the peasants who celebrate Presentation or the Virgin of Kazan, and the cultured people who celebrate this very holiday of enlightenment – ought to celebrate their holidays in quite different manners. But it turns out that the holiday of the most cultured of people in no way differs from that of the most savage of men, except in external forms. The peasants stick to Visitation or the Virgin of Kazan, without the slightest reference to the meaning of the holiday, in order to eat and drink; the cultured use as a pretext the day of St. Tatyana, in order to stuff themselves with food and drink, without the slightest reference to St. Tatyana. The peasants eat gelatine and noodles; the cultured eat sea crabs, different kinds of cheese, soups, fillets, etc. The peasants drink vodka and beer; the cultured drink liquors of every description: wines, vodkas, liqueurs – dry, and strong, and weak, and bitter and sweet, and white and red – and champagne. The cost of each peasant's treat is from twenty kopeks to one ruble; the treat of the cultured costs from six to twenty rubles for each. The peasants talk of their love for their gossips, and sing Russian songs; the cultured speak of loving their Alma Mater, and with faltering tongues sing senseless Latin songs. The peasants fall into the mud, and the cultured – upon velvet divans. The peasants are taken and dragged home by their wives and sons, and the cultured – by scornful, sober lackeys.

Indeed, it is terrible! Terrible, because people who, in their opinion, stand on the highest level of human education, are not able in any other way to celebrate the holiday of enlightenment except by eating, drinking, smoking, and shouting senselessly for several hours in succession. What is terrible is this, that old men, the guides of the young, contribute to poisoning them by means of alcohol – which poisoning, like quicksilver poisoning, never disappears entirely and leaves traces for the rest of one's life.[21]

Lev Tolstoy, "The Holiday of Enlightenment of the 12th of January" (1889)

2

Everybody Drinks

Не с нужды и не с горя пьет русский народ, а по извечной потребности в чудесном и чрезвычайном, пьет, если угодно, мистически, стремясь вывести душу из земного равновесия и вернуть ее в блаженное бестелесное состояние.

It is not out of poverty or grief that the Russian people drink, but out of an age-old thirst for the miraculous and the extraordinary; they drink, if you will, mystically, striving to lift the soul out of its earthly equilibrium and to return it to a blissful, incorporeal state.[1]

Abram Tertz, *Unguarded Thought* (1966)

VODKA IS PART OF everyday life. In Nikolai Gogol's *The Overcoat*, the narrator complains about the smell of alcohol in staircases: "an inevitable adjunct to all back stairways in St. Petersburg houses."[2] The fact that almost everyone drinks does not detract from the fact that many people, including some prominent figures, saw vodka as Russia's downfall. Lev Tolstoy, for example, was harshly critical of drinking during the second half of his life. And Fyodor Dostoyevsky was afraid that drinking would ruin the Russian soul. His character Verkhovensky grumbles:

Русский бог уже спасовал пред "дешевкой". Народ пьян, матери пьяны, дети пьяны, церкви пусты, а на судах: "двести розог, или тащи ведро". О, дайте, дайте, взрасти поколению. Жаль только, что некогда ждать, а то пусть бы они еще попьянее стали! Ах как жаль, что нет пролетариев! Но будут, будут, к этому идет...

The Russian God has already been vanquished by cheap vodka. The peasants are drunk, the mothers are drunk, the children are drunk, the churches are empty, and in the peasant courts one hears, "Two hundred lashes or stand us a bucket of vodka." Oh, this generation has only to grow up. It's only a pity we can't afford to wait, or we might have let them get a bit more tipsy! Ah, what a pity there's no proletariat! But there will be, there will be; we are going that way...[3]

Fyodor Dostoyevsky, *Demons* (1871)

Thus, everyone drinks, no matter their rank, class, gender, or age.

CHILDREN

From time immemorial, drinking in Russia has been a social and ceremonial activity in which all members of the village community participated. In 1853, the scientist Preobrazhensky wrote that it was acceptable for peasants to drink, "but they also teach their children to drink. You cannot help but be surprised when a child who can barely walk or talk reaches for a glass of vodka, asks for it with gestures, gets it and then drinks it down. A four- or five-year-old is already drinking by the glassful..."

Всему у нас этому делу учитель и заводчик был уездный наш лекарь. Этот человек был подлинно, доложу вам, необыкновенный и на все дела преостроумнейший! Министром ему быть настоящее место по уму; один грех был: к напитку имел не то что пристрастие, а так – какое-то остервенение. Увидит, бывало, графин с водкой, так и задрожит весь. Конечно, и все мы этого придерживались, да все же в меру: сидишь себе да благодушествуешь, и много-много что в подпитии; ну, а он, я вам доложу, меры не знал, напивался даже до безобразия лица.

– Я еще как ребенком был, – говорит, бывало, – так мамка меня с ложечки водкой поила, чтобы не ревел, а семи лет так уж и родитель по стаканчику на день отпущать стал.

Так вот этакой-то пройда и наставлял нас всему.

In all these things our teacher and guide was the district doctor. This man, I can tell you, was really an extraordinary fellow, and uncommonly sharp at such business. A minister's place would have suited him; but he had one vice – he had a passion, or rather an infatuation, for drinking. The sight of a decanter of vodka would set him shaking all over. Of course we all drank a bit, but always in moderation. We used to have a sit and enjoy ourselves, but it was an exception to be even half-seas over; whilst he, I can tell you, knew no moderation, and drank till he made a beast of himself.

"I was still a child," he would say, "my mother used to give me teaspoonfuls of vodka to stop my mouth; and when I was seven years old, my father allowed me one small glass a-day." This was the sort of rogue who put us up to everything.[4]

Mikhail Saltykov-Shchedrin, "Times of Yore" (1856)

Infants often got alcohol from the milk of their mother or wet-nurse. Or they came in contact with it without actually drinking it. For example, in the Poltava region (Ukraine), small children had their feet dipped in vodka before their first haircut so that they would learn to run fast. Nikolai Pomyalovsky, a writer who died of alcoholism at age 27, wrote in 1863, shortly before his death: "I first got drunk at age seven. From then until the end of my schooling, my passion for vodka developed crescendo and diminuendo." Some children began drinking because the distilleries where they worked paid in liquor. And even if they themselves did not drink, they certainly witnessed addiction to drink.

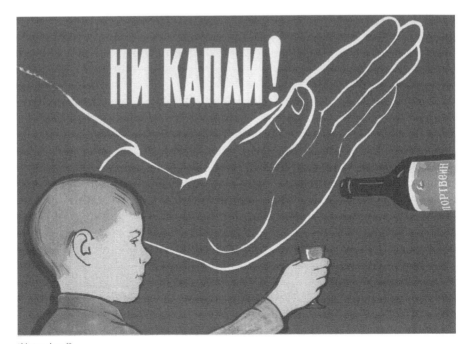

"Not a drop!"

Бабушка поселилась со мною на чердаке. Окно его выходило на улицу, и, перегнувшись через подоконник, можно было видеть, как вечерами и по праздникам из кабака вылезают пьяные, шатаясь, идут по улице, орут и падают. Иногда их выкидывали на дорогу, словно мешки, а они снова ломились в дверь кабака; она хлопала, дребезжала, взвизгивал блок, начиналась драка, – смотреть на все это сверху было очень занятно.

Grandmother and I had established ourselves in the attic. Its window gave on to the street, and one could see, by leaning over the sill, in the evenings and on holidays, drunken men crawling out of the tavern and staggering up the road, shouting and tumbling about. Sometimes they were thrown out into the road, just as if they had been sacks, and then they would try to make their way into the tavern again; the door would bang, and creak, and the hinges would squeak, and then a fight would begin. It was very interesting to look down on all this.[5]

Maxim Gorky, *My Childhood* (1913-1914)

YOUNG PEOPLE

Learning to drink, and to do so properly, is part of a good upbringing.

ЛЕБЕДЕВ. Да, Авдотья Назаровна, трудно теперь с женихами. Не то что жениха – путевых шаферов достать негде. Нынешняя молодежь, не в обиду будь сказано, какая-то, господь с нею, кислая, переваренная... Ни поплясать, ни поговорить, ни выпить толком...

АВДОТЬЯ НАЗАРОВНА. Ну, пить-то они все мастера, только дай...

ЛЕБЕДЕВ. Не велика штука пить – пить и лошадь умеет... Нет, ты с толком выпей!.. В наше время, бывало, день-деньской с лекциями бьешься, а как только настал вечер, идешь прямо куда-нибудь на огонь и до самой зари волчком вертишься... И пляшешь, и барышень забавляешь, и эта штука. (Щелкает себя по шее.) Бывало, и брешешь, и философствуешь, пока язык не отнимется... А нынешние... (Машет рукой.) Не понимаю... Ни богу свечка, ни черту кочерга.

LEBEDEV Yes, Avdotya, husbands are hard to find these days. You can't lay your hands on a decent best man, let alone an eligible groom. No offence meant, but young men are a pretty spineless, wishy-washy crew nowadays, God help them. Can't dance, can't talk, can't drink properly.

AVDOTYA Can't drink? Oh yes they can, given the chance.

LEBEDEV Drinking? There's nothing to it, even a horse can drink. No, the thing is to drink properly. Now, in our time you'd sweat away at your lectures all day long, then you'd make for the bright lights in the evening and buzz around till crack of dawn. You'd dance and amuse the girls and there'd be a bit of this business. [*Pretends to drink.*] Sometimes you'd jabber away nineteen to the dozen. But young men these days – . [*Makes a gesture of dismissal.*] I can't make them out, they're no use to man or beast.[6]

Anton Chekhov, Ivanov (1887)

WOMEN

The German traveler Adam Olearius visited Russia in 1634, 1636, and 1639. He saw how women would play deaf when their drunk husbands wanted to leave a drinking establishment. The men would fall down, and the women would continue imbibing until they sank to the ground next to their husband. For better or worse, women could be just as enthusiastic tipplers as their male counterparts.

МАША. Любить безнадежно, целые годы все ждать чего-то... А как выйду замуж, будет уже не до любви, новые заботы заглушат все старое. И все-таки, знаете ли, перемена. Не повторить ли нам?

ТРИГОРИН. А не много ли будет?

МАША. Ну, вот! (Наливает по рюмке.) Вы не смотрите на меня так. Женщины пьют чаще, чем вы думаете. Меньшинство пьет открыто, как я, а большинство тайно. Да. И все водку или коньяк. (Чокается.) Желаю вам! Вы человек простой, жалко с вами расставаться. (Пьют.)

MASHA. Loving hopelessly, waiting and waiting for years on end for something... But once I'm married, there'll be no room for love, new problems will blot out the old one. And anyhow, you know, it makes a change. Shall we have another?

TRIGORIN. Aren't you overdoing it?

MASHA. Oh, go ahead! [*Fills two glasses*] Don't look at me like that. Women drink more often than you think. A few drink openly, like me, but most of them do it on the sly. Yes. And it's always vodka or brandy. [*Clinks glasses*] Here's to you! You're a nice man. I'm sorry you're going away. [*They drink.*][7]

Anton Chekhov, The Seagull (1895-1896)

In the debate over moderating alcohol consumption that flared up at the end of the nineteenth century, some preachers of abstinence upbraided women for driving their husbands to alcoholism with their enabling attitude. Others reproached them for providing too little diversion at home, leading their husbands to seek refuge elsewhere.

In fact, many women see vodka as an essential part of Russian hospitality.

За столом любимый общажный спор: почему живем так скудно и бедно, если такая богатая, можно сказать, чудовищно богатая страна. Старенький вопросец, Василий Замятов уже встал, чтобы всех перекричать – на вилке огурец, Замятов явно не успел закусить и орет на нас (прораб на стройке): – ... Надо работать! Ра-бо-та-аать! Так кричал, что я даже не видел, были ли у Замятова руки и ноги. Только рот. И огурец на вилке.

И вдруг Зинаида стопку с водкой к небу и весело кричит: – ... Мужик должен все время пи-ииить!

Кричит звонче: – Вино! Чай! Кофе! Водку помаленьку! Пиво! Мужик без дела и питья – свихивается. Что угодно, но пи-и-ииить!

Все в восторге, подхватывают – пить, ах, как важно! Пить, чтобы жить!.. – Орут, вопят, воздавая должное здравому женскому уму, ура, женщине! ура!.. Какой дикий ор. Они чокаются: пьем, все пьем!..

At the table, the favorite topic of communal debate was why we live such a meager, impoverished existence if the country is so rich, even monstrously rich. A time-honored little question. Vasily Zamyatov was already standing up so he could outshout us all – there was a cucumber on his fork, and Zamyatov had obviously forgotten to eat it – and was yelling at us like a construction foreman: "You have to work! W-O-R-K!" He was shouting so loud that I couldn't even see whether Zamyatov had arms or legs. He was all mouth. And a cucumber on a fork.

And suddenly Zinaida raises a glass of vodka skywards cheerfully shouting: "A man should always driiiiiiiink!"

Her shouting became even more resonant: "Wine! Tea! Coffee! Vodka, in moderation! Beer! A *muzhik* with nothing to do and nothing to drink goes bananas. Doesn't matter what, but he must driiiiiink!"

Everyone joins in ecstatically. To drink – oh, how vital! They howl, they scream in recognition of these words of feminine wisdom – hurrah for the woman! Hurrah!... What wild yelling. They clink glasses: let's drink, everyone, drink![8]

Vladimir Makanin, *The Underground, or a Hero of Our Time* (1999)

Marriages fell apart because the hubby would immediately convert his hard-earned monthly wages into vodka, with some of them even drinking the shirt off their own back. Many women developed a fatalistic attitude toward such behavior, whereas others became debauched themselves.

Provided that the household was not at risk, many women tolerated their husband's drinking. But on the other hand... There were some women who put ammonia in the vodka bottle or added alkola to their man's tea: This was a mixture of bromide, soda, licorice water, and dandelion root that was advertised in cheap newspapers and was supposed to take away the desire for vodka. Other women would appear at the factory gates on payday in order to take the pay envelope straight from their husbands' hands. They were known as *buksiry* (tugboats). Sometimes, women took collective action. The nineteenth century

I Won't Let You,
Vladimir
Makovsky
(1892)

saw several instances of a *babi bunt* (an uprising of peasant women). In 1907, a group of women in one village in Novgorod province demanded that the local liquor store be closed. When the authorities did not react, the women took matters into their own hands and closed the store themselves. Sixteen women were arrested the next day.

After the 1917 revolution, women fared better, the standard of living gradually improved, and the Soviets proudly provided all sorts of amenities. Medical services, education, and child care were free. Women in the Soviet Union had it so good that they could work in any number of worthy vocations, such as tractor driver or crane operator. Many doctors were women, and women were also the mainstay of education. Unfortunately, these latter two professions were not very prestigious in the Soviet Union. Besides working their job and bearing children, women were also responsible for the household and had to do their husband's bidding. When women asked each other how their marriage was going, the first question was usually, "And does he drink?" A negative response elicited jealousy from the other woman and a dreamy gaze into the distance. One of the characters in Sergei Dovlatov's story "Driving Gloves" (1986) puts it this way: "My wife is convinced that 'not drinking' should be considered one of the principal marital duties."[9]

After World War II, women were the backbone of the Soviet economy – inevitably, since so many men had been killed or were interned in camps. They discharged their duties admirably. As Marius Broekmeyer writes in *Russia's Sorrow*: "Women are always available. A peasant woman is not incapacitated by being drunk for three straight days."[10] But it was not all sorrow and misery;

The Vodka Lover is the Labor Union's Enemy (1959)

in some villages, women had good lives. Broekmeyer continues: "Seven of them pool their resources to keep a cow and an apparatus for distilling alcohol (otherwise they do not bring you wood, they do not plow your land), and they keep only two pigs. The pension is for sugar and bread. They say that they have never lived so well."

According to historian Barbara Alpern Engel, around 1975 there was a growing realization that men in the Soviet Union were frustrated. They drank too much to be of any use, and because their wives were working, they lost their traditional role as breadwinner and master of the household. Men also felt that their wives had lost their femininity, writes Alpern Engel. "Marriage with a really feminine girl instills in a man two things. On the one hand, he becomes more masculine from the need to protect and defend her, and on the other hand, sharp traits in his character soften; gradually, he becomes more tender and kind."[11] Which is to say that if women would take better care and be more feminine, men would no longer have any need to drink and everything would work out fine. And if men drink anyway, women should be understanding and obliging. Nowhere in the world are women as willing to gloss over their men's failings as they are in Russia.

И не было для меня красивее и желанней ее, не было на свете и не будет!

Придешь с работы усталый, а иной раз и злой, как черт. Нет, на грубое слово она тебе не нагрубит в ответ. Ласковая, тихая, не знает, где тебя усадить, бьется, чтобы и при малом достатке сладкий кусок тебе сготовить. Смотришь на нее и отходишь сердцем, а спустя немного обнимешь ее, скажешь: "Прости, милая Иринка, нахамил я тебе. Понимаешь, с работой у меня нынче не заладилось". И опять у нас мир, и у меня покой на душе. А ты знаешь, браток, что это означает для работы? Утром я встаю как встрепанный, иду на завод, и любая работа у меня в руках кипит и спорится! Вот что это означает – иметь умную жену-подругу.

Приходилось кое-когда после получки и выпивать с товарищами. Кое-когда бывало и так, что идешь домой и такие кренделя ногами выписываешь, что со стороны, небось, глядеть страшно. Тесна тебе улица, да и шабаш, не говоря уже про переулки. Парень я был тогда здоровый и сильный, как дьявол, выпить мог много, а до дому всегда добирался на своих ногах. Но случалось иной раз и так, что последний перегон шел на первой скорости, то есть на четвереньках, однако же добирался. И опять же ни тебе упрека, ни крика, ни скандала. Только посмеивается моя Иринка, да и то осторожно, чтобы я спьяну не обиделся. Разует меня и шеп-чет: "Ложись к стенке, Андрюша, а то сонный упадешь с кровати". Ну, я, как куль совсем, упаду, и все поплывет перед глазами. Только слышу сквозь сон, что она по голове меня тихонько гладит рукою и шепчет что-то ласковое, жалеет, значит...

Утром она меня часа за два до работы на ноги подымет, чтобы я размялся. Знает, что на похмелье я ничего есть не буду, ну, достанет огурец соленый или еще что-нибудь по легости, нальет граненый стаканчик водки. "Похмелись, Андрю-ша, только больше не надо, мой милый". Да разве же можно не оправдать такого доверия? Выпью, поблагодарю ее без слов, одними глазами, поцелую и пошел на работу, как миленький. А скажи она мне, хмельному, слово поперек, крикни или об-ругайся, и я бы, как бог свят, и на второй день напился. Так бывает в иных семьях, где жена дура; насмотрелся я на таких шалав, знаю.

And for me there was no more beautiful woman in the whole world, and there never will be.

I'd come home from work tired, and bad-tempered as hell sometimes. But no, she'd never fling your rudeness back at you. She'd be so gentle and quiet, couldn't do enough for you, always trying to make you something nice to eat, even when there wasn't enough to go round. It made my heart lighter just to look at her. After a while I'd put my arm round her and say, "I'm sorry, Irina dear, I was damn rude to you, I had a rotten day at work today." And again there'd be peace between us, and my mind would be at rest. And you know what that means for your work, mate? In the morning I'd be out of bed like a shot and off to the factory, and any job I laid hands on would go like clockwork. That's what it means to have a real clever girl for a wife.

Sometimes I'd have a drink with the boys on payday. And sometimes, the scissor-legged way I staggered home afterwards, it must have been frightening to watch. The main street wasn't wide enough for me, let alone the side streets. In those days I was tough and strong and I could hold a lot of drink, and I always got home on my own. But sometimes the last stretch would be in bottom gear, you know. I'd finish it on my hands and knees. But again I'd never get a word of reproach, no scolding, no shouting. My Irina, she'd just laugh at me, and she did that careful like, so that even drunk as I was I wouldn't take it wrong. She'd pull my boots off and whisper, "You'd better lie next to the wall tonight, Andrei, or you might fall out of bed in your sleep." And I'd just flop down like a sack of oats and everything would go swimming round in front of me. And as I dropped off to sleep, I'd feel her stroking my head softly and whispering kind words, and I knew she felt sorry for me.

In the morning she'd get me up about two hours before work to give me time to come round. She knew I wouldn't eat anything after being drunk, so she'd get me a pickled cucumber or something like that, and pour me out a good glass of vodka – a hair of the dog, you know. "Here you are, Andrei, but don't do it any more, dear." How could a man let someone down who put such trust in him? I'd drink it up, thank her without words, just with a look and a kiss, and go off to work like a lamb. But if she'd said a word to cross me when I was drunk, if she'd started snapping at me, I'd have come home drunk again, believe me. That's what happens in some families, where the wife's a fool. I've seen plenty of it and I know.[12]

Mikhail Sholokhov, The Fate of a Man (1957)

Father Mirtov, who campaigned for abstinence in the early twentieth century, regarded that very casualness as the source of the whole problem:

Look at the loving care with which the Russian people regard the "little drunken ones" (*pyanenkiye*).... Does not the popular proverb "whoever is drunk and clever has a double advantage" directly reflect the kindly attitude of the Russian towards alcoholism? Let us look further at how the so-called pious Russian becomes indignant when he sees a lighted cigarette in the hands of an Orthodox priest. He does not forgive the priest this weakness... But this same pious parishioner will treat his own priest to a drink and forcibly get him dead drunk... Alcohol has apparently entered into the people, becoming its flesh and blood... it has bought up the Russian, gaining his friendship; and in it, the Russian seeks inspiration, forgetfulness, the easing of his sorrows and his own happiness... Here now is the root of the evil.[13]

Initially, it was primarily peasants who drank to excess. But during the final decades of the nineteenth century, the landowners made up for lost ground. The impoverishment of the lower gentry, through the abolition of the vodka monopoly, certainly played a role in this. In his 1942 memoirs, the academician and shipbuilder Alexei Krylov quotes a landowner who talks about his proper and moderate lifestyle:

Летом встаю я в четыре часа и выпиваю стакан (чайный) водки; мне подают дрожжи, я объезжаю поля. Приеду домой около 6½ часов, выпью стакан водки и иду обходить усадьбу – скотный двор, конный двор и прочее. Вернусь домой часов в 8, выпью стакан водки, подзакушу и лягу отдохнуть. Встану часов в 11, выпью стакан водки, займусь до 12 со старостой, бурмистром. В 12 часов выпью стакан водки, пообедаю и после обеда прилягу отдохнуть. Встану в 3 часа, выпью стакан водки... и т.д.

In the summertime I arise at four in the morning and drink a (tea) glass of vodka. They bring around the *drozhky* and I survey the fields. I arrive home by half past six and drink a glass of vodka before inspecting the estate: the barnyard, the stables, etc. I return home at eight, drink a glass of vodka, have a bite to eat, and take a nap. I arise at eleven, drink a glass of vodka, and work with the steward, the bailiff until noon. At noon I drink a glass of vodka, have supper, and after supper I take a nap. I arise at three, drink a glass of vodka...and so on.[14]

There were also many drinkers among the creative intelligentsia. According to Anton Chekhov, the following menu was known as the "journalist's dinner":

1) Рюмка водки
2) Суточные щи с вчерашней кашей
3) 2 рюмки водки
4) Поросенок с хреном
5) 3 рюмки водки
6) Хрен, кайенский перец и соя
7) 4 рюмки водки
8) 8 бутылок пива

1) Glass of vodka
2) Cabbage soup with yesterday's kasha
3) 2 glasses of vodka
4) Suckling pig with horseradish
5) 3 glasses of vodka
6) Horseradish, cayenne pepper and soy sauce
7) 4 glasses of vodka
8) 8 bottles of beer[15]

Well-known drinkers included the poets Alexander Blok, Konstantin Balmont, and Sergei Yesenin, the writers Alexander Kuprin, Alexander Fadeyev, and Mikhail Sholokhov, composer Modest Mussorgsky, and painter Alexei Savrasov.

Merchants were famous for their drinking stamina, especially if they came from the lower classes. According to the statutes governing social classes, they even had a right to "binges." The "little binge" could go on for a week, and a "big binge" could last a month (see Chapter 6). Merchants as a class disappeared after the revolution, but the expression "to binge like a merchant" lived on.

– Какой же вы... Извозчики, а не пьете... Холостому человеку невозможно, чтоб не пить. Выкушайте!

Извозчик косился на водку, потом на ехидное лицо няньки, и лицо его самого принимало не менее ехидное выражение: нет, мол, не поймаешь, старая ведьма!

– Не пью-с, увольте-с... При нашем деле не годится это малодушество. Мастеровой человек может пить, по тому он на одном месте сидит, наш же брат завсегда на виду в публике. Не так ли-с? Пойдешь в кабак, а тут лошадь ушла; напьешься ежели – еще хуже: того и гляди, уснешь или с козел свалишься. Дело такое.

"What a man!... A cabman and not drink!... A bachelor can't get on without drinking. Help yourself!"

The cabman looked askance at the bottle, then at nurse's wily face, and his own face assumed an expression no less cunning, as much as to say, "You won't catch me, you old witch!"

"I don't drink; please excuse me. Such a weakness does not do in our calling. A man who works at a trade may drink, for he sits in one place, but we cabmen are always in view of the public. Aren't we? If one goes into a pothouse, one finds one's horse gone; if one takes a drop too much, it is worse still; before you know where you are, you will fall asleep or slip off the box. That's where it is."[16]

Anton Chekhov, "The Cook's Wedding" (1885)

Before the revolution there were various occupations in which the use of vodka was all but obligatory, or at least characteristic. Nearly all coachmen, concierges, shoemakers, butlers, tailors, footmen, merchants, bakers, smiths, and officers – especially in the cavalry – were notorious lushes. They drank because their work was so hard. You had to drink, because alcohol was a pick-me-up. Doctors even prescribed it for that purpose. Some drank because it was cold outside; after all, vodka warms you up. This is an illusion: alcohol does bring blood to the surface of the skin, which makes you feel warmer, but the internal temperature of the blood drops and the drinker in fact becomes more vulnerable to cold. Others drank because it was hot and they were thirsty. People would choke if their throats were not lubricated. There is something to this: there often was no clean water available, and as a result workers in dusty professions had to find another way to dampen their throats. And under extremely warm conditions, the body processes alcohol very quickly.

Мастер был, разбойник... Видом был важный, сановитый... Пьянствовал только сильно, но ведь это, внучка, кому как... Кому вредно, а кому и пользительно. Певче-му надо пить, потому – от водки голос гуще становится...

He was masterful, the brigand... He was proud, dignified... The only thing was, he drank a lot, but, my child, for some people that's how it is... For some, it harms; for some, it helps. A singer has to drink, since vodka adds richness to the voice...[17]

Anton Chekov, "In the Asylum for the Sick and Aged" (1894)

After the revolution, some of the above occupations disappeared, but hunters and fishermen, soldiers, actors, artists, masters of ceremony, athletes, gravediggers, plumbers, bank employees, and criminals stood ready to take over from them. The famous writer Venedikt Erofeev noted that one had to consider drinking opportunities when choosing one's profession.

Надо уметь выбирать себе работу, плохих работ нет. Дурных профессий нет, надо уважать всякое призвание. Надо, чуть проснувшись, немедленно чего-нибудь выпить, даже нет, вру, не «чего-нибудь», а именно того самого, что ты пил вчера, и пить с паузами в сорок-сорок пять минут, так, чтобы к вечеру ты выпил на двести пятьдесят больше, чем накануне. Вот тогда не будет ни дурноты, ни стыдливости, и сам ты будешь таким белолицым, как будто тебя уже полгода по морде не били.

Вот видите, сколько в природе загадок, роковых и радостных. Сколько белых пятен повсюду!

You have to know how to choose your profession. Bad professions don't exist; you should respect every calling. In the morning, upon waking, you should immediately drink something – and not just something, but precisely the same thing you drank yesterday – and keep drinking it at intervals of 40 to 45 minutes, so that by nightfall you will have drunk 250 grams more than the day before. That's how you'll avoid feeling nauseous or ashamed, and you'll have a face so clear that one might think it's been at least half a year since it's had a good smacking.

Now you see how many mysteries there are in the world, both fateful and fun, how many blank spots throughout![18]

Venedikt Erofeev, *Moscow to the End of the Line* (1970)

It is more or less true that the 1917 revolution brought little change in the drinking behavior of Russians. The Bolshevik authorities enforced strict measures for a while, during which time they destroyed alcohol supplies, sent home-distillers to camps, and executed alcoholics. But gradually the old patterns resumed, so that the statement "everybody drinks" became the reality once more. According to a report from March 1939, the streets of Moscow were swarming with delegates after the end of the party congress. Many of them had gotten sloshed in restaurants. "As a result of those excesses, forty delegates had to be taken to a sobering-up station, where their stomachs were pumped and they were detained until they had regained consciousness."

COSSACKS

Although many people regard them as Ukrainians or Russians, Cossacks consider themselves a separate people. They are in any event of Slavic origin, having settled on the steppes of southern Russia and Ukraine in the late Middle Ages. The end of the fifteenth century saw the emergence of the Zaporozhye Sech, a republic run mostly by so-called hetmans. They had a tacit agreement with the tsar: if serfs, criminals, or people on the run for some other reason made it as far as the Cossack region, they would be left alone. This made the Cossacks a strange mix of disparate types who had one thing in common: the ability to celebrate exuberantly.

Вся Сечь представляла необыкновенное явление. Это было какое-то беспрерывное пиршество, бал, начавшийся шумно и потерявший конец свой. Некоторые занимались ремеслами, иные держали лавочки и торговали; но большая часть гуляла с утра до вечера, если в карманах звучала возможность и добытое добро не перешло еще в руки торгашей и шинкарей. Это общее пиршество имело в себе что-то околдовывающее. Оно не было сборищем бражников, напивавшихся с горя, но было просто бешеное разгулье веселости. Всякий приходящий сюда позабывал и бросал все, что дотоле его занимало. Он, можно сказать, плевал на свое прошедшее и беззаботно предавался воле и товариществу таких же, как сам, гуляк, не имевших ни родных, ни угла, ни семейства, кроме вольного неба и вечного пира души своей. Это производило ту бешеную веселость, которая не могла бы родиться ни из какого другого источника. Рассказы и болтовня среди собравшейся толпы, лениво отдыхавшей на земле, часто так были смешны и дышали такою силою живого рассказа, что нужно было иметь всю хладнокровную наружность запорожца, чтобы сохранять неподвижное выражение лица, не моргнув даже усом, - резкая черта, которою отличается доныне от других братьев своих южный россиянин. Веселость была пьяна, шумна, но при всем том это не был черный кабак, где мрачно-искажающим весельем забывается человек; это был тесный круг школьных товарищей.

The whole of the Sech presented an unusual scene: it was one unbroken revel; a ball noisily begun, which had no end. Some busied themselves with handicrafts; others kept little shops and traded; but the majority caroused from morning till night, if the wherewithal jingled in their pockets, and if the booty they had captured had not already passed into the hands of the shopkeepers and spirit-sellers. This universal revelry had something fascinating about it. It was not an assemblage of topers, who drank to drown sorrow, but simply a wild revelry of joy. Everyone who came thither forgot everything, abandoned everything which had hitherto interested him. He, so to speak, spat upon his past and gave himself recklessly up to freedom and the good-fellowship of men of the same stamp as himself – idlers having neither relatives nor home nor family, nothing, in short, save the free sky and the eternal revel of their souls. This gave rise to that wild gaiety which could not have sprung from any other source. The tales and talk current among the assembled crowd, reposing lazily on the ground, were often so droll, and breathed such power of vivid narration, that it required all the nonchalance of a *Zaporozhets* to retain his immovable expression, without even a twitch of the mustache – a feature which to this day distinguishes the Southern Russian from his northern brethren. It was drunken, noisy mirth; but there was

The Zaporozhye Cossacks Writing a Mocking Letter to the Turkish Sultan, Ilya Repin (1880-91)

no dark ale-house where a man drowns thought in stupefying intoxication: it was a dense throng of schoolboys.[19]

Nikolai Gogol, *Mirgorod*: "Taras Bulba" (1839-1842)

Another tacit arrangement that the Cossacks had with the tsar was that they would not conduct forays against the Russians. They were to look elsewhere, preferably toward the Muslims to their south. In turn, the tsar could use the fierce horsemen to defend the national frontiers. Otherwise he left them alone, and in that way the Cossacks were able to develop their independent nature, in which they took great pride. The various Cossack groups are named for the region in which they were based; for example, there were Don Cossacks, Kuban Cossacks (*Kubanskaya* was a popular Soviet brand of vodka), and the Amur Cossacks, generally dwelling at the fringes of the empire that they so often defended or even enlarged.

In the tsarist era, the Cossacks played a prominent role in the conquest of Siberia. For that, they used the power of weapons and vodka. In his book about the fur trade in the seventeenth and eighteenth century, James Gibson writes that the well-armed Cossack expeditions usually numbered a few dozen men, rarely more than a hundred. In exchange for vodka in particular, the indigenous people paid *yasak* (tribute, mostly in pelts) and pledged their allegiance to the tsar. To be on the safe side, the Cossacks often extracted a little extra cooperation by taking several people hostage from each tribe or population group.

Whether or not Cossacks are Russians, it is a fact that they resemble Russians and drink not only wine, but also vodka, preferably in large quantities. But in all regards, they are just a little bit rougher and wilder. In earlier times, Cossack settlements were temporary, and the entire community and all it possessed could be picked up and moved in no time. According to Nikolai Gogol, the Cossacks were quite dexterous.

Современные иноземцы дивились тогда справедливо необыкновенным способностям его. Не было ремесла, которого бы не знал козак: накурить вина, снарядить телегу, намолоть пороху, справить кузнецкую, слесарную работу и, в прибавку к тому, гулять напропалую, пить и бражничать, как только может один русский, - все это было ему по плечу. Кроме рейстровых козаков, считавших обязанностью являться во время войны, можно было во всякое время, в случае большой потребности, набрать целые толпы охочекомонных: стоило только есаулам пройти по рынкам и площадям всех сел и местечек и прокричать во весь голос, ставши на телегу: "Эй вы, пивники, броварники! полно вам пиво варить, да валяться по запечьям, да кормить своим жирным телом мух! Ступайте славы рыцарской и чести добиваться! Вы, плугари, гречкосеи, овцепасы, баболюбы! полно вам за плугом ходить, да пачкать в земле свои желтые чеботы, да подбираться к жинкам и губить силу рыцарскую! Пора доставать козацкой славы!" И слова эти были как искры, падавшие на сухое дерево. Пахарь ломал свой плуг, бровари и пивовары кидали свои кади и разбивали бочки, ремесленник и торгаш посылал к черту и ремесло и лавку, бил горшки в доме. И все, что ни было, садилось на коня. Словом, русский характер получил здесь могучий, широкий размах, дюжую наружность.

Their foreign contemporaries rightly marvelled at their wonderful qualities. There was no handicraft which the Cossack was not expert at: he could distill brandy, build a wagon, make powder, and do blacksmith's and gunsmith's work, in addition to committing wild excesses, drinking and carousing as only a Russian can – all this he was equal to. Besides the registered Cossacks, who considered themselves bound to appear in arms in time of war, it was possible to collect at any time, in case of dire need, a whole army of volunteers. All that was required was for the Osaul or sub-chief to traverse the market-places and squares of the villages and hamlets, and shout at the top of his voice, as he stood in his wagon, "Hey, you distillers and beer-brewers! You have brewed enough beer, and lolled on your stoves, and stuffed your fat carcasses with flour, long enough! Rise, win glory and warlike honors! You ploughmen, you reapers of buckwheat, you tenders of sheep, you danglers after women, enough of following the plough, and soiling your yellow shoes in the earth, and courting women, and wasting your warlike strength! The hour has come to win glory for the Cossacks!" These words were like sparks falling on dry wood. The husbandman broke his plough; the brewers and distillers threw away their casks and destroyed their barrels; the mechanics and merchants sent their trade and their shop to the devil, broke pots and everything else in their homes, and mounted their horses. In short, the Russian character here received a profound development, and manifested a powerful outward expression.[20]

Nikolai Gogol, *Mirgorod*: "Taras Bulba" (1839-1842)

The Cossacks certainly did not drink in moderation, but just like Russian peasants, they usually limited themselves to ritual days. Then they would go all out for a couple of days. Tolstoy writes about the Cossacks in the Caucasus:

Белецкий поднял стакан. – Алла бирды, – сказал он и выпил. (Алла бирды, значит: бог дал; это обыкновенное приветствие, употребляемое кавказцами, когда пьют вместе.) – Сау бул (будь здоров), – сказал Ерошка, улыбаясь, и выпил свой стакан. – Ты говоришь: праздник! – сказал он Оленину, поднимаясь и глядя в окно. – Это что за праздник! Ты бы посмотрел, как в старину гуляли! Бабы выйдут, бывало, оденутся в сарафаны, галунами обшиты. Грудь всю золотыми в два ряда обвешают. На голове кокошники золотые носили. Как пройдет, так фр! фр! шум подымется. Каждая баба как княгиня была. Бывало, выйдут, табун целый, за-

играют песни, так стон стоит; всю ночь гуляют. А казаки бочки выкатят на двор, за-
сядут, всю ночь до рассвета пьют. А то схватятся рука с рукой, пойдут по станице
лавой. Кого встретят, с собой забирают, да от одного к другому и ходят. Другой раз
три дня гуляют. Батюшка, бывало, придет, еще я помню, красный, распухнет весь,
без шапки, все растеряет, придет и ляжет. Матушка уж знает, бывало: свежей
икры и чихирю ему принесет опохмелиться, а сама бежит по станице шапку его
искать. Так двое суток спит! Вот какие люди были! А нынче что?

Beletsky raised his glass. "*Allah birdi!*" he said, and emptied it.

"*Saul bul!*"[21] Eroshka replied with a smile, emptying his glass. "You think this is a festival?" he said to Olenin, standing up and looking out the window. "This isn't what *I'd* call a
festival, my friend! You should have seen what they were like in the old days! The women
all came out in real finery, with gold trimmings and coin necklaces, and golden head-
dresses, and you should have heard the clink-clink-clink of the gold when they walked!
Every woman looked like a princess, and they came out in flocks, singing songs. There
was carousing all night long. The men would roll barrels into the yards and sit drinking till
dawn, and then they would all walk through the village arm in arm. They went from house
to house, and took along anyone they met. They drank and danced for three whole days.
I remember my father would come home without his hat, all bloated and red, his clothes
ripped to shreds, and lie down to sleep. Mother knew exactly what to do: She brought him
fresh caviar and some *chikhir*[22] for his hangover, and then she'd go through the village
looking for his hat. And Father would sleep for two whole days! That's how people were
back then, and look at them now!"[23]

Lev Tolstoy, *The Cossacks* (1863)

Given the relative independence that the Cossacks enjoyed under the tsars,
it is no surprise that they took the side of the Whites in the Civil War (1918-
1920), fighting against Lenin's Bolshevist rule. Later, during the Soviet era, the
Cossacks paid a steep price for their support of the Whites. Their culture was
suppressed and their numbers fell from 11 million in 1918 to scarcely 100,000
today.

In the following passage, a Red Army regiment is close on the heels of a
group of Don Cossacks. During a moment of rest, a Cossack leader wistfully
recalls his life before World War I and the 1917 revolution.

Днями летними, погожими в степях донских, под небом густым и прозрачным
звоном серебряным вызванивает и колышется хлебный колос. Это перед
покосом, когда у ядреной пшеницы-гарновки ус чернеет на колосе, будто у
семнадцатилетнего парня, а жито дует вверх и норовит человека перерасти.

Бородатые станичники на суглинке, по песчаным буграм, возле левад засевают клинышками жито. Сроду не родится оно, издавна десятина не дает больше тридцати мер, а сеют потому, что из жита самогон гонят, яснее слезы девичьей; потому, что исстари так заведено, деды и прадеды пили, а на гербе казаков Области Войска Донского, должно, недаром изображен был пьяный казак, телешом сидящий на бочке винной. Хмелем густым и ярым бродят по осени хутора и станицы, нетрезво качаются красноверхие папахи над плетнями из краснотала.

По тому самому и атаман дня не бывает трезвым, потому-то все кучера и пулеметчики пьяно кособочатся на рессорных тачанках.

Семь лет не видал атаман родных куреней. Плен германский, потом Врангель, в солнце расплавленный Константинополь, лагерь в колючей проволоке, турецкая фелюга со смолистым соленым крылом, камыши кубанские, султанистые, и – банда. Вот она, атаманова жизнь, коли назад через плечо оглянуться. Зачерствела душа у него, кан летом в жарынь черствеют следы раздвоенных бычачьих копыт возле музги степной. Боль, чудная и непонятная, точит изнутри, тошнотой наливает мускулы, и чувствует атаман: не забыть ее и не залить лихоманку никаким самогоном. А пьет – дня трезвым не бывает потому, что пахуче и сладко цветет жито в степях донских, опрокинутых под солнцем жадной черноземной утробой, и смуглощекие жалмерки до хуторам и станицам такой самогон вываривают, что с водой родниковой текучей не различить.

On fine summer days in the Don steppes, the wheat waves and rings like pure silver under the intense translucent sky. That's before the reaping, when the beard of the full-eared Garnovka wheat darkens like the fluff on the lip of a seventeen-year-old and the rye stretches up as though it would outgrow a man.

The bearded Cossack farmers sow their rye in strips on the loamy patches and sandy slopes and along the edges of the poplar groves. It never burgeons well; an acre won't yield more than six bushels, but they sow it because they can distill from it a spirit clearer than a maiden's tears, because this has been the custom for centuries, because their fathers and forefathers loved to drink, and because it was not for nothing that the Great Seal of the Don Cossack Army portrayed a drunken Cossack sitting stripped to the waist astride a barrel of wine. It's a wild and heady brew that goes around the villages and *stanitsas* in autumn and sends the Cossacks' tall red-topped hats swaying unsteadily along by the willow fences.

That's why the ataman himself is never sober; that's why the gun-crews and drivers all loll tipsily on their machine-gun carts.

It's seven years now since the ataman saw the smoke of his home fires. First, a German prison camp, then service with Wrangel, then Constantinople melting in the sun, then internment behind barbed wire, then a Turkish fellucca with its tarry, salt-caked lateen, then the rushes of the Kuban, and then – this marauding band.

That's what the ataman's life has been, if he cares to look back. His heart has hardened as the imprint of an ox's cloven hoof hardens by a steppeland pool in the heat of summer. A mysterious, hidden pain gnaws at his vitals, sickens every muscle, and he feels that this sickness can be neither forgotten nor drowned in drink. Yet still he drinks – never a day sober; for sweet and fragrant grows the rye in the Donside steppe with its black greedy belly upturned to the sun, and the brown-cheeked village women whose husbands are away make a brew so pure there's no telling it from spring water.[24]

Mikhail Sholokhov, "The Birthmark" (1924)

3

Rituals

Лучший стрелок, которого удалось мне встречать, стрелял каждый день, по крайней мере три раза перед обедом. Это у него было заведено, как рюмка водки.

The best marksman I ever met used to shoot every day, at least three times before dinner. It was as much a part of his daily routine as a glass of vodka.[1]

Alexander Pushkin, *Tales of Belkin:* "The Shot" (1830)

HOW TO DRINK VODKA

Ivan Chonkin is the somewhat bungling hero of the books by Vladimir Voinovich that bear his name. He is a true-blue Russian who enjoys a nip or two. When Chonkin drinks, he assumes a drinking posture and holds his breath, which helps the vodka do its job. Drinking is not something you do casually. You have to prepare and concentrate, like the New Year's traveler does in the Nikolai Fokht's *The Hangover Book*:

Отдаю должное – пьет новогодний путешественник красиво: крепко, но с уважением берет рюмку за ножку, подносит ко рту, а не голову клонит, коротким движением закидывает водку в организм. При этом не производит лишних звуков – не крякает, не мычит, не комментирует событие. Молча дожидается проникновения водки в желудок, держит паузу до появления характерного приятного жжения в пищеводе и лишь после этого руками (не вилкой) берет огурец и им, прикрыв глаза, хрумкает, вдумчиво жует, смешивая послевкусие «Виктора» с ароматом домашнего рассола, смиренно проглатывает огурец.

You have to give credit where credit is due – there is beauty in how the New Year's traveler drinks: he firmly, but respectfully, takes the shot glass by its little stem, brings it to his mouth, and, without tilting the head, tosses the vodka into the body with a quick movement. No superfluous sounds are made: he does not grunt, mutter, or comment on what is taking place. He silently waits for the vodka to penetrate the stomach, pauses in anticipation of the characteristic and pleasant burning sensation in the gullet, and only then takes a pickle with his hand (not his fork). With his eyelids lowered, he bites down, chewing thoughtfully, blending the aftertaste of Viktor with the aroma of homemade brine, and then serenely swallows the pickle.[2]

Nikolai Fokht, *The Hangover Book* (1997)

WASHING IT DOWN

You have to eat when drinking vodka (see Chapter 13). Many Russians also mix their drinks. They wash the vodka down, preferably with beer, but if necessary with water, juice, or lemon soda.

— Володь, ты мне скажи, я был в Москве, у родственников в гостях, и там за столом был один знакомый моих родственников. Работает за границей, в посольстве. И он сказал, что за границей не запивают. Считается очень даже некрасиво и неприлично запивать водой, или, скажем, пивом, или ситром. Ты мне скажи, никак я сам не пойму, почему за границей не запивают?

— Видишь ли, – начал было я, – предполагается, что напиток сам по себе вкусный. Он его проглотит, посмакует во рту и прислушивается к аромату. Зачем же отбивать вкус того, что кажется вкусным?

— Значит, у них водка, что ли, вкуснее нашей?

— Я б не сказал, напротив, они очень любят русскую водку. Но дело в том, что они пьют маленькими глоточками, из рюмок граммов так по двадцать. А от маленьких глоточков и от того, что не закусывают, хмелеют они очень быстро.

— Пить не умеют, вот и все, – выручил меня другой сосед. – Какие они против нас питоки. Да ему ежели вот этот тонкий стакан – его и под столом не найдешь.

— Слабаки.

— Теперь понятно. А то я все думал, почему же такое – за границей не запивают. Конечно, ежели двадцать грамм, их и во рту не найдешь. Это даже смешно, двадцать грамм водой запивать или, скажем, ситром. Двадцать грамм – это курам на смех, разве это питье?

"Explain something to me, Volodya. I was in Moscow visiting my relatives, and there was an acquaintance of theirs at the table. He works abroad, in the embassy. And he said that in other countries they don't eat or drink anything with their vodka. It's even considered crass or rude to wash it down with water or, for instance, beer or lemon soda. Explain that to me. I can't get my head around it. Why don't they wash it down?"

"You see," I attempted to explain, "the idea is that the drink tastes good all by itself. He swallows it, savors it in his mouth, and experiences the flavor. Why try to kill the taste of something that tastes good?"

"Are you saying that their vodka tastes better than ours?"

"That's not it. In fact, they like Russian vodka a lot. The point is that they drink it in tiny gulps, about twenty grams a shot. And because the gulps are so small and they aren't eating or drinking anything with them, they get drunk really fast."

"They don't know how to drink, that's the bottom line," another neighbor stepped in to help explain. "What kind of drinkers are they compared to us? Give him a little glass like this and you won't even be able to find him under the table."

"They're weaklings."

"Now I understand. Because I kept wondering why they don't eat or drink anything with their vodka in other countries. Of course, if it's a matter of twenty grams, you can't even feel that in your mouth. It's a joke, washing down twenty grams with water or, for instance, lemon soda. Twenty grams – even chickens would laugh at that. You call that drinking?"[3]

Vladimir Soloukhin, *The Ponds of Olepino* (1973)

BOTTOMS UP

Vodka is not for sipping. It's just not done. If you are a foreigner, you can dress like a Russian and speak the language fluently, but if you don't empty your glass in one gulp, you betray your non-Russian origin. Bottoms up – *do dna*, in Russian – is the norm. Not emptying your glass in one swig, especially after a toast, means bad luck for the person to whom you're drinking.

– Эй, эй! – прикрикнул он, когда после первого большого глотка я сделал второй. Забрал – и теперь сам, вслед за мной, тоже сделал несколько крепких глотков. Посидел. Отдышался от обжигающей жижи. – Неплохо пьешь, отец, а? – Да ведь русский, – оправдался я скромно. – А-аа! – пренебрежительно воскликнул он, протянув гласный звук. Мол, он тоже заглотнуть водки может как следует! или не видишь?!. Тем не менее он пьянел на глазах. И продолжал прикладываться маленькими беспаузными глотками (думаю, это была первая его ошибка).

"Hey, hey!" he cried out, when I followed my first big gulp with another. He took it from me and now he too, following my example, took several hefty swigs. He just sat there for a moment. When he got his wind back after the burning liquid he said: "You know how to drink, eh, pops?" "Well, I'm a Russian after all," I replied modestly. "Aaaaaaw!" he exclaimed dismissively, drawing out the vowel sound. He seemed to be saying that he, too, knew a thing or two about downing vodka, whether I could see it or not. But the fact of the matter was that he grew drunk before my eyes. And he continued to ply away, taking little sips one after the other (I think this was his first mistake).[4]

Vladimir Makanin, *The Underground, or a Hero of Our Time* (1999)

The protagonist Akimov in Oleg Yermakov's story "The Yellow Mountain" (1989) does know how it's supposed to be done; at any rate, he poured himself a glass of water from a carafe and "drank it down like vodka, in one gulp."

Some people contend that Russians drink in one gulp because vodka is actually nasty. In his book on Russia, the Dutch physician Pieter van Woensel wrote in 1804: "I must note in passing that the Russians' vodka, or *garelka*, leaves such an atrocious taste in my mouth that I believe that it must function as a means of preventing drunkenness."[5] And for that reason, you have to pour it down all at once. But it does take some practice to get it to go straight into your esophagus. When you're ready to do it, you press your bottom lip against the glass and purse your upper lip above it, while at the same time bending your head way back. If you do it right, you avoid all contact with your taste buds. You can also neutralize the taste by drinking the vodka ice-cold.

Wine is the sun, the earth and the grape. Vodka is a volatile sperm of a nation. It is a shock, an aggression, an epileptic attack, a blow below the belt. Drinking in Russia often ends up in scuffles and ugly fights – something that rarely happens in wine countries like Italy or France. Vodka culture is the culture of spasm and hysteria. It is happiness through nausea and disgust. No one in his right mind can claim that vodka is tasty. This is why it is gulped, not sipped. It is only the uncultured West Europeans who sip vodka, which shows their lack of understanding of vodka culture. Wine, on the other hand, is gradualness, enjoyment, delight. It is happiness through happiness. It does not lead to oblivion, but provides communication along horizontal, rather than vertical, lines.[6]

Vitali Vitaliev, *Borders Up! Eastern Europe through the Bottom of a Glass* (1999)

Meanwhile, others say that drinking in one gulp is an old trick to avoid getting drunk too quickly. They assume that drunkenness is caused by the alcohol vapors, and not by the bitter liquid itself. By tossing the vodka back all at once, the vapors supposedly have no way of rising into the head via the nose...

Француз может восхвалять аромат коньяка, шотландец – славить вкус виски. Водка – она никакая. Невидимая, бесцветная, в идеале – безвкусная. Но при этом резкая, раздражительная смесь. Русский пьет водку залпом – гримасничая и матерясь – и тут же бросается ее закусывать, занюхивать, «полировать». Важен не процесс, а результат. Водку с тем же успехом можно было бы не пить, а вкалывать в вену.

The Frenchman will praise the aroma of cognac, and the Scotsman will laud the flavor of whiskey. Vodka, however, is colorless, odorless, and tasteless. At the same time, it is an acrid and irritating drink. The Russian gulps his vodka down, grimacing and swearing, and immediately reaches for something else to "smooth it out." The result, not the process, is what's important. You might as well inject vodka into your bloodstream as drink it.[7]

Victor Erofeyev, "The Russian God" (2002)

Starting in the seventeenth century, Russians were no longer permitted to distill their own liquor, and they could drink only on established holidays. Having liquor at home was also prohibited. This meant that Russians seized every opportunity to drink, and on those occasions they would guzzle everything they could get their hands on. In his book about drinking, the English author Kingsley Amis explained: "Drinking to get drunk is probably known in every country, and there are alcoholics in most places, but even the ordinary Russian drinks to be drunk with the minimum of delay – hence the down-in-one ritual, which of course also shortens the agony of getting down the local hooch."[8] The fact that Russians sniff their sleeve if they do not have bread or something else to nibble on is also said to come from the fact that vodka is actually vile.

Рука невольно тянется к столу и шарит, ища чего-нибудь острого, отшибающего противный сивушный дух: соленого огурца, селедки, гриба, капустки... Здесь были караси, к тому же горячие. Пока донесешь разваливающуюся рыбку до рта, пока на нее подуешь, пока обсосешь острые косточки – водочный дух и вкус все еще стоит во рту, и в горле, и в самом желудке, и минута эта ужасна. Все морщатся, зажмуриваются, шарят рукой вслепую и, только спустя некоторое время, обсосав третью рыбку или удачно поддев пласт яичницы, приходят в себя. Впрочем, многие запивают водку холодной колодезной водой. Им, наверное, легче.

Your hand involuntarily shoots out to the table and fumbles around, looking for something flavorful to kill the disgusting fusel taste: pickles, herring, mushrooms, sauerkraut... Here, we had carp, and it was hot. The entire time it takes to bring the disintegrating fish to your

SOVIET ERA ANTI-ALCOHOL POSTERS

"Alcohol" in which the noose forms the first "o".

"And they say *we* are pigs...

"Let's drive drunkards from the workforce."

"When your gaze is fixed on the glass, pull your hand away: Vodka is poison!"

mouth, to blow on it, and to suck its sharp bones, that vodka smell and taste are still in your mouth, in your throat, and in your belly. That minute is awful. Everyone is contorting their faces, blinking, groping blindly with their hands. Only once a little time has passed and they've sucked the bones of their third helping of fish clean or successfully excavated down to the egg layer of the salad, only then do they come to. Then again, many people wash vodka down with cold well water. They probably have it easier.[9]

Vladimir Soloukhin, *The Ponds of Olepino* (1973)

MANLINESS

For a Russian man, the ability to drink vodka is an important gauge of masculinity. And the question "Do you drink?" is a test for whether he'll be accepted by a group of men. Answering "no" makes it difficult, if not impossible, to assimilate completely in a new workplace, athletic club, or living situation. You remain an outsider, you will never be *svoy* (*chelovek*), meaning "our type (of person)." Workers have an expression for the drink that a new colleague is expected to buy on his first day on the job or his first payday: *privalnaya*. Only after the *privalnaya* do you truly belong. And it has to be vodka. Less potent beverages are unworthy of a man, and drinking cognac is perceived as snobbish. So be careful: If you ask a Russian "Do you drink vodka?" you might get the answer, "No, I spread it on my sandwich."

Водку в белом чайнике подавал половой, и я с завистью каждый раз смотрел, как Яг ее пил из чайной чашки. Он выливал водку себе в рот, горло совсем не глотало, а лицо его после этого не только не морщилось, но всегда делалось таким, будто в него вошло что-то светлое. Я так не мог. Мокрый водочный ожог, в особенности после глотка, когда первое дыхание, холодя пылающие рот и горло, приобретало отвратительный запах спирта, был мне чрезвычайно противен. Я пил водку, потому что пьянство почиталось одним из элементов лихости, и еще потому, что кому-то и зачем-то доказывал силу: пить больше других и быть трезвее, чем другие. И хотя мне и самому уже было ужасно худо, и каждое движение нужно было себе заказывать, а уж потом только с чрезвычайной сосредоточенностью проделывать, – но я ощутил это как приятную победу, когда Яг, уже после многих чайников, выпив из чашки, вдруг закрыл глаза, начал белеть, и подперев голову ладонью, так дышал, что весь раскачивался.

The vodka was served in a white teapot, and I could not help envying Yag each time I saw him drink from his cup: he would pour the vodka down his throat without swallowing, his face showing no sign of a wrinkle and, in fact, seeming to light up from the inside. I was different. The moist vodka burn – especially the one immediately after a swallow, when the breath, cooling a fiery mouth and throat, takes on the revolting odor of alcohol

– filled me with disgust. I drank vodka because intemperance was considered one of the components of bravado and because I wanted to prove – to whom and for what reason I cannot say – that I had the ability to drink more than anyone else and remain sober longer. And even though I was in a terribly bad way myself and had to command each move I wanted to make and then carry out each command with great concentration, still I felt I had scored a victory when after many teapots Yag took a gulp from his cup and, turning pale, suddenly closed his eyes, propped his head up on his hand, and began breathing so hard his whole body shook.[10]

M. Ageyev, *Novel with Cocaine* (1983)

ABSTAINING

Back in the seventeenth century, the German traveler Adam Olearius wrote that a Russian lacks the strength to turn down a drink. And the willpower. Fortunately, refusing a drink is not an option: "None of them anywhere, anytime, or under any circumstance lets pass an opportunity to have a draught or a drinking bout. They drink mainly vodka, and at get-togethers, or when one person visits another, respect is rendered by serving one or two 'cups of wine,' that is, vodka. The common people, slaves, and peasants are so faithful to the custom that if one of them receives a third cup and a fourth, or even more, from the hand of a gentleman, he continues to drink up, believing that he dare not refuse, until he falls to the ground – and sometimes the soul is given up with the draught."[11]

Refusing a drink is more shocking than sipping: it is one of worst ways of insulting a Russian host. Whether you're a Russian or a foreigner, the host interprets your refusal as a lack of respect, as if you consider yourself superior and won't deign to have a glass with him. The question, literally, is, "*Ty menya ne uvazhayesh?*" (Don't you respect me?), and it seems to come from the depths of his already-deep soul.

И, дав такой ответ, Ахилла действительно выпил, да и все выпили пред ужином по комплектной чарке. Исключение составлял один отец Захария, потому что у него якобы от всякого вина голова кружилась. Как его ни упрашивали хоть что-нибудь выпить, он на все просьбы отвечал:

– Нет, нет, освободите! Я ровно, ровно вина никакого не пью.

– Нынче все пьют, – уговаривали его.

– Действительно, действительно так, ну а я не могу.

– Курица, и та пьет, – поддерживал потчевавших дьякон Ахилла.

– Что ж, пускай и курица!.. Глупо это довольно, что ты, братец, мне курицу представляешь...

– Хуже курицы вы, отец, – укорял Ахилла.

"No!" Perhaps the most famous Soviet anti-alcohol poster, by V.I. Govorkov (1954).

— Не могу! Чего хуже курицы? Не могу!

— Ну, если уж вина никакого не можете, так хоть хересу для политики выпейте! Захария, видя, что от него не отстают, вздохнул и, приняв из рук дьякона рюмку, ответил:

— Ну, еще ксересу так и быть; позвольте мне ксересу.

And after making that reply Achilles did just that, and right before supper all the others also had shots of vodka from identical goblets. The sole exception was Father Zacharias, because any sort of spirits apparently made him dizzy. No matter how much they begged him to drink something, anything, he replied to all their entreaties:

"No, no, let me off the hook! I absolutely, positively do not drink spirits of any kind."

"Everybody's drinking now," they cajoled him.

"That's true, that's true, but I can't."

"Even chickens drink." Deacon Achilles said, supporting the others.

"So what? Let them!... That's pretty dumb of you, my friend, to hold up chickens to me as an example…"

"You're worse than a chicken, Father," Achilles reproached him.

"I can't drink! How am I worse than a chicken? I simply can't drink!"

"Well, if you can't drink vodka, then at least be shrewd enough to have some sherry!"

Seeing that they were not about to leave him alone, Zacharias sighed, accepted a glass from the deacon, and replied:

"Well, shcherry's all right. I'll have some shcherry."[12]

Nikolai Leskov, *The Cathedral Clergy* (1872)

Thus, not drinking is a tricky thing. And it is virtually impossible if you want to get a Russian to do something. He won't take you seriously. Women can indeed refuse, but men are left to the mercy of the wolves. However, there are a few methods for getting around this. You can say that your poor health doesn't allow you to drink (feigning a liver disorder works wonders). Or you can say that you don't drink because you are an alcoholic who has stopped drinking. This latter approach might even earn you respect.

— Ну да довольно же, довольно! — ужасно вдруг опять рассердился и закричал Вельчанинов — пора вам, убирайтесь!

— Нет, не довольно-с! — вскочил и Павел Павлович, — даже хоть и надоел я вам, так и тут не довольно, потому что мы еще прежде должны с вами выпить и чокнуться! Выпьем, тогда я уйду-с, а теперь не довольно!

— Павел Павлович, можете вы сегодня убраться к черту или нет?

— Я могу убраться к черту-с, но сперва мы выпьем! Вы сказали, что не хотите пить именно со мной; ну, а я хочу, чтобы вы именно со мной-то и выпили!

Он уже не кривлялся более, он уже не подхихикивал. Все в нем опять вдруг как бы преобразилось и до того стало противоположно всей фигуре и всему тону еще сейчашнего Павла Павловича, что Вельчанинов был решительно озадачен.

– Эй, выпьем, Алексей Иванович, эй, не отказывайте! – продолжал Павел Павлович, схватив крепко его за руку и странно смотря ему в лицо. Очевидно, дело шло не об одной только выпивке.

"No, it's not enough, sir!" Pavel Pavlovich, too, jumped up. "Even though you're sick of me, it's still not enough, because first you and I must have a drink and clink glasses! We'll have a drink, and then I'll go, but now it's not enough!"

"Pavel Pavlovich, can you clear the hell out of here today or not?"

"I can clear the hell out of here, sir, but first we'll drink! You said you don't want to drink precisely with me; well, but I want that you drink precisely with me!"

He was no longer clowning, no longer tittering. Everything in him was again as if transformed suddenly and was now so opposite to the whole figure and tone of the just-now Pavel Pavlovich that Velchaninov was decidedly taken aback.

"Eh, let's drink, Alexei Ivanovich, eh, don't refuse!" Pavel Pavlovich went on, gripping him firmly by the arm and looking strangely into his face. Obviously, this was not just a matter of drinking.[13]

Fyodor Dostoyevsky, "The Eternal Husband" (1869)

Arriving at an event late in order to avoid a few drinks can fail as a ploy. The latecomer has to drink down one or more glasses as punishment, the *shtrafnoy* (penalty). It was Tsar Peter the Great who introduced this custom with his "penalty goblet."

THE TROIKA

In 1958, a new ban on the sale of alcohol in small restaurants and cafeterias went into effect. This made it difficult to obtain a small amount of vodka, except in Intourist hotels, but the goods available there were restricted to foreigners and party bosses. Ordinary Russians could get smashed at home or go to a chic restaurant and order vodka with their meal, but that was expensive and could easily require a time investment of three hours or more. It was easier to find drinking buddies, pool your money, buy a half a liter from the liquor dealer, and kill the bottle while standing in a doorway or sitting on a park bench. In view of the volume, having three drinkers was ideal. As a result, you would often see people hanging around the liquor dealers holding up two fingers against their chest as a sign that they were looking for two buddies. It was less common to see a single finger. This is how *troika* drinking became fashionable (a *troika* can

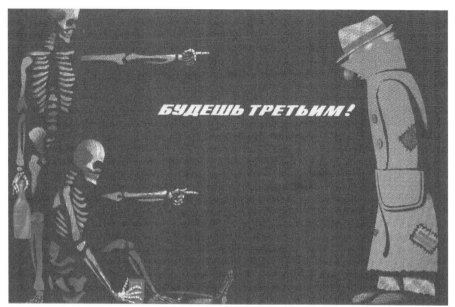

Anti-alcohol poster: "You'll be our third!"

be a coach pulled by three horses, but can also refer to three of anything). The question "Want to be the third?" is never misunderstood.

> Usually when I come to the store in the afternoon, two characters rush out to meet me. Both conspirators wink at me. One raises his arms as if ready to embrace me, the other displays his finger. With a haughty and stern expression, I pass by the wine counter, leaving the two in utter bewilderment and confusion. They are completely unable to understand why I refuse to go threes with them. Do I disdain their company? Do I not drink at all? Then why the devil did I come into the store? Is it a man's job to stand in line for butter and sausages? I in fact feel a bit uncomfortable about disappointing people in a companionable mood. I suppose it must be written on my face: "I am a ready third bird."[14]
>
> Anatoly Gladilin, "Moscow Essays" (1976)

The *troika* often drank the vodka furtively, and thus the glasses also had to be filled furtively (drinking straight from the bottle is inappropriate in all situations). Under your jacket, in a dark staircase, under the table. People had also figured out that when a half a liter is poured, exactly twenty-one air bubbles come up – glup, glup, glup. And so with three people, you had to stop after the seventh bubble, exactly one-third. "Through the seventh bubble" was a common expression among drunks.

After the collapse of the Soviet Union, the vodka industry deftly capitalized on the *troika*. Vodka brands appeared with names such as "*Troika*," "Want to be the third?" and "The three of us." A further step in this direction was the sale of vodka in plastic containers measuring ten centiliters, like the cups from which we used to drink orange juice on school field trips. From that point on, Russian alcoholics no longer depended on the *troika* and could drink in isolation. They call those containers "Russian yogurt" or "Schoolgirls." In 1995, the Russian government banned the sale of vodka in plastic packaging. The Belarusan government followed suit in 1999. Many boozers are convinced that the ban on "Russian yogurt" was the result of lobbying by glass manufacturers. Latvian or Uzbek tipplers are luckier, since "Russian yogurt" is still freely available in their countries.

In fact, *troika* drinking did not emerge out of the blue; drunks were simply resuming an old tradition. Or this is at any rate suggested by Adam Olearius, who visited Moscow in 1634:

> It is true that recently these public taverns, some of which belonged to the Tsar and some to the boyars, have been abolished, because they drew people away from work and gave them an opportunity to drink up their earnings. Now one can no longer buy two or three kopeks worth of vodka. Instead, His Tsarist Majesty ordered that each town have one *kruzhechny dvor*, which sells vodka only by the jug or tankard. The people who are appointed managers of these establishments have taken a special oath, and they annually supply an unbelievable sum of money to His Tsarist Majesty's treasury. However, daily drunkenness has hardly diminished as a result of this measure, for several neighbors pool their funds to buy a tankard or more, and do not disperse until they have emptied it to the dregs. Some of them also buy up large quantities and secretly sell it by the cup. It is true that now fewer people are seen naked, although the number of drunkards wandering about and wallowing in the gutters is not much reduced.[15]
>
> Adam Olearius, *The Travels of Olearius in Seventeenth-Century Russia* (1656)

GESTURES

Besides holding fingers against your chest to indicate how many drinking buddies you need, another much older gesture is the one that signals "let's drink." You tap your middle finger on the side of your jaw, just under the chin. Everyone knows then that you're thirsty. You can also use that gesture – in combination with a knowing look – to indicate that someone is an alcoholic.

The origin of the gesture, according to legend, was a peasant who performed a heroic deed for the people and the fatherland. The peasant was told that he could ask the tsar for anything he wanted. After briefly pondering the matter, the man decided that he wanted to be able to drink free in state-owned taverns for the rest of his life. "Fine," the tsar said, "that is within my power. I will draw up a document bearing the tsar's seal, you can show that to the tavern keeper, and he will serve you at no charge." The peasant objected that he would lose the document, especially since he could drink so much for no charge. The tsar then decided to tattoo the imperial seal in a place that was not immediately visible, on the jaw directly under the chin. In the tavern, the man had to tilt his head back a little and tap on the tattoo.

IS THE VODKA AUTHENTIC?

In the 1990s, at the onset of unbridled capitalism, adulterated and poor-quality vodka was commonplace on the market. People of questionable character reused bottles of known brands and affixed a metal cap on them using special equipment. Friends advised you to buy your vodka in a real store, and not in the market, at a kiosk, or from a passing acquaintance. Since that period, Russians have had a number of ways to check the authenticity of vodka whenever they encounter dubious bottles:

- Turn the bottle upside down: when fake vodka is inverted, it leaves a murky trace behind in the liquid just under the cap, whereas genuine vodka is crystal-clear.

- The "shake and see if it froths" method: genuine vodka will have hundreds of robust bubbles.

- Rub the bottom of the bottle hard against the palm of your hand: if the bottle leaves a black mark, that is proof that it was on a conveyor belt.

- Open the bottle: if the vodka is genuine, little air bubbles will spiral upward.

- Do the litmus test: vodka is supposed to be non-alkaline and non-acidic, which means that it has no effect on litmus paper.

- Heat up a copper wire and dip it into the glass of vodka. If the vodka is fake, it will stink horribly.

- Some producers plan to include an eight-digit number on the bottle. You can then text that number to the factory to see whether the bottle is a fake.

DRINKING AWAY A HANGOVER

One of the ways to deal with a hangover has become an established Russian custom: the morning-after drink. There is a Russian verb for the concept of "drinking away a hangover": *opokhmelitsya*. If you're lucky, *opokhmelitsya* will make the angels in your head sing:

О, эта утренняя ноша в сердце! О, иллюзорность бедствия! О, непоправимость! Чего в ней больше, в этой ноше, которую еще никто не назвал по имени? Чего в ней больше: паралича или тошноты? Истощения нервов или смертной тоски где-то неподалеку от сердца? А если всего этого поровну, то в этом во всем чего же, все-таки, больше: столбняка или лихорадки? […]

– Да мы знаем, что тяжело, – пропели ангелы. – а ты походи, походи, легче будет. А через полчаса магазин откроется: водка там с девяти, правда, а красненького сразу дадут…

«Красненького?»

– Красненького, – нараспев повторили ангелы господни.

«Холодненького?»

– Холодненького, конечно…

О, как я стал взволнован!..

«Вы говорите: походи, походи, легче будет. Да ведь и ходить-то не хочется. Вы же сами знаете, каково в моем состоянии ходить!…»

Помолчали на это ангелы. А потом опять запели:

– А ты вот чего: ты зайди в ресторан вокзальный. Там вчера вечером херес был. Не могли же выпить за вечер весь херес!..

«Да, да, да. Я пойду. Я сейчас пойду, узнаю. Спасибо вам, ангелы…»

И они так тихо-тихо пропели:

На здоровье, Веня…

А потом так ласково-ласково:

– Не стоит…

– Какие они милые!...

Oh, that morning burden in the heart! Oh, the illusory nature of calamity. Oh, the irretrievable! What's worse about this burden which no one has yet called by any name, what's worse – paralysis, or nausea? Nervous exhaustion, or mortal sorrow somewhere in the region of the heart? But if that's all equal, then all the same what's worse about it – stupefaction, or fever? [...]

Yes, we know that it's tough, the angels sang out. *But get moving, you'll feel better, and the stores will be open in half an hour – no vodka until nine, it's true, but they'll have a little red the first thing.*

"Red wine?"

A little red wine, the angels of God chorused.

"Chilled?"

Chilled, of course.

Oh, I got terribly excited.

"You say get moving, you'll feel better. But I don't feel like moving at all. You know yourselves what sort of shape I'm in... to get moving!"

The angels kept quiet about that. And then started singing again.
You know what, drop by the restaurant at the Station. They've got something there. Yesterday, they had sherry. It couldn't have been all drunk up in one evening.
"Yes, yes, yes. I'll go right now and find out. Thank you, angels."
Your health, Venya.
And then ever so gently:
Don't mention it.
They're so nice.[16]

Venedikt Erofeev, Moscow to the End of the Line (1970)

Preferably, you drink the same thing in the morning as what you ended the evening with and what (partly) caused the hangover. If that's not available, you can use any other alcoholic beverage. For example, *portveyn*, a sort of wine that is supposed to be similar to port and is popular among experienced drinkers. The trick is to stop with that one drink, because otherwise you're shifting the problem to the next morning, and you might become a binge drinker, or worse: an alcoholic.

Each morning my hangover got me out of bed as automatically as if I had been going to work. I gathered together bottles from the night before and went next door to shop No. 28 to exchange the empties for a glass of cheap fortified wine. This disgusting brew helped me control myself until ten o'clock when the spirits section opened.

In the morning, my hands shook so much that I could not hold a glass without spilling it over myself. If I had a companion with me he would pour the wine down my throat – if not I used a belt; I wrapped one end round the hand that held the glass and passed the other around my neck, pulling on it so the glass reached my lips.

On the days when the shop was out of wine we had to look for eau de Cologne or aftershave lotion. I found these hard to drink on an empty stomach. Furniture polish was the worst – that was real poison and always made me puke. However, once I had lined my stomach with a hair-of-the-dog, I could drink whatever came my way.[17]

C. S. Walton, Ivan Petrov: Russia through a Shot Glass (1999)

"BROTHERHOOD"

When you make a good friend in Russia, you can seal the relationship by drinking with your new friend "in a brotherly fashion." Both friends take a glass and hook arms, and each of them drinks his own glass at the same moment. The whole glass at once, of course, because otherwise it doesn't count. *Pit na brudershaft* is what it's called in Russian. Even the tomcat Begemot in *The Master and Margarita* is familiar with this custom.

– А простите... это ты... это вы... – он сбился, не зная, как обращаться к коту, на "ты" или на "вы", – вы – тот самый кот, что садились в трамвай?

– Я, – подтвердил польщенный кот и добавил: – Приятно слышать, что вы так вежливо обращаетесь с котом. Котам обычно почему-то говорят "ты", хотя ни один кот никогда ни с кем не пил брудершафта.

Thoroughly shaken, he looked around him and finally said to the tom: "Excuse me, was it you. ..." He broke off, not knowing how to address the tom. "Are you the tom cat who tried to board the streetcar?"

"I am," the flattered tom confirmed, and added: "It is pleasant to hear you addressing a tom so courteously. For some reason cats are usually treated with excessive familiarity, although no cat has ever drunk brudershaft with anyone."[18]

Mikhail Bulgakov, *The Master and Margarita* (1928-1940)

STYLE AND ETIQUETTE

Russians drink liberally, often in competition, because drinking heavily is proof of virility, merit, and breadth of character. For a party at home, they set out all the alcohol, preferably as much as possible, and in a restaurant they order more than they can actually afford. They live for the day, and tomorrow can bring what it may.

The biggest cliche about Russian drinking customs is that Russians smash their empty glass by throwing it over their shoulder. It appears that military officers did this in the nineteenth century. In the film version of Lev Tolstoy's novel *War and Peace* directed by Sergei Bondarchuk, officers do throw down their glasses and break them. Glass shards bring luck. But apart than that, most Russians do not smash their glasses.

- One thing that all Russians abhor is leaving behind a half-full bottle. That's simply not done.
- Similarly, you cannot do a "floating pour": the glass must sit on a table when it's being filled.
- Never, ever, raise a glass during a toast and then set it back down without drinking. That brings misery and calamity.
- Empty bottles have to be removed from the table immediately.
- One person (or "one hand," as Russians say), pours all the vodka for each round. There are light hands and heavy hands (pourers): after a light one, you wake up the next morning without a hangover.

- When you clink glasses – which is not required in larger groups – remember that men hold their glasses lower than women do.

The Russian variant of "one for the road" is *na pososhok*, which means literally "for the staff." When a guest departed, he would pick up his staff, which stood next to the door of the peasant's shack. There are a number of variations on this expression, such as "for the horse," "for the stirrup," or "for the gas pedal."

TOASTING

When German General Friedrich Paulus was captured during the Battle of Stalingrad, he made a toast to the courage of the Red Army. He was obviously familiar with Russian customs. That battle was the overture to Germany's defeat. After Stalingrad, the Allies began cooperating more closely, and in December 1943 they met in Tehran. Elliott Roosevelt attended the conference of the Big Three (Roosevelt, Churchill, and Stalin) as an assistant to his father Franklin, the U.S. president during World War II. The leaders discussed the war's progress, the timing for opening the second front in the west, and German prisoners of war.

> So there I was, at my first Russian-style banquet. And all the stories you may have heard about them are true.
>
> Of course, vodka; and fortunately also a still white wine, light and dry, and a Russian champagne, to my taste very good. I say "fortunately" for there was no conversation without a drink; it would have been a contradiction in terms. The only way we talked was through the medium of proposing a toast. It may sound cumbersome, but if your staying power is good you find that it develops into quite a lot of fun. Thus, if you want to say something on even as vapid a subject as the weather, it becomes:
>
> "I wish to propose a toast to the magnificent weather we have been enjoying!" And you are on your feet to do it, and everybody else rises to his feet, and you all drink. Quite a system. It can even be political:
>
> "I wish to propose a toast," cried a Russian, "to your future deliveries of Lend-Lease matériel which I am sure will arrive on time in the future, and will not be arriving late, as have shipments to date!" Everyone rises, glasses are emptied, everyone sits down again. In a situation like this, vodka can be your worst friend, but I noticed that Stalin stuck to vodka all through the meal, his glass being refilled each time from his own private bottle next to him. It wasn't water, either; for once he filled my glass with it, coming around the table to do so. If it was anything less than one hundred proof, I most emphatically do not wish to be offered the real thing. [...]

At the P.M's [Churchill] birthday dinner, once more the Russian custom – everyone toasting everyone else – was observed, and once again I am afraid that accurate count was lost. I do remember that a good part of the dinner was spent standing up; I do remember Stalin's cheerful habit of touching the glass of everyone in whose name we were drinking; I do remember some of the toasts themselves.

Stalin: "My fighting friend Churchill!" and later, "My fighting friend Roosevelt!"

Churchill: "Stalin the mighty!" and "Roosevelt the President – my friend!"

And Father: "To our unity – war and peace!"[19]

Elliott Roosevelt, *As He Saw It* (1946)

It was not only the bigwigs who learned about Russian toasting during World War II. When the Nazis were on the verge of defeat, the Soviet and American armies met on the Elbe River. The joy was intense and the fraternization was heartfelt. Of course, there was plenty of drinking and toasting going on, and naturally the Russians had vodka with them, since each soldier was entitled to a hundred grams a day (see "The State Ration," page 198). With the addition of whiskey and looted schnapps, a veritable drinking spree ensued.

The American journalist Ann Stringer, who was present at one such joyous meeting, described the scene:

The commander invited us to lunch. He told me that I was the first American woman he and his troops had ever seen, and seated me at the luncheon in the place of honor to

The meeting on the Elbe.

his right. Then the toasting began! Toasts to victory, enduring friendship, and everlasting peace. I soon learned that when the Russians toast, it's serious business. We drank toasts in cognac. Then wine. Then schnapps. Then vodka. Then another liquour which I couldn't quite identify, although it tasted much like grain alcohol. The luncheon itself started with creamed sardines. Then highly-seasoned meat patties. Many plates of hard-boiled eggs were passed, as well as plates of raw eggs. The Russians would break one end of the shell of the raw eggs, then suck the yolk and white out.[20]

Meanwhile, American Bill Shank did not want to be a spoilsport, so he secretly poured the vodka into his boots. Still, he drank enough to make his head feel like it would explode.

Facing the mess hall that morning took more willpower than anything I had confronted in the past three days. When I saw bottles of vodka on the breakfast table, I knew the end had come. Even W. C. Fields once said he was a man of moderation – he never took a drink before breakfast. Yet for the honor of the U.S. Cavalry, I drank my libation. Now I know why these Russians drink so much vodka. My head cleared up, and I felt great. You have to keep drinking the stuff to stay lucid.[21]

Making a toast is a mandatory ritual at the Russian table. If you drink without toasting, then you have nothing more than a drink-fest. Drinking with toasts is civilized, it is not "drinking for drinking's sake"; it's cultured drinking.

Обильная еда и крепкая выпивка. Поминальная по Тетелину пьянка – как пир старых времен. Пышно-торжественные, бархатные брежневские тосты – это стиль. Фальшиво, конечно. Но с откровенным желанием расслабиться. Так можно жить годы, десятилетия – с желанием наговорить всем и каждому (и услышать от них самому) безудержно нарастающую гору все тех же бархатных комплиментов. Передать (и переполучить) пайку добрых слов. Тех цветистых словосочетаний, что хотя бы на первое время обеспечат тебе мир, а ему покой в пугливой душе. (Или, наоборот, покой тебе, а ему – мир.) Все обнимались. Плясали лезгинку. Пили за богинь, за русских женщин, подобных которым мир никого не создал.

Ample food and strong drink: Tetelin's funeral drink-fest was like a medieval banquet. Grandiloquent, velvety Brezhnev-era style toasts – now that's style. Ring a bit false, of course, but the desire to cut loose is sincere. You can live that way for years, for decades – with a desire to heap on each and every person around you an ever-growing mountain of these very same velvety compliments (and be paid back in kind), to give (and receive) a ration of kind words, those flowery phrases that will bring you peace, at least for a while, and bring calm to his fearful soul (or maybe it's the other way around – you'll get calm and

he'll get peace). Everyone was hugging. They danced the *lezginka*. They drank to god-
desses, to Russian women, the likes of which the world has yet to create.[22]

Vladimir Makanin, The Underground, or a Hero of Our Time (1999)

At Russian gatherings that involve civilized drinking, there is usually someone in charge. He indicates when the next round will be drunk, does the pouring, decides who is to give the toast, and concludes everyone's toast by summarizing what's been said and tying it in with the evening's theme (the birthday, the victory, the anniversary, etc.). Often the identity of that person is obvious without anything being said, and if things go well he will hardly be noticed. At bigger gatherings, a head of the table is "appointed" in advance. This lends even greater luster to the refinement of the ladies and gentlemen present. The name of this person comes from Georgian: *tamadá*. In the former Soviet Union, Georgians, among whom toasting has developed into a true art, are known to be the best toastmasters.

The *tamadá* makes sure that the glasses have been emptied, and if he has good reason to do so, he can give someone permission not to drink wine or vodka. With the first toast, he introduces himself, thanks everyone for the honor of being named *tamadá*, and "blesses" the gathering. The second toast is to the family or the hostess, the third one to the reason for the gathering, the fourth one to the dead. After that, a toast is drunk to those present. Between the toasts, people eat and converse. Sometimes there is singing. The toasts themselves can range from three words – "To everyone's health" – to entire panegyrics. The finer the toasts, the more splendid the event. On official occasions in the Soviet Union, there were toasts to Lenin, to Stalin, and to whomever was party leader at the time, to the "friendship among peoples," to the "true course," to peace, to socialism, and so on.

В банкете участвовали гости и несколько заслуженных работяг. Мы были приглашены все трое. Видимо, нас считали местной интеллигенцией. Тем более что скульптор отсутствовал.

Всего за столом разместилось человек тридцать. По одну сторону – гости, напротив – мы.

Первым выступил начальник станции. Он представил мэра города, назвав его "стойким ленинцем". Все долго аплодировали.

После этого взял слово мэр. Он говорил по бумажке. Выразил чувство глубокого удовлетворения. Поздравил всех трудящихся с досрочным завершением работ. Запинаясь, назвал три или четыре фамилии. И наконец, предложил выпить за мудрое ленинское руководство.

Все зашумели и потянулись к бокалам.

Потом было еще несколько тостов. Начальник станции предложил выпить за мэра. Композитор Петров – за светлое будущее. Режиссер Владимиров – за мирное сосуществование. А штангист Дудко за сказку, которая на глазах превращается в быль.

Цыпин порозовел. Он выпил фужер коньяка и потянулся за шампанским.

– Не смешивай, – посоветовал бригадир. – А то уже хорош.

– Что значит – не смешивай, – удивился Цыпин, – почему? Я же грамотно смешиваю. Делаю все по науке. Водку с пивом мешать – это одно. Коньяк с шампанским – другое. Я в этом деле профессор.

The guests and a few honored workmen took part in the banquet. All three of us were invited. Apparently, we passed for the local intelligentsia. Especially since the sculptor was not present.

There were about thirty people at the table: guests on one side, us on the other.

The first to speak was the station chief. He introduced the mayor, calling him a "firm Leninist". Everyone applauded for a long time.

Then the mayor spoke. He read from a piece of paper. Expressed a feeling of profound satisfaction. Congratulated everyone who worked on the project on beating the deadline. Stumbled over three or four names. And, finally, proposed a toast to the wise Leninist management.

Everyone raised a cheer and reached for their glasses.

Then there were a few more toasts. The station chief drank to the mayor. Composer Andreyev to the radiant future. Director Konstantinov to a peaceful coexistence. And the weightlifter Dudko to the fairy tale that turns into reality before our very eyes.

Tsypin turned pink. He had a tall glass of brandy and reached for the champagne.

"Don't mix," Likhachev suggested, "you're in fine shape already."

"What do you mean, don't mix," Tsypin demanded. "Why not? I'm doing it intelligently. Scientifically. Mixing vodka and beer is one thing. Cognac and champagne is another. I'm a specialist in that area."[23]

Sergei Dovlatov, *The Suitcase* (1986)

In fact, what can you *not* toast? During his dinner with Stalin, Franklin Roosevelt complained that Russians have 365 different toasts: one for every day of the year. Only a couple of things are truly important for a good toast: the toast must be heartfelt, and it must be spoken ardently and as poetically as possible.

Подождав некоторое время, побыв неподвижно среди того нелепого и жуткого молчания, которое последовало после ее страшного вопроса, она поднялась и, вынув теплую руку из теплой, душистой муфты, обняла его за шею и нежно и крепко поцеловала одним из тех поцелуев, что помнятся потом не только до гробовой доски, но и в могиле. Да-с, только и всего: поцеловала – и ушла. И тем вся эта история и кончилась... И вообще довольно об этом, – вдруг резко меняя тон, сказал композитор и громко, с напускной веселостью прибавил: – И давайте по сему случаю пить на сломную голову! Пить за всех любивших нас, за всех, кого мы, идиоты, не оценили, с кем мы были счастливы, блаженны, а потом разошлись, растерялись в жизни навсегда и навеки и все же навеки связаны самой страшной в мире связью! И давайте условимся так: тому, кто в добавление ко всему вышеизложенному прибавит еще хоть единое слово, я пущу в череп вот этой самой шампанской бутылкой.

"She waited there for a little while; she sat motionless in the absurd, cruel silence that followed her terrible question. And then she stood up, removed her warm, sweet-smelling hand from her muff, slipped it around his neck, and kissed him with both tenderness and passion. It was one of those kisses a man remembers not only on his deathbed but in the grave itself. And that was all – she kissed him and left. That's how the story ends. ... And really, we've talked enough about this," the composer said, suddenly changing his tone. "In honor of my story, let's add to the fog in our brains," he continued loudly, trying to appear amused. "Let's drink to everyone who loved us and whom we – idiots that we are – didn't value. Let's make a toast to those who blessed us and made us happy and then were discarded forever from our lives, but remained forever linked to us by the most terrible link on earth. And let us agree, gentlemen, that I will smash this champagne bottle across the skull of anyone who adds even a single word to my story."[24]

Ivan Bunin, "Ida" (1924)

As a foreigner, you are not obligated to come up with such a small work of art, but you will make a deep impression if you do. You can also simply say "to your health": "*Za (vashe) zdorovye*" [pronounced *zdaróvye*]. The increasingly commonplace *na zdorovye* is technically incorrect, but any Russian will understand and not be insulted (part of the confusion comes from the fact that Czechs and Poles, for example, drink *na* rather than *za* something).

Another way to make an impression is to shout "*Poyekhali*" [pronounced *payékhali*] ("Here we go!") after glasses have been clinked. Yuri Gagarin, the first man in space and a lover of drink, uttered that now-common expression right before he was shot into space on April 12, 1961. These days, when cosmonauts are about to go on space missions, they first lay a wreath at Gagarin's grave in the Kremlin wall. The night before blastoff, they watch a bit of light Soviet cinema, the 1970s film *The White Sun of the Desert*. The next morning, they sign their name on the door of their hotel room, drink a glass of vodka, smash the glass (sure enough), and yell in unison, "*Poyekhali*!" Alcohol is strictly forbidden on their mission, but it is a ritual for one of the cosmonauts to smuggle a bottle of cognac on board.

Another way to impress is with "*Davai!*" which means something like "come on," "here we go," or "hup." Note that "*Davai!*" sounds a bit imperative, and so you can soften it by prefacing it with *Nu*: "*Nu. Davai…,*" which makes it sound more like encouragement. You can show even more courtesy by using the polite form of the verb: "*Davaite!*"

Seasoned travelers to Russia combine the two: "*Davai, poyekhali!*" ("Hup, here we go!")

THE ADMIRAL'S HOUR

Peter the Great was a phenomenal drinker. Nevertheless, the tsar was very disciplined and stuck to a strict daily routine. He arose at five o'clock and paced about his chamber for half an hour, after which he had his secretary read out a list of affairs of state, and then he ate breakfast. After that, he would tour construction projects in St. Petersburg to check on progress, and then he would go to the Senate or the Admiralty, where he met with his admirals. At eleven o'clock, he would drink a goblet of anise vodka. According to the Russian etymologist Vladimir Dal, eleven o'clock was considered midday in the navy. The admirals followed this example and also had their midday meal right after this. This habit of the tsar took root and is known as "the admiral's hour" (*admiralsky chas*). At eleven o'clock, men exchange knowing looks; one glance is enough to proclaim the admiral's hour – and if not, they simply tap their chins.

– Кушать готово! – перебил Петр Михайлыч, увидев, что на стол уже поставлена миска.

– А вы и перед обедом водочки не выпьете? – отнесся он к Калиновичу.

– Нет, благодарю, – отвечал тот.

– Как угодно-с! А мы с капитаном выпьем. Ваше высокоблагородие, адмиральский час давно пробил – не прикажете ли?.. Приимите! – говорил старик, наливая свою серебряную рюмку и подавая ее капитану; но только что тот хотел взять, он не дал ему и сам выпил. Капитан улыбнулся… Петр Михайлыч каждодневно делал с ним эту штуку.

– Ну, а уж теперь не обману, – продолжал он, наливая другую рюмку.

– Знаю-с, – отвечал капитан и залпом выпил свою порцию.

Все вышли в залу, где Петр Михайлыч отрекомендовал новому знакомому Палагею Евграфовну. Калинович слегка поклонился ей; экономка сделала ему жеманный книксен.

– Нас, кажется, сегодня хотят угостить потрохами, – говорил Петр Михайлыч, садясь за стол и втягивая в себя запах горячего.

"Dinner is ready!" Pyotr Mikhailych interrupted, after noticing that a tureen had already been placed on the table. "You don't even have a bit of vodka before you eat?" he asked, addressing himself to Kalinovich.

"No, thank you," was the response.

"As you wish, my good man! But the captain and I will have a drink. Your Honor, the admiral's hour chimed long ago – may I be at your service? Here you go!" said the old man, filling his silver cup and handing it to the captain. But as soon as the captain reached for it, he drew it back and drank it himself. The captain smiled... Pyotr Mikhailych played this prank on him every day.

"And now without trickery," he continued, filling the other cup.

"I know, my good man." the captian replied, and dispatched his portion in one gulp.

They all proceeded into the next room, where Pyotr Mikhailych introduced his new acquaintance to Palageya Yevgrafovna. Kalinovich made a slight bow to her; the house-keeper responded with an affected curtsy.

"Today, it seems, we are being treated to pluck," Pyotr Mikhailych remarked, taking his seat at the table and breathing in the smell of the hot meal.[25]

Aleksei Pisemsky, *One Thousand Souls* (1858)

GAMES

Despite the long, cold winter nights, Russians are not big on games. True, they enjoy chess, but they regard it as a sport, and they do play dominoes and cards, but rarely without betting. Cards are played with azart, which is to say with abandon and passion, just like drinking, and there too you can easily lose everything. That's what happened to Fyodor Dostoyevsky, an ardent gambler who once lost all his money gambling in Baden-Baden and who wrote The Gambler (1866) to pay off his debts.

Where drinking is involved, a Russian is capable of anything. Bring vodka into the picture and he's willing to participate in "ordinary" games. For example, there is a Russian variant of musical chairs that involves having glasses of vodka on a table, one fewer than the number of players. Everyone dances around the table, and when a signal is sounded, each person tries to reach a glass, and of course drain it. The one who cannot do so is a loser twice-over: He is eliminated from the next round, plus he missed out on a drink.

Another game is called "guess who's drinking vodka." You fill every glass with water, except one, which gets vodka – 150 grams per glass. The players have to drink the whole glass with a straw, but without revealing what they're drinking. Then they guess which lucky dog had the vodka. Next, you put vodka in two of the glasses, then three... and you keep going like this until all of the glasses contain vodka. There's also "electric train." For that you need a train schedule and a bottle of vodka. The "conductor" announces the station, and at the imaginary stopover the players drink down a whole glass. Then they go to the next station, stop, drink, etc. And soon participants decide they've had enough and "get off the train." Whoever goes the longest distance – and is still standing – is the winner.

Some rulers liked games too. For example, the Yugoslav communist Milovan Djilas described a dinner at Stalin's dacha that took place in 1948:

> The dinner began with someone – it seems to me that it was Stalin himself – proposing that everyone guess how many degrees below zero it was, and that everyone be punished by being made to drink as many glasses of vodka as the number of degrees he guessed wrong. Luckily, while still at the hotel, I had looked at the thermometer, and I added to the number to allow for the temperature drop during the night, so that I missed by only one degree. I remember that Beria missed by three and remarked that he had done so on purpose so that he might drink more glasses of vodka.[26]

Finally, there are old games based on different flavors of vodka. In the eighteenth century, noblemen and landowners showed off by having vodka in their homes for every letter of the alphabet: anise vodka, birch vodka, citrus vodka, etc. The host would choose a word, and the guests had to drink and, by guessing which vodka it was, spell the word out. Or the host would make a cocktail, and the drinker could figure out the word based on which vodkas were used in the cocktail.

THE FACETED TUMBLER (GRANYONY STAKAN)

Единственная причина, из-за которой иногда не хочется идти в гости в тот или иной деревенский дом, – водка. И хорошо бы отдать честь, поговорить по душам, но как вспомнишь... Из рюмочек почему-то не принято. Не успеешь устроиться на место, как перед тобой возникает граненый стакан, налитый доверху. Не пойти в гости никак нельзя. Тотчас скажут, что зазнался москвич, считает зазорным с нами, простыми тружениками деревни... Но пить из стакана (разумеется, не единожды) тоже ведь никак нельзя без риска помереть либо тут же за столом, либо придя домой, на кровати.

Кроме того, я узнал о завещании Ивана Дмитриевича, в котором он просил свою старуху собрать на поминки мужиков и напоить, «чтобы уводили под руки».

The only reason I sometimes don't want to go visiting in the village is vodka. It would be nice to pay my respects, to have a heart-to-heart talk, but then I remember... Nobody uses little shot glasses, for some reason. No sooner have you taken your seat than faceted tumblers filled to the brim appear before you. But you can't avoid paying visits. They'll immediately start saying that the Muscovite has a swelled head and is ashamed to be with us, simple, hardworking village folk... But to drink a whole glassful (and not just one, of course) also can't be done without risk of dying right there at the table or in your own bed after you return home.

To make matters worse, I heard that the dying wish Ivan Dmitriyevich expressed to his old woman was that at his *pominki* the *muzhiks* be given enough to drink "so that they'll need a helping hand getting home."[27]

Vladimir Soloukhin, "The Funeral Banquet" (1973)

The most famous glass from the Soviet era is the *granyony stakan*, the faceted or ribbed tumbler. It is made out of thick, cheap glass, has seventeen vertical ribs (or twelve; opinions vary), stands 90 millimeters high, has a diameter of 65 millimeters, and flares out slightly, so the top is a bit wider than the bottom. Because of the ribs, the glass can fall a full meter onto a concrete floor without breaking. It is popular with vodka drinkers because of the ideal volume of twenty centiliters: In a *troika* with a half liter, each drinker can fill it almost to the brim. The most traditional place for drinking out of such glasses is the train station restaurant.

Вот-вот. Наша запущенность во всех отраслях знания... подумать страшно! Я, например, у очень многих спрашивал: сколько все-таки граней в граненом стакане? Ведь у каждого советского стакана одинаковое количество граней. И представь себе – никто не знает. Из ста сорока пяти опрошенных только один ответил правильно, и то невзначай. Пока не поздно, я думаю, не начать ли в России эпоху Просвещения?...

Exactly. Enlighten her. Our neglect of all branches of knowledge... it's frightening. For example, I've asked many people: how many grains are there in a faceted tumbler? After all, every Soviet glass has an identical quantity of grains. And just imagine – no one knew. Out of the 145 surveyed, just one answered correctly, and only by chance. Shouldn't we begin an era of Enlightenment in Russia, before it's too late?[28]

Venedikt Erofeev, *Walpurgis Night, or "The Steps of the Commander"* (1985)

Morning Still Life,
Kuzma Petrov-Vodkin
(1918)

The glass is said to have been designed by Vera Mukhina, who sculpted the *Worker and Kolkhoz Woman* monument in Moscow. Although Mukhina did get involved in glass design in the 1940s, this modern Soviet legend has been declared an urban myth by her grandson. He points out that the glass is much older than that and has been around at least since 1918, when it was at the center of Kuzma Petrov-Vodkin's painting *Morning Still Life*. But there is even more to the legend: Mukhina is said to have designed the glass in cooperation with the artist Kasimir Malevich. The first machine-produced, genuine (count the ribs!) faceted tumblers rolled off the assembly line in the crystal-producing city of Gus-Khrustalny in 1943.

However, the basic design of the *granyony stakan* dates back to a much earlier time. In 1702, Peter the Great visited a glass factory in Vladimir. There, he is said to have been given the very first faceted tumbler (with ribs) by Yefim Smolin. He was so pleased that he exclaimed, "*Stakanu byt!*" ("The glass should be."), basically mandating its production. The noblemen who were with him are said to have misunderstood, thinking he said, "*Stakanu bit!*" or "The glass should be smashed!" That is when Russians supposedly began smashing their glasses after drinking.

4

Vodka in Russia ⁽⁹⁸⁸⁻¹⁸⁰⁰⁾

Русской человек, вижу по себе, не может без понукателя... Так и задремлет, так и закиснет".

"Странно", сказал Платонов: "отчего русской человек способен так задремать и закиснуть, что, если не смотришь за простым человеком, сделается и пьяницей, и негодяем".

"The Russian, as I can see from myself, can't get along without someone to goad him on. He'll simply doze off, he'll simply stagnate."

"It's strange," said Platonov, "that the Russian is so capable of dozing off and stagnating that if you don't keep an eye on a simple man, he'll turn into a drunkard and a ne'er-do-well."[1]

Nikolai Gogol, *Dead Souls* (1842)

VODKA DID NOT YET exist in 988, when Grand Prince Vladimir I of Kiev was baptized. Russians drank birch sap, mead (a honey-based beverage), *kvas* (made from sourdough bread), and beer, all of them products of natural fermentation. The upper classes also drank imported wine, which was used in church rituals and was all but considered a sacred drink by the ordinary people. The Tatar invasion in 1220 made it impossible to obtain wine, which disappeared from society. The Tatars allowed beer to replace wine in church and did not tax it owing to its ritual function.

Russians first encountered distilled beverages in 1386. A delegation from Kaffa (now Feodosiya), a Genoese colony in the Crimea, was on its way to Lithuania. The travelers were transporting alcohol distilled from grapes, which they called *aqua vita*. The party stopped over in Moscow in order to show off the *aqua vita* to the grand prince's court. The beverage did not make much of an impression on the invited apothecaries and boyars: it was too strong for their taste. They decided that this *aqua vita* could be used only for medicinal purposes, and only if diluted with water. Thus, it would be nearly a century before the distilling of alcohol would take root in Russia.

Already, however, the Russians were drinking an astonishing volume of alcohol. One of the first foreigners to report on that phenomenon was the Italian Ambrogio Contarini, who traveled to Moscow and Persia in 1476.

> They have no wine of any kind, but drink a beverage made of honey and the leaves of the hop, which is certainly not a bad drink, especially when old. The sovereign, however, will not grant permission to every one to make it; for, if they had that permission, they would be constantly intoxicated, and would murder each other like brutes. Their custom is to remain from morning till midday in the bazaars and to spend the remainder of the day in the taverns in eating and drinking. After midday you cannot obtain any service of them whatever."[2]

Even the construction of the Kremlin was disrupted by the general state of drunkenness. According to another Italian traveler, Giosafat Barbaro, that was one of the reasons that Grand Prince Ivan III (reigned 1462-1505) decided around 1475 to enact a ban on the making of beer and mead.

Russian culinary historian William Pokhlyobkin contends that Russians first managed to extract alcohol from their own local ingredients between 1448 and 1474. The first to do so were probably monks at the Chudov Monastery in the Kremlin in Moscow. Pokhlyobkin cites a number of arguments in support of his hypothesis. First, a delegation of Russian clergy had visited a council in Italy, where they had probably seen *aqua vita* in the monasteries, as well as the equipment for distilling it. Second, the Russians had made considerable improvements in their farming techniques in the second half of the fifteenth century, in part by practicing crop rotation. This brought greater prosperity and gave rise to grain surpluses, especially in the Duchy of Muscovy – and it was grain of excellent quality. In addition, chroniclers have recorded events that indicate that drunkenness acquired a more aggressive character in the mid-fifteenth century, which could be attributable to a new beverage. Documents have also been preserved from this period that mention a tax on vodka. Finally, society was "ripe" for a new and – especially – less time-consuming drink. Economically speaking, distilling vodka is more expedient than brewing beer or preparing mead. The latter could easily take 40 years to mature, and entire villages were involved in brewing beer for important holidays. Because of the efficient use of raw materials, the minimal manpower needed, and the rapid production process, low investments in distilling vodka yielded high returns. There was also the fact that vodka does not spoil, is easy to store, and is simple to transport.

The distillation of vodka generated an important by-product, the mash (*barda*). This was valuable animal feed, because when distilling is done efficiently, the waste product contains almost all of the nutritional value of the original grain. Considering that distilling took place during winter especially, when livestock were in stable and had to be fed, it is clear that the distilling of vodka benefited livestock farming. Some distilleries even produced vodka exclusively for the sake of the *barda*.

The Vodka Maker
Konstantin Makovsky (1871)

Vodka was an attractive product for the state too, since it was easy to tax. Such tax revenues were sorely needed because of the many wars that Russia was waging. In this way, the authorities – completely apart from the historical processes through which Russians gradually learned the art of distilling – gave substantial impetus to the development of vodka. Vodka became Russia's first industrially produced product.

It was monks who were the first distillers. In their wake came the nobility, who had been granted the royal privilege to distill vodka for their own use in 1478. From then on, production increased at such a fast pace that Grand Prince Ivan III placed the production and sale of malt wine (*khlebnoye vino*) in the state's hands between 1472 and 1478. This was the first in a long series of state vodka monopolies in Russia.

Ivan III was an energetic ruler, and under his reign Moscow rose enormously in importance. He subjugated a number of other principalities, including Novgorod in 1478, and he waged war on the Tatars. The empire of the Golden Horde collapsed once and for all, and drunk with success, Ivan had himself declared "Ruler of All the Russias" and later tsar, derived from the Latin *caesar* (emperor).

His grandson Ivan IV ("the Terrible," 1533-1584) ascended to the throne in 1533. Even though Tatar domination had ended, there were still Tatar khanates in the Crimea and Kazan from which raids were launched. Ivan made quick work of the Kazan Tatars, capturing the city and its environs in 1552. Once the smoke of battle had cleared, the Russian soldiers were surprised by the countless taverns they found in Kazan, where vodka and beer were freely served. Back in Moscow, the soldiers pressured the tsar to open such taverns there as well. This is how the *tsaryov kabak* (tsar's tavern) came into being, at first in limited locations. It soon became clear that the taverns were significantly augmenting the state treasury. So began a tradition that has essentially been a leitmotiv throughout Russian history: vodka as a mainstay of the state budget. The state monopoly on the production and sale of vodka was now vested in the tsar's taverns, and the authorities demanded precise bookkeeping by the tavern keepers, who were appointed from among the best people in the village or city and had to swear an oath by kissing the cross in church. From that point on, the tavern keeper was known as the *tselovalnik* (kisser).

Ivan IV permitted several exceptions to the monopoly, specifically in the remote areas of Russia. Elsewhere, the tavern rights could be bought through what was known as *otkup*, a sort of concession sold by Dutch auction. Who bought the rights was unimportant; the state cared only about the revenues. Thus, many taverns fell into the hands of boyars and church dignitaries. A large percentage of the sales from these taverns still flowed into the state coffers. Monasteries were also allowed to continue distilling for their own use, but sales remained in state hands, by way of the state taverns.

Ivan himself enjoyed tsar's wine, as vodka was called at the time, but he kept a firm grip on its distribution. His penal code described in exacting detail the penalties that applied to the illegal production and sale of vodka. The people and soldiers were supposed to be sober. Russians were allowed to drink, but in moderation. In the mid-sixteenth century, a book came out in Russia titled *Domostroi*, a sort of moral handbook for the ordinary Christian Russian, with tips about keeping one's household and how to behave. The book recommended keeping beer, wine, and mead in the home for "guests and holidays," as well as aromatic herbs for brandy. Alcohol abuse was also addressed: "When you are invited to a wedding, do not drink to the point of intoxication or stay late. For in drunkenness and late hours are bred quarrels, shouting matches, and fights, even bloodletting. [...] Intoxication with wine brings death to soul and body and loss of property."[3]

This warning did not come out of the blue. Fairy tales and folk stories current around the same time the *Domostroi* appeared depicted a sort of paradise that included an abundance of magnificent food and, especially, an abundance of drink. This paradise even featured "seas full of it, you can wet your face in it, you can refresh your horse with it, you can even swim in it, and no one will say anything. And if someone is completely tippled, there are beds, with soft feathers, with sheets and wool blankets. To top it all, there are all sorts of delicacies for counteracting the detrimental effects of intoxication: cabbage, pickles, and milk fungus, turnips, garlic, and onions, bowls and bowls of them..."

The death of Ivan IV in 1584 unleashed the Time of Troubles. Various dubious figures occupied the throne, including Boris Godunov. When he was deposed in 1605, huge mobs stormed the houses of his family and servants, went down into the cellars, and got rip-roaring drunk, in some cases fatally. In 1613, a congress of boyars, Cossacks, and clergy resolved to put an end to the years of chaos by appointing a tsar. Mikhail Romanov (1613-1645) was chosen, and he became the founder of the House of Romanov that was to hold sway over Russia for just over three centuries.

During the Time of Troubles, there had been little change in the policies governing alcohol: tavern keepers were still the only ones allowed to produce and sell vodka. However, oversight of their income left much to be desired, and despite the flogging that Boris Godunov specifically introduced for this form of corruption, large sums of money disappeared into their pockets. In addition, the tsar's taverns had competition in the form of illegal inns, and home-distilling was also in fashion. All in all, the tsar's taverns scarcely provided any revenues for the state treasury.

Meanwhile, the people were grumbling. The tax on basic goods such as bread, salt, and vodka was very high. In addition, many of the materials needed to make vodka were stolen, there were many fake products on the market, and state institutions were corrupt. Men sat in taverns and drank up all their money. There were instances in which they drank so much around Easter that the fields remained fallow. This only made vodka more expensive, and peasants could no longer pay their tavern debts.

На Варварке стоит низенькая изба в шесть окон, с коньками и петухами, – кружало – царев кабак. Над воротами – бараний череп. Ворота широко раскрыты, – входи кто хочет. [...] В передней избе у прилавка – крик, шум, ругань. Пей, гуляй, только плати. Казна строга. Денег нет – снимай шубу. А весь человек пропился, – целовальник мигнет подьячему, тот сядет с краю стола, – за ухом гусиное перо, на шее чернильница, – и пошел строчить. Ох, спохватись, пьяная голова! Настрочит тебе премудрый подьячий кабальную запись. Пришел ты вольный в царев кабак, уйдешь голым холопом.

– Ныне пить легче стало, – говаривает целовальник, цедя зеленое вино в оловянную кружку. – Ныне друг за тобой придет, сродственник или жена прибежит, уведет, покуда душу не пропил. Ныне мы таких отпускаем, за последним не гонимся. Иди с богом. А при покойном государе Алексее Михайловиче, бывало, придет такой-то друг уводить пьяного, чтобы он последний грош не пропил... Стой... Убыток казне... И этот грош казне нужен... Сейчас кричишь караул. Пристава его, кто пить отговаривает, хватают и – в Разбойный приказ. А там, рассудив дело, рубят ему левую руку и правую ногу и бросают на лед... Пейте, соколы, пейте, ничего не бойтесь, ныне руки, ноги не рубим...

Among the shops on the Varvarka was a low house with six windows and decorated with carved horses and cocks; over the gateway was a sheep's skull. The gates were wide open for anyone who cared to enter. [...] In the front room, near the counter, there was constant hubbub, shouting, and cursing. They could drink and enjoy themselves as long as they paid. The cashier was strict. If a man had no money – then off with his coat! And if he had drunk away everything, the tapster would wink at the Government clerk, who would sit down at the end of the table, a quill behind his ear and an inkhorn around his neck, and begin to write. Oh, beware, you drunkards! That clever clerk will prepare a serf's deed for you: though you come in a free man, you may go out a helpless serf!

"It's easier to drink nowadays," the tapster said, pouring some greenish wine into a mug. "A friend, or a relative, or your wife, comes to fetch you nowadays, before you've drunk your soul away. We let such folk go – we don't run after them nowadays. Let them go in peace. But in the late Tsar's time it was different. A man might come to take his drunken friend away before he'd spent his last kopek... It would be: Stop! This will be a loss to the treasury, and it needs that last kopek! And do you know what happened to people who tried to stop men drinking? The guard would be called in – they'd take the fellow and clap him into the criminals' guardhouse. And there, after he'd been tried, they'd cut off his left hand and his right foot and throw him out on the ice... You drink, lads, drink! There's nothing to fear, they don't chop off hands and feet now!"[4]

Aleksei Tolstoy, *Peter the First* (1934)

Under Tsar Alexei Mikhailovich (1645-1676), disaffection reached the boiling point. The disturbances began in 1648 in Moscow and quickly spread throughout the country. Besides political demands, the insurgents also wanted the abolition of the tavern and alcohol concession system and a halt to grain exports. In response, Tsar Alexei imposed tough measures, punishing some boyars and ordering that the taverns be closed. In the cities, there was one pot house (*piteyny dvor*, literally "drinking yard") where customers could drink in

Tsar Alexei

Tsar Peter I

moderation – one glass per person – and only four days a week, beginning at two in the afternoon. The gathering at which these resolutions were adopted in 1652 became known as the "Assembly on Taverns."

The abolition of the concession system essentially brought about the reintroduction of the state monopoly. The eternal paradox once again reared its head: the more state revenues came in, the worse public health became. Under the monopoly, the vodka was more expensive but of better quality, because there was less adulteration. When vodka is expensive or scarce, however, people tend to make more of it at home. This paradox plagues Russia to this day.

In 1655, the Croatian priest and scholar Juraj Križanić traveled to Moscow. Despite the recently imposed monopoly, he observed a great deal of drunkenness, for which he held the state responsible. The Catholic priest was exiled to Siberia.

Still, the pot house policy and the associated restrictions did pay off. Indeed, it seemed that Russians were scarcely even touching vodka any more. But the state coffers were running low, and after the country experienced poor harvests and the insurgent Stenka Razin began battling the upper class on the peasants' behalf, the concession system was gradually reintroduced. The number of pot houses increased rapidly, and some of them grew into huge enterprises with their own distillery and bathhouse. In addition, in 1681 the nobility was granted the function of "subcontractor," which meant that they supplied vodka to the state for a predetermined price and on a set schedule. That vodka was then collected and stored in special warehouses, to be sold later in the pot houses. During that period, one quarter of the state revenues came from alcohol.

Peter I (1682-1725), later known as Peter the Great, became tsar of Russia in 1682. He had no problem with people drinking, even heavily, as long as they

Tsarina Elizabeth

Tsarina Catherine II

remained competent. But he meted out harsh punishment for those who were so drunk that they couldn't do their job. Peter also realized that a lot of money could be made through vodka. In 1699, he abolished the position of "kisser" and replaced it with the *burmistry*, officials who managed the vodka reserves and oversaw supply operations. Because of corruption, however, revenues were less than expected. In order to secure money for his involvement in the Great Northern War, Peter then decided to reintroduce the concession system, but without fully abolishing state sales. Ten years later, in 1716, he eliminated all restrictions on vodka production: anyone could distill it, and taxes were paid both on equipment and on production.

Peter died in 1725. After numerous court intrigues, his daughter ascended to the throne sixteen years later. During her coronation, Elizabeth Petrovna (1741-1761) treated the masses to a glass of vodka. Two fountains ran in the Kremlin: one with white wine, the other with red wine. Elizabeth made alcohol more readily available to the people as well. In 1750, she introduced a fixed price for vodka: a bucket would henceforth cost one ruble and eighty-eight kopeks. The tsaritsa also decreed that the nobility could produce vodka, although they were barred from trading in it. If caught trading illegally, nobles could lose their title and even their land. Courtiers faced exile or military service, and merchants were expelled from society. Meanwhile, the wealth of the vodka concession-holders – most of whom were merchants – reached dizzying heights.

Peter's granddaughter, Catherine the Great (1762-1796), continued the concession system for vodka, and in 1765 she decreed that the nobility could continue to distill vodka without paying excise duty on it. This privilege was to remain in force for 120 years. The scope of production was rigidly defined: the higher the nobleman's title, the more barrels he could produce. Other classes had to buy their vodka from the state. Distilleries operated by merchants were seized and shut down.

For the nobility, it became a matter of honor and prestige to have one's own brand of vodka. The quality of their vodka attained a very high level, and the selection grew by leaps and bounds. Vodka became a product that Russians could be proud of. Catherine gave friendly heads of state gifts of vodka, and the same honor was also bestowed on uncrowned eminences such as Voltaire, Goethe, and Kant. Meanwhile, the people were drinking inferior state vodka, on which, of course, they got drunk. Catherine is said to have remarked that a drunken nation is easier to rule.

UNITS AND MEASUREMENTS

For years, the bucket (*vedro*) was the standard unit of measurement for vodka. The exact volume was officially defined in Russia in 1621: the "court bucket" or "Moscow bucket," which came to a little more than twelve liters. One measurement that was larger than the bucket was the barrel (*bochka*). There were barrels that measured between five and as much as forty buckets. After the bucket came the quarter (*chetvert*, approximately three liters), the *shtof* (square bottle, approximately 1.23 liters), the *kruzhka* (this was not only a mug, but also a way of measuring out one-tenth of a bucket: 1.23 liters), and "twenties" (bottles containing one-twentieth of a bucket, or approximately 0.61 liters). Then there were the *charka* (a glass holding approximately 12.3 centiliters) and the *shkalik* (a glass holding approximately 6 centiliters). This *shkalik* was in turn derived from the word *shkala* (scale, in the sense of graduated measurement), a word that was adopted from the Dutch in Peter the Great's day, just as the Dutch borrowed *pierewaaien*, meaning "going on a binge," from the Russian verb *pirovat* (to celebrate). These days, Russians drink from a *ryumka* (derived from rummer, 50 grams) or a *stakan* (always 200 grams). Drinking straight from the bottle is considered uncivilized.

Glass bottles were introduced in Russia in 1669. They did not yet have labels, although they sometimes had a chain with a metal nameplate. Until the end of the nineteenth century, the manufacture of glass remained the work of craftsmen. The Russian glass industry did not start to take shape until the 1885 *ukase* declaring that henceforth vodka had to be offered in bottles. The new bottles came in handsome shapes, with labels specially designed by graphic artists that sometimes bore messages such as "Vodka rejuvenates the old and gladdens the soul," "Enjoy, but drink in moderation," and "One more glass." The bottle caps indicated the quality of the vodka. Pyotr Smirnov (forefather of the Smirnoff vodka still drunk today) placed a black cap on the cheap varieties, a red cap on vodkas in the middle range, and a white cap on the most expensive varieties. The most prestigious brands sometimes adorned their caps with the image of a famous person.

In the Soviet Union, the standard unit for a bottle of vodka was a half-liter. That still holds true today. And for a glass, it's five centiliters. Still, anyone who travels to Russia will be struck by how Russians use grams, not centiliters, to tell you how much vodka is in a glass. If you order a hundred grams of vodka (the norm) in a good restaurant, you receive a carafe and two *ryumki*. However, a half-liter bottle is just a half a liter, not five hundred grams.

In Vladimir Voinovich's novel, *Moscow 2042*, the time traveler Kartsev journeys to Moscow in 2042, where everything is available in abundance, a fact he is not yet aware of while still in the air. Thus, he behaves like many airline passengers still do. The bottles that Voinovich writes about are also known in Russian as *merzavchiki* (little bastards).

Меня разбудила стюардесса, толкавшая перед собою тележку с напитками. Улыбнувшись в полном соответствии со служебной инструкцией, она спросила меня, что я буду пить. Разумеется, я сказал: водку. Она опять улыбнулась, протянула мне пластмассовый стаканчик и игрушечную (50 граммов) бутылочку водки Смирнофф. Она собралась уже двигать свою тележку дальше, когда я нежно тронул ее за локоток и спросил, детям примерно какого возраста дают такие вот порции. Она понимала юмор и тут же, все с той же улыбкой, достала вторую бутылочку. Я тоже улыбнулся и довел до ее сведения, что, когда я брал билет и платил за него солидную сумму наличными, мне было обещано неограниченное количество напитков. Она удивилась и высказала мысль, что неограниченных количеств чего бы то ни было вообще в природе не водится. Поэтому она хотела бы все-таки знать, каким количеством этих пузырьков я был бы готов удовлетвориться.

– Хорошо, – сказал я, – давайте десять. [...]

Когда я выставил все бутылочки перед собой, мой сосед, заказавший стакан томатного сока, снял темные очки и стал следить за моими действиями не без интереса. Потом извинился и спросил, неужели я действительно готов в себя вместить все это ужасное количество водки. Я объяснил, что пол-литра водки для русского человека есть первоначальная и, я бы даже сказал, естественная норма.

The first thing I remember is being awakened by a stewardess pushing the drink cart. Smiling precisely as she had been trained to, she asked me what I'd like to drink. Needless to say, I said vodka. She smiled again, handed me a plastic glass and a toy-sized bottle of Smirnoff. She was about to push her drink wagon on ahead when I touched her lightly on the elbow and asked her why she had given me a child's portion of vodka. She caught the humor and, with the same smile on her face, handed me a second bottle. I smiled too, and informed her that when I had purchased my ticket – paying a hefty sum for it in cash – I had been promised unlimited beverages. She expressed surprise and said that unlimited supplies of anything do not exist in nature. She then wanted to know exactly how many bottles would satisfy me.

"Alright," I said, "give me ten." [...]

As I arranged the bottles before me, the person in the seat beside me (who had ordered a glass of tomato juice) removed his sunglasses and began following my actions with some interest. Then, apologizing for the intrusion, he asked if I really intended to ingest that horrendous amount of vodka. I explained that for a Russian, half a liter of vodka was the most rudimentary and, I would even go so far as to say, natural norm.[5]

Vladimir Voinovich, *Moscow 2042* (1987)

In the 1970s, vodka bottles appeared in the Soviet Union with an aluminum cap (which could not be put back on, meaning that you had to finish the bottle). This notorious cap had a tab that made it easier to open. Suddenly, the tab disappeared: the Russians had not patented the design, so shady figures abroad did just that. Thus, the Russians had to obtain a license or leave off the originally Russian tab. The latter is what happened. From that point on, drunks had to work the bottle open with a knife or something similar.

5

Religion

– Удается это потому, – сказал он, – что вера роскошь, которая дорого народу обходится.

– Ну, однако, не дороже его пьянства, – бесстрастно заметил Туганов.

– Да ведь пить-то – это веселие Руси есть, это национальное, и водка все-таки полезнее веры: она по крайней мере греет.

"They are succeeding," he said, "because faith is a luxury that costs the common people dearly."

"No more so, however, than their drunkenness," Tuganov observed matter-of-factly.

"But drinking, why, it's the joy of Rus, it's our national pastime, and anyhow, vodka is more useful than faith: at least it warms you up."[1]

Nikolai Leskov, *The Cathedral Clergy* (1872)

IN 988, VLADIMIR I was baptized, after which he ordered his subjects to be immersed in the Dnieper River and also become Christians. From that point on, the Byzantine variant of Christianity gradually – and peacefully – spread outward from Kiev. Many historians regard the baptism of Vladimir and his people as the starting point of Russian history.

The prince, who was later canonized, took no chances with his decision. He had performed a thorough study and summoned representatives of Islam, the Roman church, the Jews, and Orthodox Christianity to make the case for their religion to him. In addition, he had sent out envoys. In Constantinople, they were so impressed by the pomp and circumstance of the Byzantine rite that they did not know if they were dwelling "in heaven or on earth." This was an important argument in favor of Orthodox Christianity. In answering the Muslims who tried to persuade him to choose their religion, Vladimir I is purported to have said, "Drinking is the joy of Rus, it cannot do without it" (Руси есть веселие пити, не может без того быти). And so Vladimir rejected Islam.

For centuries, Russian secular authorities have wrestled with the "public revenue or public health" dilemma. A similar phenomenon is discernible in the Russian Orthodox Church: On the one hand, the church often joined in the battle against vodka, while on the other hand drinking was widespread among the lower clergy in particular. Priests were sarcastically referred to as "the drinking class," which had a disastrous effect on their moral authority. During a 1551 ecclesiastical council, Ivan the Terrible gave a speech filled with references to debaucheries committed by priests and monks. They cursed and fought, and they drank up the income that they took in for the church or monastery. A year later, Ivan issued an order mandating that "priests and monks not go to the tavern, nor become intoxicated."[2]

Travelers to Russia repeatedly confirmed the image of "the drinking class." Adam Olearius describes a typical scene: "When we passed through Novgorod, during the second embassy, I saw a priest in a robe or underwear (he had undoubtedly pawned his cloak in a tavern) staggering along the streets. When he came opposite my inn, he wanted to bestow the customary blessing upon the *streltsy* who were standing guard. When he extended his hand while endeavoring to bend over somewhat, his head proved too heavy, and he pitched over into the mud. After the *streltsy* picked him up, he blessed them anyway with his besmeared fingers. Since such spectacles may be seen daily, none of the Russians are astonished by them."[3]

The clergy's reputation as the drinking class can be attributed most of all to the parish priest. Not that monks did not drink, but with them it was less conspicuous. Priests were part of the community; they were involved in all important events in the village, and those events always involved a great deal of alcohol. There was simply no escaping it for the priest. In *Living Water*, David Christian quotes from the memoirs of parish priest Ivan Belyustin:

Say it is a holiday like Easter, and the priest conducts an icon procession. Each house offers hospitality, that is, vodka and something to eat. If the priest refuses, everyone in the family falls to his knees and will not rise until the priest has had a drink. This, too, does not work: the priest implores his hosts to rise and leaves without drinking. The host is terribly offended, of course; fuming with indignation, he gives the priest something for the prayer but does not accompany him to the next house. Afterward, if the priest should dare approach the peasant about some need, it would just evoke a rude refusal: "You didn't pay respects to me, and, well, I'm not your servant." That is the way it was in one house, then a second, then a third, and so on. If the priest accepts the vodka, by the time he has gone through the whole village even the most cautious, sturdiest soul hardly has the strength to perform his duty. A priest who is less cautious or whose constitution is weaker simply passes out. And what scandals do not occur when the priest is in such a condition![4]

In the short story "Makar's Dream" (1883), Vladimir Korolenko describes a drunken priest who decides to have a smoke. "He got up and staggered toward the great, fiercely heated fireplace to light his pipe at the blaze. But he was too drunk, he swayed and fell into the fire. When his family returned, all that remained of the little Father were his feet."[5] It's no surprise that priests drink; after all, they too experienced drinking from an early age, and seminaries were known as breeding grounds of alcoholism. And within the seminary, the choirs were notorious. Parents didn't like it when their children joined the choir, because that meant that their offspring were off the straight and narrow path once and for all.

Хоры, делая мальчиков дураками, в то же время развращают их. Присутствуя очень часто на поминках, на которых, как известно, наш православный люд не ест, а лопает, не пьет, а трескает, дети не только видят пьяных, но привыкают и сами пить водку. Равным образом, они нередко бывают при кутежах больших певчих, слышат цинические рассказы о полуведерных, любовных похождениях, картежной игре, о драках и разного рода скандалах.

Being in a chorus, on top of turning boys into fools, also has a corrupting effect. Since they attend a lot of *pominki* – at which, as is well-known, our Orthodox folk don't eat, but shovel it in, don't drink, but guzzle to the point of bursting – the children not only see the inebriated, but get used to drinking vodka themselves. Furthermore, they often witness the debauchery of older choristers and hear cynical tales about half-bucket binges, amorous adventures, card playing, fistfights, and all manner of outrage.[6]

Nikolai Pomyalovsky, *Seminary Sketches* (1863)

As ye sow, so shall ye reap. But after a life of drinking, some priests are still unable to resist. Father Ioann is no exception:

Как он ни старался всею жизнию привыкнуть к употреблению большого количества сивухи, он не мог победить ее действия, и поэтому он после полудня был постоянно пьян. Пил он до того, что часто со свадьбы или с крестин в соседних деревнях, принадлежавших к его приходу, крестьяне выносили его замертво, клали, как сноп, в телегу, привязывали вожжи к передку и отправляли его под единственным надзором его лошади. Клячонка, хорошо знавшая дорогу, привозила его преаккуратно домой. Матушка попадья также пила допьяна всякий раз, когда бог пошлет. Но замечательнее этого то, что его дочь, лет четырнадцати, могла, не морщась, выпивать чайную чашку пенника.

Try as he might to grow accustomed to drinking large quantities of *sivukha*, his whole life he was never able to overcome its effect. As a result, he was drunk every afternoon. He drank so much that after a wedding or christening in one of the parish villages, the peasants often had to load him dead-drunk into his cart like a sheaf. They would tie the reins to the cart and send him home in the sole charge of his horse. The old nag, who knew the way well, delivered him home just fine. His wife also took any opportunity to get herself drunk. What was more striking was the fact that his daughter, who was around fourteen, could down a teacup of liquor without batting an eye.[7]

Alexander Herzen, *My Past and Thoughts* (1855)

Overall, drinking decreased among the clergy over the course of the nineteenth century. Morals improved, with more and more priests opposing alcohol abuse and becoming active in the temperance movement. The church itself took a stricter stance toward drinking priests, and the clergy realized that it needed to set its own house in order. At the first church congress opposed to drunkenness, held in 1910, a priest from Ryazan said the following:

Before we can fight against alcoholic excesses, we must say to ourselves: "*medicus curat ipse.*" It is painful to admit that the clergy is still considered "the drunken estate," even though drunkenness has diminished in comparision with the past. Priests still justify drinking as necessary for maintaining good relations with their parishioners, among whom drinking habits are so widespread. To this day the Holy Synod [the supreme body of the Orthodox Church] considers many cases of drinking by priests. I have seen priests on whom neither prayers, supplications, nor threats had any effect and who drank even during services. In fact, deacons find it completely normal to get drunk before the Easter liturgy and other services. Priests still see nothing improper in drinking in company, at railroad stations, in hotels, inns and even clandestine taverns. One priest of my acquaintance tried to convince a teetotalling parishioner to drink, saying "I give you permission." Another, speaking about the temperance societies, said "it's all stupidity." A third stated at this very conference that "drinking cannot be avoided." But in our age of growing criticism of the Church, the role of the priest's character has become very important. If at an earlier time, the peasants, carting their drunken priest, removed their hats out of respect for the clergyman's cassock, now the people condemn priests who do not adhere to moral principles in their personal lives. Intemperate behavior on the part of individual servants of the Church undermines its authority.[8]

The Amsterdam merchant Nicolaas Witsen, who would later become friends with Peter the Great, visited Russia in 1664. He called on Patriarch Nikon, who was building a monastery just to the west of Moscow that was known as New Jerusalem. Witsen noticed that the walls surrounding the monastery had no window openings. He writes that this was "to keep the monks from hauling brandy through them." The monks were notorious:

Там, при въезде в него, – древний мужской монастырь... все говорят, что в нем, в каждой келье, у каждого монаха, всегда есть за образом и водочка и колбаса. Глебочку очень занимает, носят ли монахи под рясами штаны, я же, думая о монастыре, вспоминаю то болезненно-восторженное время, когда я постился, молился, хотел стать святым.

There, at the entrance to the city, stands an ancient monastery... People say that every monk in it always keeps a little vodka and sausage behind the icon in his cell. Glebochka is very curious to know whether the monks wear pants under their cassocks, while I, thinking of the monastery, recall that tender, rapturous period when I would fast, and pray, and dream of becoming a saint.[9]

Ivan Bunin, *The Life of Arseniev* (1933)

In 1858, the French author Alexandre Dumas (the elder) also witnessed the frequent secular goings-on at monasteries. He once visited a monastery that ran a restaurant. According to him, the good eating and drinking boosted the number of visitors, attracting pilgrims. "The monastery owns various properties outside its walls, and one of the most surprising is the Troitsa Restaurant in Moscow, much frequented for its celebrated sterlet soup. There one can eat and drink – even get drunk – as in other cabarets, and the only indication of its monastic ownership is the rule that the doors of private rooms must not be shut. (If the same rule were observed at the hostelry attached to the monastery, I fancy there would be a marked falling off in the numbers of men and women pilgrims visiting Troitsa.)"[10]

The Meal at the Monastery (detail), Vasily Perov (1865-76)

In the second half of the nineteenth century, the call for abstinence grew ever louder, often with priests leading the way. Priests had drunkards sign a statement that they would stop drinking, or they would try to get at least an oral pledge. Other drunkards went to church and made their promise before the icon of St. Sergius of Radonezh. It was rumored that the only way to successfully stop drinking was to go to the Church of the Intercession of the Most Holy Mother of God (*Pokrova Presvyatoy Bogoroditsy*), which had dedicated a side altar to Sergius. The church was located 28 versts from Moscow, in the village of Nakhabino. Pilgrims usually arrived drunk, because they had downed a few final drinks along the way. The journey to the village was generally a merry and colorful event. The village of Tushino served as the last way station before Nakhabino, and it was bursting at the seams with taverns. It was where two groups of men met: happy, celebrating pilgrims on their way to the church, and serious, respectable people who were on their way home. In some years, the church had 30,000 visitors.

Pilgrimages and processions were a good pretext for drinking. As on church holidays, there was no fasting. Adam Olearius witnessed this in the seventeenth century:

> After drinking wine to excess, they are like unbridled animals, following wherever their passions lead. I recall in this connection what the Grand Prince's interpreter told me at Great Novgorod: "Every year there is a great pilgrimage to Novgorod. At that time a tavern keeper, for a consideration given by the Metropolitan, is permitted to set up several tents around the tavern; beginning at daybreak, the pilgrim brothers and sisters, as well as local people, gather to toss off several cups of vodka before the service of worship. Many of them stay all day and drown their pilgrim devotion in wine. On one such day it happened that a drunken woman came out of the tavern, collapsed in the street nearby, and fell asleep. Another drunken Russian came by, and seeing the partly exposed woman lying there, was inflamed with passion, and lay down with her to quench it, caring not that it was broad daylight and on a well-peopled street. He remained lying by her and fell asleep there. Many youngsters gathered in a circle around this bestial pair and laughed and joked about them for a long time, until an old man came up and threw a robe over them to cover their shame."[11]

The Russian Orthodox Church has an entire canon of saints to whom prayers can be directed for personal salvation. Many believers have a favorite, often the saint of their name-day. As with Sergius of Radonezh, they can be venerated in order to rid oneself of an affliction.

> – Вот первое: об исцелении от отрясовичной болезни – преподобному Марою.
> – Преподобному Марою, – повторил за ним, соглашаясь, отец Бенефактов.
> – От огрызной болезни – великомученику Артемию, – вычитывал Ахилла, заломив тем же способом второй палец.
> – Артемию, – повторил Бенефактов.
> – О разрешении неплодства – Роману Чудотворцу; если возненавидит муж жену свою – мученикам Гурию, Самону и Авиву; об отогнании бесов – преподобному Нифонту; об избавлении от блудныя страсти – преподобной Фомаиде...
> – И преподобному Моисею Угрину, – тихо подставил до сих пор только в такт покачивавший своею головкой Бенефактов.
> Дьякон, уже загнувший все пять пальцев левой руки, секунду подумал, глядя в глаза отцу Захарии, и затем, разжав левую руку, с тем чтобы загибать ею правую, произнес:

– Да, тоже можно и Моисею Угрину.

– Ну, теперь продолжай.

– От винного запойства – мученику Вонифатию...

– И Моисею Мурину.

– Что-с?

– Вонифатию и Моисею Мурину, – повторил отец Захария.

– Точно, – повторил дьякон.

"Here's the first one: to cure fever and chills you pray to St. Maro."

"St. Maro," Father Benefaktov repeated after him in agreement.

"To cure the gnawing disease you pray to the great martyr Artemy," said Achilles, bending back his index finger in the same manner as he continued to count them off.

"Artemy," Benefaktov repeated.

"To remedy barrenness, you pray to Roman the Miracle Worker; if a husband starts hating his wife, it's the martyrs Gury, Samon, and Aviv; to drive out demons, St. Nifont; to get rid of sensual passion, St. Fomaida – ."

"And St. Moses Ugrin," Benefaktov, who until then had merely been nodding his head each time, quietly put in.

The deacon thought for a moment, looking Father Zacharias in the eye, and then, having already bent back the fingers and thumb of his left hand, he released them in order to count with his right hand and said:

"Yes, you can also pray to Moses Ugrin, too."

"Well, keep going then."

"To cure hard drinking you pray to the martyr Bonifaty – "

"And to Moses the Black."

"How's that, sir?"

"To Bonifaty and to Moses the Black," Father Zacharias repeated.

"True," repeated the deacon.[12]

Nikolai Leskov, *The Cathedral Clergy* (1872)

Because of the large amount of incense, the candles, and the mysterious singing, outsiders regard the Orthodox Church as mystical. Then there are the icons. Beholding icons is like praying; the believer has his eyes open and looks at the image. Through the blessed icon, which has been produced in accordance with strict rules, the beholder comes into contact with the depicted saint, and thus with the essence of Christianity as well. The icon opens the door to heaven. While praying before an icon, one can ask for the easing of an affliction. Thus, the icon known as the "Inexhaustible Chalice of the Mother of God" helps deal with drunkenness and other addictions. It hangs in the Vysotsky Monastery in the city of Serpukhov, a hundred kilometers south of Moscow.

Вот уже больше полвека тянутся по лесным дорогам к монастыри крестьянские подводы. Из-за сотни верст везут сюда измаявшиеся бабы своих близких – беснующихся, кричащих дикими голосами и порывающихся из-под веревок мужиков звериного образа. Помогает от пьяного недуга "Упиваемая Чаша". Смотрят потерявшие человеческий образ на неописуемый лик обезумевшими глазами, не понимая, что и кто Эта, светло взирающая с Золотой Чашей, радостная и влекущая за собой,– и затихают. А когда несут Ее тихие девушки, в белых платочках, следуя за "престольной", и поют радостными голосами – "радуйся, Чаше Неупиваемая!", – падают под нее на грязную землю тысячи изболевшихся душою, ищущих радостного утешения. Невидящие воспаленные глаза дико взирают на светлый лик и исступленно кричат подсказанное, просимое – "зарекаюсь!". Бьются и вопят с проклятиями кликуши, рвут рубахи, обнажая черные, иссыхающие груди, и исступленно впиваются в влекущие за собой глаза. Приходят невесты и вешают розовые ленты – залог счастья. Молодые бабы приносят первенцев – и на них радостно взирает "Неупиваемая".

For almost a half century now, peasant wagons have been plying the forest roads to the convent. Women at their wits' end bring their loved ones across hundreds of versts – raving, frightful-looking *muzhiks*, crying out in wild voices and struggling out of the ropes that hold them. The Exhaustible Cup helps against the infirmity of drunkenness. People who have lost all human appearance look with mad eyes at the indescribable image without understanding what and who She is, gazing radiantly with a Golden Cup, joyous and enjoining – and they are soothed. And when gentle girls in white kerchiefs carry Her, walking behind the patron saint, and they sing with joyous voices – "Rejoice, the Inexhaustible Cup!" thousands of tormented souls seeking joyous comfort fall down onto the muddy ground as she passes. Unseeing, fevered eyes wildly gaze at the radiant face and cry out in a frenzy words suggested to them for what they seek – "I vow!" Hysterical women beat themselves and howl with curses, tear their clothing, revealing blackened, withered breasts and deliriously drink in the eyes that compel them to follow. Prospective brides come and hang pink ribbons – a token of happiness. Young peasant women bring their first born, and the Inexhaustible joyously gazes down at them.[13]

Ivan Shmelyov, *The Inexhaustible Cup* (1918)

The story of this miraculous icon dates back to 1878, when a former soldier was ordered in a dream to visit the icon. The man, an incorrigible lush who was slowly losing all sensation in his legs, ignored the order. But when the dream returned for a third time, he crawled to Serpukhov on his hands and knees. When he arrived at the convent, no one had ever heard of the icon. However, an icon of the Mother of God showing a chalice was hanging in a corridor of the cathedral. Someone turned the icon around, and on the reverse they found the inscription "Inexhaustible Chalice of the Mother of God." As prayers were recited, the rediscovered icon was returned to the cathedral proper. The old soldier recovered from his drunkenness and regained the feeling in his legs. The people of Serpukhov were so impressed that they founded a Sobriety Society. The icon was destroyed under Soviet rule. But around 1990 the thread was picked up again, the icon was repainted, and to this day dozens of drunkards come to Serpukhov each Sunday to recover from their addiction.

The best-known saint who heals drunkenness is Boniface of Tarsus, the slave and lover of the wealthy Roman lady Aglaida. After he witnessed the torture of Christians in the city of Tarsus, he was filled with compassion and sympathy for the martyrs, and he threw himself at their feet. Having spontaneously converted to Christianity, Boniface himself was subjected to all sorts of horrors by the Romans. However, he survived the molten tin that was poured into his mouth, and he was unscathed even when they threw him into a cauldron of boiling tar. It was only after he was beheaded and his limbs were severed that he succumbed. The fact that Boniface can be invoked against drunkenness probably has its origins in a fit of rage by Aglaida, when she called him a drunkard. Or perhaps it was because he withstood the molten tin. Whatever the case, he died in 290 or 307, and his name-day is December 19 (January 1 new-style).

VODKA AS A REMEDY

When Russians first encountered distilled beverages in the fourteenth century, they initially saw them as medicine above all else. Physicians and pharmacists were enthusiastic about the strong stuff, and ordinary people also discovered its curative effects. The beverage that later became known as vodka assumed a place in the national medicine cabinet, and there it would stay. Three centuries later, Adam Olearius wrote, "In general, people in Russia are healthy and long-lived. They are rarely sick, but if someone is confined to bed, the best cure among the common people, even if there is high fever, is vodka and garlic."[14]

In the mid-nineteenth century, vodka was expensive, or in any event too expensive for ordinary people, who generally endured miserable living conditions. A discussion about those people and their circumstances was under way in progressive circles, and the revolutionary writer Nikolai Chernyshevsky contributed to that discussion.

В нашем сыром и холодном климате вино также необходимо простолюдину, как кислая капуста и квас. Долго смеялись над любовью русского мужика к щам и квасу, пока не узнали, что эта пища и это питье служат для него единственными предохранительными средствами от цынги. Точно так же нелепы лицемерные толки против потребности мужика выпить стакан вина после работы в сырости и холоде при малой питательности употребляемой им пищи, при неудобствах его жилища и недостаточности его одежды. [...] Теперь народ не может обходиться без вина.

In our cold, damp climate vodka is as necessary for ordinary people as pickled cabbage and *kvas*. People used to laugh at the Russian peasant's love for *shchi* and *kvas* until they discovered that this diet is the sole protection against scurvy. Hypocritical complaints about the peasant's need for a glass of vodka after working in the cold and damp are equally inapposite, given the low nutritionial value of most peasant food, and the poor standards of peasant housing and clothing. [...] At present, the people cannot do without vodka.[15]

Nikolai Chernyshevsky, "The Concession System" (1858)

Vodka was considered so beneficial that it was even administered to women in labor, which meant that the mother's first milk was imbued with alcohol. It helped the children sleep as well. Crying babies were given vodka directly into their mouths to get them to sleep. An advantageous side effect, they thought, was that the babies became accustomed to strong drink.

Poor peasants were not the only ones who thought this way. Russia's most famous poet, Alexander Pushkin, also considered it beneficial for children to get used to alcohol early on. He wrote his wife, Natalya Goncharova, the most beautiful woman in Russia, who had even attracted the tsar's eye:

Forgive me, dear wife. I thank you for promising not to play the coquette: even though I gave you leave to do so, it's still better if you do not take advantage of my permission. I'm happy to hear that Sashka has been weaned. He was long overdue. And the fact that the wet nurse was in the habit of drinking before bed is no great misfortune. The boy will grow accustomed to vodka and will be a fine fellow, taking after Lev Sergeyevich [Pushkin's brother].[16]

Pushkin was well-acquainted with the Caucasus. It may have been there that he learned the custom of giving young children a glass of wine. Or even vodka, which was believed to be a way of preventing alcoholism. To this day, there are still some "good" parents who acquaint their offspring – boys especially – with the taste of vodka and wine at around age three. They are given a half a glass at bedtime in the naive belief that "later they will no longer have a taste for vodka."

But you could start even earlier too. Stalin was from the Caucasus, a Georgian to be precise. His father was a shoemaker and a notorious lush.

Khrushchev claimed that Stalin himself had told him that his father used to come to the cradle, dip his finger into his wine, and dribble it into the little Joseph's mouth. Stalin himself certainly didn't think it was a bad idea to get children accustomed to drinking. But his second wife Nadya saw things differently. The British historian Simon Sebag Montefiore writes: "Stalin often gave Vasily, and later Svetlana, sips of wine, which seems harmless (though Vasily died of alcoholism), but this infuriated the stern Nadya. They constantly argued about it. When Nadya or her sister told him off, Stalin just chuckled: 'Don't you know it's medicinal?'"[15]

These were mostly *profilakticheskiye* (preventive) uses of vodka. However, it was also a medicine that you took when you were sick or didn't feel well. For example, a vodka compress on the chest was traditionally considered the best remedy for the flu; for angina, it was worn around the neck. You smeared vodka on wounds, which caused a certain amount of narcosis. Lost appetite could be stimulated, and it was good for the blood (because it dilated the blood vessels). The folklore hero Ilya Muromets triumphed over his illness by drinking a glass of vodka. In Alexander Kuprin's 1915 story "The Pit," someone who has fainted is revived with valerian drops in brandy. If you have a toothache, rub it with horseradish and vodka. Or it might be enough to simply rinse your mouth with vodka. If you're tired, rub vodka in your eyes. Depressed? Have a swig of vodka. Russians also refer to vodka as an "antimelancholic."

– Вам бы перцовки выпить... – сказал он, подумав. – В сей юдоли как выпьешь, оно и ничего. И ежели бы мамаше влить в ухо перцовки, то большая польза.

"You should drink some pepper-brandy," he said after a moment's thought. "A drink won't never do you harm in this vale of tears. And if Nanny had a drop of that stuff in her ear it would do her the world of good."[18]

Anton Chekhov, "My Life" (1896)

In Chekhov's 1883 story "From the Diary of an Assistant Bookkeeper," the title character notes the following: "Ginger – ten grams; galangal – seven grams; pepper vodka – four grams; Semibratovo blood coral – twenty grams. Combine with a liter of vodka to cure catarrh and drink one *shtof* on an empty stomach."[19]

Combined with all manner of ingredients, vodka was also used to treat rabies, scurvy, kidney stones, and diarrhea. Smallpox (*ospa*) was treated by placing a bottle of vodka and seven pastries outside the door. Mother Ospa Ivanovna would then take the bottle and drink it down, making the smallpox disappear. Around 1865, a certain Doctor Kuryayev was especially popular; he cured his patients with large quantities of vodka. This seems to be the origin of the common expression: "What's the big deal, dad? I'm not drinking, I'm having a cure." An anonymous contribution to a collection of adages from that same period said this:

> Grain vodka improves the health, serves as a medicine, and cheers the soul. A *charka* of vodka on a damp, wet day has saved many from colds, or has saved those with colds from fever. If a man is tired from heavy labor, a *charka* of vodka will restore his strength. Cuts and bruises can be cured by rubbing them with vodka. Wounds can be cured by washing them in a mixture of vinegar and vodka. And why not enjoy oneself occasionally? A *charka* of vodka makes the blood flow faster, brings a song to the throat of any youth, and enlivens the *khorovod* [folk singing and dancing].[20]

There are just as many types of vodka as there are ailments. Gogol provides a nice summary:

> – Вот это, – говорила она, снимая пробку с графина, – водка, настоянная на деревий и шалфей. Если у кого болят лопатки или поясница, то очень помогает. Вот это на золототысячник: если в ушах звенит и по лицу лишаи делаются, то очень помогает. А вот эта – перегнанная на персиковые косточки; вот возьмите рюмку, какой прекрасный запах. Если как-нибудь, вставая с кровати, ударится кто об угол шкапа или стола и набежит на лбу гугля, то стоит только одну рюмочку выпить перед обедом – и все как рукой снимет, в ту же минуту все пройдет, как будто вовсе не бывало.

> "This," she would say, taking a cork out of a bottle, "is vodka distilled with milfoil and sage – if anyone has a pain in the shoulder blades or loins, it is very good; now this is distilled with centaury – if anyone has a ringing in the ears or a rash on the face, it is very good; and this now is distilled with peach stones – take a glass, isn't it a delicious smell? If anyone getting up in the morning knocks his head against a corner of the cupboard or a table and a bump comes up on his forehead, he has only to drink one glass of it before dinner and it takes it away entirely; it all passes off that very minute, as though it had never been there at all."[21]

Nikolai Gogol, *Mirgorod*: "Old-World Landowners" (1835)

In an 1883 issue of the magazine *Strekoza* (*The Dragonfly*), "purified" vodka is described as "a universal remedy for all diseases; it endows strength and courage, excites the imagination, and knocks you out; with its help it's possible to see a green snake and even white elephants. [...] It is drunk from little shot glasses, little tumblers, and straight from the bottle. People try to strangle it, spoil it, and knock it over, but it can never be destroyed."[22]

Vodka to which gunpowder or ash has been added is called the Dance of Death. It is said to lend vigor and be therapeutic (other variants contain fly agaric or tobacco).

Иваш взял на ладонь щепотку пороха, велел татарченку налить горилки, размещал и выпил. Остальной порох он бережно сунул в карман, а флягу положил за пазуху. Он чувствовал порядочную слабость, но обыкновенное запорожское лекарство оживило его, а желание спастись возвратило энергию и бодрость.

Ivash took a pinch of gunpowder into the palm of his hand, ordered the Tatar woman to pour in some vodka, shook it up, and drank it. He carefully returned the rest of the gunpowder to his pocket and tucked the flask into his shirt. He felt quite weak, but the standard Zaporozhian remedy perked him up, and the desire to save himself returned his energy and vigor.[23]

Olga Rogova, *Bogdan Khmelnitsky* (1905)

Cossacks are not known for their discipline, but there are hetmans who beat discipline into their men in the following way while out in the field:

Да вот вам, панове, вперед говорю: если кто в походе напьется, то никакого нет на него суда. Как собаку, за шеяку повелю его присмыкнуть до обозу, кто бы он ни был, хоть бы наидоблестнейший козак изо всего войска. Как собака, будет он застрелен на месте и кинут безо всякого погребенья на поклев птицам, потому что пьяница в походе недостоин христианского погребенья. Молодые, слушайте во всем старых! Если цапнет пуля или царапнет саблей по голове или по чему-нибудь иному, не давайте большого уваженья такому делу. Размешайте заряд пороху в чарке сивухи, духом выпейте, и все пройдет – не будет и лихорадки; а на рану, если она не слишком велика, приложите просто земли, замесивши ее прежде слюною на ладони, то и присохнет рана. Нуте же, за дело, за дело, хлопцы, да не торопясь, хорошенько принимайтесь за дело!

I tell you this beforehand, gents, if any one gets drunk on the expedition, he will have a short shrift: I will have him dragged by the neck like a dog behind the baggage wagons, no matter who he may be, even were he the most heroic Cossack in the whole army; he shall be shot on the spot like a dog, and flung out, without burial, to be torn by the birds of prey, for a drunkard on the march deserves no Christian burial. Young men, obey the old men in all things! If a ball grazes you, or a sword cuts your head or any other part, attach no importance to such trifles. Mix a charge of gunpowder in a cup of brandy, quaff it heartily, and all will pass – you will not even have any fever; and if the wound is large, put simple earth upon it, mixing it first with spittle in your palm, and that will dry it out. And now to work, to work, lads, and look well to all, and without haste.[24]

Nikolai Gogol, *Mirgorod*: "Taras Bulba" (1839-1842)

The fact that vodka is used as medicine does not mean that it does not get you drunk or put you to sleep. All sorts of things can happen, as in Dostoyevsky's *The Brothers Karamazov*, where a murder has been committed. At the time of the murder, Grigory Vasilyevich was suffering from lumbago and had a salve applied to his back. Five hundred pages later, the attorney Fetyukovich interrogates him about that.

– Теперь могу ли обратиться к вам с вопросом, если только позволите, – вдруг и совсем неожиданно спросил Фетюкович, – из чего состоял тот бальзам, или так-сказать та настойка, посредством которой вы в тот вечер, пред сном, как известно из предварительного следствия, вытерли вашу страдающую поясницу, надеясь тем излечиться?

Григорий тупо посмотрел на опросчика и, помолчав несколько, пробормотал: "был шалфей положен".

– Только шалфей? Не припомните ли еще чего-нибудь?

– Подорожник был тоже.

– И перец может быть? – любопытствовал Фетюкович.

– И перец был.

– И так далее. И все это на водочке?

– На спирту.

В зале чуть-чуть пронесся смешок.

– Видите, даже и на спирту. Вытерши спину, вы ведь остальное содержание бутылки, с некоею благочестивою молитвой, известной лишь вашей супруге, изволили выпить, ведь так?

– Выпил.

– Много ли примерно выпили? Примерно? Рюмочку, другую?

– Со стакан будет.

– Даже и со стакан. Может быть и полтора стаканчика? Григорий замолк. Он как бы что-то понял.

– Стаканчика полтора чистенького спиртику – оно ведь очень недурно, как вы думаете? Можно и "райские двери отверзты" увидеть, не то что дверь в сад?

"Now, with your permission I'll ask you a question," Fetyukovitch said, suddenly and unexpectedly. "Of what was that balsam, or, rather, decoction, made, which, as we learn from the preliminary inquiry, you used on that evening to rub your lumbago, in the hope of curing it?"

Grigory looked blankly at the questioner, and after a brief silence muttered, "There was sage in it."

"Nothing but sage? Don't you remember any other ingredient?'

"There was plantago in it, too."

"And pepper perhaps?" Fetyukovitch queried.

"Yes, there was pepper, too."

"Et cetera. And all dissolved in vodka?"

"In spirit."

There was a faint sound of laughter in the court.

"You see, in spirit. After rubbing your back, I believe, you drank what was left in the bottle with a certain pious prayer, only known to your wife?"

"I did."

"Did you drink much? Roughly speaking, a wine-glass or two?"

"It might have been a tumbler-full."

"A tumbler-full, even. Perhaps a tumbler and a half?"

Grigory did not answer. He seemed to see what was meant.

"A glass and a half of neat spirit is not at all bad, don't you think? You might see the gates of heaven open, not only the door into the garden?"[25]

Fyodor Dostoyevsky, *The Brothers Karamazov* (1880)

The large amount of alcohol in vodka acts as a disinfectant. Thus, vodka can be very useful when eating food of dubious quality. If you have an upset stomach from food poisoning that came from drinking *chal* (camel's milk) in Turkmenistan, you have a glass of vodka with salt. Or at least that's what Vitali Vitaliev says. Another writer, Gustav Krist, was given so much vodka with quinine to treat malaria that his "body resembled a vat of quinine." He would have been better off rubbing vodka all over his body, to ward off mosquitoes – just as beekeepers do to prevent stings. And by the way: If your elephant is sick, feed him two liters of vodka and one kilogram of sugar a day (see *Tussen Russen* [Among Russians] by Derk Sauer and Ellen Verbeek). He'll feel better in no time.

Vodka is also reputedly a remedy for exposure to radiation. After the nuclear reactor in Chernobyl exploded in April 1986, the rescue workers were given red wine mixed with vodka. That was supposed to counteract the radiation, a belief that was encouraged by the authorities at the time. Following the nuclear disaster, rumors circulated in Moscow that free red wine was being dispensed in Kiev to treat the radiation poisoning. Many people traveled to Kiev.

In her book *Night of Stone*, the British author Catherine Merridale makes a connection between the Chernobyl disaster and submarines:

"There were no village folk remedies for radiation poisoning, but this was a society that had lived by improvisation for decades. A story got about that vodka cleaned the organism of radioactive particles, and that a ration of the stuff was always given to the crews of Soviet nuclear submarines. The treatment was particularly effective, ran the tale, if red wine were consumed at the same time. [...] Now there was a minor panic among the intellectuals. A friend, who was seven months pregnant at the time, begged me to buy some vodka for her in a foreign-currency shop. It was in vain that I told her about the wisdom of my own culture, which teaches that hard spirits are dangerous for an unborn child. How did I know, the family conference asked, that my British government was not weaving lies of its own?"[26]

Simple, straight vodka is also effective – in treating ptomaine poisoning, for example.

Позапрошлой весной он копал яму внизу, на пятнадцатом, и, стоя в грязи, не видя куда, саданул с размаху в заплывший прибывающей жижей подбой. Из гроба чуть брызнуло, и вонь, рванувшаяся из щели, выпихнула его из ямы.

Копал, как любил, без верхонок - брызги чиркнули по пальцам, по его навсегда драным в кровь заусеницам.

Потом он болел. Врагу не пожелал бы. Болело все: глаза, руки, волосы, туловище, нутро – все болело беспрерывно каменной, налитой болью.

Ребята говорили: заражение тухлым ядом. Врача не звал: боялся, подтвердит. Водка стояла в графине, как вода, все время. Томка, тогдашняя его, подливала в стакан день и ночь.

Last spring he had to dig a grave down below, in section 15, and standing in mud, unable to see anything, he whacked into the ground, which was filling with slush. There was a little squirt out of the coffin, and the stench that was steaming through the crack ejected him from the hole.

He didn't like to use work gloves – the spray struck at his fingers, his perpetually blood-crusted hangnails.

Later, he fell ill. He wouldn't have wished this on his worst enemy. Everything hurt: his eyes, his arms, his hair, his torso, his insides – everything hurt with a relentless, stone-hard pain.

The guys said he had ptomaine poisoning. He didn't call the doctor: he was afraid they were right. The carafe was always filled with vodka, as if it were water. Tomka, his girl back in those days, kept his glass full day and night.[27]

Sergei Kaledin, "The Humble Cemetery" (1987)

Russians pride themselves on their independent resourcefulness, because the government is not always reliable. Moreover, doctors like Mikhail Astrov also drink. In Chekhov's play, he is visiting Ivan Voynitsky, better known as Uncle Vanya.

астров. Как? Да... Надо сознаться, – становлюсь пошляком. Видишь, я и пьян. Обыкновенно, я напиваюсь так один раз в месяц. Когда бываю в таком состоянии, то становлюсь нахальным и наглым до крайности. Мне тогда все нипочем! Я берусь за самые трудные операции и делаю их прекрасно; я рисую самые широкие планы будущего; в это время я уже не кажусь себе чудаком и верю, что приношу человечеству громадную пользу... громадную! И в это время у меня своя собственная философская система, и все вы, братцы, представляетесь мне такими букашками... микробами. [...]

соня. А ты, дядя Ваня, опять напился с доктором. Подружились ясные соколы. Ну, тот уж всегда такой, а ты-то с чего? В твои годы это совсем не к лицу.

войницкий. Годы тут ни при чем. Когда нет настоящей жизни, то живут миражами. Все-таки лучше, чем ничего.

ASTROV What do you mean? Yes, I must confess I'm getting vulgar, but then, you see, I'm drunk. I usually only drink like this once a month. At such times my audacity and impertinence know no bounds. I feel capable of anything. I attempt the most difficult operations and do them magnificently. The most brilliant plans for the future take shape in my head. I'm no longer a poor fool of a doctor, but mankind's greatest benefactor. Greatest! I evolve my own system of philosophy and all of you seem to crawl at my feet like so many insects or microbes. [...]

SONYA Uncle Vanya, you and the doctor have been drinking again! The old boys have been getting together! It's all very well for him, he's always done it, but why do you follow his example? It looks bad at your age.

VOYNITSKY Age has nothing to do with it. When real life is missing, one must create an illusion. It is better than nothing.[28]

Anton Chekhov, *Uncle Vanya* (1896)

6

Why?

мужик. Что ж ты сделаешь?

работник. Да питье сделаю. Такое питье, что если сил нет, силы прибавится; если есть хочется, сыт сделаешься. Если сон не берет, заснешь сейчас; если скучно, весело станет. Если заробел, смелости даст. Вот какое питье сделаю!

PEASANT Why, what would you make of it?

LABORER A kind of drink. Drink, that would give you strength when you are weak, satisfy you when you are hungry, give you sleep when you are restless, make you merry when you're sad, give you courage when you're afraid. That's the drink I'd make![1]

Lev Tolstoy, *The First Distiller* (1886)

WHEN YOU ASK WHY Russians drink so much, or rather why they drink with such abandon, the answer often involves factors such as the Byzantine Christian tradition, where mysticism, wine, and ascetic fasting play a major role; the Mongol invasion (1220-1380), which led to servitude and passivity, and the repressive regimes that followed the Mongol yoke (Russians are submissive and patient during periods of a well-structured environment and political repression, but once they gain political freedom, they descend into violence and anarchy); Russia's huge territorial expanse; the fickle climate with its long nights during the cold winters; and the capricious harvests and poor soil.

The Mongols left behind a destitute Russia. Age-old traditions had been all but destroyed. Children were not being educated, the populace was servile, and morality was undermined. Villages were no longer allowed to brew beer or make mead. The incidence of violence increased dramatically. It was in that atmosphere that Russians turned to vodka, which quickly supplanted the weaker traditional drinks. Vodka became the national drink in no time. There was also the fact that Russia's grand princes needed funds. In order to fill the coffers, they abolished the traditional tavern (or *korchma*), which also served food, and replaced it with the imperial tavern, which served only alcohol. This move weakened the community function of the tavern, and, according to temperance activist Dmitry Borodin, friendly conversation gave way to solitary drinking: "Singers and musicians were silenced. Only the wild cries of drunken revelers began to resound in our homeland. [...] After three centuries of enduring the heavy burden of taxes and enslavement to a savage and alien people, our forefathers were unable to relinquish the habit of strong beverages. They drank this bitter cup to the dregs and attributed it to the spiritual suffering they had undergone during the Tatar yoke."[2]

The Mongols were replaced by autocratic grand princes, the future tsars. As a result, the Russians knew little else than an oppressive state, and they were never inspired to take the initiative or assume responsibility. Besides being oppressive, the state was also expansionist and thus hungry for money. The priest and pan-Slavist Križanić wrote in the seventeenth century of "terrible Russian drunkenness." He too blamed the tavern (*kabak*):

And the fault for this is the monopoly on alcohol, which is to say, the *kabaks*. Because of this monopoly, the people cannot brew their own spirits without permission. But even if they do obtain permission, they are told to drink everything within three or four days and must not keep anything in their homes beyond that time. And so, to comply with this order, they drink beyond their capacity and neighbors who have nothing to drink at home visit them shamelessly to drink everything down to the last drop. The common people who are not permitted to brew their own spirits do not even have any inns of their own. Thus, they are forced to go to imperial *kabaks*, which are worse than pigsties, where drinks are revolting and sold for a ridiculously high price. But even these hellish *kabaks* are too few, for each large city has only one or two of them. And so, because the people are denied spirits, they thirst so greatly for drink that, forgetting all shame, they become like madmen. No matter the size of the draught, they drink it down at once and without stopping, for they believe that this is their duty before God and Tsar... And when they gather together enough money, they go to the infernal *kabak*. And here they go mad, selling for drink what they have brought from their homes and even the clothes on their backs. Thus, it is from these accursed *kabaks* that all abominations, sins, poverty and baseness come to the people.[3]

Drinking is something that befalls one – one being, in this case, the Russian. It "happens" to him. With no will of his own, he is a victim of tradition, of social pressure, of politics, of invasions by foreign peoples, of climate, or of social injustice.

HEREDITY AND CUSTOM

In 1898, the physician Alexei Korovin established a connection between the ability to tolerate liquor and early exposure to it. From an early age, children see adults drinking and they learn that alcohol is a normal thing. When they're a little older, they imitate that behavior and begin drinking, or they might even start earlier, in childhood. At temperance congresses in the early twentieth century, adages such as "the apple doesn't fall far from the tree" and "as ye sow, so shall ye reap" were quite popular.

Children emulate their parents, who in turn emulated their own parents. But surely this all started somewhere? Enter the Mongols once again. At one point, a theory gained popularity among Russian scientists to the effect that a particular gene entered the Russian gene pool in the thirteenth century, when the Mongol hordes led by Genghis Khan sowed death and destruction across the Eurasian steppes. The Mongols took control of Russia and intermarried with the indigenous population, and over the course of the centuries a growing number of Russians acquired Mongol blood. As a result, the notorious ADH2-2 enzyme, which slows the breakdown of alcohol in the blood, entered their genetic makeup. The same scientists claim that research has shown that nearly half of all Moscow residents carry Mongol genes that make them more susceptible to the effects of alcohol and to addiction to it. This theory has since been disproved.

POVERTY

Soviet propagandists repeatedly claimed that alcoholism and other social disorders, such as crime and prostitution, had been vanquished with the advent of a socialist society. Those social disorders were in turn partly attributable to the church and capitalists, which together with the aristocracy were out to acquire power and wealth that would enable them to oppress the people. The people had little more than the church, the tavern, and scarce food, and they lived in dire poverty. Or in the words of the character Semyon Marmeladov:

– Милостивый государь, – начал он почти с торжественностию, – бедность не порок, это истина. Знаю я, что и пьянство не добродетель, и это тем паче. Но нищета, милостивый государь, нищета – порок-с. В бедности вы еще сохраняете свое благородство врожденных чувств, в нищете же никогда и никто. За нищету даже и не палкой выгоняют, а метлой выметают из компании человеческой, чтобы тем оскорбительнее было; и справедливо, ибо в нищете я первый сам готов оскорблять себя. И отсюда питейное!

"Honored sir," he began almost with solemnity, "poverty is not a vice, that's a true saying. Yet I know too that drunkenness is not a virtue, and that that's even truer. But beggary, honored sir, beggary is a vice. In poverty you may still retain your innate nobility of soul, but in beggary – never – no one. For beggary a man is not chased out of human society with a stick, he is swept out with a broom, so as to make it as humiliating as possible; and quite right, too, forasmuch as in beggary I am ready to be the first to humiliate myself. Hence the pot house."[4]

Fyodor Dostoyevsky, Crime and Punishment (1866)

Maxim Gorky believed that oppression of the workers and their impoverished state would ultimately lead to revolution. They were numbed by their inhumane existence, so they went out drinking and were numbed even more. It was a vicious cycle that they were unable to break on their own. Herzen wrote:

Вино оглушает человека, дает возможность забыться, искусственно веселит, раздражает; это оглушение и раздражение тем больше нравятся, чем меньше человек развит и чем больше сведен на узкую, пустую жизнь. Как же не пить слуге, осужденному на вечную переднюю, на всегдашнюю бедность, на рабство, на продажу? Он пьет через край – когда может, потому что не может пить всякий день. [...] Пить чай в трактире имеет другое значение для слуг. Дома ему чай не в чай; дома ему все напоминает, что он слуга; дома у него грязная людская, он должен сам поставить самовар; дома у него чашкам отбитой ручкой и всякую минуту барин может позвонить. В трактире он вольный человек, он господин, для него накрыт стол, зажжены лампы, для него несется с подносом половой, чашки блестят, чайник блестит, он приказывает – его слушают, он радуется и весело требует себе паюсной икры или расстегайчик к чего.

Alcohol stupefies a man, it enables him to forget himself, stimulates him, and induces an artificial gaiety; this stupefaction and stimulation are the more agreeable the less the man is developed and the more he is bound to a narrow, empty life. How can a servant not drink when he is condemned to the everlasting waiting in the hall, to perpetual poverty, to being a slave, to being sold? He drinks to excess – when he can – because he cannot drink every day. [...] Drinking tea at the eating-house means something quite different to servants. Tea at home is not the same thing for the house-serf; at home everything reminds him that he is a servant; at home he is in the dirty servants' room, he must get the samovar himself; at home he has a cup with a broken handle, and any minute his master may ring for him. At the eating-house he is a free man, he is a gentleman; for him the table is laid and the lamps are lit; for him the waiter runs with the tray; the cup shines, the tea-pot glitters, he gives orders and is obeyed, he enjoys himself and gaily calls for pressed caviar or a turnover with his tea.[5]

Alexander Herzen, *My Past and Thoughts* (1856)

CULTURAL BACKWARDNESS

Some writers, students, and scholars have suggested that unsatisfied intellectual curiosity is at the root of the extreme drinking habits encountered among Russians. If you cultivate the individual and satisfy his intellectual needs, he will forgo alcohol. During the latter part of the nineteenth century, students and artists went into the countryside to spread literacy to the masses. Numerous temperance groups called for the construction of libraries and theaters, for the placement of reading desks in tearooms, and for museums – based on the notion that drinking behavior would change if alternatives to the tavern were available.

– Ну, ладно, ладно – выпил и потерпи! Поговори со мною как человек с человеком. Отвечай: почему я жулик и пьяница, а не стыдно мне в жизни нисколько? Нет, ты скажи, зачем русский человек всегда украсть норовит? Украсть или выпить? Откуда такая потребность души у русского человека?..

На это Соломон Моисеевич знал научный ответ и, застенчиво кусая огурчик, заходил в изыскании первопричин аж до татарского ига, откуда повелись на русской земле и кабак и тюрьма: все благодаря культурной отсталости.

– Вот в Англии вы, Константин Петрович, были бы изобретателем... Или депутатом парламента... министром без портфеля...

"Alright then, alright, you've had your drink and now hear me out. Talk to me like one man to another. Tell me: what makes me a crook and a drunkard, who supposedly goes through life without experiencing the slightest shame? No, instead, you tell me this: why is the Russian man always drawn to stealing? Stealing or drinking. How would you explain this almost spiritual need in the Russian man?"

To this Solomon Moiseyevich had a scientific answer and, nibbling timidly on a pickle, he would take his search for the causal origin all the way back to the Tatar Yoke, which had first brought the tavern and the prison to Russian soil: in short, it was all thanks to cultural backwardness.

"Now in England, Konstantin Petrovich, you would have been an inventor … or a member of Parliament… a minister without portfolio…"[6]

Abram Tertz, *Fantastic Stories*: "At the Circus" (1955)

Following the 1917 revolution, the People's Commissar for Health, Nikolai Semashko, wrote, "For centuries the tsar kept the people drunk and ignorant by depriving them of knowledge. The worker and the peasant often had no choice but to spend their free time getting drunk to help them forget the nightmare of their vulnerable, enslaved existence. He had no cultural pastimes, took no interest in life because tsarism was as afraid of culture as darkness is of light."[7]

Meanwhile, cultivated Russians fell prey to despair because they were unable to lift up the illiterate masses. In short, the masses drank out of ignorance and intellectuals drank because they couldn't do anything about it.

Они без стакана не могли написать ни строки! Я читал, я знаю! Отчаянно пили! Все честные люди России! И отчего они пили? – с отчаяния пили! Пили оттого, что честны! Оттого, что не в силах были облегчить участь народа! Народ задыхался в нищете и невежестве, почитайте-ка Дмитрия Писарева! Он так и пишет: «народ не может позволить себе говядину, а водка дешевле говядины, оттого и пьет русский мужик, от нищеты своей пьет! Книжку он себе позволить не может, потому что на базаре ни Гоголя, ни Белинского, а одна только водка, и монопольная, и всякая, и в разлив, и на вынос! Оттого он и пьет, от невежества своего пьет!»

They couldn't write a line without a glass. I've read it, I know. They drank desperately. All the honest men of Russia. And why did they drink? They drank in desperation. They drank because they were honest, because they were not up to lightening the burden of the people. The people were suffocating in poverty and ignorance. Read Dmitry Pisarev. He writes the same thing: "The people cannot permit themselves beef, but vodka is cheaper than beef, so the Russian peasant drinks because of his poverty. They cannot permit themselves a book, because at the marketplace there is neither Gogol nor Belinsky – just vodka, both government vodka and other kinds, and from the barrel, and to take home. Therefore he drinks, because of his ignorance he drinks."[8]

Venedikt Erofeev, *Moscow to the End of the Line* (1970)

It is true that illiteracy was eliminated and people made more money under communism. But that led to a new problem, simply because the Soviet state did not have enough to offer its citizens: they got bored. The literary magazine *Literaturnaya Gazeta* described the situation in 1966 as follows: "This state of mind, in which people do not know what to do with themselves, is one which has spread far and wide. And, compounded with intellectual immaturity, it is this state of mind that lures people to the backstreets of the city. It is in this state of mind that they fill their glasses to the brim. Drunk, and, as a consequence, indifferent to all that happens around them, they lose their self-control, and this must not be tolerated for it gets them into trouble with the law."[9]

CLIMATE

The severe Russian climate, with its long winters, is often cited as one reason that Russians drink. This is something that even the authorities can do little about. It's cold, so you drink. Montesquieu concluded as early as the eighteenth century that the drinking habits of northern peoples were related to the climate. And he was not alone.

> And in fact I have never seen so many happy faces in Berlin as on the streets of Moscow at minus twenty degrees. And my fellow countrymen looked even more pleased at minus twenty-five. After thorough examination, however, I came to the conclusion that Russian friendliness at extremely low temperatures has to do not only with the joy of overcoming hardship, but also, to a large extent, with heavy alcohol consumption.
>
> Russian winters are harsh. Still, most men have to leave the house in order to earn money and buy their wives fur coats, which are stylish but expensive. Fur is an absolute necessity there. It is like the burqa in Afghanistan or the scarf and the pension fund in Germany: In my native country, the fur coat is a part of a woman's basic gear. A Russian woman without a fur coat is only half a woman. So the men go off to work. But after a few minutes of fresh air, they understand that they won't make it on their own – they need refueling. Vodka is cheaper than tea and helps protect against the cold: A tenth of a liter costs only one euro. For two euros you can also get a bit of lemon or marinated garlic. That ration is enough for about an hour, after which you need reheating. This is how the men get by and even manage to bring some of their earnings home. Then it's the women's turn: They put on their furs and go shopping.[10]
>
> Wladimir Kaminer, *Die Reise nach Trulala* (2002)

AN IMMENSE COUNTRY

Stanislav Sheverdin, the editor in chief of the magazine *Trezvost i Kultura* (*Sobriety and Culture*), which survived the end of *perestroika*, understands why Russians drink: "Euphoria and oblivion – reason enough for drinkers to drink. No doubt it has something to do with the austerity of daily living and the immenseness of Russia. Its colossal expanse somehow relativizes concepts such as death and time. Our surroundings negate our importance and this awareness of one's own insignificance turns one to drink." The sheer size of the country means that you also have little contact with your neighbors.

Огромная культура русского разговора (с выпивкой) затеялась уже в XIX, если не раньше: по причине гигантских расстояний меж усадьбами люди по полгода не виделись, а встретившись, говорили день и ночь напролет. Говорили, уже запахнувшись в шубу. Пока не зазвенит под окнами колокольчик тройки. Пока не отключат телефон за неуплату.

The immense culture of Russian conversation (while boozing) originated back in the nineteenth [century], if not earlier. Because of the vast distances between estates, people would not see one another for months at a time, so once they got together, they talked all day and all through the night. Even after they'd put on their fur coats; even after the sleigh bells were heard out the window; and until the telephone line was cut off for non-payment.[11]

Vladimir Makanin, *The Underground, or a Hero of Our Time* (1999)

The Russian philosopher Nikolai Lossky (1870-1965) studied the Russian national character in great depth. He concluded that it features a number of contradictory traits: passion, extremism, and maximalism, but also fatalism, passivity, servility, and laziness. He believed that these fundamental contradictions lay at the heart of the Russian national character. Another philosopher, Nikolai Berdyayev (1874-1948), drew similar conclusions. He spoke of the Russian as a heathen by birth who is full of contradictions, combining a Dionysian outlook with that of an ascetic. Berdyayev referred to contrasts such as good versus evil, individualism versus impersonal collectivism, universalism versus xenophobia, piety versus atheism, rebellion versus slavery, and kindness versus boorishness. Russian drinking behavior fits this paradigm: Russians drink to get drunk. Here too, another contrast can be identified: dead-drunk versus stone-sober. In addition to the plethora of holidays that sometimes bore a resemblance to orgies, Russians also maintained long periods of complete abstinence. They could not drink on fast days, and their routine was often disrupted by wars or crop failures, so that there was no money or simply nothing to drink. Many people attribute the Russians' extreme drinking habits to such uncertainties of life. If drink was available, then it had to be drunk as quickly as possible.

Человек, по моему мнению, вообще гадок, а матрос, признаться, бывает иногда гаже всего на свете, гаже самого скверного животного, которое все-таки имеет оправдание, так как подчиняется инстинкту. Может быть, я и ошибаюсь, так как жизни не знаю, но мне кажется, все-таки у матроса больше поводов ненавидеть и бранить себя, чем у кого-либо другого. Человеку, который каждую минуту может сорваться с мачты, скрыться навсегда под волной, который знает бога, только когда утопает или летит вниз головой, нет нужды ни до чего, и ничего ему на суше не жаль. Мы пьем много водки, мы развратничаем, потому что не знаем, кому и для чего нужна в море добродетель.

In my opinion, man is, as a rule, foul; and the sailor can sometimes be the foulest of all the creatures of the earth – fouler than the lowest beast, which at least has the excuse of obeying its instincts. It is possible that I may be mistaken, since I do not know life, but it appears to me that a sailor has more occasion than anyone else to despise and curse himself. A man who at any moment may fall from a mast to be forever hidden beneath a wave, a man who knows God only when he is drowning or falling head-first, has need of nothing and feels no pity for anything that happens on dry land. We sailors drink a lot of vodka and sin left and right because we do not know what good virtue does anyone at sea.[12]

Anton Chekhov, "At Sea – A Sailor's Story" (1883)

In her book *Vodka*, the Russian-born German writer Sonja Margolina says that Russians exhibit a religious disdain for earthly things. They are fatalistic: Outside or heavenly forces are stronger than man himself, and they cannot be opposed – resistance is futile. That too generates uncertainty. She writes that rational behavior and being in control of one's emotions are regarded as a sign of pride or conceit. Moreover, in the Soviet period the Orthodox ideal of humility was recast as self-sacrifice to the radiant communist future. The ideal is everything, the individual is unimportant, and so why make any effort?

Inducements to drink are usually collective, which often makes it seem that drinking is unavoidable. The individual doesn't stand a chance in the face of destiny. But there are certainly Russians who do not drink. In fact, most Russians do not have a drinking problem. Does that mean that they're superhuman, heroes, apples that *did* fall far from the tree? Or could it be that there are personal considerations, individual states of misery or joy, that induce drinking?

Lev Tolstoy saw the desire or need to escape reality as an important cause of alcoholism. In the following passage, Fedya Protasov comes from a well-to-do background.

ФЕДЯ. [...] Всем ведь нам в нашем круге, в том, в котором я родился, три выбора – только три: служить, наживать деньги, увеличивать ту пакость, в которой живешь. Это мне было противно, может быть не умел, но, главное, было противно. Второй

– разрушать эту пакость; для этого надо быть героем, а я не герой. Или третье: забыться – пить, гулять, петь. Это самое я и делал. И вот допелся. (Пьет.)

FEDYA In the society in which I was born there are only three careers open to a man – only three. The first is to enter the civil or military service, to earn money and increase the abominations amid which we live. That was repulsive to me. Perhaps I had not the capacity for it; but above all it repelled me. Then the second is to destroy those abominations. To do that you must be a hero; and I am not a hero. And the third is to forget it all by going on the spree, drinking and singing. That is what I did. And this is what my singing has brought me to! [*Drinks*].[13]

Lev Tolstoy, *The Living Corpse* (1900)

In the Soviet Union under Stalin, many drank out of fear, another form of escapism. Danger lurked everywhere one turned, and an innocent joke could prove fatal. People were not even safe in their own beds. The secret police liked to make arrests at night; people were preferably whisked away in the notorious "black marias" between midnight and six a.m. In Tatyana Tolstaya's 1987 story "Date with a Bird," a little boy asks his aunt what she's drinking. "'*Panacea*,' Tamila said, and drank some more. 'Medicine for all evil and suffering, earthly and heavenly, for evening doubts, for nocturnal enemies.'"[14]

WEAKNESS OF CHARACTER

Drinking is seductive. But if it's not the right moment, the temptation must be resisted. And resisting temptation is not the Russian's strong point; he prefers to have things land in his lap and longs for the mythical land of plenty.

О, мы непосредственны, мы зло и добро в удивительнейшем смешении, мы любители просвещения и Шиллера, и в то же время мы бушуем по трактирам и вырываем у пьянчужек, собутыльников наших, бороденки. О, и мы бываем хороши и прекрасны, но только тогда, когда нам самим хорошо и прекрасно. Напротив, мы даже обуреваемы, - именно обуреваемы, - благороднейшими идеалами, но только с тем условием, чтоб они достигались сами собою, упадали бы к нам на стол с неба и, главное, чтобы даром, даром, чтобы за них ничего не платить. Платить мы ужасно не любим, зато получать очень любим, и это во всем. О дайте, дайте нам всевозможные блага жизни (именно всевозможные, дешевле не помиримся) и особенно не препятствуйте нашему нраву ни в чем, и тогда и мы докажем, что можем быть хороши и прекрасны. Мы не жадны, нет, но однако же подавайте нам денег, больше, больше, как можно больше денег, и вы увидите, как великодушно, с каким презрением к презренному металлу мы разбросаем их в одну ночь в безудержном кутеже. А не дадут нам денег, так мы покажем, как мы их сумеем достать, когда нам очень того захочется.

Oh, he is spontaneous, he is a marvellous mingling of good and evil, he is a lover of culture and Schiller, yet he brawls in taverns and plucks out the beards of his boon companions. Oh, he, too, can be good and noble, but only when all goes well with him. What is more, he can be carried off his feet, positively carried off his feet by noble ideals, but only if they come of themselves, if they fall from heaven for him, if they need not be paid for. He dislikes paying for anything, but is very fond of receiving, and that's so with him in everything. Oh, give him every possible good in life (he couldn't be content with less), and put no obstacle in his way, and he will show that he, too, can be noble. He is not greedy, no, but he must have money, a great deal of money, and you will see how generously, with what scorn of filthy lucre, he will fling it all away in the reckless dissipation of one night. But if he has not money, he will show what he is ready to do to get it when he is in great need of it.[15]

Fyodor Dostoyevsky, *The Brothers Karamazov* (1880)

Most Russians glorify their national drink; they are proud of it, to the point of waxing lyrical about it, proud to the depths of their soul. It is a drink that brings pleasure. Vodka is undoubtedly a source of tears, but they are tears that warm the heart, God's tears.

Во многом, во многом был он сын своего отца, недаром говорившего после двух – трех рюмок водки: – Нет, отлично! Люблю выпить! Замолаживает! Замолаживает – это слово употреблялось когда-то на винокурнях, и человек выпивший хотел им сказать, что в него вступает нечто молодое, радостное, что в нем совершается некое сладкое брожение, некое освобождение от рассудка, от будничной связанности и упорядоченности. Мужики так и говорят про водку "Как можно! От ней в человеке развязка делается!" Знаменитое "Руси есть веселие пита" вовсе не так просто, как кажется. Не родственно ли с этим "веселием" и юродство, и бродяжничество, и радения, и самосжигания, и всяческие бунты – и даже та изумительная изобразительность, словесная чувственность, которой так славна русская литература?

In many ways he was a son of his father who would say, very appropriately, after a couple of glasses of vodka, "How splendid! I love drinking. It rejuvenates!" "Rejuvenates" – the word had once upon a time been used at the distilleries, and the man who had drunk meant by it that something young and joyous entered into him, that there was going on within him a certain sweet fermentation, a release from reason, from the bonds and rules of everyday life. So the peasants say of vodka, "Why, then, it loosens a man up inside!"

The famous dictum "Russia's joy is in drinking" is by no means so simple as it may seem. Aren't the holy-foolery, and the tramping, the ritual orgies, the self-immolations, and all sorts of revolts akin to that "joy" – or even that amazing picturesqueness, that verbal sensuality for which Russian literature is so famous?[16]

Ivan Bunin, *The Life of Arseniev* (1933)

It is hard to imagine a situation in which a Russian can find no reason to drink. The Russian language even has words for vodka that is drunk to celebrate a large purchase or the sealing of a deal: *magarych* or *litotska*. David Christian quotes a priest from Yaroslavl who wrote this about the inhabitants of his parish at Pokrovsko-Sitskaya:

Even on days which are not festivals, the Sitskarets will try not to miss an opportunity of getting drunk. If he has contracted to build a boat, [the main local industry] or chop wood, he has to drink a *litotska* [i.e. a toast, or *magarych*]; if someone is hired, again a drink; if someone has concluded a contract, a drink; or bought logs to start building, or sold something... and so on. In a word, nothing can be done without a *litotska*. So, when work is going well, on Sundays after service, the people drink, as they say, 'to extinction' [*na propaluyu*]. And then, if one elbows another he gets it straight around the ear. The Sitskari do not like court cases; but not one drinking session goes without a fight. Indeed, even if someone is badly beaten up, the victim will not go to court. The matter is over, except that the offender had better avoid the victim for a bit, particularly if he is drunk. Sometimes it happens that rivals, after exchanging several full-blooded blows without understanding why, will ask each other: "What are you fighting about?" and "What are you on about?" and they then drown their enmity in a half bottle of *polugar*. It must also be said that in spite of their inclination towards drunkenness, there are extremely few or even no drunkards. Even the most hardened drinker will return home at midnight, or early in the morning, sleep, sober himself up with kvas, and work as hard as ever until the next Sunday.[17]

RECONCILIATION

Villagers often drank vodka while discussing their general affairs – when sentencing criminals, for example. If a thief was apprehended, the sentencing by the community was an almost ritual ceremony. After the sentence was pronounced, the victim would buy vodka for everyone, which showed that he was satisfied with the punishment. The thief could also treat everyone to vodka in hopes that he would be forgiven and allowed back into the community. But vodka could bring people together on a smaller scale too, as illustrated in Walter Horn's *Wodka & Kaviar* (*Vodka & Caviar*), in which he quotes Wilhelm Müller, a traveler to Russia:

This famous anti-alcohol poster (1959) also sought to increase distrust of foreigners: *"Foreign Spies Actively Seek Out Those Who Love to Drink. There is a rather well-known proverb: 'What's on the sober man's mind is on the drunkard's tongue.'"*

Two figures with long, dignified beards sit off to one side at a small table, with a half a quart of *gerafeika* (pepper vodka) between them. Their faces glow, almost as if they were painted on; they regard each other with a wondrously friendly expression, hold hands, and kiss tenderly, and in this blissful state tears flow down their heated cheeks.

You might think that they are two close friends who have reunited after years of separation. But no! They are neighbors who, to their great annoyance, see each other almost every day and make each other's life miserable. But the great peacemaker, vodka, has reconciled them, and they are happy to have the opportunity to ask each other for forgiveness. They are now completely mellow, feeling no rancor, with only sweet words passing their lips, and their moist, buoyant eyes radiate heavenly rapture. Almost always, with only very few exceptions, spirits call forth a mellow mood in Russians.[18]

Wilhelm Müller, *Russische Lebensbilder* (1844)

Vodka warms the soul, sets people free, makes them sing and dance, and helps them break down barriers. At its best, it induces a state of euphoria, of absolute bliss. It made Pierre Bezukhov, a character in *War and Peace*, "ecstatic to the point of delirium." One of Chekhov's characters becomes "hot-tempered, candid, and self-sacrificing." Others go where "the birds never stop singing," "where all the roses in the world bloom together," where one feels as fresh "as a magnolia just in bloom." And in the case of old people, it "makes your bones straight."

Получилось опьянение, какого я именно и хотел, когда ехал к графу. Я стал чрезмерно бодр душою, подвижен, необычайно весел. Мне захотелось подвига неестественного, смешного, пускающего пыль в глаза... В эти минуты, мне казалось, я мог бы переплыть все озеро, открыть самое запутанное дело, победить любую женщину... Мир с его жизнями приводил меня в восторг, я любил его, но в то же время хотелось придираться, жечь ядовитыми остротами, издеваться...

It gave me just the sort of inebriation I wanted when I was going to the Count's. My soul was filled with exceptional vigor, I was spry, and extraordinarily cheerful. I wanted to perform a supernatural, ridiculous feat that would dazzle... In these minutes it seemed to me that I could swim across the entire lake, unravel the most convoluted affair, conquer any woman... The world with its lives brought me to a state of ecstasy. I loved it, but at the same time I wanted to take issue with it, to scorch it with devastating witticisms, mock it...[19]

Anton Chekhov, *A Hunting Drama* (1884)

HOSPITALITY

In the old days, visitors were offered bread (*khleb*) and salt (*sol*) by their hostess. The guest would break off a piece of the round loaf, dip it in the salt, and eat it. Bread symbolizes prosperity, and salt is a talisman. That tradition lives on as an important part of the wedding ceremony. In rural areas, the parents of the bridegroom would offer the newlyweds bread and salt after the wedding, since the bride would be coming to live with them from then on. A customary supplement to the "bread and salt" is a glass of vodka. Important guests would also be offered a glass on leaving, but without a snack.

Adam Olearius's party traveled to Russia by way of the Swedish fort of Nyenskans in the delta of the Neva. They were met there by a regiment of marksmen representing Tsar Michael Fyodorovich. "By way of welcome, the ambassadors were offered several cups of very strong vodka, two kinds of bad-tasting mead, and some pieces of gingerbread. They gave me some to try, too, saying [in Latin]: 'add a pinch of sulphur, and you'd have a drink fit for Hades.'"[20]

Though technically still on Swedish soil, they were received by a boyar at a fort a little further up the river. This Russian nobleman's wife and a lady friend were present at the reception: "Each lady had to sip a cup of vodka in honor of each of the ambassadors, then hand it over and bow to him. The Russians consider it the greatest honor they can pay a guest to show him in this manner that he has been agreeable and welcome. Where friendship and intimacy are very great, the guest is permitted to kiss the wife on the mouth."[21]

BINGE DRINKING

Whether you drink vodka out of joy or sadness, eventually too much of it will make you unhappy. A hangover is the rough physical and mental condition that occurs between the last drink you have before going to bed and the first one after you wake up. If this next drink comes on the following evening, then you're in danger of becoming an alcoholic. If it's a few days later, then you're just a partier. But if you have your first drink right after waking up in order to get rid of that unpleasant hangover, you run the risk of getting trapped in a permanent state of inebriation. And if you have that morning drink only periodically, with long pauses in between – even up to a year – then you suffer from dipsomania, and you're a "periodic" or a binge drinker.

Считается, что в питии алкоголя с утра есть что-то криминальное. Как делать секс с сестрой или после сладкого есть суп и острое мясо. Нельзя, поспав лишь три часа, начинать день с двухсот граммов текилы в бистро у Московского вокзала. А он начинал и удивлялся: почему нельзя?

Человек, пьющий с утра, знает: опьянение приходит и уходит волнами. Уж мы-то с вами знаем ритм этого прибоя! Первый глоток, самый прекрасный, распускающийся в мозгу, как цветок орхидеи. Четвертая бутылка пива, после которой понимаешь, что к работе уже не вернешься, вечер посвятишь алкоголю. Двенадцатая бутылка, после которой кажется, что пьян смертельно и пора спать... и после которой лучше пить уже водку. Самые ужасные утренние глотки, когда никто уже не пьет из удовольствия, а ты думаешь только о завтрашней головной боли. По этому морю он доплывал приблизительно до Папуа-Новой Гвинеи. Но знал туров хейердалов, на счету которых несколько кругосветок за сутки. Главное здесь – доверие. Положитесь на алкоголь, и он вознесет вас к безднам, о существовании которых вы, проводя день на работе, а вечер у телевизора, никогда бы не догадались.

Drinking first thing in the morning is regarded as a criminal act. Like having sex with your sister or eating soup and a spicy meat dish after dessert. After a mere three hours of sleep, you can't begin your day with two hundred grams of tequila in a bistro by some Moscow train station. But then it dawned on him: Why not?

The morning drinker knows: intoxication comes and goes in waves. You and I surely know the rhythm of that surf! The first gulp is the most beautiful; it fans out across the brain like an orchid blossom. The fourth bottle of beer, after which it becomes clear you're not going back to work, that the evening will be devoted to alcohol. The twelfth bottle, after which it seems like you're fatally drunk and it's time for sleep... and after which it's better to switch to vodka. Those dreadful swallows in the morning, by which time nobody is drinking for pleasure, and all you can think about is tomorrow's headache.

He had sailed this sea to approximately Papua New Guinea. But he knew a few Thor Heyerdahls who had been around the world several times in a single day. The most important thing here is trust. Put your faith in alcohol and it will take you to depths you never dreamed existed when you were spending your day at work and your evening in front of the television.[22]

Ilya Stogov, *Machos Don't Cry* (1999)

The Russian word for binge drinking is *zapoy*. It's most commonly encountered in the instrumental case: *zapoyem*. Egbert Engberts, a Russian of Dutch origin who fled his fatherland after the 1917 revolution and wrote his memoirs in the Netherlands, was familiar with the concept of binge drinking:

Others have written about alcohol abuse, and all I want to add here is that Russians were often cursed with a particular drinking affliction: Many of them drank *zapoyem*. As far as I know, this affliction exists only in Russia. What does drinking *zapoyem* mean? It means drinking sporadically, but for days on end and to the point of unconsciousness. It is up to science to say whether this is a form of illness or nothing more than a temporary flagging of one's willpower. *Zapoyem* drunks would say that it is truly an illness, that they could feel it coming on and that there was nothing they could do about it. One acquaintance of mine who occasionally suffered from this malady would disappear during the "illness" for three or more days, much to the dismay and distress of his wife and children. One time he was returned in stages from Moscow to St. Petersburg, a distance of some six hundred kilometers, and he could not remember how he had ended up in Moscow. At normal times, he was a very proper, hard-working man, an exemplary husband and father.[23]

Egbert Engberts, *Herinneringen aan Rusland* (1929)

These boozers have no idea how, why, and when they traveled to another city. Their memories have been wiped clean. The moment they realize this normally marks the end of that particular binge.

С Николаем Максимычем Путохиным приключилась беда, от которой широким и беспечным российским натурам так же не следует зарекаться, как от тюрьмы и сумы: он невзначай напился пьян и в пьяном образе, забыв про семью и службу, ровно пять дней и ночей шатался по злачным местам. От этих беспутно проведенных пяти суток в его памяти уцелел один только похожий на кашу сумбур из пьяных рож, цветных юбок, бутылок, дрыгающих ног. Он напрягал свою память, и для него ясно было только, как вечером, когда зажигали фонари, он забежал на минутку к своему приятелю поговорить о деле, как приятель предложил выпить пива...

Nikolai Maksimych Putokhin suffered a mishap of the sort that the expansive and carefree Russian nature must be as ever-ready to endure as jail or poverty: he inadvertently got dead drunk, and in a drunken manner, with no thought of family or position, spent five full days and nights staggering through the seedy parts of town. All that was left in his memory of these five days of dissipation was a hazy muddle of drunken faces, colorful skirts, bottles, and floundering legs. He probed his memory, but the only thing that was clear was that as the street lamps were being lit, he stopped in on his friend for just a minute to discuss some business and his friend suggested they go out for a beer...[24]

Anton Chekhov, "An Mishap" (1886)

It's no surprise that Anton Chekhov – a doctor by profession – describes the *zapoy* so vividly and sympathetically, since he had a brother who suffered from it. He called it "a psychosis analogous to morphine addiction, onanism, nymphomania, etc."[25] In a letter to a friend, Chekhov wrote that he had brought up the subject of *zapoy* with his brother:

Я написал, что в пьяном образе ты склонен к гиперболам и экстазу: ты туманишься, забываешь чин свой и звание, оттягиваешь вниз губу, несешь чепуху, кричишь всему миру, что ты Чехов, и наутро рвешь... Вечером и ночью врешь, а утром рвешь... [...] Да и на какой леший пить? Пить так уж в компании порядочных людей, а не solo и не черт знает с кем. Подшофейное состояние – это порыв, увлечение, так и делай так, чтоб это было порывом, а делать из водки нечто закусочно-мрачное, сопливое, рвотное – тьфу!

I explained to him that "when you are drunk you are inclined to indulge in hyperbole and ecstasy: you become vague, forget where you are, your lower lip droops, you brag to all and sundry, cry to the world that you are Chekhov and puke as morning approaches. In the evening and at night you show off, in the morning you throw up. [...] Anyway, why the devil do you have to drink? All right, so drink in the company of good men, but don't drink alone and don't drink with any old riff-raff. A clouded state of mind is the consequence of a surge of emotion, ecstasy, – suffer the surge; but turn vodka into something dismal, blubbering, spewing, – never, ugh!"[26]

THE TAVERN

The history of the tavern in Russia closely parallels developments in government finance. Sometimes the tsars collected large amounts of money through the taverns, only to shut them down because of the unbridled alcohol abuse. Or they would decide that taverns could not serve food because that would make people drink more. The first type of tavern to exist in Russia was the *korchma*, where ordinary people could go to eat and drink. The *korchma* was the focus of social life; there was singing, and it was often the place where government decrees were read aloud, judgments were handed down, and so on. It was a sort of community center. The owner ran the business as he saw fit and did not have to pay taxes. When Ivan III conquered Novgorod, he closed the private inns there and replaced them with royal *korchmas*. What was new about this was that food was no longer served. Some people claim that the bad habit of not eating while drinking dates back to this era. Meanwhile, many tavern owners opened illegal businesses, because of which drunkenness among the masses assumed epidemic proportions. Archbishop Feodosy even called for the closure of all taverns... Ivan heeded the call and imposed restrictions on the sale of alcohol. He ordered that people in Novgorod who flouted the ban be thrown off the bridge into the river. After his grandson Ivan IV captured Kazan, the first *tsaryov kabak* (imperial tavern) opened its doors in Moscow in 1552, intended for Ivan's palace guards (*oprichniki*). This was soon followed by more *kabaks*, and as of 1590 only those state-owned taverns were permitted to produce and sell spirits. The *tselovalnik* (tavern manager, literally "kisser") had to kiss the cross and swear that he would respect the imperial treasury, that he would not substitute his own alcohol for the imperial alcohol, that he would not change the prices, accept extra money, or alter the volume of the glasses,

Morning at a Tavern, Leonid Solomatkin (1873)

and that he would not dilute or mix the beverage. The proceeds flowed directly into the treasury, and so heavy drinking was in the national interest.

Unlike the *korchma*, the *kabak* was no place for "respectable women." They were indeed frequented by prostitutes. The Englishman Giles Fletcher visited Moscow in the latter part of the sixteenth century. In his 1591 book *Russia at the Close of the Sixteenth Century,* he had this to say about the *kabak*:

> In every great towne of his realme he [the tsar] hath a caback or drinking house, where is sold aquavitæ (which they call Russe wine) mead, beere, &c. [...] Wherein, besides the base and dishonourable meanes to encrease his treasurie, many foule faultes are committed. The poore labouring man and artificer, manie times spendeth all from his wife and children. Some use to lay in twentie, thirtie, fourtie rubbels or more into the caback, and vowe themselves to the pot till all that be spent. And this (as he will say) for the honour of hospodare [lord] or the emperour. You shall have manie there that have drunk all away to the verie skinne, and so walk naked (whom they call naga). While they are in the caback none may call them foorth whatsoever cause there be, because he hindereth the emperours revenue.[27]

Those who held the monopoly on alcohol gained access to money and power, with corruption as the inevitable result – as well as protests against the system. In 1648, a "tavern rebellion" erupted, which was brutally suppressed, and the Assembly on Taverns was formed to address – not for the last time – reforms of the liquor system in Russia. The halfhearted measures, such as a ban on selling vodka on credit and the closing of a number of taverns, had little effect, and little would change over the century that followed. The tavern did get a new name: *piteyny dvor* (pot house or "drinking yard").

Adam Olearius traveled to Russia three times with a delegation from Holstein that had managed to extract concessions from Tsar Michael for an overland route to Persia.

> When, in 1643, I stopped at the Lübeck house in Novgorod, I saw such besotted and naked brethren come out of the nearby tavern, some bareheaded, some barefooted, and others only in their nightshirts. One of them had drunk away his cloak and emerged from the tavern in his nightshirt; when he met a friend who was on his way to the same tavern, he went in again. Several hours later he came out without his nightshirt, wearing only a pair of underdrawers. I had him called to ask what had become of his nightshirt, who had stolen it? He answered, with the customary 'Fuck your mother', that it was the tavern keeper, and that the drawers might as well go where the cloak and his nightshirt had gone. With that, he returned to the tavern, and later came out entirely naked. Taking a handful of dog fennel that grew near the tavern, he held it over his private parts, and went home singing gaily.[28]
>
> Adam Olearius, The Travels of Olearius in Seventeenth-Century Russia (1656)

There are known cases of wealthy noblemen who drank away their estates. They could not count on mercy from the tavern owners, who were under enormous pressure to meet the imposed quota and thus were more likely to encourage heavy drinking.

Adam Olearius also describes the goings-on near a bar that was threatened by a major fire raging in the city.

> The whole city, including the Kremlin, was placed in the greatest jeopardy. Not a person wanted to escape or could, since all were as drunk as could be from the vodka they had pillaged from the cellars during the fire. They knocked the bottoms out of the barrels that were too large to take out, drew off the vodka into hats, caps, shoes, and gloves, and got so drunk that the blackened streets were covered with them. Many who completely lost consciousness were suffocated by the smoke and fumes, and burned up.[29]

Fyodor Dostoyevsky was also a witness to an effort by villagers to put out a church fire. When it began to threaten the tavern next door, the proprietor promised vodka to everyone who helped extinguish the fire. The crowd abandoned the church and rushed over to the tavern.

Some taverns had an area that was off-limits to customers, as in a church, but in most of them there were simply two separate areas for customers: the "black" part for the ordinary people, and the "clean" part for the well-to-do. The black part was sometimes situated in the cellar, the "hole."

Вероятно, не многие из моих читателей имели случай заглядывать в деревенские кабаки; но наш брат, охотник, куда не заходит! Устройство их чрезвычайно просто. Они состоят обыкновенно из темных сеней и белой избы, разделенной надвое перегородкой, за которую никто из посетителей не имеет права заходить. В этой перегородке, над широким дубовым столом, проделано большое продольное отверстие. На этом столе, или стойке продается вино. Запечатанные штофы разной величины рядком стоят на полках, прямо против отверстия. В передней части избы, предоставленной посетителям, находятся лавки, две-три пустые бочки, угловой стол. Деревенские кабаки большей частью довольно темны, и почти никогда не увидите вы на их бревенчатых стенах каких-нибудь ярко раскрашенных лубочных картин, без которых редкая изба обходится.

Probably few of my readers have had a chance of seeing the inside of a rural tavern; but we hunters drop in anywhere and everywhere! They are exceedingly simply arranged. They consist usually of a dark entrance and a parlor divided in two by a partition beyond which none of the patrons has the right to go. In this partition, above a wide oak table, there is a big longitudinal opening. The drink is sold at this table, or counter. Labelled bottles of various sizes stand in rows on the shelves directly opposite the opening. In the forward part of the hut, which is given over to the patrons, there are benches, one or two empty barrels and a corner table. Rural taverns are for the most part fairly dark, and you will hardly ever see on the log walls any of those brightly colored popular prints with which most peasant huts are adorned.[30]

Ivan Turgenev, *Sketches from a Hunter's Album*: "Singers" (1852)

A coat of arms hung over the tavern door, joined by a red flag on holidays. Sometimes there would be a broom on a post next to the tavern and a sign with the inscription "Spirits served in this house." Another common feature was a depiction of a pine tree, or two spruces by the entrance. Most rural taverns did not have signs; the trees spoke for themselves. The Russian word for spruce is *yolka*, and thus the tavern became known colloquially as the *Yolkin*, or *Ivan-Yolkin* and even *Ivan Ivanovich Yolkin*. The origins of this usage are unknown; one interpretation is that *yolka* has the same origin as *øl*, the Danish word for beer.

After 1886, only establishments that served meals were permitted. There were many different kinds: the *traktir*, the *gerberg*, the *kukhmisterskaya*, and the *restoran*. These businesses had signs from which you could tell right away what sort of license they had.

The licensed bars had signs in two colors: one half running the entire length in green and the other in yellow. The crown depots for spirits were identifiable by green signs. A yellow sign indicated a place where only beer was dispensed, whereas the cheap inns that were not entitled to sell beer or liquor had red signs.

Some signs for licensed bars also had the old-fashioned and long-obsolete inscription: "Spirits sold – come and be served, tobacco sold – come and smoke." This dated back to a time when you could not smoke in just any inn and tavern, let alone on the street.[31]

Egbert Engberts, *Herinneringen aan Rusland* (1929)

By the end of the nineteenth century, the *kabak* had apparently disappeared from public memory. In any event, it was with a certain nostalgia that Moscow writer Vladimir Gilyarovsky described the interior of a *kabak*:

В кабаках тогда запрещалось иметь не только что столы, но даже скамьи. Пугливое начальство больше всего трусило, чтобы кабак не обратился в народный клуб, и для этого заботилось, чтобы в нем не засиживались, а выпивали, стоя у прилавка. [...]

В кабаках, кроме иконы в углу, обязательно висел всегда в позолоченной раме царский портрет для того, чтобы в присутствии его величества не пели в кабаках песен, не буйствовали и не ругались "скверно матерными словами". Чуть что не так – кабатчик указывал на портрет, предупреждая, чтобы при царе "не выражались", а в ответ получал от пьяного буяна:

– На кой он нам? Ну, его...

А отсюда иногда политическое дело, и "за оскорбление величества" немало мужиков сгнило в Сибири за одно пьяное слово. Когда же в половине семидесятых годов по высочайшему повелению приказано было убрать царские портреты, то и "политические" преступления этого рода сами собой прекратились.

Back then, *kabaks* were not only prohibited from having tables, they could not even have benches. More than anything else, the cowards running things were afraid that the *kabak* might turn into a people's club, and so they took pains to make sure that nobody would be able to sit down, and would have to drink standing at the counter. [...]

In addition to the icons in the corner, *kabaks* were required to always have a portrait of the tsar hanging in a gilt frame. The idea was that in His Majesty's presence, people would not sing, roughhouse, or use "nasty, dirty words." At the first sign of trouble, the *kabak* keeper would point to the portrait and warn against "expressing oneself" in the presence of the tsar. The rowdy's usual response was:

"What's he to us? Who gives a…"

And from there, matters grew into a political case, and no small number of *muzhiks* rotted away in Siberia for a single drunken word "insulting His Majesty." In the mid-seventies, when the tsar's portrait was removed by royal command, "political" crimes of this sort also came to a halt.[32]

Vladimir Gilyarovsky, "The Goat and The Seagull"

Many eateries and drinking establishments were shut down after the revolution. The New Economic Policy caused a brief revival, but then more drudgery ensued. In Moscow and Leningrad especially, it was hard to drink outside the home. Canteens were a consolation for drinkers, as shown by a report published in *Pravda* on July 30, 1940:

На дверях – вывеска: "Чайная – кафе – закусочная." Но ни чаю, ни кофе здесь не бывает. Из закусок же чаще всего налицо лишь селедка: потому что торгуют здесь в основном водкой и пивом. Красующийся на стене плакат "Гражданам в нетрезвом виде ничего не подается" вызывает веселую улыбку, ибо трезвых здесь почти никогда не бывает.

On the door hangs a sign: "Tearoom – cafe – snackbar." But here, one will find neither coffee nor tea. And the only snack that is usually on hand is pickled herring, because the tearoom sells mostly vodka and beer. A poster crowning the wall reads "Citizens in a non-sober state will not be served" and elicits joyful smiles, for sober customers are almost never to be found here.[33]

And as in so many places around the world, a thirsty drinker could enjoy the convenience of the train station restaurant. *Pravda* also shed light on this phenomenon. The March 28, 1940, issue reported:

Moreover, spirits are sold not only at the buffet, but also by the waiters on the platforms and in the trains. Some buffets sell only vodka. Lately standard packages that include alcohol have been available at South station. Many of the sales outlets for alcohol at the most important stations are in a dire state of neglect. At the Losovaya station, for example, there is a bar with a display case from which the glass is missing; the kiosks are filthy, and the station waiters go through the cars with wine and cognac instead of food.[34]

Until the early 1980s, there was also the *pivnaya*, the beer bar, a smoky lair where men grimly downed glasses of beer. Drinking vodka outside the home was extremely inconvenient. In the waning days of the Soviet Union, there were no bars whatsoever in Moscow. The only place where the man on the street could drink was in restaurants. But restaurants were pricey and scarce, so that one usually had to stand in line. Even knocking back a glass was impossible. The elite was better off. The political *nomenklatura* had elegant establishments in the Kremlin; writers had a good café at the Writers Union, with something equivalent for musicians at the Composers Union; and scientists usually had a top-rate eating and drinking establishment at their institute. By necessity, the ordinary Russian drank at home. This made kitchens the country's most convivial spots.

7

Vodka in Russia (1800-1917)

– Пьешь и никакой веселости, – сказал Фролов. – Чем больше в себя вливаю, тем становлюсь трезвее. Другие веселеют от водки, а у меня злоба, противные мысли, бессонница. Отчего это, брат, люди, кроме пьянства и беспутства, не придумают другого какого-нибудь удовольствия?

"One drinks and is none the merrier," said Frolov. "The more I pour into myself, the more sober I become. Other people grow festive with vodka, but I suffer from anger, disgusting thoughts, sleeplessness. Why is it, old man, that people don't invent some other pleasure besides drunkenness and debauchery?"[1]

Anton Chekhov, "Drunk" (1887)

UNDER TSAR ALEXANDER I (ruled 1801-1825), the production and sale of vodka came under the jurisdiction of the newly established Ministry of Internal Affairs. Concession holders gained more rights and could also open taverns. They once again evaded taxes, and "traveling taverns" even came on the scene. As a result, Alexander reintroduced a state monopoly in 1819. He made an exception for Siberia, since controlling vodka production there was next to impossible.

Alexander's successor, Nicholas I (1825-1855), again abolished the vodka monopoly and allowed some forms of concessions. This ultimately worked out badly for the lower classes, especially those who lived by the motto *Ne pit, tak i na svete ne zhit* (If you do not drink you are not alive). This is because the vodka was of poorer quality and was more expensive. Russian Finance Minister Yegor Kankrin advocated drinking in moderation. He was opposed to prohibition for economic reasons: distilling vodka was helpful during grain gluts, since it kept "grain mountains" from developing and thus ensured stable prices on the grain market.

The aim so passionately pursued by Peter and Catherine finally came to pass in the nineteenth century: Russia became part of Europe. By 1814, after the victory over Napoleon, Russian military officers had been to Paris, where they introduced vodka. More importantly, they encountered the ideas of the French Revolution. In 1825, the Decembrist Revolt led by Russian army officers was brutally suppressed by Nicholas I. He saw to it that the *Dekabristy* were sentenced to death or exiled. Nevertheless, a cultural flowering took place in the upper stratum of society. The poet Pushkin, the "sun of poetry," appeared on the scene and propelled Russian literature to new heights; Mikhail Glinka wrote his first compositions; and philosophy flourished. The nobility immersed itself completely in French language and culture.

But Russia was still a feudalistic land of peasants – serfs who had no rights and who were bound to their lord's land. The serfs could buy their freedom, but it cost a fortune.

Нет, Константин Федорович, что уж откупаться. Возьмите нас. Уж у вас всякому уму выучишься. Уж эдакого умного человека нигде во всем свете нельзя сыскать. А ведь теперь беда та, что себя никак не убережешь. Целовальники такие завели теперь настойки, что с одной рюмки так те живот станет драть, что воды ведро бы выпил. Не успеешь опомниться, как все спустишь. Много соблазну.

"No, Konstantin Fyodorovich, why should we buy our freedom? You take us. With you any man'll learn all sorts o' smart stuff. The whole problem now is that people don't know where to turn. The barmen nowadays have started sellin' the sort o' booze that rips out your guts after just one glass and makes you want to drink a whole pail o' water. Before you know it, you've gone and blowed every kopek you had. There's lots of temptations."[2]

Nikolai Gogol, *Dead Souls* (1842)

In 1859, "drunken revolts" (*piteynye bunty*) erupted. In many locales, the common people damaged buildings in protest against high vodka prices. Meanwhile, the quality still left much to be desired. The state produced the vodka and the concession holders sold it, with concessions and taverns accounting for 43 percent of the state budget. The intelligentsia started giving thought to moderation, sobriety, and the state's dual role.

Правда ли, что преступление трезвости дошло до того в Тамбовской губернии, что губернатор Данзас выслал военную команду для усмирения непьющих? Бедное войско, бедные офицеры, мало было им защищать трон и алтарь, помещичьи розги и чиновничий разбой – пришлось теперь защищать кабак с его штофной и распивочной продажей. Уже не дадут ли им потом ведерные кавалерии через плечо, полуштофные крестики в петлицу, а нижним чинам медали с изображением голубя, сходящего на откупоренный штоф и с надписью: «Spiritus sanctus – spirito vini»!

Is it true that the crime of sobriety has reached a point in Tambov Province that Governor Danzas has dispatched a military detachment to subdue the abstainers? Poor troops, poor officers! Did they not have enough to do defending the throne and the altar, the landowners' rod and looting by government officials – now they have to defend the *kabak*, with its by-the-*shtof* and on-the-premises sales? Soon are they going to begin awarding order-of-the-bucket sashes or half-*shtof*-crosses, or, for the lower ranks, medals with the image of a dove alighting on an open *shtof* with the inscription "Spiritus sanctus – spirito vini"![3]

Alexander Herzen, *The Bell* (1859)

Alexander II (1855-1881) is known as the "Tsar Liberator." In 1861, he abolished serfdom. In addition, the accursed concession system, which had created a class of filthy rich vodka barons, was replaced in 1863 by a system involving excise duty. For the first time, vodka was distilled by private companies, such as those of Pyotr Smirnov (Smirnoff) and his uncle Ivan, who competed with each other. Other well-known brands that are still in existence were Eristoff and Keglevich.

The political debate grew more intense. Should Russia look inward, as the Slavophiles urged, or were the westerners correct in their contention that Russia had to find its salvation in Europe? In this heated discussion, the self-evident role of religion also came under fire.

– Удается это потому, – сказал он, – что вера роскошь, которая дорого народу обходится.
– Ну, однако, не дороже его пьянства, – бесстрастно заметил Туганов.

– Да ведь пить-то – это веселие Руси есть, это национальное, и водка все-таки полезнее веры: она по крайней мере греет.

Туберозов вспыхнул и крепко сжал рукав своей рясы; но в это время Туганов возразил учителю, что он ошибается, и указал на то, что вера согревает лучше, чем водка, что все добрые дела наш мужик начинает помолившись, а все худые, за которые в Сибирь ссылают, делает водки напившись.

– Впрочем, откупа уничтожены экономистами, – перебросился вдруг Препотенский. – Экономисты утверждали, что чем водка будет дешевле, тем меньше ее будут пить, и соврали. Впрочем, экономисты не соврали; они знают, что для того, чтобы народ меньше пьянствовал, требуется не одно то, чтобы водка подешевела. Надо, чтобы многое не шло так, как идет.

"They are succeeding," he said, "because faith is a luxury that costs the common people dearly."

"No more so, however, than their drunkenness," Tuganov observed matter-of-factly.

"But drinking, why, it's the joy of Rus, it's our national pastime, and anyhow, vodka is more useful than faith: at least it warms you up."

Tuberozov seethed with anger and clutched the sleeves of his cassock, but at that moment Tuganov retorted that the teacher was mistaken, pointing out that faith warmed better than vodka, that Russian peasants began all good deeds after praying and all bad ones, for which they were sent to Siberia, after getting drunk on vodka.

"The liquor business, by the way, has been destroyed by economists," Prepotensky suddenly threw in. "The economists claimed that the cheaper vodka became, the less people would drink, and that was a lie. And yet the economists weren't lying; they know that in order for the people to cut down on drunkenness, it will take more than just lowering the price of vodka. Lots of things must be done differently from the way they're done now."[4]

Nikolai Leskov, *The Cathedral Clergy* (1872)

The reign of Alexander II saw a continued surge in cultural development. In literature, Dostoyevsky, Turgenev, and Tolstoy became masters of their art. Music had eminences such as Tchaikovsky and Mussorgsky. The visual arts had Repin, Surikov, Levitan, and Serov as standard-bearers. Many intellectuals idolized the peasantry, who were less liberated in practice than they were in theory. A number of artists sought inspiration in the countryside. The nobility did not fare well in this period; the rural nobility in particular grew poorer. That class had suffered from the abolition of serfdom and had also lost its exclusive right to distill vodka.

Reading of the Manifesto (Liberating the Serfs), Boris Kustodiev (1909)

ТРОФИМОВ. Вся Россия наш сад. Земля велика и прекрасна, есть на ней много чудесных мест. (Пауза.) Подумайте, Аня: ваш дед, прадед и все ваши предки были крепостники, владевшие живыми душами, и неужели с каждой вишни в саду, с каждого листка, с каждого ствола не глядят на вас человеческие существа, неужели вы не слышите голосов... Владеть живыми душами – ведь это переродило всех вас, живших раньше и теперь живущих, так что ваша мать, вы, дядя уже не замечаете, что вы живете в долг, на чужой счет, на счет тех людей, которых вы не пускаете дальше передней... Мы отстали по крайней мере лет на двести, у нас нет еще ровно ничего, нет определенного отношения к прошлому, мы только философствуем, жалуемся на тоску или пьем водку.

TROFIMOV. All Russia is our orchard. The land is great and beautiful, there are many marvelous places in it. [*Pause*] Think, Anya, your grandfather, your great-grandfather, and all your ancestors were serf-owners, they owned living souls; and now, doesn't something human look at you from every cherry in the orchard, every leaf and every stalk? Don't you hear voices...? Oh, it's awful, your orchard is terrible; and when in the evening or at night you walk through the orchard, then the old bark on the trees sheds a dim light and the old cherry-trees seem to be dreaming of all that was a hundred, two hundred years ago, and are oppressed by their heavy visions. Still, at any rate, we've left those two hundred years behind us. So far we've gained nothing at all – we don't yet know what the past is to be to us – we only philosophize, we complain that we are dull, or we drink vodka.[5]

Anton Chekhov, The Cherry Orchard (1903)

Under Tsar Alexander III (1881-1894), the uninhibited vodka trade flourished. Competition was intense, and so both prices and treasury revenues plummeted. The quality of the vodka followed the same downward spiral, and an increase in drunkenness was again seen. Slowly the realization grew that the culprit was not so much the quality or the price of the vodka, but rather the Russians' drinking behavior. In the final analysis, Russians did not drink that much compared to most Europeans, who drank nearly every day. The total volume of alcohol consumed per capita was lower in prerevolutionary Russia than it was in comparable European countries such as Germany, France, or even Belgium, but because vodka was the alcohol that Russians consumed the most, and because it was drunk in one gulp without food accompanying it, and because nearly all of the drinking took place on a number of specific days – weddings, carnivals, funerals, and religious holidays – the consequences were more obvious and the overall effect was much more devastating. All in all, the alcohol-related mortality rate in the latter years of the tsarist regime was four to five times greater than in western Europe.

In 1885, the authorities made the first attempts to grapple with drinking behavior. The Council of Ministers decided to replace taverns with something resembling inns, where people could get food with their vodka. At the same time, the ministers turned their attention to "carry-out vodka." Could they allow quantities of less than a bucket to be sold in special liquor stores? In that case, people could drink not only in taverns, but also at home. Maybe they would eat something as they drank. Moreover, they would not have to drink an entire bucket in one "sitting." Bottles were in short supply, as the Russian glass industry was still in its infancy. Nevertheless, the sale of vodka in bottles became commonplace in Moscow and St. Petersburg. This scarcely had any effect on alcohol consumption: Drunkards would find one or two buddies to help finish off the entire bottle so that they could get their bottle deposit back right away. And they didn't eat anything with it. To make matters worse, a new profession came into being: the "glass-man." He rented out glasses and had an instrument for uncorking the bottles. The Soviet-era custom of giving the bottom of the bottle a hard knock so that the cork or cap would fly off (and sometimes the bottom would as well) dates to this period.

In 1894, the last year of Tsar Alexander III's reign, a state monopoly on spirits was reintroduced, this time not only for the sake of revenues, but also to combat cheap vodka, with its harmful effects on public health, as well as "home brew" (*samogon*). The state took control of the vodka trade and established special stores to sell it.

Винная лавка, которую в просторечии именовали "казенкой", "монополькой" или "винополькой", была нисколько не похожа на обыкновенные лавки. Над входом ее красовалась темно-зеленая вывеска с двуглавым орлом и строгой, четкой надписью:

КАЗЕННАЯ ВИННАЯ ЛАВКА

Частая железная решетка разделяла помещение на две половины. В одной, куда не было доступа посторонним, царил чинный и даже торжественный порядок, точно в аптеке, в казначействе или в банке. На многочисленных полках стояли, выстроившись, как солдаты по ранжиру, сороковки, сотки и двухсотки, которым потребители дали свои, более сочные и живописные прозвища – шкалики, мерзавчики, полумерзавчики и т. д. А по ту сторону решетки толклась самая разношерстная публика. Людям, которые были, как говорится, "на взводе" или "под мухой", отпускать водку не полагалось, но завсегдатаи казенки не сдавались и подолгу, заплетающимся языком, убеждали сиделицу, что они "как стеклышко". Если уговоры и мольбы не действовали, они переходили к угрозам и к самой отборной ругани. В таких случаях сиделица имела право вызвать городового, который всегда дежурил неподалеку от казенки.

The liquor store that simple folk called the "*kazyonka*" [from the word *kazna*, or state treasury], the "*monopolka*" [monopoly shop], or "*vinopolka*" [combining *vino* (liquor) and the ending of *monopolka*], bore little resemblance to an ordinary shop. Above the entrance proudly hung a dark-green sign displaying a double-headed eagle and sternly and austerely proclaiming:

STATE LIQUOR STORE

A heavy iron grate divided the establishment into two halves. In one half, the one into which the public was not allowed, an atmosphere of solemnity and even decorum reigned, like in an apothecary, a treasury, or a bank. On rows of shelves stood, ordered like soldiers by rank, 40-grammers, 100-grammers, and 200-grammers that had been assigned much pithier and expressive names by the customers: *ouncies*, *bastards*, and *half-bastards*, etc. And on the other side of the grate jostled a most motley assemblage. According to the rules, anyone who was, so to speak, "tipsy" or "three sheets to the wind" was not be sold vodka, but the *kazyonka's* habitués did not give up so easily and marshaled all their eloquence to convince the saleslady that they were "sober as a judge." If their arguments and pleadings failed to achieve the desired effect, they switched to threats and the most select grade of swearing. In such cases, the saleslady had the right to summon a policeman, one of whom was always posted close by the *kazyonkas*.[6]

Samuil Marshak, *At Life's Beginning* (1960)

The initiator of the new measures was Count Sergei Witte, the minister of finance. Two years earlier, he had called vodka a national calamity:

Since 1864, the government, having become convinced of the inapplicability of the principle of free trade in relation to alcoholic beverages, was compelled to undertake a series of measures to restrict the number of locations in which alcohol could be sold and to reduce excessive drinking – this national calamity. In the course of 30 years, more than ten different resolutions designed to restrict this trade and protect the populace were issued... but none of them produced the desired result... because they contained an internal contradiction. The interests of the government and of national health require the judicious consumption of wine and the termination of abuses. But... the interest of the tavernkeepers consists only in having the people drink as much in a given time as possible... [and] to transform the populace, crazed with drink and morally broken, into their slaves.[7]

The merchants who had profited from the free trade in liquor began to rise up in revolt. They suspected that the introduction of the liquor monopoly was not a selfless act, but was instead intended solely to enrich the Ministry of Finance. They were not entirely off the mark. In 1902, liquor still accounted for 28 percent of state revenues. Ivan Bunin, who was later awarded the Nobel Prize for literature, has one of his characters grouse:

Когда пропала надежда на детей, стало все чаще приходить в голову: "Да для кого же вся эта каторга, пропади она пропадом?" Монополия же была солью на рану. Стали трястись руки, болезненно сдвигаться и подниматься брови, стало косить губу, – особенно при фразе, не сходившей с языка: "Имейте в виду". По-прежнему он молодился – носил щеголеватые опойковые сапоги и расшитую косоворотку под двубортным пиджаком. Но борода седела, редела, путалась...

А лето, как нарочно, выдалось жаркое, засушливое. Совсем пропала рожь. И наслаждением стало жаловаться покупателям.

– Прекращаем-с, прекращаем-с! – с радостью, отчеканивая каждый слог, говорил Тихон Ильич о своей винной торговле. – Как же-с! Монополия! Министру финансов самому захотелось поторговать!

– Ох, посмотрю я на тебя! – стонала Настасья Петровна. – Договоришься ты! Загонят тебя, куда ворон костей не таскал!

When all hope of having children was lost, one thought began to come to him more and more frequently: "then what's all this punishment for, devil take it?" The state monopoly only rubbed salt into his wound. Soon his hands began to shake, his brows began to painfully knit and rise, and his lip began to droop, especially at the phrase that was constantly on his tongue: "bear it in mind." As always, he tried to appear younger than he really was, sporting stylish calfskin boots and an embroidered *kosovorotka* under a double-breasted jacket. But his beard grew greyer, and thinner, and tangled...

To make matters worse, the summer turned out to be hot and rainless. The rye crop failed completely. And griping to his customers became his new pastime.

"We're closing down, sir, closing down!" Tikhon Ilyich would say of his alcohol business, delightedly enunciating every syllable. "What did you expect? State monopoly, after all! The Minister of Finance himself fancies doing some selling!"

"Oh, just look at you!" groaned Nastasya Petrovna. "One of these days you'll go too far. Then they'll send you somewhere the crows don't fly!"[8]

Ivan Bunin, *The Village* (1910)

Count Witte was able to immediately eliminate one of the opposition's hobbyhorses, namely that tsarism was founded on a "drunken budget." But he also realized that combating alcoholism had to be coupled with improving the people's living conditions, whereby cultural development in particular merited attention. The government created a commission that was to make recommendations about both improving the people's drinking culture and purifying vodka. The aim was to get Russians to see spirits as a culinary element of a meal, not merely a means for getting drunk. At the same time, restraints were introduced on the vodka trade. It could now be sold only between seven in the morning and ten in the evening. Moreover, sales were completely prohibited on special occasions, such as elections. Home distillers faced stiff penalties.

NEW FACTORIES

The new measures led to a slight decline in drinking. There was also less consumption of alcohol-based medicines such as Children's Balsam and Hoffmann's Drops. However, critics contended that there was now more drinking going on underground, in illegal establishments, and that vodka had also become part of family life, the result being that women and even children had started drinking.

The monopoly also led to the construction of 350 new vodka factories, including Number 1 in Moscow, which was also dubbed Kristall. As a result, per capita consumption of alcohol did not end up decreasing, even if the cheaper vodka was of better quality. The authorities had established more stringent requirements for the packaging, ingredients, and strength of the vodka, but the vodka that the ordinary people drank was still inferior, mostly distilled from beets or potatoes or imported from Ukraine. The better Russian vodka (including Pyotr Smirnov's product) went to the West. In 1910, average annual per capita consumption in Russia came to six liters of pure alcohol.

Count Witte himself admitted in 1914 that the monopoly had not worked. The revolutionary opposition spoke mockingly of "aqua Witte" and produced caricatures depicting tsarism as a vodka bottle poised atop a house of cards.

When Alexander III died in 1894, his successor, Nicholas II (reigned 1894-1917), made a generous gesture by offering a free meal to the poor of St. Petersburg. Nicholas's decree made it emphatically clear what the people should eat and drink. "It is desirable that the meal consist of cabbage soup, pies, and thick currant juice and that mead and beer be dispensed, but no vodka." A year and a half later, his official coronation took place under a less auspicious star. Moscow organized a big party with free beer. There was a mass rush for the beverage, and 1,389 people were killed in the crush. Rumor had it that the people had overindulged the night before with free Smirnov vodka and were already drunk when the free beer was being handed out.

The first major disturbances of the twentieth century took place in 1905, during the war with Japan. The war had turned into a debacle, and revolts erupted throughout the country. The revolution that followed is also known as the drunk revolution, because mutinous troops in Odessa, Kronstadt, and other places mostly went after liquor shops. In the end, a not-so-unfavorable peace treaty was signed with Japan and the country got a parliament – the State Duma – and a constitution.

On August 2, 1914, shortly after World War I broke out, the tsar instituted a measure that was without precedent in all of Russian history: He banned the sale of vodka throughout the entire country (with the exception of elegant clubs) for the duration of the war. Only ethyl alcohol could be produced, for military and medicinal purposes. Nicholas and his government wanted to "strengthen morals and combat poverty, violence, and crime" and to demonstrate that they were willing to forgo enormous tax revenues from the alcohol monopoly to avoid exploiting the weak willpower of Russian drinkers. But just as Catherine the Great had concluded, alcohol was a political "sedative" that had a stabilizing effect, because it numbed people and kept them from engaging in subversive behavior. Disturbances broke out all across the country. Hundreds of liquor shops were raided, and sloshed soldiers plundered cities and villages. In the southern Siberian city of Barnaul, the rioting claimed more than a hundred lives.

After that wave of violence passed, people in the cities and countryside alike did drink substantially less. There was a decline in vandalism and in domestic violence. To be sure, illegal liquor distilling and bootlegging increased, sales of cologne and medicinal tonics were up, Moscow shops sold twenty times as much shellac, and the state treasury suffered. But the overall picture was clear: It did Russia good. The idea of extending the ban on vodka to peacetime was never put to a vote.

PEASANTS

These days, a self-respecting (large-scale) farmer is known as a *fermer*. Previously he was a *krestyanin*, derived from *khristyanin* (Christian), or simply a *muzhik*, even though that term applied basically to all men in rural areas apart from the nobility and clergy. The term *muzhik* – especially the plural form – is still used colloquially in the sense of "men, guys." Before the revolution, the *muzhiks* were the dominant presence in rural Russia, accounting for around 95 percent of the male population, and thus around half of the total population. Nevertheless, the upper classes regarded them as backward, lazy, and uncivilized.

> – А отчего недоимка за тобой завелась? – грозно спросил г. Пеночкин. (Старик понурил голову.) – Чай, пьянствовать любишь, по кабакам шататься? (Старик разинул было рот.) Знаю я вас, – с запальчивостью продолжал Аркадий Павлыч, – ваше дело пить да на печи лежать, а хороший мужик за вас отвечай.
>
> – И грубиян тоже, – ввернул бурмистр в господскую речь.
>
> – Ну, уж это само собою разумеется. Это всегда так бывает; это уж я не раз заметил. Целый год распутствует, грубит, а теперь в ногах валяется.

> "And why did you get into arrears?" Mr. Penochkin asked threateningly. (The old man bowed his head.) "Suppose it's because you like getting drunk, like roaming about from tavern to tavern?" (The old man was on the point of opening his mouth.) "I know your sort," Arkady Pavlych continued vehemently, "all you do is drink and lie on the stove and let good peasants answer for you."
>
> "And insolent as well," the Bailiff inserted into his master's speech.
>
> "Well, that goes without saying. That's always the way of it – I've noticed that more than once. He'll spend the whole year lazing about and being insolent and now he flops down on his knees at your feet!"[9]

> Ivan Turgenev, *Sketches from a Hunter's Album*: "Bailiff" (1852)

Around the time of Catherine II, drinking behavior among the moneyed class became more "civilized" under the influence of French drinking culture, and gentlemen began seeing heavy drinking as a "peasant's vice." Meanwhile, peasants didn't drink when there was sowing and planting to be done or when the crops were ready for harvesting. They adhered strictly to the schedule of holidays for their drinking sprees. In contrast, the rural nobility drank vodka as they had always done, without paying much attention to the seasons.

The influential writer Vissarion Belinsky (1811-1848) was also not very optimistic about the peasantry. He called them subservient and docile, saying that if they were liberated they would fall into anarchy. Peasants would start stealing and boozing and thus pose a threat to the intelligentsia.

Under the authoritarian Nicholas I – the policeman of Europe – Belinsky was one of the few critical voices heard. In contrast, Alexander II was open to liberal ideas, and after he ascended to the throne in 1855 he loosened his autocratic grip. The position of the *muzhik*, who still had no rights whatsoever, became part of the debate that was reenergized under Alexander. Among the participants in that debate were nihilists, meeting in backrooms.

– А потом мы догадались, что болтать, все только болтать о наших язвах не стоит труда, что это ведет только к пошлости и доктринерству; мы увидали, что и умники наши, так называемые передовые люди и обличители, никуда не годятся, что мы занимаемся вздором, толкуем о каком-то искусстве, бессознательном творчестве, о парламентаризме, об адвокатуре и черт знает о чем, когда дело идет о насущном хлебе, когда грубейшее суеверие нас душит, когда все наши акционерные общества лопаются единственно оттого, что оказывается недостаток в честных людях, когда самая свобода, о которой хлопочет правительство, едва ли пойдет нам впрок, потому что мужик наш рад самого себя обокрасть, чтобы только напиться дурману в кабаке.

– Так, – перебил Павел Петрович, – так: вы во всем этом убедились и решились сами ни за что серьезно не приниматься.

– И решились ни за что не приниматься, – угрюмо повторил Базаров.

Ему вдруг стало досадно на самого себя, зачем он так распространился перед этим барином.

– А только ругаться?

– И ругаться.

– И это называется нигилизмом?

– И это называется нигилизмом, – повторил опять Базаров, на этот раз с особенною дерзостью.

Павел Петрович слегка прищурился.

– Так вот как! – промолвил он странно спокойным голосом. – Нигилизм всему горю помочь должен, и вы, вы наши избавители и герои. Но за что же вы других-то, хоть бы тех же обличителей, честите? Не так же ли вы болтаете, как и все?

– Чем другим, а этим грехом не грешны, – произнес сквозь зубы Базаров.

"Then we suspected that talk and only talk about our social diseases was not worthwhile, that it led to nothing but hypocrisy and pedantry; we saw that our leading men, our so-called advanced people and reformers, are worthless; that we busy ourselves with rubbish, talk nonsense about art, about unconscious creation, parliamentarianism, trial by jury, and the devil knows what – when the real question is daily bread, when the grossest superstitions are stifling us, when all our business enterprises crash simply because there aren't enough honest men to carry them on, while the very emancipation which our government is struggling to organize will hardly come to any good, because our peasant is happy to rob even himself so long as he can get drunk at the pub."

"Yes," broke in Pavel Petrovich, "indeed, you were convinced of all this and you therefore decided to undertake nothing serious yourselves."

"We decided to undertake nothing," repeated Bazarov grimly. He suddenly felt annoyed with himself for having been so expansive in front of this gentleman.

"But to confine yourselves to abuse."

"To confine ourselves to abuse."

"And that is called nihilism?"

"And that is called nihilism," Bazarov repeated again, this time in a particularly insolent tone.

Pavel Petrovich screwed up his eyes a little. "So that's it," he murmured in a strangely composed voice. "Nihilism is to cure all our woes, and you – you are our saviors and heroes. Very well – but why do you find fault with others, including the reformers? Don't you do as much talking as anyone else?"

"Whatever faults we may have, that is not one of them," muttered Bazarov between his teeth.[10]

Ivan Turgenev, *Fathers and Children* (1862)

The *muzhiks* played a central role in the intelligentsia's vehement discussion of Russia's destiny. Although the nobility, intellectuals, and townspeople still did not have a high opinion of them, some people – led by Tolstoy and Dostoyevsky – believed that they embodied the moral superiority of the Russian nation. According to them, the Russian peasant was pure, spontaneous, good-natured, and deeply pious – in short, his unspoiled nature made him a model for many westernized urbanites.

Что ж делали до сих пор все эти Пушкины, Лермонтовы, Бороздны? Удивляюсь! Народ пляшет комаринского, эту апофеозу пьянства, а они воспевают какие-то незабудочки! Зачем же не напишут они более благонравных песен для народного употребления и не бросят свои незабудочки? Это социальный вопрос! Пусть изобразят они мне мужика, но мужика облагороженного, так сказать, селянина, а не мужика. Пусть изобразят этого сельского мудреца в простоте своей, пожалуй, хоть даже в лаптях – я и на это согласен, – но преисполненного добродетелями, которым – я это смело говорю – может позавидовать даже какой-нибудь слишком прославленный Александр Македонский. Я знаю Русь, и Русь меня знает: потому и говорю это. Пусть изобразят этого мужика, пожалуй, обремененного семейством и сединою, в душной избе, пожалуй, еще голодного, но довольного, не ропщущего, но благословляющего свою бедность и равнодушного к золоту богача.

What have all these Pushkins, Lermontovs, Borozdnas been doing up to now? I am astonished! People are dancing the *kamarinsky*, this apotheosis of drunkenness, and all we get from them are the praises they sing to forget-me-nots! Why don't they compose more edifying songs for the use of the people, and give up their forget-me-nots? Here we have a social problem! Let them portray a peasant, but an ennobled peasant, a settled and responsible villager and not simply a peasant. Let them portray a rural sage in all his simplicity, wearing bast shoes if need be – I'll accept even that – but enhanced by virtues, which – I say this without fear – may even be the envy of some greatly overrated Alexander the Great. I know Russia and Mother Russia knows me: that's precisely why I'm saying this. Let them portray this peasant, if they like, burdened by family responsibilities, advancing old age, cooped up in a stuffy hut and maybe starving too, yet perfectly content and uncomplaining, glorifying his poverty and indifferent to the gold of the wealthy.[11]

Fyodor Dostoyevsky, *The Village of Stepanchikovo* (1859)

Alexander abolished serfdom in 1861. Of course, that did not immediately solve all problems; peasants did not become civilized and developed overnight – that would take generations to accomplish. Moreover, many people thought that serfdom had been abolished without much forethought.

Если оно рационально, то вы можете наймом вести его, – сказал Свияжский. – Власти нет-с. Кем я его буду вести? позвольте спросить.
"Вот она – рабочая сила, главный элемент хозяйства", – подумал Левин.
– Рабочими.
– Рабочие не хотят работать хорошо и работать хорошими орудиями. Рабочий наш только одно знает – напиться, как свинья, пьяный и испортит все, что вы ему дадите. Лошадей опоит, сбрую хорошую оборвет, колесо шинованное сменит, пропьет, в молотилку шкворень пустит, чтобы ее сломать. Ему тошно видеть все, что не по его. От этого и спустился весь уровень хозяйства. Земли заброшены, заросли полынями или розданы мужикам, и где производили миллион, производят сотни тысяч четвертей; общее богатство уменьшилось. Если бы сделали то же, да с расчетом... И он начал развивать свой план освобождения, при котором были бы устранены эти неудобства.

"If it's rational, you'll be able to keep up the same system with hired labor," said Sviazhsky.
"We've no power over them. With whom am I going to work the system, allow me to ask?"
"There it is – the labor force – the chief element in agriculture," thought Levin.
"With laborers."

"The laborers won't work well, and won't work with good implements. Our laborer can do nothing but get drunk like a pig, and when he's drunk he ruins everything you give him. He makes the horses ill with too much water, cuts good harness, barters the tires of the wheels for drink, drops bits of iron into the thrashing-machine, so as to break it. He loathes the sight of anything that's not after his fashion. And that's how it is the whole level of husbandry has fallen. Lands gone out of cultivation, overgrown with weeds, or divided among the peasants, and where millions of bushels were raised you get a hundred thousand; the wealth of the country has decreased. If the same thing had been done, but with care that..."

And he proceeded to unfold his own scheme of emancipation by means of which these drawbacks might have been avoided.[12]

Lev Tolstoy, *Anna Karenina* (1878)

Tolstoy believed that vodka was responsible for the misery in the countryside. The emancipation of the serfs had not reduced their use of alcohol, quite the contrary. The October 27, 1881, issue of the publication *Selsky vestnik* (*The Village Herald*) contained a letter to the editor:

As a true peasant who knows the liquor business firsthand, since that is my current line of work, I would like to speak frankly about the harm that this business has caused our villagers. The harm is great, and it weighs on us more heavily than crop failure or taxes. Our village, which has a thousand souls, pours nearly seven thousand rubles [a year] into its tavern.... And compared with neighboring villages, ours is not considered one of the wildest when it comes to drinking.... Our teenage boys and girls have stopped doing folk dances on holidays... [instead] they pool their resources in order to buy a bottle and drink it in the backyard. Even little children nine years old swarm like locusts around the tavern and pretend to be intoxicated. In short, drunkenness has come to permeate our lives.[13]

The Belgian social democratic politician Emile Vandervelde visited Russia early in the twentieth century. He too got to know *muzhiks*: "In Russia, the man of the people – if he is sober – is much more peaceful and docile, i.e., more social, than workers or farmers in our countries. But he must not be drunk. In 1905, when vodka was available on every street corner, the revolt began in many cities with the raiding of liquor stores."[14]

The *muzhiks* did not end up getting the generations they needed to develop into a healthy farming class. Around the turn of the century, most *muzhiks* were still dirt farmers. Larger operations did exist, and things may have been improving, but the revolution – followed by civil war, *de-kulakization*, and forced collectivization – spelled the end of a positive trend. At present, something similar is going on. Through their extended labor contracts in *kolkhoz*es and *sovkhoz*es, rural Russians have a different connection to the land. You can hardly call them peasants any longer. But there is hope, just as there was hope a hundred years ago...

Каким бы неуклюжим зверем ни казался мужик, идя за своею сохой, и как бы он ни дурманил себя водкой, все же, приглядываясь к нему поближе, чувствуешь, что в нем есть то нужное и очень важное, чего нет, например, в Маше и в докторе, а именно, он верит, что главное на земле – правда, и что спасение его и всего народа в одной лишь правде, и потому больше всего на свете он любит справедливость.

Yes, the peasant did resemble some great clumsy beast as he followed his wooden plough; he did stupefy himself with vodka. But when one took a closer look, he seemed to possess something vital and highly important, something that Masha, for example, and the doctor lacked. What I'm talking about is his belief that truth is the chief thing on earth and that he and the whole nation can be saved only by the truth. Therefore he loves justice more than anything in the world.[15]

Anton Chekhov, "My Life" (1896)

8

Vodka and Power

I never noticed any signs of drunkenness in him, whereas I could not say
the same for Molotov, let alone Beria, who was practically a drunkard.[1]

Milovan Djilas, *Conversations with Stalin* (1962)

IVAN THE TERRIBLE

The first in the series of drinking potentates was Ivan IV (better known to
history as "the Terrible"). When he was crowned tsar in 1547 at age seventeen,
all of Moscow celebrated. The people partied in the streets and the elite was
served up a huge banquet in the Kremlin. The guests ate and drank with
abandon. The grand finale at the banquet was the appearance on the stage of a
dignitary accompanied by a number of servants, who carried buckets of mead
and vodka (which was still known as "tsar's wine" at the time). "They tried to
give the envoys as much to drink as possible, something at which the Russians
were very adept," the Austrian envoy Siegmund Freiherr von Herberstein
wrote in his *Rerum moscoviticarum commentarii*, published in 1549.[2]

Ivan ordered the construction of a fortress in the woods near Moscow.
Together with his palace guard, the so-called *oprichniki*, he parodied monastical
life there. For example, the *oprichniki* wore cassocks under which they concealed

their weapons. They listened to the tsar's sermons on God and faith, after which they engaged in drinking bouts. Whenever the group had prayed enough and the goblets were empty, Ivan would go to the prison to watch his henchmen mercilessly thrash countless "traitors." He had no scruples about torturing and killing the people who were closest to him.

PETER THE GREAT

Of all the tsars, Peter the Great was the biggest drinker. Sources say that he drank between 30 and 40 glasses a day. Peter had his first contact with alcohol as a child, by way of his teacher who instructed him from age five onward. The teacher, Nikita Zotov, was personable, erudite, and not averse to a drink or two. The fact that Peter never got drunk when he was older was said to be attributable to this early contact.

In 1691, Peter introduced the "Most Drunken Synod of Fools and Jesters," which featured a ranking system that matched (but subverted) the church hierarchy, complete with cardinals, bishops, and archimandrites. Its most important motto was: "be drunk every day and never go to bed sober." In gratitude for his services, Peter's former teacher Zotov was named "Prince-Pope," or chairman of the Council and "greatest fool." He wore a bottle around his neck, and with his retinue of cardinals Zotov paid visits in the city while riding an ox or a donkey. In the winter, he traveled about in a sleigh drawn by pigs, bears, or goats. The Synod's gatherings were full of (church) rituals and drinking obligations. For example, it was required that Bacchus be revered through excessive drinking, and sober sinners were anathematized and denied admittance to all of the empire's taverns. The church authorities were not amused by Peter's initiative, nor were the common masses, many of whom thought that Peter was the Antichrist incarnate. However, the tsar took no notice of the clergy; indeed, through a series of reforms, he subjugated the church to his secular authority.

Peter's favorite drink was anise vodka, of which he could put away enormous quantities without getting drunk. He also never suffered from a hangover. There was one famous dinner that he had with his Swiss friend Franz Lefort, who later served as an admiral in the Russian navy. Eighty-five guests were confined to Moscow's Lefortovo Palace for three whole days. Afterward, Prince Boris Kurakin related that "everyone was so drunk that words cannot describe it. Many of them even died." Those who did survive were sick for days. Peter himself was as fit as a fiddle the next day.

The tsar loved this sort of unconstrained social gathering and was eager to chat everyone up. In the new capital of St. Petersburg, he institutionalized such gatherings in the form of "assemblies," which involved plenty of lobbying and drinking. Anyone of rank was required to attend and drink vodka – even pregnant women. Peter believed that drunk people told the truth, and he rarely punished candor expressed while the speaker was drunk. Harsh punishment awaited anyone who broke the rules or arrived late. The offender had to empty the "penalty goblet" in one gulp, it being a vessel holding two liters of Madeira and bearing the image of an eagle and, at the bottom, the words "*ad fundum.*" The Danish ambassador underwent this punishment. He had disrupted the informal character of the assemblies by addressing the tsar as "Your Majesty." Another victim was Peter's close friend Alexander Menshikov, whose transgression was drinking a light Rhine wine. After draining the "Great Eagle," the number-two man in the empire collapsed unconscious, amid loud wailing by his wife.

Peter the Great had focused his attention on the West and

Ivan the Terrible, by Victor Vasnetsov (1897)

thus brought many foreigners into his employ. One of them was the Frenchman François de Villebois, like Peter a huge boozer. Heavy drinking was not a problem for Peter, as long as people did their job.

One day, when the Tsar was at his castle of Strelna, in the bay of St. Petersburg, he entrusted Villebois with a mission to the Empress Catherine, who was at Kronstadt. It was in the depth of winter, the temperature was ten or twelve degrees below zero, and the gulf was frozen, so Villebois set out in a sleigh, taking a bottle of brandy with him to keep out the cold. When he reached Kronstadt the bottle was empty, but for Villebois that was sobriety, and he seemed perfectly composed to all the officers of the guard when he presented himself and asked to be taken to the Tsarina.

The Empress was asleep, and while her maids of honor prepared to wake her, Villebois sat waiting in a room as over-heated as rooms always are in St. Petersburg in winter, and the change of temperature had a profound effect on him. When Catherine's maids conducted him to her bed-chamber and left him alone in her presence, he forgot he was looking at an Empress, saw her only as a very lovely woman, and immediately felt a strong urge to express his admiration for her beauty. Villebois was a man of rapid execution, and though the Tsarina called her women, he had already given proof of that admiration by the time they arrived.

Instantly he was arrested and a swift courier despatched to tell the Tsar as tactfully as possible what had occurred. The Tsar listened to the whole story with no sign of anger, and then asked:

"What have you done with him?"

"Sire," replied the messenger, "he was bound hand and foot and thrown into prison."

"What did he do then?"

"The moment the cell door closed behind him he fell fast asleep."

"That's my Villebois!" cried the Tsar. "I'll wager that when he wakes in the morning he will have forgotten why he is there." To the courtier's amazement, Peter gave no sign of anger, but stalked up and down the room in perplexity. Then he went on: "I suppose I must make an example of him, though the great dolt is innocent enough and had no idea what he was doing. But the Tsarina would be furious if he were not punished. Let me see. Suppose I send him to the galleys for a couple of years and then forget all about it." But before Villebois had been away six months, the Tsar found he could not do without him and recalled him to court, begging the Tsarina to pardon him as a favor to her husband. Thereafter, Villebois was as much in the Tsar's confidence as he had been before being sent on the mission that ended in such a singular fashion.[3]

Alexandre Dumas, *Adventures in Tsarist Russia* (1860)

STALIN

After Peter the Great, vodka was never again to play a major role in the personal lives of the tsars. That did not happen again until Stalin. When Iosif Vissarionovich Dzhugashvili bid farewell to training for the priesthood as a young man in Tbilisi in 1898, he joined the Bolsheviks. He was soon arrested, and during his exile he had frequent contact with criminals. They regularly had drinking bouts, for which he was once even sentenced by a Bolshevik court. Cynics say that after that, Koba – his pseudonym at the time – preferred criminals over politicians.

Stalin not only terrorized ordinary Soviet citizens, but everyone in his immediate vicinity walked on egg shells as well. And drinking was a means of exercising power. One stray remark while drunk, one wrong toast, one glass left unemptied – anything could bring a death sentence. Stalin liked to hold meetings at night, inviting the most important members of the Politburo to his dacha. Besides Vyacheslav Molotov, Lavrenty Beria, and Kliment Voroshilov, the guests would include Andrei Zhdanov, Anastas Mikoyan, Nikita Khrushchev, and Georgy Malenkov. Alexander (Sasha) Poskryobyshev was not a member of the Politburo, but as Stalin's personal secretary he did attend the nighttime extravagances. He was the butt of countless jokes by his boss. In his book *Stalin: The Court of the Red Tsar*, Simon Sebag Montefiore describes this scene: "Stalin dared Poskryobyshev to drink a glass of vodka in one gulp without a sip of water or to see how long he could hold up his hands with burning paper under each nail. 'Look!' Stalin would laugh, 'Sasha can drink a glass of vodka and not even wrinkle his nose!'"[4] Stalin himself always drank from a separate carafe, and if for some reason no such vessel was available, he had others test his drink first.

When Stalin was younger, he always forced his guests to drink alcohol. Anyone who refused was his enemy. Thus, Boris Shumyatsky, the director of the state film enterprise Sovkino, suffered dire consequences in 1937 when he refused to empty his glass after Stalin had made a toast. Shumyatsky was arrested the next day and executed not long after. Khrushchev would later contend that initially Stalin didn't make such a big deal about it: If you wanted to drink, you drank; but if not, you simply didn't. Later, that changed. You had to drink. According to Khrushchev, a prosecutor would not have treated even an inveterate criminal the way that Stalin treated his drinking companions.

Stalin admired Molotov's capacity to drink, but sometimes even the People's Commissar for Foreign Affairs got drunk. Sebag Montefiore writes that Poskryobyshev was the most notorious vomiter:

> Beria, Malenkov and Mikoyan managed to suborn a waitress to serve them "coloured water" but they were betrayed to Stalin by Shcherbakov. After swallowing some colossal brandies, Mikoyan staggered out of the dining-room and found a little room next door with a sofa and a basin. He splashed his face with water, lay down and managed to sleep for a few minutes, which became a secret habit. But Beria sneaked to Stalin who was already turning against the Armenian: "Want to be smarter than the rest, don't you!" Stalin said slowly. "See you don't regret it later!" This was always the threat *chez* Stalin.
>
> Stalin's Mitteleuropean vassals coped no better. Gottwald became so inebriated that he requested that Czechoslovakia join the USSR. His wife, who came with him, heroically volunteered: "Allow me, Comrade Stalin, to drink in my husband's place. I'll drink for us both." [...]

Sometimes Stalin himself "got so drunk he took such liberties," said Khrushchev. "He'd throw a tomato at you." Beria was the master of practical jokes along with Poskryobyshev. The two most dignified guests, Molotov and Mikoyan, became the victims as Stalin's distrust of them became more malicious. Beria targeted the sartorial splendor of the "dashing" Mikoyan. Stalin teased him about his "fancy airs" while Beria delighted in tossing Mikoyan's hat into the pine trees where it remained. He slipped old tomatoes into Mikoyan's suits and then "pressed him against the wall" so they exploded in his pocket. Mikoyan started to bring spare pairs of trousers to dinner. At home, Ashken found chicken bones in his pockets. Stalin smiled as Molotov sat on a tomato or Poskryobyshev downed a vodka full of salt that would make him vomit. Poskryobyshev often collapsed and had to be dragged out. Beria once wrote "prick" on a piece of paper and stuck it on to Khrushchev's back. When Khrushchev did not notice, everyone guffawed. Khrushchev never forgot the humiliation."[5]

In August 1939, the Soviet Union and Germany signed the notorious Molotov-Ribbentrop pact, in which the two countries agreed not to attack each other while dividing up Poland. The agreement also spelled out each country's spheres of influence. Stalin saw the nonaggression pact as a triumph that had to be celebrated effusively. Sebag Montefiore said the following about how Stalin ordered vodka and made toasts:

"I know how much the German nation loves its Führer. He's a good chap. I'd like to drink his health." [...] Before anyone could eat, Molotov started to propose toasts to each guest. Stalin stalked over to clink glasses. It was an exhausting rigmarole that would become one of the diplomatic tribulations of the war. When Molotov had run through every guest, the Germans sighed with relief until he announced: "Now we'll drink to all members of the delegations who couldn't attend this dinner."

Stalin took over, joking: "Let us drink to the new anti-Comintern Stalin" and he winked at Molotov. Then he toasted Kaganovich, "our People's Commissar of Railways." Stalin could have toasted the Jewish magnate across the table but he deliberately rose and circled the table to clink glasses so that Ribbentrop had to follow suit and drink to a Jew, an irony that amused Stalin. Forty years on, Kaganovich was still telling the story to his grandchildren.

When Molotov embarked on another toast to his *Vozhd*, Stalin

Brüderschaft, for now. Stalin and Molotov raise a toast with Ribbentrop after the signing of the 1939 Nazi-Soviet Nonaggression Pact.

chuckled: "If Molotov really wants to drink, no one objects but he really shouldn't use me as an excuse."[6]

Ribbentrop described that evening in his 1953 book *Zwischen London und Moskau*:

Excellent food was set out, and everyone was served an especially strong brown vodka – so strong that it almost took your breath away. But Stalin seemed to be utterly unaffected by the brown vodka. When I expressed admiration for the drinking capacity of Russians compared to Germans, Stalin laughed and told me a secret with a wink: His beverage was only Crimean wine, but it had the same color as the infernal vodka!"[7]

The German diplomat Gustav Hilger had a tiff with Beria, who wanted him to drink more than he wished to. Hilger later wrote about the incident: "Stalin soon noticed that Beria and I were in dispute about something, and asked across the table: 'What's the argument about?' When I told him, he replied, 'Well, if you don't want to drink, no one can force you.' 'Not even the chief of the NKVD himself?' I joked. Whereupon he answered, 'Here, at this table, even the chief of the NKVD has no more to say than anyone else.'"[8]

Marshal Alexander Golovanov was a young confidant of Stalin's, and as such he was present at one of the meetings with Churchill during World War II. Golovanov was well aware of the English prime minister's propensity for drink, but he was more concerned about Stalin. Could he keep up with the British prime minister? Writing in his memoirs, Golovanov described his feelings at the time:

Тосты продолжались. Черчилль на глазах пьянел, в поведении же Сталина ничего не менялось. [...] Встреча подошла к концу. Все встали. Распрощавшись, Черчилль покинул комнату, поддерживаемый под руки. Остальные тоже стали расходиться, а я стоял как завороженный и смотрел на Сталина. Конечно, он видел, что я все время наблюдал за ним. Подошел ко мне и добрым хорошим голосом сказал: «Не бойся, России я не пропью. А вот Черчилль будет завтра метаться, когда ему скажут, что он тут наболтал...» Немного подумав, Сталин продолжил: «Когда делаются большие государственные дела, любой напиток должен казаться тебе водой, и ты всегда будешь на высоте. Всего хорошего». – И он твердой, неторопливой походкой вышел из комнаты.

The toasts continued. Churchill was getting drunker by the minute, but Stalin's demeanor did not change in the least. [...] The meeting drew to a close. Everyone rose. After saying his farewells, Churchill needed help walking out of the room. The others also began to go their separate ways, but I stood watching Stalin, utterly captivated. Of course, he saw that I had my eye on him. He walked up to me and in a friendly voice said, "Have no fear, I won't drink Russia away. Churchill, on the other hand, will be sweating tomorrow when they tell him everything he just said..." After pausing to think, Stalin continued: "When important affairs of state are at stake, any drink should be just like water to you, and you'll always come out on top. Take care." And he left the room with a steady, unhurried gait."[9]

Alexander Golovanov, Long-Range Bombing (1969)

In 1943 the Russians won the Battle of Stalingrad, in April 1945 they captured Berlin, and on May 8 of that year Germany capitulated. The celebration in the Soviet Union was subdued, as the nation licked its many war wounds. But in light of the victory, the following New Year's celebration at the Kremlin was a big one. The toasts came one after another, as evidenced by rumors that consumption averaged two liters of vodka per person. Stalin himself drank in moderation, and because of that everyone was completely sloshed, but no one could leave. After all, no one could leave before Stalin did.

KHRUSHCHEV

Nikita Khrushchev was a heavy drinker. In his younger days, he was once kicked off a soccer team for drunkenness. His favorite drink was pepper vodka, and in 1962 he personally commissioned the makers of Stolichnaya to market a variety of that flavor. At his dinners, guests had to drink as much as under Stalin, and the pressure was just as great. On one of these occasions, the Czechoslovak leader, Antonín Novotný, drank so much that he passed out. Khrushchev's servants pumped his stomach and placed him in a bath. The Soviet leader himself often couldn't remember what had happened at his dinners. The next morning he would ask his personal secretary how things had gone.

Khrushchev was not known as a connoisseur of art and culture. In fact, he didn't like artistic types, and he positively despised abstract art. The writer Vladimir Tendryakov described a number of scoldings that the "creative intelligentsia" had to endure during a gathering at Khrushchev's dacha.

Хрущев тогда во время обеда, что называется, стремительно заложил за воротник и... покатил "вдоль по Питерской" со всей русской удалью.

Сначала он просто перебивал выступавших, не считаясь с чинами и авторитетами, мимоходом изрекая сочные сентенции: "Украина – это вам не жук на палочке!.." И острил так, что, кажется, даже краснел вечно бледный до зелени, привыкший ко всему Молотов.

Затем Хрущев огрел мимоходом Мариэтту Шагинян. Никто и не запомнил за что именно. Просто в ответ на какое-то ее случайное замечание он крикнул в лицо престарелой писательнице: "А хлеб и сало русское едите!" Та строптиво оскорбилась: "Я не привыкла, чтоб меня попрекали куском хлеба!" И демонстративно покинула гостеприимный стол, села в пустой автобус, принялась хулить шоферам правительство. Что, однако, никак не отразилось на ходе торжества.

During dinner, Khrushchev had really been putting it away, so to speak, and expressed a truly Russian spirit by taking a spirited musical jaunt "Down the Petersburg Road."

At first he limited himself to breaking in on the speakers, without the slightest regard for rank or position, and volunteering juicy asides, such as "Ukraine is not some chicken for the cooking!" His witticisms were even enough to bring a blush to the cheeks of the preternaturally pale-green Molotov, who had seen it all.

Khrushchev then set his sights on Marietta Shaginyan. Nobody could recall what got him started. But in response to some random comment she made, he shouted into the aging writer's face: "You're eating bread and Russian fatback!" The writer was outraged: "I am not accustomed to being reproached for a crust of bread!" She then demonstratively quit the festivities, climbed into an empty bus, and began badmouthing the government to the drivers. Her departure, however, did nothing to dampen the revelry.[10]

Vladimir Tendryakov, "On the Blessed Island of Communism" (1974)

Nikita's oldest son Leonid once bragged about his talent as a sharpshooter while drunk, and friends then challenged him to shoot a bottle off a pilot's head. With his first attempt, he hit the neck of the bottle. With the second one, he struck the officer in the forehead, killing him.

BREZHNEV

As secretary general of the Central Committee of the Communist Party, Leonid Brezhnev had his favorite vodka brought in from Belarus: Zubrovka. He liked to drink – or rather, drinking was the norm. Andrei Gromyko, the perennial foreign minister in the late Soviet period and one of Brezhnev's most important advisers, once tried to discuss with him the Russian drinking problem: "Socialism and the enslavement of the people to vodka do not go together. Why has the Politburo not raised its voice against this?" Brezhnev listened to him patiently and then said, "You know, Andrei, the Russian has always drunk vodka. He cannot do without it."[11]

The leaders of West and East Germany, Helmut Schmidt and Erich Honecker, both admitted that they were afraid to keep pace with the Soviet leader. Brezhnev's alcohol consumption was terrifying; on holidays, assistants had to help him leave the room. The only one who could come close to keeping up with him was Konstantin Chernenko. Chernenko was himself the party leader for a brief period in 1984 and 1985, before he died of cirrhosis of the liver. Dutch historian Elbert Toonen wrote:

> Chernenko was famous for never getting drunk. When Brezhnev later had to stop drinking because of his heart and liver ailments, Chernenko would serve him mineral water. Brezhnev would then signal a servant, who would give him what he wanted from a hip flask. Brezhnev also asked his guests to smoke so that he could at least enjoy the smell. During the 1970s, French counterespionage officers reportedly conducted a clandestine operation in which they tapped into the discharge from his bathroom in a Copenhagen hotel room. That was when it became clear that he was dying. But his death did not result from a heart ailment; it was caused by problems with his liver, owing to excessive vodka use.[12]

The French actress Marina Vlady was married to the hugely popular, semi-banned singer Vladimir Vysotsky, who was to die of alcoholism and drug abuse in 1980 at age 42. After his death, she committed her memories of him to writing. For example, she described a visit that the two of them paid to Brezhnev.

> Мы слушаем традиционную речь. Брежнев держится свободно, шутит, роется в портсигаре, но ничего оттуда не достает, сообщает нам, что ему нельзя больше курить, и долю рассказывает об истории дружбы между нашими народами. Ролан Леруа мне шепчет: "Смотри, как он поворачивается к тебе, как только речь заходит о причинах этой дружбы..." Действительно, я замечаю понимающие взгляды Брежнева. Я знаю, что ему известно все о нашей с тобой женитьбе. Когда немного позже мы пьем шампанское, он подходит ко мне и объясняет, что водка – это другое дело, что ее нужно пить сначала пятьдесят граммов, потом сто и потом, если выдерживаешь, – сто пятьдесят, тогда хорошо себя чувствуешь. Я отвечаю, что мне это кажется много. "Тогда нужно пить чай", – заключает он, и я получаю в память об этой встрече электрический самовар, к которому все-таки приложены две бутылки старки.

> We listened to a traditional speech. Brezhnev appeared relaxed. He joked around and went through the motion of taking a cigarette out of his cigarette case, which was actually empty, and then told us that he is not able to smoke anymore. He also spent time talking about the history of friendship between our peoples. Roland Leroy whispered in my ear: "Look how he turns to you whenever he starts to talk about the reasons for this friend-

ship..." He was right. I could see the look of understanding on Brezhnev's face. I knew that he knows all about our marriage. A little later, when we were drinking champagne, he came up to me and explained that vodka is another matter, that it should be drunk first fifty grams at a time, then a hundred, and then, if you can stand it, one hundred fifty – then you'll feel good. I told him that seemed like a lot to me. "Then you should drink tea," he pronounced, and I received an electric samovar as a memento of our meeting – but not without two bottles of *starka* attached to it.[13]

Marina Vlady, *Vladimir, or the Aborted Flight* (1987)

GORBACHEV

The "secretary mineral" was not a drinker. His dealings with vodka are addressed elsewhere in this book.

YELTSIN

In 1991, many Russians breathed a sigh of relief. Now that the Soviet Union no longer existed, a normal drinking man returned to power in Russia: Boris Nikolayevich Yeltsin. It was no secret that he was a heavy drinker. According to his grandson Boris, Yeltsin's favorite drink was a "northern lights": champagne and vodka. From 1976 to 1985, during the period when he was party leader in Sverdlovsk (which has returned to its tsarist-era name, Yekaterinburg), before he became a nationally known figure, he commissioned the development of a vodka that left no trace on the drinker's breath.

Russians could relate to the president's sense of humor. For foreigners, it took some getting used to:

На охоте царит особый, бодрый, здоровый дух. Никогда не забуду, как один зарубежный гость, когда плыли на катере по озеру, все посматривал на черный чемоданчик на дне лодки. Думал, что ядерный. Старался держаться от чемоданчика подальше, все норовил на краешек лодки отсесть. Я его не разубеждал. А когда на острове чемоданчик открыли и достали оттуда две бутылки водки и соленые огурчики, гость долго смеялся. Ядерный же чемоданчик "плыл" в соседнем катере, под охраной офицеров.

I'll never forget one time when I was sailing around the lake with a foreign guest. He kept glancing at my black briefcase on the bottom of the boat. He thought it was the nuclear briefcase, and he tried to stay as far away from it as possible, squeezing to the edge of the boat. When we got to the island, the briefcase was opened, and two bottles of vodka and some pickled cucumbers were taken out. The guest laughed for a long time. The nuclear suitcase was in the next boat, under the guard of officers.[14]

Boris Yeltsin, *Midnight Diaries* (2000)

The president was jokingly referred to as "Boris Yolkin." (Historically, a bar was known colloquially as an "Ivan-Yolkin," derived from the word *yolka* [spruce], because there would often be two spruces standing next to a tavern's entrance, protruding above the roof of the establishment.) Once, when Yeltsin was asked if he drank, he inquired as to whether that was a question or a proposal. To the former he would have replied "no," to the latter "yes, please."

В свое время я, как и большинство людей, не считал зазорным поднять на празднике рюмку-другую за здоровье. Но какой же вал слухов, сплетен, политической возни поднимался в обществе, на страницах газет по этому поводу! Теперь даже трудно в это поверить...

Традиционно русский образ жизни жестко диктовал: не пить на дне рождения – нельзя, не пить на свадьбе друга – нельзя, не пить с товарищами по работе – нельзя. Я к этой обязаловке всегда относился с тоской, пьяных людей не выносил, но... в какой-то момент почувствовал, что алкоголь действительно средство, которое быстро снимает стресс.

In my day, like the majority of people, I considered it quite acceptable to raise a shot glass or two to someone's health on a special occasion. But what a wave of rumors, gossip, and political turmoil has been kicked up in public and in the newspapers over this issue! It's hard to believe now.

The traditional Russian lifestyle dictates that it's impossible not to drink at a birthday; it's impossible not to drink at a friend's wedding; it's impossible not to drink with your co-workers. I always regarded this as a tiresome obligation, and I couldn't bear to put up with drunks, but fairly early on I concluded that alcohol really was a means of quickly getting rid of stress.[15]

Boris Yeltsin, *Midnight Diaries* (2000)

There are countless anecdotes about official occasions where Yeltsin was obviously under the influence: during a one-on-one with Bill Clinton, for example, or the time he missed an appointment in Ireland because he was sitting drunk in the airplane at Shannon Airport and refused to come out. His vice president, Alexander Rutskoy, was once accused of being in a "permanent state of visiting Ireland."

Yeltsin also once fell into a Moscow canal under "obscure circumstances." It was said that hoodlums had thrown him in. But the best-known incident is certainly the time in Berlin when he spontaneously stood before an orchestra and began conducting. It was the Berlin police band, which was playing Kalinka on the occasion of the Russian troop withdrawal from Germany.

The French named a vodka for him: Boris Yeltsin Vodka.

Yeltsin's memoirs show that afterward he himself was not very happy about his spontaneous behavior.

Стресс, пережитый в конце 93-го года, во время путча и после него, был настолько сильным, что я до сих пор не понимаю, как организм вышел из него, как справился. Напряжение и усталость искали выхода. Там, в Берлине, когда вся Европа отмечала вывод наших последних войск, я вдруг почувствовал, что не выдерживаю. Давила ответственность, давила вся заряженная ожиданием исторического шага атмосфера события. Неожиданно для себя не выдержал. Сорвался...

Что я чувствую сейчас, когда показывают ставшие уже журналистским штампом кадры, на которых я дирижирую тем злополучным оркестром? Не стыд, не безразличие, не раздражение, тут другое какое-то чувство. Я кожей начинаю ощущать состояние тревоги, напряжения, безмерной тяжести, которая давила, прижимала меня к земле. Я помню, что тяжесть отступила после нескольких рюмок. И тогда, в этом состоянии легкости, можно было и оркестром дирижировать.

После этого случая группа помощников президента обратилась ко мне с письмом: я своим поведением, своими экспромтами наношу вред самому себе, наношу вред всей нашей совместной работе. Извиняться перед помощниками не стал. Вряд ли кто-то из них мог помочь мне. Дистанция между нами была слишком велика. Я ходил по сочинскому пляжу и думал: надо жить дальше. Надо восстанавливать силы. Постепенно пришел в себя.

С тех пор все, что вызывало изменения в моем обычном состоянии – бессонницу, простуду, обычную слабость, – списывали на влияние алкоголя. Я знал об этих разговорах, но отвечать на них считал ниже своего достоинства.

The stress I underwent in late 1993, during the White House rebellion and thereafter, was so great that to this day I don't understand how I managed to survive it. The tension and exhaustion required some outlet. There, in Berlin, when all of Europe was celebrating the withdrawal of our last forces, I suddenly felt that I couldn't take it anymore. The responsibility and the whole atmosphere of the event, tense with the expectation of a historical step, weighed upon me. I snapped.

How do I feel now, when that all-too-familiar footage of me conducting that ill-fated orchestra is shown? I don't feel shame or indifference or irritation. But I can begin to feel my skin crawl as I think of that alarm, tension, and immeasurable weight of stress that pressed down upon me in those days, pushing me to the ground. I remember that the weight would lift after a few shot glasses. And in that state of lightness I felt as if I could conduct an orchestra.

AN ENCOUNTER WITH STALIN

Before or after the revolution, before or after church, before or after breakfast – it makes no difference. Turning down a drink was, is, and remains highly inappropriate, peculiar, or suspicious.

После ужина вышли из-за стола размяться. И вот мы, группа старших офицеров, стоим так это у окна, курим, разговариваем, когда мой друг, Васька Серов, толкает меня локтем в бок. Я оборачиваюсь: ты чего толкаешься? Смотрю, батюшки! – передо мной сам товарищ Сталин в таком это, знаете, темно-сером мундире. А на груди одна Золотая Звезда – и все, и ничего больше. Вот так, как вы от меня, стоит, даже ближе. В руке стакан с водкой. А рядом с ним Молотов Вячеслав Михайлович, Маленков Георгий Максимилианович и маршал Конев Иван Степанович. И представляете, товарищ Сталин водку из правой руки в левую переложил, правую протягивает мне и говорит: "Здравствуйте, я Сталин". Так прямо и сказал: "я Сталин". Как будто я могу не знать, кто он. А я опешил и стою с открытым ртом. Он говорит: "А вас как зовут?" А я, знаете, хочу ему ответить, а язык точно, как говорят, прилип к горлу. А товарищ Сталин стоит, смотрит и ждет. И тут хорошо, меня Конев выручил. Это, говорит, товарищ Сталин, полковник Бурдалаков.

А он переспрашивает:

– Бурдалаков? Федор Бурдалаков? Командир сто четырнадцатой гвардейской мотострелковой? Бывший разведчик?

Тут я совсем онемел. Вы представляете, генералиссимус, Верховный Главнокомандующий, сколько у него дивизий, людей и разведчиков, и неужели он каждого по имени и фамилии? А он говорит: "А вы, товарищ Бурдалаков, что же, непьющий?" Я, можете себе представить, перепугался и не знаю, что сказать. Скажу, что пьющий, подумает – пьяница. Непьющий – тоже как-то нехорошо. Стою и молчу. А товарищ Сталин опять к Коневу:

– Он у вас, видать, и немой, и непьющий.

И тут Иван Степанович опять помог. "Как же, товарищ Сталин, – говорит, – фронтовик-разведчик может быть непьющим?" "Вот я и подумал, – говорит Сталин, – что непьющих разведчиков не бывает. Пьющий человек может не быть разведчиком. Немой человек может быть разведчиком, ему лишь бы видеть и слышать, но не может быть непьющим. Непьющий человек не может быть разведчиком никогда". – Вот он такие слова мне сказал, и я на всю жизнь их запомнил. – Федор Федорович, держа перед собой кусок чурчхеллы, задумался, помолчал и опять оживился. – И вы представляете, после этого он мне говорит. "Если вы, товарищ Бурдалаков, – говорит, – не против, то давайте с вами выпьем". Можете вообразить? Не против ли я! А еще говорят, мания величия. Да какая может быть мания, если он полковника спрашивает, не против ли он с ним выпить. Да я бы, если б он сказал: выпей, Бурдалаков, ведро водки, да хоть керосина, я выпил бы. Я даже и не помню, как у меня стакан с водкой оказался в руках. "Ну, – говорит он, – за что пьем?" Я набрался храбрости и говорю, глядя ему прямо в глаза: "За товарища Сталина". А он опять улыбнулся и говорит: "Ну что ж, за товарища Сталина, так за товарища Сталина, товарищ Сталин тоже не самый последний товарищ". Протянул стакан, мы чокнулись, он свою водку немного пригубил и на меня смотрит.

"After supper we got up from the table to stretch our legs, and there we are, a group of officers, standing near the window and talking, when my friend Vaska Serov nudges me in the side with his elbow. I turn around and ask: 'Why are you shoving me?' I look, and blow me! Standing right there in front of me is Comrade Stalin in that, you know, dark gray uniform. And just a single Gold Star on his chest, nothing else. Standing as close to me as you are, or even closer. Holding a glass of vodka. And there beside him are Vyacheslav Mikhailovich Molotov, Georgy Maximilianovich Malenkov and Marshal Ivan Stepanovich Konev. And can you imagine, Comrade Stalin shifts the vodka from his right hand to his left, holds out his right hand to me and says: 'How do you do? I'm Stalin.' That just what he said, 'I'm Stalin.' As though I might not know who he was. I was dumbstruck and just stood there with my mouth open. He says: 'And what's your name?' And you know, I tried to answer him, but my tongue just stuck in my throat, as they say. Comrade Stalin stood there, looking at me and waiting. But then, all right, Konev came to my rescue. 'Comrade Stalin,' he said, 'this is Colonel Burdalakov.'

"And then he asked: 'Burdalakov? Fyodor Burdalakov? Commander of the 114th Motorized Infantry Guards Regiment? The former intelligence scout?'

"Well, at that I was totally stupefied. Can you imagine it, a generalissimo, the Supreme Commander – the number of divisions, people and intelligence officers he has, how can he possibly remember every one by name? And he said: 'Tell me, Comrade Burdalakov, are you a nondrinker then?' You can just imagine how scared I was, I didn't know what to say. If I say I do drink, he'll think I'm a drunk. But being a nondrinker's not so good either, somehow. I stand there and say nothing. And Comrade Stalin says to Konev again: 'Seems like you've got a mute teetotaler here.'

"Then Ivan Stepanovich helped me out again. 'Certainly not, Comrade Stalin,' he said, 'how could a front-line scout be a nondrinker?' 'That's what I thought,' said Stalin, 'there aren't any scouts who don't drink. A drinking man might not be a scout. A mute might be a scout, all he has to do is see and hear, but he can't be a nondrinker. A nondrinker could never be a scout.'

"Those were the very words he said to me, and I'll never forget them as long as I live."

Holding up a piece of *churchkhella* in front of him, Fyodor Fyodorovich pondered in silence for a moment and then he brightened up again. "And just imagine, after that – after that he says to me: 'If you have no objections, Comrade Burdalakov, let's take a drink together.' Can you just imagine that? If I have no objections!' And they talk about him being a megalomaniac. But what kind of manias has he got if he asks a colonel if he has no objections to taking a drink with him? If he'd told me: 'Burdalakov, drink a pailful of vodka,' or even kerosene, I'd have drunk it. I don't even remember how the glass of vodka ended up in my hand. 'Right,' he says, 'what are we drinking to?' I plucked up my courage, looked him straight in the eye and said: 'For Comrade Stalin.' And he smiled again and said: 'Why not, Comrade Stalin it is then – Comrade Stalin's no slouch, after all.' I held up my drink, we clinked glasses, he sipped a bit of his vodka and looked at me."[17]

Vladimir Voinovich, *Monumental Propaganda* (2000)

After that incident a group of my aides wrote me a letter saying that my behavior and my impromptu remarks were harming me and all our mutual work. I didn't apologize to my aides. None of them was able to help me. The distance between us was too great. I walked along the beach in Sochi and realized that I had to go on living. I had to regain my strength. Gradually, I came to myself.

Ever since then, whatever provoked a change in my usual behavior – insomnia, a cold, or ordinary tiredness – would be ascribed to the influence of alcohol. I knew about those rumors, but I considered it beneath my dignity to respond to them.[16]

Boris Yeltsin, *Midnight Diaries* (2000)

PUTIN

Although there is a vodka named for him – even if that's not officially so, since the Russian brand Putinka is said to be derived from *putina* (fishing season) – Putin prides himself on his healthy lifestyle. Vladimir Vladimirovich drinks just as many non-drinking Russian men do: only if he can't get around it.

9

Army and Prison

Кошевой дал приказ собраться всем, и когда все стали в круг и затихли, снявши шапки, он сказал: Так вот что, панове-братове, случилось в эту ночь. Вот до чего довел хмель! Вот какое поруганье оказал нам неприятель! У вас, видно, уже такое заведение: коли позволишь удвоить порцию, так вы готовы так натянуться, что враг Христова воинства не только снимет с вас шаровары, но в самое лицо вам начихает, так вы того не услышите.

The Koshevoy ordered a general assembly; and when all stood in a ring and had removed their caps and became quiet, he said: "See what happened last night, brother gentles! See what drunkenness has led to! See what shame the enemy has put upon us! It is evident that, if your allowances are kindly doubled, then you are ready to stretch out at full length, and the enemies of Christ can not only take your very trousers off you, but sneeze in your faces without your hearing them!"[1]

Nikolai Gogol, *Mirgorod*: "Taras Bulba" (1839-1842)

IN THE BARRACKS

The Russian Army and alcohol are not a happy combination. It is a story of calamitous defeats, of rations, of hazing and discharge rituals, and of heroism. Centuries before our own era, the Scythians in the South slaughtered drunken troops. The Russians themselves experienced the first disastrous consequences of mass drinking in 1377. While in an obvious state of intoxication, they were slaughtered near the Pyana River (whose name means "drunken") by the Tatar prince Arapsha. Is this the origin of the name of the river, a branch of the Sura River in Nizhny Novgorod Province? Writer Pavel Melnikov contends that the river owes its name to the way in which it meanders like a "drunken woman"; others say that there was no Russian name for the river until the dramatic defeat, and that afterward it was dubbed the Pyana.

Another mishap occurred five years later, in 1382, when the Muscovites lost their city to the Tatar Khan Tokhtamysh. They had spent two days indulging in mead, and in response to false pledges by the Tatars, they recklessly opened the city gates. The city was all but leveled.

Toward the end of the seventeenth century, Peter the Great, Tsar of All the Russias, decided to pursue access to the Baltic Sea. He needed a port that would also be navigable in the winter. To that end, he first had to defeat the Swedes, who held the area around present-day St. Petersburg. In 1701, the Dutch artist Cornelis de Bruijn witnessed one of the confrontations between the Russians and the Swedes in Arkhangelsk. The Swedes were about to attack when, for unknown reasons, they departed with the job left undone.

> The Russians gleefully overindulged in wine, of which they found large stores, and during the reckless celebration of their victory a cask of gunpowder was set on fire, blowing up part of the ship. Four Russians were killed and twenty were injured. The Swedes, as best as anyone could tell, lost only one man, who was shot dead by the Ship in the river, and thus fell into the Russians' hands.[2]
>
> Cornelis de Bruijn, *Reizen over Moskovie* (1711)

Tsar Peter the Great drank a great deal, and his officers and soldiers were also not averse to boozing. They brought huge amounts of vodka along on military campaigns – mostly for their own consumption, but they might sell what they didn't use. In 1721, the tsar went so far as to issue an edict instructing that each sailor should receive a certain amount of vodka every day (the "state ration" – see below). He didn't forget the ordinary people either. From then on, the workers of St. Petersburg received a glass of vodka every day. This vodka, however, was of significantly poorer quality than what the sailors got, and it became known as "the tsar's Madeira" (the "penalty goblet" during Peter's assemblies generally contained Madeira), "*Petrovskaya vodka*," or "fourteenth-rate French vodka."

Russian soldiers sometimes looted alcohol during battle. In 1758, for example, victorious Russian troops came across barrels of vodka during the war with Prussia. That prompted the obligatory toasts, the battle was lost, and the Prussians captured 20,000 Russian soldiers.

There were some officers who recognized that vodka and war were not a good mix, and some of them even learned lessons from that:

– Не хотите ли подбавить рому? – сказал я своему собеседнику, – у меня есть белый из Тифлиса; теперь холодно.

– Нет-с, благодарствуйте, не пью.

– Что так?

– Да так. Я дал себе заклятье. Когда я был еще подпоручиком, раз, знаете, мы подгуляли между собой, а ночью сделалась тревога; вот мы и вышли перед фрунт навеселе, да уж и досталось нам, как Алексей Петрович узнал: не дай господи, как он рассердился! чуть-чуть не отдал под суд. Оно и точно: другой раз целый год живешь, никого не видишь, да как тут еще водка – пропадший человек!

"Have some rum in it?" I asked my companion. "I've got some white rum from Tiflis. It's turned cold now."

"Thanks all the same, I don't drink."

"How is that?"

"I just don't. I took an oath. Once when I was a second lieutenant, you know how it is, we'd had rather a lot to drink, and that night there was an alarm. We went out on parade half-tipsy and didn't half catch it when Aleksei Petrovich found out. He was furious. Very nearly had us court-martialed. That's the way of it – you might go a whole year sometimes without seeing a soul, and with vodka on top of that – you're done for."[3]

Mikhail Lermontov, *A Hero of Our Time* (1840)

In 1807, during the war against Napoleon, a battle took place at Preussisch Eylau (present-day Bagrationovsk, in Kaliningrad Province). In his memoirs, Russian General Alexei Yermolov described how four regiments of Russian infantrymen found casks of wine that had been left behind by merchants. The regiments fell into total disarray; they halted en masse when they were supposed to continue on, and when they were supposed to fall back, they pressed forward. The French noticed this and made mincemeat of the regiments. Napoleon himself remarked in an 1805 report that the Russian troops had spent the evening before the Battle of Austerlitz (today's Slavkov u Brna, in the Czech Republic) "in drunkenness, tumult, and rivalry."

В другой, более счастливой роте, так как не у всех была водка, солдаты, толпясь, стояли около рябого широкоплечего фельдфебеля, который, нагибая бочонок, лил в подставляемые поочередно крышки манерок. Солдаты с набожными лицами подносили ко рту манерки, опрокидывали их и, полоща рот и утираясь рукавами шинелей, с повеселевшими лицами отходили от фельдфебеля.

In another, more fortunate company, since not all of them had vodka, soldiers crowded around a pockmarked, broad-shouldered sergeant major, who, tipping a keg, poured into the canteen caps that the soldiers held out in turn. The soldiers, with pious faces, brought the caps to their mouths, upended them, and, rinsing their mouths and wiping them on their greatcoat sleeves, walked away from the sergeant major with cheered faces.[4]

Lev Tolstoy, *War and Peace* (1867-1869)

Universal conscription was introduced in Russia in 1874. Before that, soldiers had been recruited from the lower class, with tours of duty ranging from twenty-five years to life. Conscription shortened this period significantly, although the soldiers did have to remain available as reservists. Before the recruits reported to their unit, they did a celebratory tour from village to village, squandering the money that they had been given by their distressed parents. They played the accordion, danced, guzzled vodka, and fought with guys from other villages. "As drunk as a recruit" is a common expression in Russian.

Drinking played a crucial role in the Russo-Japanese War of 1904-1905. Indeed, wags contend that it was the principal cause of Russia's defeat. The drinking began right after mobilization. Entire trainloads of soldiers reported to their regiments inebriated. They could not get enough to drink, according to a newspaper report from 1904: "The reservists searched every man as he entered the barracks. All had vodka. The searchers always threw it into the street. In one peasant's rags eleven bottles were found. His eyes ran with tears when he saw them broken. The heap of shattered glass grew. A dirty stream of vodka flowed through the courtyard. Many threw themselves on their knees and, in spite of the dirt, tried to drink from the pools. They were kicked back. Three truckloads of broken glass were transported."[5]

Writer Vikenty Veresayev was a military doctor: "Next to a tremendous barrel whose top had been knocked out stood an official dipping spirits out with a scoop for all who wished... More and more frequently, we were overtaking staggering, dead-drunk soldiers; and in all the following days, during the costly retreat, our army swarmed with drunkards as though some joyous general holiday were being celebrated."[6] In Mukden (Shenyang), the Japanese came across thousands of drunken soldiers, whom they slaughtered with their bayonets. Almost all of the armed forces drank. From a Russian engineer's diary: "The crews of the ships at Port Arthur asked leave to go to the advanced positions, and returned under the influence of liquor. No one could understand how they became drunk. In the towns liquors were not sold, and yet men went to the advanced positions and returned intoxicated. At last it was discovered, and how do you suppose? It appears that the sailors went to the front in order to kill one of the enemy and to take away his brandy-flask. Just imagine such a thing. They risked their lives to get drunk! They did all this without thinking anything of it, and contrived to conceal it from the authorities."[7]

When World War I broke out, Nicholas II imposed nationwide prohibition. The edict also applied to soldiers deployed abroad. Once Russian troops occupied a city, under no circumstances could they be supplied with alcohol. Of course, the Germans were aware of the Russian troops' vice, and so they left vodka in the Russian trenches or served it during "fraternization." Nevertheless, prohibition was a success. Even the foreign press wrote about the improved discipline in the army. In 1915, a correspondent from *The Times* called it "essentially nothing short of a revolution."

The civil war that followed the October 1917 revolution was also supposed to be a dry war. There was much alcohol present, however.

– Самогон варите по всем помещениям, с противогазов понаделали себе змеевиков. Патроны тратите на забаву да злодеянство, когда их недостает на фронте для борьбы против вольных украинских атаманов!

"Making home-brew in every barrack, taking apart gas masks to fashion coils! Wasting cartridges for your own amusement, or worse, when there aren't enough to go around to fight the free Ukrainian atamans!"[8]

Konstantin Paustovsky, *The Beginning of an Unknown Age* (*The Story of a Life*) (1956)

The sources have nothing to say about alcohol consumption in the military during the first years of Stalin's rule. However, we can assume that the heavy boozing continued. One incident made it into the record: During a May Day parade in Moscow, a soused cavalry officer fell off his horse in the middle of Red Square. This prompted Kliment Voroshilov, the People's Commissar for Defense, to order that all Red Army soldiers and officers found to be drunk while on duty be court-martialed and that military pilots who flew while inebriated be executed, with no chance of pardon.

Then came World War II. On June 22, 1941, Hitler's troops launched a surprise attack on the Soviet Union. Stalin was stunned and secluded himself for days. Moreover, right before the war began he had purged the entire military brass, which meant that the most experienced officers were no longer available.

Yet drinking before leaving for the barracks is a time-honored tradition, and the "Great Patriotic War" against Nazi Germany was no exception.

Новиков и Неудобнов одновременно поглядели в окно: по путям, пронзительно выкрикивая, шарахаясь и спотыкаясь, шел пьяный танкист, поддерживаемый милиционером с винтовкой на брезентовом ремне. Танкист пытался вырваться и ударить милиционера, но тот обхватил его за плечи, и, видимо, в пьяной голове танкиста царила полная путаница, – забыв о желании драться, он с внезапным умилением стал целовать милицейскую щеку.

Новиков сказал адъютанту:

– Немедленно расследуйте и доложите мне об этом безобразии.

– Расстрелять надо мерзавца, дезорганизатора, – сказал Неудобнов, задергивая занавеску.

На незамысловатом лице Вершкова отразилось сложное чувство. Прежде всего он горевал, что командир корпуса портит себе аппетит. Но одновременно он испытывал и сочувствие к танкисту, оно содержало в себе самые различные оттенки, – усмешки, поощрения, товарищеского восхищения, отцовской нежности, печали и сердечной тревоги. Отрапортовав:

– Слушаюсь, расследовать и доложить, – он, тут же сочиняя, добавил: – Мать у него тут живет, а русский человек, он разве знает меру, расстроился, стремился со старушкой потеплей проститься и не соразмерил дозы.

Novikov and Neudobnov both looked out of the window. A policeman, a rifle hanging from his shoulder strap, was marching a drunken soldier across the tracks; the soldier was stumbling, lurching about and letting out piercing screams. He tried to hit out and break free, but the policeman just grabbed him firmly by the shoulders. Then – God knows what thoughts were passing through his befuddled mind! – he began kissing the policeman's cheek with sudden tenderness.

"Find out what the hell all that's about," Novikov ordered Vershkov, "and report back immediately!"

"He's a saboteur. He deserves to be shot," said Neudobnov as he drew the curtain.

You could see a number of different feelings on Vershkov's usually simple face. In the first place, he was sorry that his commanding officer had had his appetite spoiled. At the same time he felt sympathy for the soldier, a sympathy that included nuances of amusement, approval, comradely admiration, fatherly tenderness, sorrow and genuine anxiety. After saluting and saying that of course he'd report back immediately, Vershkov began embroidering:

"His old mother lives here and... Well, you know what we Russians are like. He was upset, he wanted to mark his departure and he misjudged the dose."[9]

Vasily Grossman, *Life and Fate* (1959)

The book *The Soviet Union and Its Vodka* by Dr. Friedrich Seekel was published shortly after the 1941 German invasion. Its last paragraph reads as follows: "The alcohol problem is only one link in a chain of wanton infamies. The vast proletarianization that has spread there over the last twenty-five years has increased the capacity for suffering of the masses united in the Soviet federation to an almost inhuman degree. Millions upon millions of blood sacrifices are atoning today for their political bondage. The tormented East must follow this course through to its conclusion."[10] Seekel ends the paragraph with the reassuring declaration that the German sword will bring the long-awaited relief and finish off the criminal clique in the Kremlin.

The Germans were certainly militarily superior at the beginning of the war, but they also tried to cleverly exploit the Soviets' weaknesses. Vodka-related propaganda developed into a powerful weapon. German airplanes dropped leaflets intended to win over the Soviet soldiers with texts such as "Red Army soldiers! How much longer do you want to suffer? Break free of these monsters! We will see that you have enough to eat and drink!"[11] They even dropped pamphlets in the shape of a bottle labeled as vodka addressing Soviet women:

Wives and mothers of Red Army commanders and soldiers! Is it not a base trick to give a man vodka so that he, in a drunken haze, without knowing what he's doing, will stumble into battle that promises him certain death. This is exactly what the Red Army command is doing with your husbands and sons at the front line. Read the order [...] and you will understand how despicable its actions are. Tell your loved ones not to believe the lies of Stalinist propaganda, not to follow orders that urge them toward inevitable destruction. We are already near! We bring you liberation from Stalinist oppression, terror, and lies![12]

The turning point of the war was the Battle of Stalingrad, in January 1943. The fighting claimed the lives of 146,000 German soldiers, and another 90,000 were taken prisoner. The Russians regained their self-confidence, and old customs from the tsarist era were revived. Marius Broekmeyer writes about this in his book *Stalin, the Russians, and Their War*:

Officers could henceforth also have an orderly who took care of all sorts of business for them. Captain Rubenshteyn's orderly provided him with a mug of vodka and baked apples every morning. Throughout the day as well, there was vodka whenever he received guests. "No one was drunk, but everyone was certainly tipsy." After the war Rubinshteyn was out of it for a few years owing to alcoholism, which he had picked up in the military."[13]

Heroic deeds were performed in order to get a bottle. Solzhenitsyn describes a "hero of the Soviet Union" who rode up a flight of stairs into the military commissar's office on horseback to demand vodka. Afterward, this hero, Koverchenko, kept the Germans from blowing up a bridge and started collecting a toll on it, to pay for vodka.

In Stalingrad, the fighting in the streets progressed house-by-house.

"Today, for example, two soldiers came to me. It turned out that they had been fighting for fourteen days in a house surrounded by German houses. And these two, so quietly, you know, demanded rusks, ammunition, sugar, tobacco, loaded it all in their rucksacks and went off. They said: 'There are two more of our men there, guarding the house, and they need a smoke.' Actually, it is such a peculiar affair, this war in houses," he smiled. "I don't know whether I should tell this to you, but a funny incident happened yesterday. The Germans captured a house, and there was a barrel of spirits in its basement. And our guards soldiers became angry about [the idea of] the Germans drinking this barrel, so twenty men attacked the house, seized it back and rolled the barrel away, while almost the whole street was held by the Germans. All this caused a great sense of triumph..."[14]

Vasily Grossman, *A Writer at War* (1945)

After Germany was defeated, the Soviet troops behaved brutally in some cases, often while under the influence. Soldier Grigory Pomerants was embarrassed by their conduct in Berlin. "Soldiers drank and the officers drank. Military engineers used mine detectors to search for alcohol hidden in bushes. They drink methyl alcohol and go blind. When prisoners are interrogated, the first words are 'ring, watch, bicycle, wine!'" In *Ivan's War*, Catherine Merridale quotes a Soviet lieutenant: "When our soldiers find alcohol [...] they take leave of their senses. You can't expect anything from them until they have finished the last drop. [...] If we hadn't had drunkenness like this we would have beaten the Germans two years ago."[15]

It would be unseemly to talk only about vodka and its disastrous effects, because millions of Soviets fought in the war and the vast majority of them preserved their dignity. Andrei Sokolov was a prisoner of war held by the Nazis. He said something wrong and was called to account by officers who were dining on bread, fatback, and schnapps. Herr Kommandant Müller offered Andrei a glass of vodka, which he drank without eating anything:

Но он смотрит внимательно так и говорит: "Ты хоть закуси перед смертью". Я
ему на это отвечаю: "Я после первого стакана не закусываю". Наливает он второй,
подает мне. Выпил я и второй и опять же закуску не трогаю, на отвагу бью, думаю:
"Хоть напьюсь перед тем, как во двор идти, с жизнью расставаться". Высоко
поднял комендант свои белые брови, спрашивает: "Что же не закусываешь, русс
Иван? Не стесняйся!" А я ему свое: "Извините, герр комендант, я и после второго
стакана не привык закусывать". Надул он щеки, фыркнул, а потом как захохочет
и сквозь смех что-то быстро говорит по-немецки: видно, переводит мои слова
друзьям. Те тоже рассмеялись, стульями задвигали, поворачиваются ко мне
мордами и уже, замечаю, как-то иначе на меня поглядывают, вроде помягче.
Наливает мне комендант третий стакан, а у самого руки трясутся от смеха. Этот
стакан я выпил врастяжку, откусил маленький кусочек хлеба, остаток положил на
стол. Захотелось мне им, проклятым, показать, что хотя я и с голоду пропадаю, но
давиться ихней подачкой не собираюсь, что у меня есть свое, русское достоинство
и гордость и что в скотину они меня не превратили, как ни старались.

But he was looking at me sharply. "Have a bite to eat before you die," he said. But I
said to him, "I never eat after the first glass." Then he poured out a second and handed it
to me. I drank the second and again I didn't touch the food. I was staking everything on
courage, you see. "Anyway," I thought, "I'll get drunk before I go out into that yard to die."
And the commandant's fair eyebrows shot up in the air. "Why don't you eat, Russian Ivan?
Don't be shy!" But I stuck to my guns, "Excuse me, *Herr Kommandant,* but I don't eat after
the second glass either." He puffed out his cheeks and snorted, and then he gave a roar
of laughter, and while he laughed he said something quickly in German, must have been
translating my words to his friends. The others laughed, too, pushed their chairs back,
turned their big mugs round to look at me, and I noticed something different in their looks,
something a bit softer-like.

The commandant poured me out a third glass and his hands were shaking with laughter. I drank that glass slowly, bit off a little bit of bread and put the rest down on the table. I
wanted to show the bastards that even though I was half dead with hunger I wasn't going
to gobble the scraps they flung me, that I had my own, Russian dignity and pride, and that
they hadn't turned me into an animal as they had wanted to.[16]

Mikhail Sholokhov, *The Fate of a Man* (1957)

Valentin Rasputin's novel *Live and Remember* is set in Buryatiya, which
lies to the east of Lake Baikal. The Buryats are a people related to the Mongols
who were originally nomadic. The book tells the story of a Russian deserter,
Andrei, who, during World War II (after four years of fighting and twice being
wounded), returns to his native region along the Angara River because he can
no longer cope with his homesickness. He hides in the local forests. Only his

wife Nastyona is aware of his return. She had pictured his return differently, as one of triumph, and it was specifically for that celebratory occasion that her family had hidden away a bottle of *tarasun*, a beverage that was originally made from fermented mare's milk.

Это была обыкновенная самогонка, из довоенных еще богатых хлебов, но ее здесь испокон веку называли бурятским словом "тарасун". Настена знала, где он стоит: по ранней весне, отгребая картошку, она разглядела торчащую из земли, как фитиль, затычку и под ней нащупала бутыль, которую прятали не от нее, не от Настены, и не от кого-то еще, а просто прятали, чтобы до поры не попадалась на глаза и не тревожила понапрасну душу. После Настена отлила из бутылки в четушку, а четушку подсунула в мешок Андрею: все, может, на час, на другой утешит, пободрит мужика, позастит ему глаза. Чем ему больше отвлечься, куда кинуться от тоски и беды? Один и один. Недели и месяцы один.

It was ordinary home-brewed liquor from the rich prewar grains, but here they had always used the Buryat word *tarasun* for it. Nastyona knew where it was: in early spring when she was digging out the potatoes, she saw the stopper sticking out of the ground like a wick, and found the bottle, which they were hiding, not from her, or anyone else for that matter, they were just hiding it so that it wouldn't fall under their eyes too often, troubling the soul. Nastyona had poured some off into a pint and tucked it into a sack for Andrei: it might make an hour or so of his life more bearable, cheer him up. What else was there for him, where else could he go to forget his depression and bad luck? He was always alone. Weeks and months on end.[17]

Valentin Rasputin, Live and Remember (1974)

Tombs of the unknown soldier appeared throughout the Soviet Union, as did war memorials with an eternal flame and sometimes an honor guard. During remembrances, the veterans always drink their first glass of vodka standing, in silence, in memory of their fallen comrades-in-arms. But it was often the case that villages had no veterans – because not one man had come back alive – and in those situations the war was commemorated soberly, to put it mildly.

And so they lived, without pensions or privileges. And it was only on Victory Day that they placed a little table in front of their *izba*, setting out photographs of their family members killed in action, with a bottle of vodka and glasses so that every passerby could commemorate the fallen. They didn't even have a nice snack to go along with it.[18]

Anatoly Ananyev, "We Remain Weak – There Will Be No Rest" (1995)

These days, the compulsory tour of duty in Russia is twelve months. The traditional practice is for the military brass to send recruits to barracks far away from their native region. They are granted leave only once. The living conditions in the Russian barracks are simply miserable, and there is a good chance of being sent to a war zone such as Chechnya. In addition, the older soldiers bully the newcomers. Russian has a word for this: *dedovshchina*, which could be described as a month-long hazing ritual. It usually involves vodka. (For more details, see *The Color of War* (2006) by Arkady Babchenko.)

The *dedovshchina* was just one of the miseries associated with serving in the Russian military. In 2007, some 341 soldiers committed suicide. No wonder young men go to great lengths to try to get out of serving, often through self-mutilation.

> They went there together, with a bottle of vodka and an ax. Once they were in the woods, Vadim took a big swig for encouragement, and then he sprinkled the rest of the alcohol on his right hand, laid it on a log, and cut off his index finger. After that, his girlfriend made him a loving bandage, and they buried the finger under the log and went to the dacha.[19]
>
> Wladimir Kaminer, *Militär Musik* (2001)

Kaminer finishes the story: Vadim goes to the hospital, the finger is found, and the doctors sew it back on. All that effort for nothing: Vadim still has to serve in the army.

Soldiers are not allowed to drink in the barracks, but there's always a way to get vodka. They smuggle it in past the sentries in jars of jam, tubes of toothpaste, or thermos bottles. It can also happen on a larger scale. In 1984, a search was conducted in Czechoslovakia for four missing tank crewmen. After two days, they were found asleep in the woods. Their tank was gone. They had traded it in a bar for two cases of vodka. The bar owner intended to dismantle it and sell the parts to a scrap metal dealer.

Despite everything, the recruit's sendoff to the barracks is still celebrated. Family and friends gather the night before to have a glass, and everyone writes his name on the label of a full bottle of vodka. Once the conscript has completed his tour of duty, they ceremonially partake of that bottle, in the presence of everyone who signed it at the sendoff.

For a military man, being promoted to officer is a high point of his career. This calls for exuberant celebration, which means a lot of alcohol. The star that will later be sewed to his epaulet is presented to him in a glass of vodka. The new officer drains the glass, takes the star from his mouth, salutes, and declares that he is ready. He repeats the ritual with each subsequent promotion. And even though the official penalties are extraordinarily harsh, he continues to merrily drink for the rest of his career. In the words of a former officer in the Soviet army:

> There is a television set there but I already know that the whole of today's program is about Lenin. Yesterday it was about the danger of abortion and the excellence of the harvest, tomorrow it will be about Brezhnev and the harvest or Ustinov and abortion. As I enter the living room, I am greeted with delighted cries... Around the table sit fifteen or so officers. They have just begun a game... A place is made for me at the table and a large glass of vodka put down beside me. I drink it, smiling at my companions, and push a large sum of money over the bank. Here we go. Some time after one o'clock, officers returning from night exercises burst noisily into the room, dirty, wet, and worn out. They are found places at the table and someone brings them glasses of vodka... Three hours later, the commander of a neighboring company appears... He is greeted with delighted cries. Someone produces a full glass of vodka for him. We have already got through a good deal and we have begun to drink only a half a glass at a time... By tradition, the loser buys drinks for everyone else... we drink all that... someone is coming... they are pouring out more drinks... Another round... At six o'clock the clear notes of a bugle float out over the regiment – reveille for the soldiers. When we hear it we all get up, throw our cards on the table, and go off to bed.[20]

IN PRISON

The step from military camp to prison camp is not as big as it might seem. Both situations involve large groups of (predominantly) men who are cut off from the outside world and spend their days in close quarters. Boredom sets in, bossing each other around offers diversion, and the resulting patterns of behavior show similarities.

The first Russian penal colonies arose in the mid-nineteenth century as a supplement to exile, forced labor, and imprisonment. The convicts lived in barracks within a fenced-in area. They worked during the day, but the rest of their time was mostly free. The prisoner spent the period before his conviction in a regular prison, in anticipation of his trial, which could take a long time. The camp was mostly a relief compared to the prison cell. That remains the case today.

One of the first people to be sent to a prison camp in Russia was Fyodor Dostoyevsky. His novel *Memoirs from the House of the Dead* shows that life in prison and in the camp has a lot in common with life on the outside. The prisoners' emotions and needs are similar to those of free men; they work, eat, sleep, and drink...

Я остановился на том: почему в кармане у арестанта не залеживались деньги. Но, кроме труда уберечь их, в остроге было столько тоски; арестант же, по природе своей, существо до того жаждущее свободы и, наконец, по социальному своему положению, до того легкомысленное и беспорядочное, что его, естественно, влечет вдруг "развернуться на все", закутить на весь капитал, с громом и с музыкой, так, чтоб забыть, хоть на минутку, тоску свою. Даже странно было смотреть, как иной из них работает, не разгибая шеи, иногда по нескольку месяцев, единственно для того, чтоб в один день спустить весь заработок, все дочиста, а потом опять, до нового кутежа, несколько месяцев корпеть за работой. [...] Впрочем, кутеж развертывался постепенно. Пригонялся он обыкновенно или к праздничным дням, или к дням именин кутившего. Арестант-именинник, вставая поутру, ставил к образу свечку и молился; потом наряжался и заказывал себе обед. Покупалась говядина, рыба, делались сибирские пельмени; он наедался как вол, почти всегда один, редко приглашая товарищей разделить свою трапезу. Потом появлялось и вино: именинник напивался как стелька и непременно ходил по казармам, покачиваясь и спотыкаясь, стараясь показать всем, что он пьян, что он "гуляет", и тем заслужил всеобщее уважение. Везде в русском народе к пьяному чувствуется некоторая симпатия; в остроге же к загулявшему даже делались почтительны. [...] Арестант, начиная гулять, мог быть твердо уверен, что если он уж очень напьется, то за ним непременно присмотрят, вовремя уложат спать и всегда куда-нибудь спрячут при появлении начальства, и все это совершенно бескорыстно. С своей стороны, унтер-офицер и инвалиды, жившие для порядка в остроге, могли быть тоже совершенно спокойны: пьяный не мог произвести никакого беспорядка. За ним смотрела вся казарма, и если б он зашумел, забунтовал – его бы тотчас же усмирили, даже просто связали бы. А потому низшее острожное начальство смотрело на пьянство сквозь пальцы, да и не хотело замечать. Оно очень хорошо знало, что не позволь вина, так будет и хуже.

I had come to the question of why money did not remain long in the prisoner's pocket. Apart from the difficulty of keeping it safe, there is so much misery in the prison, and the prisoner in the nature of things has such a thirst for freedom and is rendered by his position in respect to society so irresponsible and undisciplined, that he is naturally open to the temptation to have his fling, to "blue in" all his wealth in one wild noisy revel and so to forget his anguish if only for a fleeting moment. It was quite strange to see one of them keep his nose to the grindstone, sometimes for several months on end, simply in order to squander all his earnings, down to the last kopek, in one day and then once more plod away at work for months, until the next outbreak. [...] A "binge", however, developed gradually. It would usually take place on a holiday or a man's name-day. The prisoner whose saint's day it was, on getting up in the morning, lit a candle before the ikon and said his prayers; then he dressed himself up and ordered dinner for himself. Beef and fish would be bought and Siberian meat dumplings made; he would eat steadily through it all like an ox, almost always alone, but very occasionally inviting his friends to share his table. Then vodka would make its appearance: the man would get as drunk as a lord; then he absolutely must go reeling and staggering all through the barracks in an effort to show everybody that he was drunk and "having a good time" and thus earn general respect. All over Russia the common people feel sympathy with a drunken man; in the prison he was even treated almost with respect. [...] Any prisoner who set out to get drunk could confidently rely on being looked after if he went too far, put to bed at the right time and hidden somewhere if ever anybody in authority put in an appearance, and all quite disinterestedly. For their part the sergeant and the old soldiers living in the prison to keep order might also be quite easy in their minds: the drunken man would not create any disturbance. The whole barrack would take care of him and if he began to be noisy or disorderly he would be violently suppressed, even bound if necessary. Therefore the lower authorities turned a blind eye on drunkenness and refused to notice anything. They knew very well that if they did not allow vodka, worse things would happen.[21]

Fyodor Dostoyevsky, *Memoirs from the House of the Dead* (1860-1862)

Russians also harbor sympathy for prisoners. After all, anyone can suffer misfortune. Prior to the 1917 revolution, it was traditional on the most important holidays to send gifts to the prisons, for "the poor wretches." The generous donors hoped that the prisoners would remember them in their prayers – because God is especially receptive to a prisoner's prayer. The guards were usually not forgotten either. They were often not much better off than those whom they were guarding. The gifts were so generous that the job of prison guard was especially popular right before major holidays.

In Moscow, most gifts went to the Butyrka central prison, which served as a temporary holding place for inmates who were to serve their sentences in Siberia. From there, they were marched several times a year to the notorious "transfer prison" in Vladimir. As the motley procession made its way through the streets of Moscow, thousands of people assembled along the route. They would cross themselves and throw rolls and cookies at the prisoners. Just outside the gates of Moscow, the people would bid farewell to the convicts and slip them all sorts of things. Middlemen would in turn buy the presents from them, because there were only two things that mattered to the prisoners: money and vodka. Vladimir Gilyarovsky described this sort of nineteenth-century scene in his 1926 book *Moscow and Muscovites*:

Затем происходила умопомрачительная сцена прощания, слезы, скандалы. Уже многие из арестантов успели подвыпить, то и дело буйство, пьяные драки...

Наконец конвою удается угомонить партию, выстроить ее и двинуть по Владимирке в дальний путь.

This was followed by an amazing farewell spectacle, tears and angry outbursts. Many of the arrestees had already managed to do some drinking, so you could count on there being disorder and drunken brawls... Finally the convoy managed to subdue the party, create orderly ranks, and get it to set out on its journey along the Vladimir Highway.[22]

The first systematic penal colonies in the Soviet Union – or corrective labor camps, as they were officially called – came into being around 1925. The most famous ones were the camps on the Solovetsky Islands, in the White Sea. Several years later, the camp system had developed to such an extent that a special administration was needed to run it: the Gulag (Chief Administration of Camps). Nobel Prize laureate Aleksandr Solzhenitsyn described the camps exhaustively in his magnum opus, *The Gulag Archipelago* (1958-1967). Varlam Shalamov, an author who is not as well known in the West and who spent 20 years in the camps, gave the Gulag inmates a human face in his *Kolyma Tales* (1954-1973).

The nadir of Stalin's terror came in 1937. Hundreds of thousands of people were executed, and millions more ended up in the camps, which had in the meantime spread across the entire country. The executioners who carried out the death sentence were given a ration of vodka to keep them from becoming giddy with death. In his book *The Unquiet Ghost*, Adam Hochschild quotes a victim of Stalin's terror, who in turn quotes an executioner:

"The 'special facility,'" Niazov said, had no purpose besides killing; prisoners were never kept there more than two or three days before being shot. "We took them about twelve kilometers, to a small hill... We'd shout: 'Get out! Line up!' They'd climb out, and in front of them there was already a pit dug for them. They'd climb out, huddle... We shot them, and if anyone was still moving, we would finish them off and get back into the trucks. We would go back to the camp, leave our weapons in the guardroom, and drink as much as we wanted, for free... I always drank one glass, went to the cafeteria, ate something hot, and then went back to the barracks to sleep."[23]

During the great terror, the camps grew at such a brisk pace that a manpower shortage loomed. Selection procedures for recruiting suitable people were nonexistent or were simply disregarded. The Gulag became the last refuge for people who were "incompetent, drunk, or simply stupid." In her book *Gulag*, Anne Applebaum quotes Izrail Pliner, the head of the Gulag, who complained in 1937: "We get the leftovers from other sections; they send us people based on the principle 'you can take what we do not need.' The cream of the crop are the hopeless drunkards; once a man goes over to drink, he's dumped on to the Gulag... From the point of view of the NKVD apparatus, if someone commits an offense, the greatest punishment is to send him to work in a camp."[24]

For the prisoners, meanwhile, it's no problem if a guard drinks in excess – quite the contrary. In Shalamov's 1959 story "Committees for the Poor," the best guard is a little older and has a low rank. Someone like that is more likely to turn a blind eye. "It's even better if he drinks. Such a person is not trying to build a career. The career of a prison guard – and especially of a camp guard – must be lubricated with the blood of the prisoners."[25]

The most notorious camps were situated in the Kolyma mining region in Magadan Province, in the extreme northeast of Russia. Being thousands of kilometers away from Moscow, the bosses had free rein. For those at the very top, vodka was not good enough; they had delicacies flown in, such as wine from the Caucasus and bear meat. For camp boss Bogdanov, as Shalamov writes in the 1965 short story of the same name, prisoners had even constructed a special wooden road across the taiga, over which he was supplied alcohol in 200-liter barrels.

Shalamov spent nearly 17 years in Kolyma. One of the few ways to survive was to get a job in the camp's kitchen as a servant to a camp chief. Shalamov found another solution: He was admitted to the hospital, and after he recovered he was able to continue working there as a nurse. The following scene takes place in 1948. The skilled doctor Rubantsev is the head of the surgery department. However, he is unable to get along with the administration and is transferred.

Александр Александрович Рубанцев уехал. На третий же день в процедурной была устроена пьянка – хирургический спирт пробовал и главный врач Ковалев, и начальник больницы Винокуров, которые побаивались Рубанцева и не посещали хирургическое отделение. Во врачебных кабинетах начались пьянки с приглашением заключенных – медсестер, санитарок, словом, стоял дым коромыслом. Операции чистого отделения стали проходить с вторичным заживлением – на обработку операционного поля не стали тратить драгоценного спирта. Полупьяные начальники шагали по отделению взад и вперед.

Rubantsev left, and three days later a drunken party was held in the treatment room. Even the principal doctor, Kovalyov, and the hospital director, Vinokurov, helped themselves to the surgical alcohol. They hadn't visited the surgical ward earlier, because they were afraid of Rubantsev. Drunken parties began in all the doctors' offices, and nurses and cleaning women were invited. In a word, there were a lot of changes. Secondary adhesion began to occur in operations in the surgical ward, since precious grain alcohol could not be wasted on patients. Half-drunk hospital officials strolled back and forth through the ward.[26]

Varlam Shalamov, "Descendant of a Decembrist" (1962)

Under orders from Stalin, Soviet troops that had been prisoners of war abroad were sent to the Gulag. These former POWs were much more articulate and tougher than the political prisoners and were not as likely to be doormats for the criminals. Strikes and revolts took place right before Stalin died, and others followed after his death. The prisoners demanded better clothing and working conditions, and there was also a case, in 1954, of criminal prisoners demanding better food and vodka. Otherwise they would rebel.

Relatively few people escaped from the camps, even though the security was usually not that good and the guards who had direct contact with the prisoners did not carry weapons. The soldiers who manned the guard towers were indeed armed, as were those who patrolled outside the camp. There was no point attempting escape, since most of the camps were situated in the middle of nowhere. In fact, the inhabitants of Kolyma called the rest of Russia "the mainland." If a prisoner in Kolyma tried to escape, he had to contend with the endless coniferous forests of the taiga – known as the "green prosecutor" – from whom escape was virtually impossible. Whatever the case, if you did want to escape, you could take advantage of the desire for vodka:

План такой: сейчас же в поселке брать машину. Остановить, сказать шоферу: заработать хочешь? Нам нужно из Старого Экибастуза подкинуть сюда два ящика водки. Какой шоферюга не захочет выпить?! Поторговаться: поллитра тебе? Литр? Ладно, гони, только никому! А потом по дороге, сидя с ним в кабине, прихватить его, вывезти в степь, там оставить связанного. Самим рвануть за ночь до Иртыша, там бросить машину, Иртыш переплыть на лодке – и двинуться на Омск.

The plan was to take a lorry as soon as they reached the settlement. Stop one and say to the driver, "Do you want to earn something? We have to bring two cases of vodka up here from old Ekibastuz." What driver would refuse drink? They would bargain with him. "Half a liter, all right? A liter? Right, step on it, but not a word to anybody." Then on the highway, sitting with the driver in his cab, they would overpower him, drive him out into the steppe, and leave him there tied up. While they tore off to reach the Irtysh in a single night, abandon the lorry, cross the river in a little boat, and move on towards Omsk.[27]

Aleksandr Solzhenitsyn, *The Gulag Archipelago Three* (1958-1967)

Vodka was the shortest escape route, but if you weren't careful it could also be the shortest route back to prison. Some people were not actually interested in escaping, but only wanted an evening of boozing. Otherwise they were doing just fine in the camp. Seasoned criminals often said, "Prison is my home." There are also tattoos that communicate the same thing: once they are free, they end up back in the camp within a couple of days. Irina Ratushinskaya is a dissident poet who was held in the camp complex near the city of Potma in Mordovia District in the early 1980s:

Что они думали в последнюю свою тюремную ночь? Многим ли было куда возвращаться, ждал ли их кто-нибудь? Я уже знала, что в дни освобождений под тюрьмой стоят местные бабки с самогоном и продают втридорога, чтоб было чем немедленно отпраздновать. И многие, напившись, даже не успевают с Потьмы уехать, а уже попадаются милиции.

What were they thinking their last night in prison? How many of them had someplace to go, someone waiting for them? I already knew that on release days local women waited outside with home brew, which they sold for three-times the regular price, so that people would be able to celebrate without delay. Many got so drunk they never made it out of Potma before they again wound up in the hands of the police.[28]

Irina Ratushinskaya, *Gray is the Color of Hope* (1988)

Russians sometimes use the slang word *zek* to refer to a prisoner. This is derived from the abbreviation *ZK* for *zaklyuchonny kanaloarmeyets* (imprisoned canal builder) – referring to the forced laborers who built the White Sea Canal in the early 1930s. In order to survive in the camps, the *zeks* tried to secretly observe certain "outside" rituals or celebrations. For example, the Russian prisoner Yuri Zorin recalled with amazement how well the Lithuanians in his camp organized the Christmas service, a holiday for which they had spent the entire year preparing. "Just imagine, in the barracks, a table loaded with everything: vodka, ham, everything."

But how does that vodka or home-distilled alcohol make it into the camp? Where is the leak? The camp inmates are quite resourceful, and sometimes a true story is hard to tell apart from an urban legend:

Вам расскажут и как один зэк пошел к начальнику дрова колоть для кухни – начальникова дочка сама прибежала к нему в сарай. И как хитрый дневальный сделал лаз под барак и подставлял там котелок под слив, проделанный в полу посылочной комнаты. (В посылках извне иногда приходит водка, но на Архипелаге – сухой закон, и ее по акту должны тут же выливать на землю (впрочем никогда не выливали) – так вот дневальный собирал в котелок и всегда пьян был.)

They will tell you how a certain zek went to the chief to split wood for the kitchen – and how the chief's daughter ran out to him in the woodshed. Or how a sly orderly made a crawl hole underneath the barracks and put a pot under the drain in the floor of the parcel room. (There was sometimes vodka in parcels from outside, but there was a prohibition law on the Archipelago, and, with due documentation, they were supposed to pour out all the vodka right on the ground – but they never ever did pour it out – and so this duty orderly supposedly collected it in his pot and was always drunk.)[29]

Aleksandr Solzhenitsyn, *The Gulag Archipelago Two* (1958-1967)

Smuggling vodka into the camp is a time-honored tradition. Fyodor Dostoyevsky, who was sentenced to death in 1849 for revolutionary activities (he was standing in front of a firing squad when the news of his pardon was read aloud and his sentence was commuted to four years of hard labor and five years of exile), described the "dealers" who supplied vodka to the camp population by way of a variety of middlemen.

К этому-то поставщику и являются указанные ему наперед от острожного целовальника проносители, с бычачьими кишками. Эти кишки сперва промываются, потом наливаются водой и, таким образом, сохраняются в первоначальной влажности и растяжимости, чтобы со временем быть удобными к восприятию водки. Налив кишки водкой, арестант обвязывает их кругом себя, по возможности в самых скрытых местах своего тела. Разумеется, при этом выказывается вся ловкость, вся воровская хитрость контрабандиста. Его честь отчасти затронута; ему надо надуть и конвойных и караульных. Он их надувает: у хорошего вора конвойный, иногда какой-нибудь рекрутик, всегда прозевает. Разумеется, конвойный изучается предварительно; к тому же принимается в соображение время, место работы. Арестант, например печник, полезет на печь: кто увидит, что он там делает? Не лезть же за ним и конвойному. Подходя к острогу, он берет в руки монетку – пятнадцать или двадцать копеек серебром, на всякий случай, и ждет у ворот ефрейтора. Всякого арестанта, возвращающегося с работы, караульный ефрейтор осматривает кругом и ощупывает и потом уже отпирает ему двери острога. Проноситель вина обыкновенно надеется, что посовестятся слишком подробно его ощупывать в некоторых местах. Но иногда пролаз ефрейтора добирается и до этих мест и нащупывает вино. Тогда остается одно последнее средство: контрабандист молча и скрытно от конвойного сует в руки ефрейтора затаенную в руке монетку. Случается, что вследствие такого маневра он проходит в острог благополучно и проносит вино. Но иногда маневр не удается, и тогда приходится рассчитаться своим последним капиталом, то есть спиной.

The smugglers, pointed out to him beforehand by the dealer, then come to the agent, bringing with them ox-guts. These have first been rinsed out and then filled with water to keep them in their original moist and elastic state, so that in due course they can be used to hold vodka. Having filled the gut with vodka the smuggler fastens it round his body as inconspicuously as possible. Needless to say, this is an opportunity for displaying all the smuggler's skill and thievish cunning. His honour is involved; he must cheat both guards and sentries. He does cheat them; the guard, sometimes a raw recruit, is never any match for a good thief. The prisoner has, of course, studied the guard beforehand and taken into consideration the time and place of work. The prisoner is a stove-setter, for example, and he climbs up on top of a stove; who is to see what he does there? The guard cannot be expected to climb up after him. When he comes to the prison, the prisoner takes a little money – fifteen or twenty silver copecks – in his hand, just in case, and waits at the gates for the corporal. The corporal of the watch inspects every prisoner returning from work and runs his hand over him before he unlocks the prison door for him. The smuggler usually hopes that delicacy will prevent a too detailed investigation of certain parts of his body. But sometimes a wily corporal probes as far even as these parts and feels the vodka. Then there remains one last expedient: the smuggler silently and without the notice of the guard thrusts the money he has been holding into the corporal's hand. Sometimes in consequence of this manoeuvre he gets safely into prison carrying his vodka. But sometimes the manoeuvre is unsuccessful and then he must settle his debts with his sole capital, his back.[30]

Fyodor Dostoyevsky, *Memoirs from the House of the Dead* (1860-1862)

Anton Chekhov, who visited a labor camp on Sakhalin Island toward the end of the nineteenth century, wrote in his 1895 work *Sakhalin Island* that "liquor was brought in using cylindrical candy tins and samovars, using just about everything but people's belts, but most often in barrels and ordinary bottles, since the low-level bosses were bribed and the higher-ups looked the other way."[31]

When Solzhenitsyn got to know the Soviet camps, little had changed in terms of alcohol, although perhaps there was less risk involved. After all, guards were still eager to get their hands on vodka or *samogon*. In the following passage, Solzhenitsyn talks about the "freemen," citizens who worked in the penal colony.

Эти вольняшки второго разряда, простые работяги, как и зэки, тотчас и запросто сдруживались с нами, и делали все, что запрещалось лагерным режимом и уголовным законом: охотно бросали письма зэков в вольные почтовые ящики поселка; носильные вещи, замотанные зэками в лагере, продавали на вольной толкучке, вырученные за то деньги брали себе, а зэкам несли чего-нибудь пожрать; вместе с зэками разворовывали также и производство; вносили или ввозили в производственную зону водку. (При строгом осмотре на вахте – пузырьки с засмоленными горлышками спускали в бензобаки автомашин. Если вахтеры находили и там, – то все же никакого рапорта начальству не следовало: комсомольцы-охранники вместо того предпочитали трофейную водку выпить сами.)

These second-class *"volnyashki,"* ordinary sloggers like the zeks, made friends with us right away without nonsense, and did everything forbidden by the camp regimen and by criminal law: they willingly deposited the zeks' letters in the free mailboxes of the settlement; they took and sold at the local free markets clothes the zeks had pinched in camp and kept the money, bringing the zeks some grub; together with the zeks they also plundered the project: they brought vodka into the work compound. (Despite very strict inspection at the gatehouse, they would drop flasks of vodka with tarred necks into the gasoline tanks of automobiles.) [...] And if it happened that the guard found them, there would still be no official report filed with the chief; the Komsomol guards preferred to drink any contraband vodka themselves.[32]

Aleksandr Solzhenitsyn, *The Gulag Archipelago Two* (1958-1967)

The smuggling methods went even further:

Наиболее благонадежные уголовники отправляются на дневные работы вне лагеря – поднимать отечественное сельское хозяйство, колоть начальству дрова и мыть посуду, ну и так далее. На ночь они возвращаются в зону. И умудряются иногда пронести через обыск до трех литров спирта. Как? На это разработана целая технология. Берется презерватив и соединяется герметично с тонкой пластиковой трубкой (кембриком). Затем расконвоированный все это хозяйство заглатывает, оставляя наружный конец кембрика во рту. Чтоб его не затянуло внутрь, он крепится в щели между зубами (зэки со всеми тридцатью двумя зубами вряд ли встречаются в природе). Через кембрик с помощью шприца в проглоченный презерватив закачивают эти самые три литра – и зэк идет в зону. Если соединение сделано неловко или презерватив вдруг порвется в зэковском желудке – это верная и мучительная смерть. Тем не менее рискуют и носят – ведь из трех литров спирта получится семь литров водки! Когда герой является в зону, ожидающие его приятели начинают процесс выкачивания. Зэка подвешивают за ноги к балке в бараке, конец кембрика вынимают наружу и подставляют посудину, пока все не вытечет. Потом вытаскивают пустой презерватив – он свое отслужил. И весь барак гуляет...

The more reliable criminals were allowed out of the camp for day labor – to boost Soviet agricultural output, cut wood for the camp bosses, wash dishes, and so forth. They returned to the zone at night. Sometimes they got it into their heads to smuggle three liters of pure alcohol past the guards. How did they do it? They had an elaborate system. They would take a condom and hermetically seal it to a thin plastic (cambric) tube. Then the day laborer would swallow this contraption, leaving the outer end of the tube in his mouth. To prevent it from slipping down, he affixed it to the space between teeth (zeks with all thirty-two teeth are a rare breed). Using a syringe, the three liters were pumped through the tubing into the swallowed condom – and then the zek went back to the zone. If the tube was not securely attached or the condom suddenly broke in the zek's stomach, a certain and torturous death awaited him. But this didn't stop anybody from taking the risk. After all, three liters of pure alcohol yield seven liters of vodka! When the hero appeared in the zone, his eager buddies would begin the extraction process. The zek would be hung by his legs from a beam in the barracks, the tip of the tube was pulled out, and a basin was put in place until everything had flowed into it. The empty condom would then be pulled out – it had served its purpose. It was party time in the barracks...[33]

Irina Ratushinskaya, *Gray is the Color of Hope* (1988)

In the Soviet Union, there were different types of camps designed to hold all sorts of criminals based on the seriousness and nature of the crime committed. Murderers and repeat offenders were held in the harshest camps. At present, there are also special camps for young people, women, foreigners, white-collar criminals, and those with infectious diseases (such as HIV or tuberculosis). There are also rehab camps where people undergo forced recovery from their addiction to drugs or alcohol. This is not to say that alcohol or drugs are unavailable there. One method for smuggling them in is to fill condoms with alcohol and place them in fuses filched from ovens.

Then they threw the fuses over the fence into the living zone. Dogs ran over the ploughed earth between the fences but they were quite stupid. They ran up barking when prisoners shouted, "water!", only to have hot water poured on their noses. After that the animals stayed away when they heard the cry. When the zeks were ready to throw the fuses over one of their mates would start a fight to distract the guards. Most of us had played skittles at some time in our lives so we could throw far and accurately.[34]

C. S. Walton, *Ivan Petrov: Russia through a Shot Glass* (1999)

THE STATE RATION

Heavy drinking in the military is not an exclusively Russian phenomenon. What is indeed typically Russian is the fact that the authorities mandated that certain ranks had a right to vodka; the military brass considered alcohol a mental and physical pick-me-up. Sailors were the first ones to enjoy a prescribed glass of vodka. In 1721, Tsar Peter the Great issued an edict declaring that sailors had the right to a serving of vodka every day, known as the state ration (*kazyonnaya charka*). At first they received four glasses of vodka per week and later one glass a day. Less than a century later, Paul I officially reaffirmed the policy.

In contrast, soldiers were entitled to a state ration only in times of war, and they also received less: two or three glasses a week, depending on whether they were involved in combat. In addition, they received vodka during inclement weather, in order to counter the "physical discomfort." During campaigns, exercises, and the like, officers were at liberty to decide on their own whether to "prescribe" extra vodka for their men, because vodka ensured additional valor and strength amid the rigors of military life. Doctors also routinely prescribed vodka for sick soldiers. *The Handbook for the New Recruit* from 1875 even contained a separate entry concerning vodka: "Beneficial when used in moderation, harmful when used in excess." It was recommended in the event of bad weather and scarce food supplies. Yet the argument that vodka warms the body is nonsense. Vodka dilates the blood vessels, making the body more susceptible to hypothermia.

During peacetime, soldiers received only 15 state rations a year: on religious, royal, and specifically military holidays, such as "regiment day," when the officers were required to treat the soldiers. The commander would make a toast, scoop vodka from a bucket using a special ladle, and drink to the soldiers' health. The soldiers would thank him, after which the next officer would repeat the ritual. Only after all the officers had had their turn were the soldiers themselves allowed to eat and drink. The state rations were usually drunk ceremonially, in one gulp, and without food.

Soldiers could request money instead of vodka. Only a few availed themselves of that right, and those who did were objects of derision. That choice was more common in the navy, because more state rations were distributed, which made it worthwhile.

For officers, however, refusing vodka was out of the question. The prevailing opinion was that officers who were unable to congratulate their soldiers on a holiday by having a glass were incompetent and should not serve in the military. Alcoholism among officers was the order of the day in the tsarist army, to a much greater extent than among soldiers.

Кузьма Васильевич действительно отличался благоразумием и, несмотря на свои молодые годы, вел себя примерно; всяких неприличных поступков избегал тщательно, не прикасался карт, вина не пил и даже общества чуждался, так что товарищи его, смирные – прозывали его красною девицей, а буйные – мямлей и рохлей.

Kuzma Vasilyevich certainly was distinguished by his prudence and, in spite of his youth, his behavior was exemplary; he studiously avoided every impropriety of conduct, did not touch cards, did not drink and, even shied from society, so that the quieter of his comrades called him "a regular girl" and the rowdy ones called him a muff and a noodle.[35]

Ivan Turgenev, "Lieutenant Yergunov's Story" (1868)

In his 1942 memoirs, Lieutenant General Count Alexei Ignatyev described the drinking behavior of tsarist officers:

Умение выпить десяток стопок шампанского в офицерской артели было обязательным для кавалергарда. Таков был и негласный экзамен для молодых – надо было пить стопки залпом до дна и оставаться в полном порядке.

Для многих это было истинным мучением. Особенно тяжело приходилось некоторым молодым в первые месяцы службы, когда старшие постепенно переходили с ними на "ты": в каждом таком случае требовалось пить на брудершафт. [...] На одном празднике меня подозвал к себе старейший из бывших командиров полка генерал-адъютант граф Мусин-Пушкин и предложил выпить с ним на брудершафт. Однако после традиционного троекратного поцелуя он внушительно мне сказал:

– Теперь я могу тебе говорить "ты", но ты все-таки продолжай мне говорить: "ваше сиятельство".

The ability to drink ten glasses of champagne in the officer's mess was mandatory in the Cavalry Guard. Such was the tacit examination that young officers had to endure: they were compelled to down a glassful in one gulp and remain completely collected.

For many, this was pure torture. It was especially hard for some of the young fellows in the first months of their service, when their superiors were gradually switching to the familiar *ty* in addressing them. Each such occasion called for downing a glassful to *Brüderschaft* with linked arms. [...] During one celebration, I was called over by the oldest of the former regimental commanders, General-Adjutant Count Musin-Pushkin, who proposed that we perform the brotherhood ritual. But after the three kisses on the check that are part of this rite, he told me quite emphatically:

"Now I can call you *ty*, but you will continue to address me as 'your Excellency.'"[36]

After conscription was introduced in 1874, the military became even more of a national school for alcoholism. Ordinary soldiers were now at risk as well. Many of them had never drunk before entering the service. A survey of St.

Petersburg alcoholics found that of the 450 respondents, 255 said that they started drinking while in the military. In 1899, drinking in the military became a subject of public debate. Military doctors made spirited arguments in favor of abolishing the state ration, replacing it with tea and offering the soldiers a different sort of amusement. But it was not until 1908 that the state ration came to an end, partly as a consequence of the defeat in the Russo-Japanese War. And perhaps the officials in St. Petersburg had read the words of Kaiser Wilhelm II, who had said that victory in the impending war would go to the more sober side. Vodka was also banished from the mess halls. The navy followed suit in 1913, and in 1914 there was no drinking anywhere.

The state ration did not disappear for long. In 1940, it was reintroduced by Kliment Voroshilov, the People's Commissar for Defense, namely 100 grams of vodka for the men fighting the Finns and 100 grams of cognac for pilots. The state ration was now known as "Voroshilov's 100 grams" or "the people's commissar's 100 grams."

As of September 1, 1941, all soldiers were entitled to a state ration. On November 12, 1942, Stalin went so far as to devote an official order to this, No. 2507, which specified that all troops directly involved in hostilities would receive one hundred grams of vodka a day – 100 grams for "the front," whereas reservists got 50 grams. A brisk trade in vodka arose because the officers in charge of weighing the portions were required to account for the surplus amounts only once every ten days. They usually drew up the portions on the spot by adding water to the pure alcohol. But often they did not do that and simply gave the men pure alcohol, which they themselves washed down with water. Sometimes the soldiers saved up their rations so that they could later get dead drunk.

Свои «боевые» сто грамм, разведенные в пути до последнего градуса, я, как правило, отдавал «дядькам» и только в лютые холода в крайнем уж случае выпивал – для согрева. Один раз, под Христиновкой, в Винницкой области, в метель, когда и палку-то в костер негде было найти, орлы огневики раздобыли где-то ящик с флаконами тройного одеколона. Я так продрог и устал, что мне было все равно, что пить, чем греться, и выпил из кружки беловатой жидкости – на всю жизнь отбило меня от редкостного в ту пору напитка, и по сей день отрыгивается одеколоном и от горшка ароматно пахнет; я боюсь в парикмахерских облеваться, когда меня освежают.

I usually gave away my "combat" hundred grams, which along the way had been diluted down to the final proof, to the "old-timers," and only when the cold was really brutal, when things got really desperate – only then would I drink to warm up. Once, outside Khristinovka, in Vinnitsa Province, during a snowstorm when there wasn't a stick to be found to make a fire, the bucks from artillery managed to get their hands on a carton full of triple-essence eau de cologne. I was exhausted and frozen to the bone, and I didn't care what I had to drink to warm up, so I drank the whitish liquid from a cup – and that was enough to put me off the stuff, which was quite prized in those days, for the rest of my life. To this day, when I regurgitate, it smells like eau de cologne, and when I go to the barbershop I'm afraid of puking when they splash it on me.[37]

Viktor Astafyev, *The Jolly Soldier* (1998)

During hostilities, the portions were generally distributed after the fighting, whereby the survivors laid claim to the portions of their fallen comrades. In *Ivan's War*, Catherine Merridale quotes a soldier: "'It was always good to serve with the infantry,' a survivor remembered. 'The infantry or the artillery. The death rates among them were highest. And no one was checking how much vodka we sent back.'"[38] But there are also many veterans who claim that the stress following battle was often so great that they could not hold anything down, be it food or vodka.

Right after the war, the state ration was again abolished. Which is not to say, of course, that servicemen no longer drank. To this day, the military is still known as a school for alcoholism.

10

Samogon and Surrogates

Где пьют? Везде. Дома, на работе само собой, в дороге, в поле, в лесу, на берегу реки или озера, на вокзале, в машине, в магазине...

Что пьют? Все, что возможно. Перечислять нет смысла, все равно список будет не полон. Удивляет лишь необыкновенная живучесть, стойкость организма ко всяким кислотам и растворителям, которые легко плавят и камень, и стекло, и любой металл, но не могут побороть нутро российского алкоголика.

Where do they drink? Everywhere. At home, at work (obviously), on the road, in the field, in the forest, by the river or lake, at the train station, in the car, in the store...

What do they drink? Everything conceivable. There's no sense in making a list, because it could never be complete. The surprising thing is the body's extraordinary durability and hardiness when it comes to all sorts of acids and solvents that easily break down stone and glass and any metal but are no match for the insides of the Russian alcoholic.[1]

Anatoly Pristavkin, *Valley of the Shadow of Death* (2000)

THROUGH THE AGES, VODKA has often been scarce or simply too expensive for the common man, but Ivan Ivanovich still likes to drink. And so he has two options: distill his own or drink something else. There are some people who prefer home-distilled alcohol anyway, because it can have an almost divine character.

– После жаркого человек становится сыт и впадает в сладостное затмение, – продолжал секретарь. – В это время и телу хорошо и на душе умилительно. Для услаждения можете выкушать рюмочки три запеканочки.

Председатель крякнул и перечеркнул лист.

– Я шестой лист порчу, – сказал он сердито. – Это бессовестно!

– Пишите, пишите, благодетель! – зашептал секретарь. – Я не буду! Я потихоньку. Я вам по совести, Степан Францыч, – продолжал он едва слышным шепотом, – домашняя самоделковая запеканочка лучше всякого шампанского. После первой же рюмки всю вашу душу охватывает обоняние, этакий мираж, и кажется вам, что вы не в кресле у себя дома, а где-нибудь в Австралии, на каком-нибудь мягчайшем страусе...

"After eating something hot a person develops a sense of satiety and descends into a delightful fog," the secretary continued. "At that moment the body is content and the soul is uplifted. For delectation, you can take two or three glasses of spiced brandy."

The chairman grunted and crossed out the sheet of paper he was writing on.

"This is the sixth sheet I've ruined," he said angrily. "This is unconscionable!"

"Keep writing, keep writing, my good man!" whispered the secretary. "I'll stop! I'll be very quiet. I'm telling you in all honesty, Stepan Frantsych," he continued in a barely audible whisper. "A home-made spiced brandy is better than any champagne. After the first glass, your entire soul becomes engulfed in the smell, a sort of mirage, and it seems to you that rather than being in an easy chair in your own home, you are somewhere in Australia, seated on the softest imaginable ostrich..."[2]

Anton Chekhov, "The Siren" (1887)

The Russian word for homemade alcohol is *samogon*. *Sam* means self or own, and *gon* is derived from *gnat* (to distill). Russians have been doing their own distilling for centuries, and they are not about to stop. When the excises increase, distillers make substantial profits. Moreover, Russians don't take official prohibitions against *samogon* seriously, although the fact that they avoid calling it by its true name – which is replaced with euphemisms like *neylonovka* (derived from the nylon used as a filter) or *krasnoye* (literally "red"; *samogon* often has a reddish tint) – shows that they recognize a certain need for discretion.

Many Russians simply consider *samogon* more reliable than the vodka available at a kiosk or market. In the years following the collapse of the Soviet Union in particular, fake vodka that had been decanted into a "real" bottle with a chic label was commonplace. Sometimes it was nothing short of life-threatening. *Samogon* can be trusted: You know who made it and what went into it. Knowing how to make *samogon* is a handy skill to have.

Та же бригада [...] начала ходить в поля и из бункеров комбайнов или прямо из куч уносить, а то и с помощью станичников "исполу" увозить зерно, забрасывая его в известные им хаты. Заквашивается самогонка и ночью же где-нибудь ломается забор, тын, сваливаются старые телеграфные столбы на дрова, "бо з дровамы здись цила проблэма", и начинается производство самогонки.

Потом, опять же в определенных хатах, собираются бабы, ранбольные на бал, начинаются песни, танцы и все, что дальше, после гулянки, полагается.

That same brigade [...] began to go out into the fields and carry grain by hand from the hoppers or right from the stacks, or in some cases promised the villagers "halves" to help haul grain and drop it off at particular huts. The *samogon* would be set to ferment and at night they would break down some fencing or lathing, or take down an old telegraph pole to use for firewood, "seein' as how feerwood hereabouts's right skars" – and then the *samogon* production would get underway.

Later, in those same particular huts, the women and wounded got together for a ball, and the singing and dancing began, followed by everything else you would expect to come after merrymaking.[3]

Viktor Astafyev, *The Jolly Soldier* (1998)

As early as the nineteenth century, there were some people who knew how to process products containing alcohol, such as lacquer and cleaning products, in order to make them potable, but it was not until prohibition during World War I that the Russians began applying those techniques on a large scale. It was a golden age for drug stores, with sales of alcoholic medicines reaching phenomenal heights. During the first year of the war, the 150 drug stores in Petrograd – as St. Petersburg was known from 1914 to 1924 – saw a tenfold increase in sales: They sold pure alcohol in quantities equivalent to 300,000 buckets of vodka. Some medicines were even available in liter bottles.

The figures remained staggering in the 1920s, even after the prohibition of vodka had been lifted. In 1925, 225,000 *samogon* stills were confiscated. Three years later, 48,005 people were fined in the month of January alone on charges of bootlegging, and 1,320 people were sent to penal colonies. In March of that same year, Moscow radio stations aired appeals in the breaks between programs calling on the rural population to stop producing *samogon*.

The absolute zenith was probably the period during Gorbachev's temperance campaign in the mid-1980s. The party leader ordered the closure of vodka factories or had them converted to soft drink factories, and he also curbed the glass industry. In Moldova and Georgia, he ordered the destruction of entire vineyards. The impact is being felt to this day. The staggering amount of *samogon* being distilled caused an acute shortage of sugar, which is a good base ingredient for *samogon*. As a result, the distillers substituted taffy for sugar. Bottles were also universally in short supply: At parties, the host would dispense alcohol from samovars or mineral water bottles. Drug stores experienced shortages of medicines containing alcohol, and alcoholics paid pensioners to obtain those substitutes for them. *Samogon* also replaced vodka as a means of payment.

In 1987, the authorities confiscated more than one million stills, including one at a research station near the South Pole. Nevertheless, the production of *samogon* in 1988 was around fifty percent greater than vodka production by the state. The impact of prohibition on the production of *samogon* is reflected in the number of arrests on bootlegging charges: 80,000 in 1985, 158,000 in 1986, and 400,000 in 1987.

The distilling of *samogon* was – and is – women's work. Prohibition was in effect during World War I while the men were at the front, and thus women had to do the distilling themselves. The fact that more women than men work in vodka factories to this day is attributable to this – besides the miserable wages and their ability to withstand temptation.

Ivan Bunin describes an old woman who sells spirits, probably *samogon*. The story is set in a small Russian village at the beginning of the twentieth century. However, it could have taken place a century earlier or later in any Russian village.

Мимо садового вала, по задворкам, он [Игнат] поплелся на деревню, черневшую обтаявшими избами на косогоре. Желтоватые, замасленные санями горбы сугробов, с гладко втертым в них конским навозом, и выбоины, полные студеной вешней воды, тянулись между избами и пуньками. Игнат стукнул в окошечко особенно черной и хилой избы, под стенкой которой, нахохлившись, дремали куры. Изнутри примкнуло к окошечку старое, желтое лицо. Игнат показал двугривенный. И, надернув на босые ноги старые валенки, с головой накрывшись полушубком, баба провела Игната через дорогу в холодную пахучую пуньку с железной дверкой и сунула в подставленный карман его растянувшихся порток четверть бутылки.

За пунькой, на скате косогора, покрытом зернистым снегом, он постоял, думая о Любке. Потом запрокинул голову и, не переводя духа, выпил все до капельки. И, пряча пустую посуду в карман, почувствовал, как горячо, хорошо пошла отрава по всему его телу. Он присел на корячки и стал ждать дурману; потом упал, хохоча, наслаждаясь тем, что пьян.

Past the garden wall and through the backyards, Ignat began to make his way toward the village, whose thawing huts blackened the hillside. The expanse between the huts and sheds was dotted with potholes filled with the icy melt of spring and slopes of yellowish, sled-worn snow covered in a smooth layer of horse manure. Ignat knocked on the window of a particularly dark and dingy hut, whose wall sheltered a brood of fluffed-up, slumbering chickens. Inside, an aged and yellow female face came to the window. Ignat showed her his twenty kopeks. After pulling her worn felt boots onto her bare feet and hooking a short fur coat behind her head, the old *baba* led Ignat across the road into a cold, musty shed with a metal door and stuck into the already waiting pocket of his threadbare trousers a quarter-full bottle of vodka.

Behind the shed, on a hillside slope covered in granular snow, Ignat stood for a while and thought about Lyubka. Then he threw back his head and, in one gulp, drained the bottle to the last drop. Hiding the empty bottle in his pocket, he felt how warmly and well the poison spread through his entire body. He squatted on the ground and began to wait for the dizziness; then he fell, laughing, reveling in the fact that he was drunk.[4]

Ivan Bunin, "Ignat" (1912)

If you know what you're doing, almost anything can be used as the base ingredient for *samogon*. In the nineteenth century, for example, a Professor Spassky invented a method for extracting alcohol from peat and wood chips. And according to connoisseur par excellence Venedikt Erofeev, even Lenin concerned himself with the base ingredients for alcoholic beverages. He thought that potatoes and grain should be used to feed the people. "I am decidedly against the use of potatoes for alcohol. Alcohol can and should be made from peat. The production of alcohol from peat should be developed," Lenin declared on September 11, 1921.

Just before the outbreak of World War II, soldier Ivan Chonkin, Voinovich's famous creation, is ordered to guard a crashed airplane in a remote village. Everyone forgets about him completely. Chonkin moves in with a peasant woman and leads the uncomplicated life of the simple farmer that he is. One day, he is visiting his neighbor Gladyshev, who is married to Aphrodite. As always, there is a foul stench in their house and on their property.

Гладышев... достал с горки два пропыленных стакана, посмотрел на свет, поплевал в них, протер тоже майкой, поставил на стол. Сбегал в сени, принес неполную бутылку, заткнутую скрученной в жгут газетой, налил полстакана гостю и полстакана себе.

– Вот, Ваня, – сказал он, придвинув к себе табуретку и продолжая начатый разговор, – мы привыкли относиться к дерьму с этакой брезгливостью, как будто это что-то плохое. А ведь, если разобраться, так это, может быть, самое ценное на земле вещество, потому что вся наша жизнь происходит из дерьма и в дерьмо опять же уходит.

– Это в каком же смысле? – вежливо спросил Чонкин, поглядывая голодными глазами на остывающую яичницу, но не решаясь приступить к ней раньше хозяина.

– А в каком хошь, развивал свою мысль Гладышев, не замечая нетерпения гостя.

– Посуди сам. Для хорошего урожая надо удобрить землю дерьмом. Из дерьма произрастают травы, злаки и овощи, которые едим мы и животные. Животные дают нам молоко, мясо, шерсть и все прочее. Мы все это потребляем и переводим опять на дерьмо. Вот и происходит, как бы это сказать, круговорот дерьма в природе. И, скажем, зачем же нам потреблять это дерьмо в виде мяса, молока или хотя бы вот хлеба, то есть в переработанном виде? Встает законный вопрос: не лучше ли, отбросив предубеждение и ложную брезгливость, потреблять его в чистом виде, как замечательный витамин? Для начала, конечно, – поправился он, заметив, что Чонкина передернуло, – можно удалить естественный запах, а потом, когда человек привыкнет, оставить все, как есть. Но это, Ваня, дело далекого будущего и успешных дерзаний науки. И я предлагаю, Ваня, выпить за успехи нашей науки, за нашу Советскую власть и лично за гения в мировом масштабе товарища Сталина.

– Со встречей, – поспешно поддержал его Чонкин.

[...]

– Из хлеба или из свеклы? – поинтересовался Чонкин.

– Из дерьма, Ваня, со сдержанной гордостью сказал Гладышев. Иван поперхнулся.

– Это как же? спросил он, отодвигаясь от стола.

– Рецепт, Ваня, очень простой, – охотно пояснил Гладышев. – Берешь на кило дерьма кило сахару...

Опрокинув табуретку, Чонкин бросился к выходу. На крыльце он едва не сшиб Афродиту с ребенком и в двух шагах от крыльца уперся лбом в бревенчатую стену избы. Его квало и выворачивало наизнанку.

[...]

– О господи! с беспросветной тоской высказалась вдруг Афродита. – Еще одного дерьмом напоил, ирод проклятый, погибели на тебя нету. Тьфу на тебя! Она смачно плюнула в сторону мужа. Он не обиделся.

– Ты, чем плеваться, яблочка моченого из погреба принесла бы. Плохо, вишь, человеку.

Gladishev.... got two dusty glasses from the cabinet, held them to the light, spat in them, wiped them with his T-shirt too, and placed them on the table. Then he dashed out to the passageway and came back with a partially full bottle of home brew that had a twist of newspaper for a stopper. Gladishev poured his guest half a glass, then poured himself half a glass also.

"There you go, Vanya," he said, pulling the stool up to him and picking up their conversation. "We usually react squeamishly to shit as if it were something bad. But if we look into the matter we see that it could be the most valuable substance on earth, because all life comes from shit and returns to shit."

"In what sense?" Chonkin asked politely, gazing with hungry eyes at the cooling omelet, but then deciding not to begin before his host.

"Any sense you like." Gladishev developed his idea without taking any notice of his guest's impatience. "Judge for yourself. The ground must be fertilized with shit for a good harvest. All the herbs, grains, and fruits that we and the animals eat grow up out of shit. The animals give us milk, meat, wool, and all the rest of it. We use it all and then change it back into shit again. That's the origin of – how should I put it – of the circulation of shit in nature. Let's ask ourselves for a moment why we should use shit in the form of meat or milk or even this bread here, that is, in processed form. A legitimate question arises: Wouldn't it be better to rid ourselves of our biases and false squeamishness and use shit itself in pure form as a sort of wonder vitamin? In the beginning of course," Gladishev corrected himself, noticing Chonkin wince, "we could remove its natural smell and then, when man was used to it, leave it just the way it is. But, Vanya, that task belongs to the distant future and to future exploits of science. Vanya, I propose we drink a toast to the success of our science, to Soviet power, and to the person of Comrade Stalin, a genius of worldwide fame."

"To our meeting." Chonkin hastily seconded the toast.

[...]

You make it from grain or from beetroot?" asked Chonkin curiously.

"From shit, Vanya," said Gladishev with restrained pride.

Chonkin choked. "What do you mean?" he asked, moving away from the table.

"Very simple recipe, Vanya." Gladishev was eager to explain. "You take a kilo of sugar to a kilo of shit..."

Knocking his stool over, Chonkin dashed for the door. He almost knocked Aphrodite and the baby down on the porch. Two steps from the porch he braced his forehead against the log wall of the hut, where he vomited himself inside out.

[...]

"Oh, Lord!" said Aphrodite suddenly, in hopeless anguish. "You've gone and given another one shit to drink, you goddamned tyrant, there's no getting rid of you. I spit on you!" she said and spat juicily in her husband's direction.

Gladishev, however, did not take offense.

"Instead of spitting you'd be better off bringing a marinated apple up from the cellar. Can't you see the man's not feeling well?"[5]

Vladimir Voinovich, The Life and Extraordinary Adventures of Private Ivan Chonkin (1969)

Scientists got to work on Lenin's idea of using peat to distill vodka. They came up with various methods for distilling from anything – including manure and human feces. This inspired the poet Demyan Bedny to come up with a little rhyme:

Вот настали времена:
Что ни день – то чудо.
Водку гонят из говна,
По три литра с пуда.
Русский ум изобретет
В зависть всей Европы:
Скоро водка потечет
В рот из самой жопы.

Who'd have ever thought of it:
Never-ceasing wonders.
Vodka's now distilled from shit,
A pood will yield three liters.
Russian ingenuity –
Much to Europe's envy –
Soon will figure how to pass
Vodka straight to mouth from ass.[6]

"Out with *Samogon!*" At the bottom, a poem:
He who uses a *samogon* apparatus
To make profits for himself
Is turning sugar to poison
People's health to ruin!

Just as the Russians were being allowed to drink again, in the mid-1920s, the United States was going through a period of prohibition. The American mafia eagerly took advantage of the situation and became powerful thanks to the capital coming from bootlegging. Of course, they had to look to Russia for a good recipe for *samogon*. After all, who had more experience with prohibitions on alcohol?

Ostap Bender, the hero of Ilf and Petrov's *The Little Golden Calf*, knew many recipes for *samogon* that he was eager to market to ritzy customers from Chicago, if only they would pay...

Переводчик стал жаловаться на иностранцев.

– Поверите ли, на меня стали бросаться: расскажи да расскажи им секрет самогона. А я не самогонщик. Я член Союза работников просвещения. У меня в Москве старуха-мама.

– А вам очень хочется обратно в Москву? К маме?

Переводчик жалобно вздохнул.

– В таком случае заседание продолжается, – промолвил Бендер. – Сколько дадут ваши шефы за рецепт? Полтораста дадут?

– Дадут двести, – зашептал переводчик. – А у вас, в самом деле, есть рецепт?

– Сейчас же вам продиктую, то есть сейчас же по получении денег. Какой угодно: картофельный, пшеничный, абрикосовый, ячменный, из тутовых ягод, из гречневой каши. Даже из обыкновенной табуретки можно гнать самогон. Некоторые любят табуретовку. А то можно простую кишмишевку или сливянку. Одним словом-любой из полутораста самогонов, рецепты которых мне известны.

Остап был представлен американцам. В воздухе долго плавали вежливо приподнятые шляпы. Затем приступили к делу.

Американцы выбрали пшеничный самогон, который привлек их простотой выработки. Рецепт долго записывали в блокноты. В виде бесплатной премии Остап сообщил американским ходокам наилучшую конструкцию кабинетного самогонного аппарата, который легко скрыть от посторонних взглядов в тумбе письменного стола. Ходоки заверили Остапа, что при американской технике изготовить такой аппарат не представляет никакого труда. Остап со своей стороны заверил американцев, что аппарат его конструкции дает в день ведро прелестного ароматного первача.

The interpreter started complaining about the foreigners: "Believe it or not, now they've started getting on my case: 'Tell us the secret of making moonshine, tell us!' But I'm a member of the Educational Workers' Union, not a bootlegger. My elderly mama lives with me in Moscow…"

"So you really want to get back to Moscow, then? Back to your mama?"

The interpreter sighed plaintively.

"If that's the case, then the meeting is still in session," Bender said. "How much will your bosses there give for the recipe? Will they give a hundred and fifty?"

"They'll give two hundred," the interpreter whispered. "What, do you really have a recipe on you?"

"I'll dictate it to you this minute, well, the minute I get the money. Whatever kind you want: from potatoes, wheat, apricots, barley, mulberries, buckwheat kasha… you can even make moonshine out of an ordinary wooden stool. Some people really like moonshine distilled from wooden stool mash. Or I could give you plain old Afghan-style hooch, or else plum brandy. In a word, any one of the hundred and fifty moonshine recipes I happen to know by heart."

Ostap was introduced to the Americans. Their politely raised hats floated in the air for a long time. Then everyone commenced the work at hand.

The Americans picked wheat-mash moonshine, which attracted them with the ease of its production. They spent a long time writing down the recipe. As a kind of free bonus, Ostap told the American peasant petitioners how best to construct a personal still that could be easily hidden in the deep bottom drawer of a desk, away from prying eyes. The petitioners assured Ostap that with American technology it would be no trouble at all to make a still like that. Ostap, for his part, assured the Americans that a still of his design would yield a bucket a day of marvelous, aromatic *pervach*.[7]

Ilya Ilf and Evgeni Petrov, The Little Golden Calf (1931)

Fortunately, not all products had to undergo "processing" before use. Cologne, lotions, dandruff shampoo, and "hygienic alcohol" – for washing your hands, for example, or rinsing your mouth – could be drunk straight out of the container. Extracts of lemon or juniper berry were added in. (If necessary, you could also dump in a cooked egg yolk to absorb the filth. Discard after using.) Cologne was highly popular in the 1960s and 1970s in particular, specifically for treating a hangover. It was a cheap product and could be obtained in the early hours too, unlike real alcohol, which was available only after nine o'clock in the morning.

None of this was healthy. Boris Segal noticed this when he worked in a clinic as a psychiatrist in the 1970s: "The extent to which drinking is indulged in at wine-producers and vodka distilleries, and at factories where alcohol is used for technical purposes, is unbelievable. Russian workers do not hesitate to drink technical spirits that contain toxic admixtures. In 1970, 27 Moscow workers poisoned by spirits containing phosphoric compounds were admitted to a hospital where I was a consulting psychiatrist. Many of those patients died."[8]

Russians know dozens of methods for extracting alcohol from all sorts of things and for purifying the alcohol contained in harmful substances, *all of them dangerous and best avoided*. One of them goes back to days of yore, when they knew how to make malt spirits but had not yet heard of distilling. They would let the mash stand for a little while, then heat it and quickly take it outside, into the cold. The vaporized alcohol was collected and filtered. It stank to high heaven. This method was not forgotten and is still used to make *samogon*. The "vodka" is poured into special barrels and frozen. Then a spigot is turned on, the unfrozen alcohol flows out, and the water with the fusel oil can be discarded as a block of ice. Alcoholics sometimes employ the same principle with brake fluid, lotions,

Vladimir Mayakovsky's *"Samogon Be Gone!"* Cover for a 1923 anti-*samogon* poem (with *lubok* style illustrations by the author).

cleaners, medical products, and the like. Only a few tools are needed: a cold environment, a bucket (or a glass), and an iron rod. The brake fluid (or whatever) is carefully poured over the rod as it is held over the bucket; the unwanted elements freeze to it while the alcohol drips into the bucket. After that, the liquid is poured through a cotton cloth, which adds another step of filtration. Another option is to spread shoe polish on a slice of bread and lay the "sandwich" in the sun upside down. The alcohol is drawn into the bread. Then you take a knife, turn the sandwich right side up, scrape the shoe polish off, and you're left with your own version of French toast... You can do something similar with insecticide used to kill cockroaches. All you have to do is spray that on a slice of brown bread and eat it. *(Or so they say. Don't try this at home.)*

There was nothing but Benedictine on the shelf of shop No. 28.

"Let's buy a bottle," I said.

"Are you crazy?" my mate Tarzan exploded. "That's a women's drink. Let's get some cucumber face lotion from Auntie Dusya."

"But Benedictine's stronger than vodka. I used to drink it in Riga."

"Okay, you win."

Tarzan and I wandered off to the park with our Benedictine. We were on our third bottle when Pashka Plaksin joined us. Pashka was famous in Chapaevsk as an alcoholic and a master sewer of felt boots. Many people made boots on the quiet for it was as absurd to look for them in the shops as it would have been to ask for a ferry boat at a chemist. Pashka's boots were the best in town – to own a pair was like having a Pierre Cardin suit in your wardrobe. Those who wanted to jump the queue would slip him a bottle of something. That is how Pashka became a drunkard. In the mornings he shook so much he could not even pull up a glass with his scarf. Someone had to slip a stick between his lips and pour the wine straight down his gullet.

Pashka produced two bottles of pure surgical spirit donated by a grateful customer. The next thing I knew was an agonizing pain in my head and back. I opened my eyes to see someone giving me an injection.

"What did you drink?" a voice asked.

"Surgical spirit," I rasped.

"You can't get that in the chemists. Where did it come from?"

"A friend gave it to me."

"That was no friend. If the police had not found you and brought you here you would have died. That was industrial spirit and it has burned up your kidneys."

It seemed that after leaving Tarzan and Pashka I had fallen info a snowdrift. Some passing police had pulled me out and hauled me in to the sobering-up station.[9]

C. S. Walton, *Ivan Petrov: Russia through a Shot Glass* (1999)

There are several methods for purifying furniture polish. The easiest one involves pouring the polish into a bucket or pan. You light the liquid and wait until the orange flame turns blue. At that point, the harmful chemical substances have burned off and the polish is ready for consumption. ***Do not do this: it is harmful to the immune system.***

There is also a brand of glue called BF. This popular glue has been nicknamed Boris Fyodorovich, which calls up an association with Yeltsin, whose name was Boris Nikolayevich. Using BF, you can separate the alcohol in, say, a cleaning product from the chemicals. If you add BF and salt to the mix and stir it vigorously with a stick, a lump forms in the liquid. After you remove the lump, you can drink what's left.

The narrator in Vladimir Makanin's novel *The Underground* is a down-and-out writer, a *yaryga*, someone who has drunk away his high social and economic status. He even ends up in a psychiatric institution. The staff is happy to have this erudite patient, and he is allowed to drink with them.

Я сел.

– А раз сели, то и выпьем!

– Холин-Волин повел глазом на пустой (уже пустой) графинчик на столе.

Я, конечно, осторожничаю, спрашиваю – а можно ли мне пить сегодня?

Холин-Волин в хохот:

– Вот какой деликатный больной пошел нынче!

Но Иван Емельянович становится на миг серьезным:

– Обеденный укол вам следует пропустить. А ваш утренний – выпивке не помеха. Вы не спьянеете быстро?

Я улыбнулся.

– Тогда поехали! – уже умоляюще вскрикнул Холин-Волин.

Не так уж они оба были пьяны, скорее, возбуждены предстоящей им выпивкой – почему бы и нет? Большие начальники, волею случая вынужденные дежурить в праздник, пьют себе в удовольствие. (Могут себе позволить. Еще и меня позвали. Могли не позвать.) Иван Емельянович с серьезным видом извлек из шкафа емкий медицинский сосуд с красной сеткой делений. Спирта там на треть. Иван всмотрелся в черточки делений, черпнул ковшиком в другом сосуде (вода) и строгой рукой доливает до нужных градусов – как я понял, до сорока любимых и привычных. Смешивает ложечкой, сбросив туда маленькую щепотку марганцовки. ("Серебряная! – подмигнул мне про ложечку Холин-Волин.) Теперь капля молока из пакета. Иван Емельянович (улыбнулся) помешивает. И, наконец, пропускает через снежно-белую марлю, отцеживая редкие хлопья.

Было общеизвестно, что продажная водка в этот год в магазинах всюду плоха, так что академический ее эквивалент созидался прямо на глазах: с улыбкой и без объяснений. Виртуозно, но не торопясь.

I took a seat.

"Well, since you sat down, that calls for a drink!"

Kholin-Volin's eyes darted toward the empty (already) decanter on the table.

Naturally, I play it safe. I ask, "May I have a drink today?"

Kholin-Volin chuckles:

"Look at the well-mannered sort of patient we have nowadays!"

But Ivan Yemelyanovich turns serious for a moment:

"We should skip your lunch-time injection today. However a little drink won't interfere with your morning one. You don't become quickly inebriated, do you?"

I smiled.

"Then let's get going!" Kholin-Volin exclaimed, starting to sound a bit desperate.

They were not so much drunk as just excited by the prospect of drinking – and why not? When circumstances compel the higher-ups to do a shift over a holiday, they are certainly entitled to a drink. (They can permit themselves. But they also invited me. They didn't have to.) With an earnest look on his face, Ivan Yemelyanovich took a large medical flask crisscrossed with a network of red lines. It was one-third full of pure alcohol. Ivan peered closely at the scale markings, scooped a dipper into another container (water), and with a scrupulous hand poured it in until it reached the proper percentage (as far as I could tell the ever-popular and familiar forty). He mixed it with a spoon, adding just a pinch of manganese. ("Silver! – Kholin-Volin winked at me in regard to the spoon.) Now, a drop of milk from a packet. Ivan Yemelyanovich (he smiled) stirs it. And, finally, he pours it through some snow-white gauze, filtering out any flakes.

Everyone knew that the vodka you could buy in stores that year was universally bad, so its academic equivalent was being produced right before our eyes: with a smile and without explanation. Masterfully, but without haste.[10]

Vladimir Makanin. *The Underground, or a Hero of Our Time* (1999)

In *The Curse of Usovo*, Reinout van der Heijden writes about several men who had the good fortune to "work as welders at the Khrunichev rocket factory. Every morning, they were given a pine resin solution for cleaning the weld surfaces. In this case, salt was added and the mixture was stirred until all of the resin stuck to the stirring implement. This cocktail was known as a 'piner,' because the user's belches smelled of conifers. As for cleaning the weld points... Well, many a regulation was violated in the venerable space industry."[11] Even the Red Army was not immune to Gorbachev's temperance campaign, as evidenced by an article that appeared in *The Times* on October 25, 1985:

LITERARY TIPPLERS

Евгения Ивановна поднесла ко рту рюмку, по-мужицки вставила ее в рот и опрокинула в горло, а затем, сморщившись, стала чистить копченую рыбку. – Вот так надо пить! Бравурно, прибавила она.

Yevgeniya Ivanovna raised the shot glass to her lips, inserted it right into her mouth like a real *muzhik*, tossed its contents down her throat, shuddered, and then turned to cleaning the smoked fish. "That's how you drink! With bravado," she added.[14]

Nikolai Leykin, *The First Steps* (1901)

Нет, теперь я пил без тошноты и без бутерброда, из горлышка, запрокинув голову, как пианист, и с сознанием величия того, что еще только начинается и чему предстоит быть.

No, now I drank without nausea and without a sandwich, straight from the bottle, throwing back my head like a pianist, conscious both of the grandeur of the fact that it was just beginning and of what lay ahead.[15]

Venedikt Erofeev, *Moscow to the End of the Line* (1970)

Вот бутылка с водкой, так называемый спиртуоз. А рядом вы видите Николая Ивановича Серпухова.

Вот из бутылки поднимаются спиртуозные пары. Посмотрите, как дышит носом Николай Иванович Серпухов. Поглядите, как он облизывается, и как он щурится. Видно, ему это очень приятно, и главным образом потому, что спиртуоз.

Here we have a bottle of vodka, the so-called *spirituoso*. And next to it we have Nikolai Ivanovich Serpukhov.

Spirituosic vapors emanate from the bottle. See how Nikolai Ivanovich Serpukhov breathes them in with his nose. Take a look at how he licks his lips and squints his eyes. It appears that he takes great pleasure in this, mainly because it is *spirituoso*.[16]

Daniil Kharms, "On Phenomena and Existences No. 2" (1934)

Остановясь, раздвинув ноги, от которых столбами пала тень на жниве, Захар вынул из глубокого кармана полушубка бутылку, глянул на нее против солнца и весело ухмыльнулся, увидав, что и бутылка и водка в ней зарозовели. Закинув голову, он вылил водку в разинутый рот, не касаясь бутылки губами, и хотел было запустить ее выше самого высокого, самого легкого дымчатого облачка в глубине неба.

He stopped with legs spread wide, and their shadow fell in huge pillars upon the crop stubble. Removing the bottle from the deep pocket of his sheepskin, he held it up against the sunlight and grinned with pleasure when he noticed that the bottle and the vodka inside it had turned a rosy pink. Throwing back his head he poured out the vodka into his gaping mouth, not touching the bottle with his lips, and then he reared back to launch that bottle higher than the highest and most delicate hazy cloudlet in the depths of the heavens above.[17]

Ivan Bunin, "Zakhar Vorobyov" (1912)

"As a result of the rising price of vodka and diminished sales, Soviet troops are increasingly deprived of their favorite beverage. They are reacting to these restrictions by stealing and consuming fluids from tanks and aircraft containing alcohol. Fighter pilots in particular are stealing deicing fluid." The deicing fluid was distilled before it was drunk. And in order to cover up the theft, water was substituted. Not surprisingly, this could have dramatic consequences. When the deicing tanks were used, the water froze on the wings and the aircraft became too heavy. Besides requiring deicing fluid, a MiG-25 bomber also uses dozens of liters of alcohol for its brake systems. This is why it was known as the "flying restaurant." Because such alcohol was very pure and had a very high market value, it was also known as "white gold."

Пить просто водку, даже из горлышка, – в этом нет ничего, кроме томления духа и суеты. Смешать водку с одеколоном – в этом есть известный каприз, но нет никакого пафоса. А вот выпить стакан «ханаанского бальзама» – в этом есть и каприз, и идея, и пафос, и сверх того еще метафизический намек. [...]

Пьющий просто водку сохраняет и здравый ум, и твердую память или, наоборот, теряет разом и то и другое. А в случае со «слезой комсомолки» просто смешно: выпьешь ее сто грамм, этой «слезы» – память твердая, а здравого ума как не бывало. Выпьешь еще сто грамм – и сам себе удивляешься: откуда взялось столько здравого ума? И куда девалась вся твердая память?..

Даже сам рецепт «слезы» благовонен. А от готового коктейля, от его пахучести, можно на минуту лишиться чувств и сознания. Я, например, лишался.

Лаванда – 15 г.
Вербена – 15 г.
«Лесная вода» – 30 г.
Лак для ногтей – 2 г.
Зубной эликсир – 150 г.
Лимонад – 150 г.

Приготовленную таким образом смесь надо двадцать минут помешивать веткой жимолости. Иные, правда, утверждают, что в случае необходимости жимолость можно заменить повиликой. Это неверно и преступно! Режьте меня вдоль и поперек – но вы меня не заставите помешивать повиликой «слезу комсомолки», я буду помешивать ее жимолостью. Я просто разрываюсь на части от смеха, когда вижу, как при мне помешивают «слезу комсомолки» не жимолостью, а повиликой...

To drink vodka, even from the bottle, is nothing other than weariness of spirit, and vanity. To mix vodka with eau de cologne, there is a certain caprice, but no pathos whatsoever. But if you drink a glass of "Balsam of Canaan" there is caprice and an idea and pathos, and beyond that a hint of the metaphysical. [...]

Somebody drinking just vodka will keep his right mind and a clear head or he'll lose them both at once. But in the case of a "Tear of a Komsomol Girl" it's funny – you drink 100 grams of this "Tear" and your head is clear and it's as if you never had a right mind. You drink 100 more grams and you'll be surprised at yourself. Where did all the right mind come from? And where did your clear head get to?

Even the "Tear"'s recipe itself is fragrant. And from the prepared cocktail, from its odorousness, it is possible to lose consciousness for a moment. I did, for example.

Lavender Toilet Water	15 g.
Verbena	15 g.
Herbal Lotion	30 g.
Nail Polish	2 g.
Mouthwash	150 g.
Lemon Soda	150 g.

The mixture prepared this way must be stirred for twenty minutes with a sprig of honeysuckle. Some, it is true, maintain that in case of necessity it is permissible to substitute dodder for honeysuckle. But this is both incorrect and criminal. Cut me up left and right, but you won't get me to stir it with dodder. The "Tear" I'll stir with honeysuckle. I simply die laughing when I see somebody stirring a "Tear of a Komsomol Girl" with dodder and not honeysuckle.[12]

Venedikt Erofeev, *Moscow to the End of the Line* (1970)

It is certainly not the case that freeloaders and drifters are the only ones who like to drink and that they were the only ones who had problems during restrictions on the sale of vodka. Sana Valiulina writes about student life in Moscow in the 1980s. The students also did plenty of experimenting with cocktails.

For Aliya, the worst was when he would drink cologne for lack of an alternative. At such times he would look her straight in the eye, squint, and dramatically throw his head back. She would see his Adam's apple convulsing, and he would again look her in the eye defiantly and blow the cologne vapors into her face. Sometimes Anton would make his signature cocktail – cologne mixed with beer – and force a strong-smelling drink into Aliya's hands, but even then he respected her wishes and simply snorted contemptuously when she poured it down the sink.

LUSHES

Когда он опять посмотрел на Алферова, тот уже крепко спал, навзничь раскинувшись и странно выбросив одну руку.

Так в русских деревнях спят шатуны пьяные. Весь день сонно сверкал зной, проплывали высокие возы, осыпая проселочную дорогу сухими травинками, – а бродяга буйствовал, приставал к гулявшим дачницам, бил в гулкую грудь, называя себя сынком генеральским, и наконец, шлепнув картузом оземь, ложился поперек дороги, да так и лежал, пока мужик не слезет с воза. Мужик оттаскивал его в сторонку и ехал дальше; и шатун, откинув бледное лицо, лежал, как мертвец, на краю канавы,– и зеленые громады возов, колыхаясь и благоухая, плыли селом, сквозь пятнистые тени млеющих лип.

When he looked at Alfyorov again the man was already sound asleep, flat on his back with one arm oddly thrown out.

This was how drunken tramps used to sleep in Russian villages. All day in the shimmering, sleepy heat tall laden carts had swayed past, scattering the country road with bits of hay and the tramp had lurched noisily along, pestering girl vacationists, beating his resonant chest, proclaiming himself the son of a general and finally, slapping his peaked cap to the ground, he had lain down across the road, and had stayed there until a peasant climbed down from his hay wagon. The peasant had dragged him to the verge and driven on; and the tramp, turning his pale face aside, had lain like a corpse on the edge of the ditch while the great green bulks, swaying and sweet-smelling, had glided past, through the dappled shadows of the lime trees in bloom.[18]

Vladimir Nabokov, *Mary* (1926)

Я не говорю, что пьяных у нас много. Пьяных не так чтобы много. За весь месяц май я всего одного в лежку пьяненького встретил.

А лежал он поперек панели. И чуть я на него, на черта, в потемках не наступил.

Гляжу – лежит выпивший человек, ревет и шапкой морду утирает.

– Вставай,– говорю,– дядя! Ишь разлегся на двухспальной.

Хотел я его приподнять – не хочет. Ревет.

– Чего,– говорю,– ревешь-то, дура-голова?

– Да так,– говорит,– обидно очень...

– Чего,– говорю,– обидно?

– Да так,– говорит,– люди – какая сволота.

– Чем же сволота?

Да так, мимо шагают... Прут без разбору... Не могут тоже человеку в личность посмотреть: какой это человек лежит – выпивший, или, может, несчастный случай...

I'm not saying that we have a lot of drunks. There aren't so many drunks that you'd call it a lot. The whole month of May I only ran into one drunk flat on his back.

And he was lying right across the sidewalk. I almost stepped on him in the dark, the devil.

I look, and there's a drunk person lying there, howling and wiping his face with his hat.

"Get up, fella'!" I say. "That's no double bed ya' got there."

I wanted to help him get up, but he didn't want to. He kept howling.

"What are ya' howling about, knucklehead?" I say.

"Ya' know," he says, "it really hurts my feelings..."

"What hurts your feelings?" I say.

"Ya' know." he says. "People are such swine."

"How so?"

"Ya' know, they walk right by... They push on no matter what... They can't take a look at a man's personality, look at what kind of man's lying there – whether he's drunk, or maybe had an accident..."[19]

Mikhail Zoshchenko, "Sober Thoughts" (1928)

Эти люди вовсе бесстрастны: идут, ни на что не обращая глаз, молчат, ни о чем не думая. В комнате их не много добра; иногда просто штоф чистой русской водки, которую они однообразно сосут весь день без всякого сильного прилива в голове, возбуждаемого сильным приемом, какой обыкновенно любит задавать себе по воскресным дням молодой немецкий ремесленник, этот удалец Мещанской улицы, один владеющий всем тротуаром, когда время перешло за двенадцать часов ночи.

These people are utterly impassive: they walk along looking neither to right nor to left, saying nothing and thinking nothing. In their rooms you will not find much in the way of belongings, at most, there may be a bottle of pure Russian vodka, which they mechanically sip away at all day without ever experiencing that rush of blood to the head induced by a more vigorous intake of liquor, such as young German craftsmen, the cavaliers of Meshchanskaya Street, enjoy when they lord it alone over the pavements in the small hours of the morning after their Sunday binge.[20]

Nikolai Gogol, "The Portrait" (1834)

Бывало, как наш Хохрюков запьет, так не то что люди, даже собаки воют. Посудин же – хоть бы тебе нос у него покраснел! Запрется у себя в кабинете и лакает... Чтоб люди не приметили, он себе в столе ящик такой приспособил, с трубочкой. Всегда в этом ящике водка... Нагнешься к трубочке, пососешь, и пьян... В карете тоже, в портфеле...

When our Khokhryukov used to drink, not only the people, even the dogs would howl; but Posudin, his nose doesn't even turn red! He shuts himself up in his study and laps. He has arranged a little kind of box on his table with a tube, so that no one can know what he's up to, and this box he keeps full of vodka. All one has to do is to stoop down to the little tube, suck, and get drunk. And out driving, too, in his portfolio.[21]

Anton Chekhov, "Murder Will Out" (1885)

"As long as he's still not resorting to toothpaste, there's hope," Aliya told Vera. Diluted Pamarin-brand Bulgarian toothpaste was the last and lowest circle in the career of any Russian alcoholic, and what followed was undefined oblivion.[13]

Sana Valiulina *Het Kruis* (2000)

When the Soviet Union ceased to exist in 1991, the fifth state monopoly on vodka was immediately terminated. In 1992, everything was liberalized: production, importation, sales, scale of production, and prices. The market was awash in vodka, especially vodka of dubious quality. And perhaps for the first time in Russian history, the normal state of affairs was turned on its head. Vodka was rubbed on shoes to improve comfort; farmers applied a mix of vodka and mint to their skin to ward off bees; vodka-based ointments were sold for dying hair and treating dandruff. People cleaned their furniture, applied a coating to keep their glasses from freezing over, and removed ice from their car windows. All with vodka.

To this day, countless Russians drink *samogon* and surrogates. There is a good chance that the government will reintroduce a vodka monopoly in order to protect the populace. But will the people allow themselves to be protected?

11

Vodka in Russia (1917-Present)

После печального эпизода с упившимся арестантом – ввели строгий лимит: 150 грамм на брата. Полностью упразднить эту моду – на такую затею даже Тихомиров не решался: попробуй отмени вино в России – революция вспыхнет...

Ever since the death of the drunken jailbird, consumption had been strictly limited to 150 grams a head. Not even Makepeace ventured to introduce total prohibition in a Russian city: try it and you'll get a revolution at once.[1]

Abram Tertz, *The Makepeace Experiment* (1963)

WORLD WAR I WAS still raging when the February 1917 revolution occurred. The tsar was deposed and the Provisional Government led by Alexander Kerensky took control. It continued the sobriety policy imposed by Nicholas II, banning beverages with an alcohol content of more than one-half percent. Harsh prison sentences awaited those found guilty of public drunkenness. But the law and reality do not necessarily coincide in Russia. Ivan Bunin recalls what it was like in the famous Moscow restaurant Praga: "Spring of '17. The Prague Restaurant is filled with people, music, and waiters. Wine is forbidden, but almost everyone is drunk. The music brings sweet agony to one's soul."[2]

The political situation changed again dramatically when Vladimir Ilyich Lenin (1917-1924) and his Bolsheviks toppled the Provisional Government in October. Russia became the world's first communist country. The takeover involved relatively little bloodshed, but the anarchy that followed was staggering. In Petrograd (which was renamed Leningrad in 1924 and then changed back to St. Petersburg in 1991), soldiers and sailors got plastered after they had expelled the government from the Winter Palace. People literally drowned in cellars flooded with wine. Others tore down the walls of liquor stores. In her memoirs of the revolution, the Bolshevik Maria Joffe wrote that there "were puddles of vodka next to the stores. All of Petrograd was drunk. During those days, one regiment would have sufficed to capture the city. Soldiers had been sent into the city to calm the people, but the soldiers got drunk."[3] A report to the Ministry of Defense states that during a raid on a wine store "twenty-two soldiers died of heart attacks, twenty-six were killed when the tank containing alcohol exploded, and nine were downed by bullets fired at the tank." Dozens of cities suffered from "drunken pogroms." In Veliky Ustyug, for example, a historic town in northern Russia, there was a big vodka factory with enormous stores of alcohol left over from the prohibition period. A couple of months after the October Revolution, the stores were looted by residents. An enormous explosion resulted, with an estimated death toll of more than four hundred.

While chaos reigned throughout the country, the Bolsheviks continued the battle against alcohol unabated. "It was under the banner of abstinence that the communist workers and peasants party of Russia was born and is consolidating," read one slogan. In November 1917, the authorities decided to "liquidate" the stores of alcohol in Petrograd. To that end, they created a new position: People's Commissar to Combat Alcohol. But behind the scenes the partying continued full throttle, as evidenced in the testimony provided by Konstantin Paustovsky, who described the years of revolution, civil war, and the young Soviet state at great length:

Москва была полна слухами о разгульной жизни анархистов в захваченных особняках. Чопорные старушки с ужасом шептали друг другу о потрясающих оргиях. Но то были вовсе не оргии, а обыкновеннейшие пьянки, где вместо шампанского пили ханжу и закусывали ее окаменелой воблой.

Moscow was rife with rumors about wild living by anarchists in expropriated mansions. Prim ladies with horror whispered to one another about shocking orgies. But these were no orgies, just ordinary drink-fests, where instead of champagne they were drinking home brew accompanied by dried fish as hard as stone.[4]

Konstantin Paustovsky, *The Beginning of an Unknown Age* (1956)

Advertisement for the "First All-Russian BookLotto," in which the value of every winning ticket could be redeemed for books. The 30-kopek ticket quotes Lenin: "They (vodka and other narcotics) will draw us back to capitalism, rather than forward to communism."

Maxim Gorky, the patriarch of Soviet letters, wrote about liquor stores that were raided and "pigs" who got drunk. People drowned in vats of vodka "while their comrades kept drinking from the same vats." In his study *The Drunken Society*, Boris Segal refers to a conversation that he had with witness Roman Goul, a writer who later emigrated to the West: "After the manager of a liquor factory ordered the alcohol to be removed from the containers into manure fields, peasants squeezed the spirit out of the manure with their feet and drank it."[5]

Bolshevik leader Lenin was initially consistent in his approach to alcohol abuse. He had an aversion to alcohol and drank rarely, standing by his motto that "vodka and other narcotics will draw us back to capitalism, rather than forward to Communism." He believed that wholesale drunkenness was a threat to the revolution and ordered that drunkards and looters be shot without mercy. Slogans sound nice, but bullets are more effective. The poet Demyan Bedny wrote:

Аль ты не видел приказов на стене –
о пьяницах и вине?
Вино выливать велено,
а пьяных – сколько не будет увидено,
столько и будет расстреляно.

You did not see the orders on the wall
Concerning drunks and liquor?

The booze is to be poured out in the street,
And drunkards, however many you may meet,
That will be the number to be shot.[6]

Some people did not wait for the executions and emigrated. Or they took their own life in the realization that their class's days were over. The person in the following passage thought that drinking was over and done with.

Первым погибнул в городе Огонек-классик, честный ярыга, спившийся студент, – умер, – повесился, оставив записку: «Умираю потому, что без водки жить не могу. Граждане и товарищи новой зари! – когда класс изжил себя – ему смерть, ему лучше уйти самому. Умираю на новой заре!»
Огонек-классик умер пред новой зарей.

Ogonyok, the Classicist, was the first to die in the town, an honorable drunk, an alcoholic student – he died – he hanged himself, leaving this note:
"I'm dying because I cannot live without vodka. Citizens and comrades of the new dawn! – when a class has outlived itself – death to it! Better it should go away by itself. I am dying at the new dawn!"
Ogonyok the Classicist died before the new dawn.[7]

Boris Pilnyak, *The Naked Year* (1921)

In 1918, the authorities established Glavspirt, the state enterprise for alcohol, which reopened some of the 1,736 alcohol factories from before the revolution, with the aim of producing "technical and medicinal alcohol." In line with that move, they also stepped up efforts to combat home distillers in rural areas, declaring them "enemies of the people." In 1920, all wine, cognac, and vodka factories were nationalized, and sales of wine with alcohol content of less than 12 percent was allowed once again.

The Bolsheviks blamed the *kulaks* for turning the rural proletariat into drunkards. They also should have taken some responsibility themselves, as evidenced by Ivan Bunin's diary entries. He quotes the Kiev edition of the newspaper *Izvestiya*: "Unfortunately, the Ukrainian countryside remains just as Gogol described it – ignorant, anti-Semitic, illiterate… Among the commissars there is bribe-taking, extortion, drunkenness, and violations of every legal principle every step of the way… Soviet officials win and lose thousands at cards and support their distilleries with their drunkenness."[8]

Meanwhile, the Soviets too were having problems with the public health versus state revenues dilemma. In 1922, Lenin had a change of heart, and despite "serious moral reservations" he characterized alcohol production as a river of

"One's smart the other's a fool! One grabs a book, the other heads to a tavern."

gold. One year later, the need for revenue was so dire that the production of and trade in vodka was permitted again. At first, the vodka could not contain more than 14 percent alcohol; then that was raised to 20 percent and finally to 30. This vodka was known popularly as "Rykovka," in honor of Alexei Rykov, the chairman of the Council of Ministers. One of the official arguments for resuming production, according to Rykov, was the need to protect the country from dangerous *samogon*.

The years of civil war and War Communism took their toll. The country was still far removed from the shining future envisioned by Lenin. In his memoirs, Konstantin Paustovsky described the desperation:

> Электричество в Одессе давно не горело. О нем забыли. Лампочки обросли пыльной корой. Выключатели, если их случайно поворачивали, взвизгивали от ржавчины.
>
> Единственным человеком из нас, который радовался этому, был Володя Головчинер.
>
> – У каждого времени, – говорил он с апломбом, как будто открывал необыкновенную истину, – есть свой стиль. Стиль нашего времени – приближение к патриархальной жизни. Посудите сами, электричество ушло в невозвратное прошлое. Трамвайные рельсы зарастают крапивой. На площадях городов цветет картошка. Из воздуха исчезли последние молекулы копоти. Вместо обуви мы носим греческие котурны, а вместо водки пьем чистую воду. По-моему, это прекрасно. Начинается золотой век.

> Electricity in Odessa had not been working for a long time. It had become a distant memory. Lightbulbs were encrusted in dust. Light switches, if someone chanced to turn one, squealed with rust.
>
> The only one of us who was happy about all this was Volodya Golovchiner.
>
> "Every era," he stated with aplomb, as if he had discovered a profound truth, "has a style all its own. The style of our time is a return to patriarchal living. Judge for yourself: electricity is a thing of the past. The tramway rails are growing over with nettles. Potato plants are flowering in town squares. The last molecules of soot are disappearing from the air. Instead of shoes, we are wearing Greek buskins, and instead of vodka, we're drinking pure water. I think that's wonderful. A golden age is dawning."[9]

> Konstantin Paustovsky, *A Time of Great Expectations* (1958)

In short, it was time for drastic economic measures. With the introduction of the New Economic Policy (NEP, 1921), which temporarily permitted a free market, the struggle against alcohol faded completely into the background, and in 1925 the state monopoly on liquor was reinstated: It was once again possible to produce (state) vodka of 40 percent. This gave rise to big celebrations, and there were even calls to make October 1, 1925 – the day on which the flow of vodka was restored – a national holiday. That did not happen, but on that date in Moscow some 4,500 dead-drunk people ended up at police stations or hospitals. In Tver, the local soviet hung a sign on a newly opened bar reading "In memory of Lenin," and in the city of Sereda (the present-day Furmanov), a surcharge of 15 kopeks was paid on each bottle of vodka to defray the costs of a club building dedicated to him. Restaurants shot up like mushrooms, even though not many people could afford their prices.

Lenin's successor, Joseph Vissarionovich Stalin (1923-1953), in an uncharacteristic fit of candor while speaking to a delegation of foreign workers in 1927, said that vodka was an evil, but that he had to choose between two evils: becoming dependent on capitalists by turning a number of important factories over to them for a substantial sum, enough to provide the Soviets the working capital needed to develop industry; or instituting a vodka monopoly. Stalin opted for the second evil. To press home his argument, he alleged that Lenin himself had told him that the reintroduction of the monopoly in time of need was temporarily possible as an "unusually effective method." The liquidation of vodka sales remained the most important objective, and production was supposed to decrease steadily. Alcohol as a luxury item was to have fully disappeared from the Soviet Union within ten years.

In 1927, Stalin ended the NEP and presented his first five-year plan, in which everything was subordinated to the development of heavy industry. During the collectivization of agriculture in 1931, millions of *kulaks* were subjected to internal exile. Famine broke out. The arts came under the yoke of Socialist Realism, whereby all artistic expression had to serve the purposes of the communist ideal.

Partly because of a number of good harvests, alcohol consumption increased again in 1935. "Life has become happier," a *Pravda* headline proclaimed. Mikoyan repeated these words by Stalin in his famous toast: "Life is happier now. You cannot drink yourself blind to a good and satisfied life. Life has become happy, and thus there can be drinking, but in such a way that you don't take leave of your senses." *Pravda* ran ads for Dutch *dzhin* (gin), and Stalin was increasingly propounded as the loving father of the fatherland, who kept watch over everyone.

Гетманов, поглядев на портрет Сталина, висевший на стене, поднял рюмку и сказал: – Что ж, товарищи, первый тост за нашего отца, пускай он нам будет здоров.

Сказал он эти слова немного грубоватым, товарищеским голосом. В этом простецком тоне суть состояла в том, что всем было известно величие Сталина, но собравшиеся за столом люди пили за него, прежде всего любя в нем простого, скромного и чуткого человека. И Сталин на портрете, сощурившись, оглядывая стол и богатую грудь Галины Терентьевны, казалось, говорил: "Вот, ребята, я раскурю трубочку и подсяду к вам поближе".

– И верно, хай наш батько живет, – сказал брат хозяйки, Николай Терентьевич. – Что б мы все без него делали?

Он оглянулся на Сагайдака, придерживая возле рта рюмку, не скажет ли тот чего-нибудь, но Сагайдак посмотрел на портрет: "О чем же, отец, еще говорить, ты все знаешь", и выпил. Все выпили.

Getmanov filled the glasses with vodka. With great deliberation, the guests began choosing something to eat. Looking at the portrait of Stalin on the wall, Getmanov raised his glass and said: "Well, comrades, let's drink first of all to our father. May he always remain in good health!"

He pronounced these words in a rather bluff, free-and-easy tone of voice. The implication was that they all understood Stalin's greatness very well, but were drinking to him now as a human being, someone they loved for his straightforwardness, modesty and sensitivity. And Stalin himself, looking up and down the table and then at the ample breasts of Galina Terentyevna, appeared to say, "Very well, fellows, I'll just get my pipe going. Then I'll bring my chair up a bit closer."

"That's right, may our father live for a long time! Where would we be without him?" said Nikolai Terentyevich.

Holding his glass to his lips, Getmanov looked round at Sagaydak, as though expecting him to say something. Sagaydak just looked at the portrait as if to say, "What more needs to be said, Father? You already know everything." He downed his vodka and the others followed suit.[10]

Vasily Grossman, *Life and Fate* (1959)

Four years later, there was another decline: The Soviet Union made large-scale grain deliveries to Germany under the terms of the Molotov-Ribbentrop Pact, the August 1939 nonaggression treaty between the Soviet Union and Nazi Germany. When Germany nevertheless invaded the Soviet Union in 1941, vodka production initially dropped even further, in part because of the repurposing of factories – for example, Distillery Number 1 was now producing fuel for Molotov cocktails.

After World War II, alcohol consumption returned to previous levels. The resistance to drinking on the part of some peasants before the war had been broken during their service in the military. After all, Stalin had reinstated an old tradition by giving Red Army soldiers 100 grams of vodka a day. Back on their native soil, the former soldiers continued to drink. To this day, veterans have heated discussions about the extent to which the Red Army contributed to alcoholism in the Soviet Union.

Stalin died in 1953. Many people were genuinely moved, but there were plenty who had no reason whatsoever to mourn his loss; on the contrary, they celebrated. Secretly, unless they were already interred in a camp. As a victim of Stalin's terror says in Adam Hochschild's book *The Unquiet Ghost*: "I still regard March 5 [the day Stalin died] as a holiday. Beginning with the first day. I even managed to get vodka in camp. We chipped in: it was two hundred rubles plus ten cans of meat, and for that, a guard brought us a bottle of vodka."[11]

After Stalin, Nikita Khrushchev (1894-1971) emerged as the political leader in 1956. Politically and culturally, he loosened the reins somewhat (earning the period from the late fifties to early sixties the designation "the Thaw") and there was gradually greater prosperity, and with it greater vodka consumption. In the early 1960s, families on average spent one-fifth of their income on alcohol. Those who were less well off spent comparatively more: up to 40 percent. The state vodka came in bottles with an aluminum cap. The bottle had to be emptied in one sitting, which was no problem because no one intended to leave anything for the following day.

Meanwhile, the policy on alcohol continued to limp along based on two hoary notions: First, temperance campaigns were good, but, second, they should not be too stringent, because the national budget depended on revenues from vodka sales. At that point, a half liter cost 2.87 rubles, a quarter liter 1.47. Every Soviet citizen knew those prices. Beer vending machines and even beer halls appeared, since Khrushchev thought that after a day of hard work a laborer had the right to a mug of beer. He was deposed in 1964. He was not given a place in the Kremlin wall behind Lenin's mausoleum, and he never had a vodka named for him.

There was little change in alcohol policy under Leonid Ilyich Brezhnev (1906-1982). The authorities remained opposed to alcoholism, while they were in favor of "normal" drinking – because of the revenue it generated. Moreover, there was the danger that "a country with clear heads would pose a threat to the Soviet leaders, who were trying to poison our spirit with alcohol," as the exiled Russian writer Viktor Nekrasov wrote in 1977. Nevertheless, in 1972 Brezhnev issued regulations targeting alcohol abuse, but they were generally ignored. Alcohol consumption continued to rise during that period, and new vodka brands even came onto the market.

Although Russians initially fared better during this period, and even though many people today look back nostalgically at the relatively abundant

1970s, the last ten years under Brezhnev are known as a period of "stagnation." Revenues from the production and sale of alcohol accounted for around 20 percent of the state budget, and in some years the figure reached nearly 30 percent. In rural areas, according to Russia expert Marius Broekmeyer, even the rhythm of village life was largely driven by vodka. In *Russia's Sorrow*, he writes: "It is absurd but true: The 'cashpoint plan' has to be implemented per region and per province before the civil servants can be paid. This means that services and commerce must first raise the money needed to pay salaries. If the plan is not met, vodka is deployed since it always sells quickly. As a result, salaries are first paid in place A, where it is possible to buy alcohol, which results in revenues, and then the civil servants in place B have their turn. And so on."[12]

The period of stagnation was also a period of false appearances. Party leaders manipulated the economic data, suggesting that the harvests were more than abundant and that crime was nonexistent. Life in the world's most fortunate country was much rosier in theory than in practice. And no one said anything about alcohol abuse. Thus, in 1966 sociologist Grigory Zaigrayev wrote: "It is well known that in capitalist countries the main cause of alcohol abuse is exploitation, poverty, unemployment and lack of civil rights. [...] The establishment of the socialist system in our country eliminated the socioeconomic and political conditions that lead to drinking by the working masses in capitalist societies."[13] Professor Vladimir Rozhnov, the director of the Moscow Department of Psychotherapy, contributed to the discussion in 1969: "Prior to the October Revolution the need for alcoholic beverages was engendered by a social system oriented against the people. [...] The Great October Revolution eliminated the social causes of alcoholism for the first time in human history. [...] Yes, we have many reasons to be proud of ourselves. [...] The overwhelming majority of Soviet people are distinguished by exceptionally high moral standards. [...] Only a very small group of our people abuse alcohol."[14]

Upon Brezhnev's death in 1982, income from vodka sales accounted for one-third of the national budget. His two immediate successors did not last long. Yuri Andropov (1982-1984) did not drink much. As secretary general of the Communist Party, he did step up efforts against freeloading and drunkenness. Control commissions appeared everywhere. Vodka sales were allowed only after 11 AM, the "wolf's hour" (at the Moscow Puppet Theater, a fairy tale character would appear in a window every hour, and at eleven o'clock it was the turn of the gray wolf). At the same time, Andropov introduced inexpensive vodka. The people affectionately referred to this vodka as Andropovka and devised acronyms such as *Vsesoyuznoye Odobreniye Deyatelnosti Kommunista Andropova* (All-Soviet Approval of the Activities

Earlier Soviet vodka labels were rather simple: "Vodka" or "Spirits". Only later (right) did the Soviets introduce a bit more style.

of Communist Andropov) or **Vot On Dobry Kakoy,** Andropov (What a Great Guy This Andropov). Andropov's successor, Konstantin Chernenko (1984-1985) was party leader for too short a time to carry out real changes, even if he had wanted to. Drinking on the job remained commonplace.

It was Mikhail Sergeyevich Gorbachev (1985-1991) who finally got serious about combating alcohol, beginning in 1985. His *glasnost* (openness) and *perestroika* (reformation) policies unleashed a fresh wind as he relaxed censorship and released political prisoners. Gorbachev himself was a moderate drinker. This gave rise to the nickname "secretary mineral." And in popular parlance Gorbachevka was the name given to vodka of dubious quality. His rigorous temperance campaign created a great deal of bad blood and contributed to the economic collapse a few years later. Many Russians are convinced that the sharp decline in vodka sales threw the country's wobbly financial foundation out of kilter once and for all. Despite the freedom of expression and new opportunities for private initiative, the lion's share of the populace was not enthusiastic about *perestroika*. "Just words and no vodka," they said with displeasure. In 1987, this populace was said to have drunk one billion bottles of cologne and one million liters of glass cleaner at a time when 2.7 million liters of confiscated *samogon* were dumped.

Meanwhile, the economy went even further downhill, with scarcely any goods available in the stores. Standing in line was a daily routine. Whenever people saw a queue, they would immediately join it and only then ask what was for sale at the front of the line. Even if you yourself didn't need the product, if would certainly be something good to barter. The queues had their own subculture with their own rules and customs. It was completely normal for people to take turns in line or to ask their neighbor to reserve their spot. Many people always took along a "just-in-case" bag (*avoska*, a string shopping bag)

Soviet era ad for "bitters" (Starka, gin and Zubrovka).

and a length of string (for rolls of toilet paper). The lines for alcohol were especially notorious; they often reeked, and fistfights were more the rule than the exception. Some people made a profession out of standing in line: They would hire themselves out to others. You could also buy a bottle of vodka from those professionals before two in the afternoon.

Vladimir Sorokin described the queue subculture in a book that consists of dialogues between waiting people:

– Ин вино веритас...

– Что?

– Истина, говорю, в ханке.

– Эт точно... я на ночь хотел взять погреться, жена скурвилась, не дала...

– Ничего, щас восполнишь.

– А что там... бутылка на троих. Понюхать только.

– Ты гигант.

– Ххе... [...]

– Давай на подоконнике...

– Открывай.

– Держи сырок.

– Ага.

– Падла... теперь не делают кепочек... ровная...

– Зубами подцепи...

– Ммм... опля...

– Ну вот.

– Ну чо, пей, парень, первым.

– Спасибо.

– Держи.

– Будьте здоровы. . . . . фууу..аа

– Вась, ты теперь, я дотяну.

– . . . . хааа...

– Чтоб не последняя. . . . . . . ой бля...

– *In vino veritas*...

– You what?

– Truth is in booze, I said.

– Quite right too... I wanted to get some to keep warm for the night, but the wife wouldn't let me, the bitch...

– Never mind, you'll make up for it now.

– What d'you mean... one bottle between three. Just catch a whiff of it.

– Mr. Universe...

– Ha ha... [...]

– Put it on the window sill...

– You open it.

– Here, take the cheese.

– Uh-huh.

– Shit... don't make the tops... straight...

– Use your teeth...

– Mmmm... oopla...

– There we are.

– Okay mate, you first.

– Thanks.

– Here.

– Cheers......... phew... aah...

– You next, Vasya, I'll survive.

– .... aah...

– Here's hoping this isn't the last............ aah, shit...[15]

Vladimir Sorokin, *The Queue* (1983)

In 1990, Gorbachev's temperance measures were repealed. His policy had been a failure. To this day, Gorbachev remains unpopular in Russia, among all strata of the population. This is largely attributable to his temperance policy.

A year later, the August 1991 coup took place. Tanks rolled through the streets of Moscow and there was sporadic shooting, but, under the inspiring leadership of Boris Nikolayevich Yeltsin, the power grab failed. Many people thought that it was because the coup plotters were drunk. Premier Pavlov was even said to have suffered from alcohol poisoning. "With Vice President Gennady Yanayev's hands trembling at their press conference, the plotters looked somber, like schoolboys who expected to get punished for a prank. They had appeared increasingly paralyzed – some of them were intoxicated with vodka. Hence, they were subjected to laughter by journalists who attended their press conference, and by ordinary people who saw the conference on television," Cristoph Neidhart reports in his book *Russia's Carnival*.[16]

In December 1991, the Soviet Union imploded. Fifteen independent countries came into being, with Russia far and away the biggest one. Boris Yeltsin became its first president (1991-2000). His brave actions during the coup had made him popular among the people. Moreover, a normal, recognizable Russian was back in power, a man who enjoyed his liquor but who did revamp the wavering vodka policy by abolishing the state monopoly on vodka. All controls on production, importation, sales, quantities, and prices were lifted. A selection of vodkas flooded the market, whereby foreign brands were considered the crème de la crème. Absolut was popular, as were Finlandia and Smirnoff. New foreign vodkas with Russian names were launched, such as Rasputin, but most of them contained alcohol diluted with water. Russian pseudo-vodkas also cropped up: water diluted with industrial vodka imported from Poland, Germany, or the Netherlands. The foreign bottles were often reused and then filled with counterfeit vodka. Yeltsin stood by for a year and a half, but then on June 11, 1993, he reintroduced the state monopoly, which was now the sixth in Russian history. That same year, 1993, he was unable to keep Russia from becoming the most hard-drinking nation in the world, with average consumption of half a liter of vodka per adult male every two days. In 1996, the estimates of the number of deaths caused by alcohol poisoning varied from 60,000 to 150,000. In 1998, the inspection service that monitored enforcement of the monopoly was abolished, but there had been no controls for some time already. Around 2000, Russia achieved a new milestone: on average a new vodka came onto the market every day, ranging across all price classes, sizes, types, and qualities. Russians who had made money quickly (the "new Russians") introduced vodkas bearing their own name. Some politicians, such as the nationalist Vladimir Zhirinovsky, appeared on labels as historical figures. Regions also tried to distinguish themselves with their own vodka, such as the Bashkir region's Kalashnikov, with a bottle in the shape of a machine gun.

Late in the summer of 2006, Russia was still seeing hundreds of alcohol-related deaths. Because the government intended to introduce a new licensing system, but the new seals were not yet ready, vodka disappeared from the shelves. People again turned to home-distilling in large numbers and sold inferior alcohol. Dozens of people mysteriously turned completely yellow. It turned out that they had drunk antifreeze, a blow that most already-weakened livers could not withstand.

In 2007, there was intense lobbying in the State Duma for the introduction of a seventh vodka monopoly. Vladimir Putin, whom Yeltsin had installed as his successor in 1999, supported the idea. But it was not only for the sake of public health – the intention was also to take on the large mafia-like structures surrounding the big vodka companies and secure their revenues. In 2008, however, Putin left this up to his successor, Dmitry Medvedev, who introduced a few restrictions on sales and advertising, but did not reinstate the monopoly.

The vodka cycle is the one stable factor in Russia. Young people might well take a liking to beer, but most Russians see it as a glorified soft drink, and vodka producers need not feel threatened by it. No matter what the political situation, Russians drink (and curse) vodka. Moreover, vodka producers know how to keep up with the times. For example, a vodka glass was recently designed with a USB port. You plug it into your computer, so that your friends can check if you are drinking along with them during a virtual party.

CURRENCY

Until the end of the Soviet Union, and even after its demise, vodka offered security to the Russians. After all, vodka is as steady as a rock, because it can't lose its value in one fell swoop and because demand for it never flags, nor does the supply. People in rural areas – and increasingly the urban population as well – know how to distill it under the most difficult circumstances. Thus, vodka often functions as "currency." And of course, that means a black market. It is also a popular "gift." In Dutch, we might call that greasing the palm, or even bribery. Russians simply see it as a reward for service rendered.

Shortly before the outbreak of World War II, the virtuous soldier Ivan Chonkin is ordered to guard an airplane not far from a *kolkhoz*. He soon runs into the *kolkhoz* chairman Golubyev, who likes to drink. But at the time of their meeting he has had nothing to drink for well over a day. This deprivation was the result of sheer willpower, since Golubyev had to go the recruitment office to register for the front.

– Ты это вот чего... – начал опять Чонкин и вдруг решительно, со стуком поставил флягу перед Голубевым. – Пить будешь?

Председатель посмотрел на флягу и облизнулся. Недоверчиво посмотрел на Чонкина. – А ты это по-товарищески или в виде взятки?

– В виде взятки, – подтвердил Чонкин.

– Тогда не надо.

Иван Тимофеевич осторожно подвинул флягу назад к Чонкину.

– Ну, не надо, – так не надо, – легко согласился Чонкин, взял флягу и поднялся.

– Погоди, – забеспокоился председатель. – А вдруг у тебя такое дело, что его можно решить и так. Тогда выпить мы сможем не в виде взятки, а по-товарищески. Как ты считаешь?

Чонкин поставил флягу на стол и подвинул к председателю.

– Пей, – сказал он.

– А ты?

– Нальешь, и я выпью.

Спустя полчаса, когда содержимое фляги резко уменьшилось, Голубев и Чонкин были уже закадычными друзьями, курили папиросы "Казбек", и председатель задушевно жаловался на свои обстоятельства. [...]

Председатель безнадежно тряхнул головой и одним глотком принял в себя полстакана самогона. Чонкин сделал то же самое. Сейчас разговор дошел до самой выгодной для Чонкина точки. Надо было не упускать момента.

"Listen, here's the thing…" Chonkin began again, and then with sudden decisiveness banged the flask down in front of Golubev. "You want a drink?"

The chairman looked at the flask, licked his lips, then looked mistrustfully back up at Chonkin. "You doing this out of friendship or as a bribe?"

"As a bribe," confirmed Chonkin.

"In that case, I don't." Ivan Timofeyevich carefully pushed the flask back to Chonkin.

"If it's don't, then it's don't," agreed Chonkin readily, and he took the flask and stood up.

"Hold on there," said the chairman, beginning to feel uneasy. "Why don't we say you have a problem that can be solved through regular channels. Then we can drink out of friendship and not because there's a bribe involved. What do you think?"

Chonkin put the flask back down on the desk and pushed it. "Drink," he said.

"How about you?"

"You pour, I'll drink." Half an hour later, the contents of the flask drastically decreased, Golubev and Chonkin were already bosom buddies. They sat smoking Kazbek cigarettes, while the chairman complained about his life. […]

The chairman shook his head in despair and drained a half glass of home brew in a single gulp. Their conversation had now reached the point most advantageous for Chonkin and he could not let the moment slip by."[17]

Vladimir Voinovich, *The Life and Extraordinary Adventures of Private Ivan Chonkin* (1969)

The first tsars in the Romanov dynasty, Michael Fyodorovich and Alexei Mikhailovich, paid salaries partly in alcohol in the first half of the seventeenth century. And in the nineteenth century, Lev Tolstoy referred to vodka as a lubricant: In the following passage, the character Sergei needs to buy a cross for the grave of a deceased family member.

– Где его возьмешь, крест-то? из полена не вытешешь?

– Что говоришь-то? Из полена не вытешешь, возьми топор да в рощу пораньше сходи, вот и вытешешь. Ясенку ли, что ли, срубишь. Вот и голубец будет. А то, поди, еще объездчика пой водкой. За всякой дрянью поить не наготовишься. Вон я намедни вагу сломал, новую вырубил важную, никто слова не сказал.

"Where am I going to get a cross from? I can't chop one out of a log."

"Can't chop one out of a log – what are you talking about? Take your axe, get yourself out in the forest first thing, and you can cut one there. Go on, cut a little ash tree down… and there's your cross. Either that or buy the forester a few drinks. Doesn't mean you've got to treat him for any old bit of rubbish. Couple of days ago when I broke me splinter bar I cut meself a smashing new one, and nobody said nothing about it."[18]

Lev Tolstoy, "Three Deaths" (1859)

In the Soviet Union – especially beginning in the mid-1960s – there were certain things that you could hardly get done without vodka. An electrician would not come unless you slipped him a couple of bottles, nor would the plumber or the TV repairman. If you had to consult a doctor, you needed vodka, although that profession preferred bottles of a prestigious foreign beverage, certainly for operations. If there was some government service that you needed, you would not get anywhere without vodka. In 1969, *Literaturnaya Gazeta* published a story by Grigory Gorin depicting a head of household taking stock of the family finances for the coming month:

Нет, что ни говори, жизнь нынче трудная… Сам посуди: я зарабатываю 140 рублей, жена – 100. Всего выходит 240. Это как-никак, 80 поллитровок! Кажется, жить можно?

Но теперь считай. За квартиру платить надо? Надо! Три поллитровки долой. За свет – две поллитровки, за телефон – одну. […]

В общем, туда-сюда, считай-прикидывай, а все равно на житье 30 поллитровок остается, не больше! Говоря яснее: бутылка в день. А у меня семья – три человека!.. Что есть бутылка на троих? Не мне тебе рассказывать… Так, тьфу! Щекотание горла!

Any way you cut it, life is tough these days. Think about it: I earn 140 rubles; the wife, 100 – 240 total. That'll get you 80 bottles! You'd think that's enough to live on, right?

But do the math. Do I have to pay rent? You bet! There go three bottles. Electricity – there's another two; telephone – one more. […]

All told, with one thing and another, add it all up and all you've got left is 30 bottles to live on, maximum! To put it plainly: a bottle a day. And I have a family – three of us! What's a bottle for three people? You don't need me to tell you… It's a joke! Barely enough to tickle the throat![19]

Grigory Gorin, "On the Family Budget" (1969)

The ruble was held in low regard, and ordinary people were not allowed to accept dollars or other currencies; that was the domain of black marketeers, waiters, and taxi drivers. Things were not much different in rural areas, where drivers in particular were the big earners. That meant that alcoholism was rampant among that profession. In *Russia's Sorrow*, Marius Broekmeyer quotes writer Vladimir Kuprin: "If you want me to become a lush, then let me work as a driver, but if you take pity on me, give me a job in the stable. […] Just look at our middle-aged drivers and tractor operators. Short, thick necks, heavy rolls of fat in front and behind, beady eyes, and short, seemingly swollen hands."[20] Gorbachev's temperance campaign unleashed turmoil. It was not only alcoholics who suffered mightily; rural pensioners also had a hard time of it. As Reinout van der Heijden writes in *The Curse of Usovo*: "In the spring, they needed help turning over their vegetable garden, and that was always done by tractor operators from the *sovkhoz* after hours, in exchange for a bottle of vodka. Vodka was no longer available, and initially they refused to accept home-distilled product made by Aunt Valentina. 'I might as well drink my gasoline,' one of them sneered."[21]

Soviet citizens measured their prosperity in terms of the quantity of vodka they could buy. For many years, that meant 50 bottles of vodka for an average salary and 20 for a pension. The state price for vodka was (depending on the type) between three and five rubles, but in 1986 and 1987 the shortage forced the price up to 20 rubles on the black market. Meanwhile, the average pension remained 60 rubles a month. The erosion of the ruble's value continued unabated. By the early 1990s, a pile of Soviet currency could buy you nothing.

> Most of the complaining was about vodka. By then, a half liter cost 150 rubles, although it was not to be found in the village stores. Eggs, sausage, and dairy products were also unavailable, and meat had been gone for years. [...]
>
> Pavel Ivanov figured out that on his salary he could buy only ten bottles of vodka or a pair of new shoes, which he desperately needed. He predicted that by summer he would be walking through the village barefoot and that he might have to start drinking less. "Gorbachev and Yeltsin are identical," he complained. "Both of them betrayed the country and deprived the people of alcohol."[22]
>
> Reinout van der Heijden, *De vloek van Oesovo* (1996)

Because of the shortage, in some locales even the authorities regarded vodka as currency and paid teacher salaries in cases of vodka. In the city of Nalchik, one government institution decided to settle its five months of arrears in police salaries with vodka. Instead of real money, they received eight cases from the local vodka factory. There were reports of doctors treating blood donors to a bottle of vodka.

12

Temperance

При слове «водка» русский человек начинает вести себя непредсказуемо. Как будто дыра пробивается в подсознание, и там все начинает булькать, пузыриться, ходить ходуном, а на поверхности возникают всякие-разные жесты и мимика, глаза загораются, руки потираются; кто подмигивает, кто прищуривается, кто глуповато во весь рот улыбается, кто щелкает пальцами, кто хмурится и впадает в прострацию, но никто, от верхов до низов, не остается равнодушным, выключенным из игры. Мы все в России – заложники водки в большей степени, чем любой политической системы. Короче, водка – Русский бог.

The very mention of the word "vodka" triggers unpredictable behavior in Russians. It seems to punch a hole directly into the subconscious, setting off a range of odd gestures and facial expressions. Some people wring their hands; some grin idiotically or snap their fingers; others sink into sullen silence. But no one, high or low, is left indifferent. More than by any political system, we are all held hostage by vodka. In short, vodka is the Russian god.[1]

Viktor Erofeyev, "The Russian God" (2002)

It was on account of "the weakness of the people" that Grand Prince Ivan III (1440-1505) became the first Russian ruler to tackle alcohol abuse. He ordered the closing of all public places where alcohol was served, and Muscovites were allowed to drink only on holidays. His son and successor, Vasily III, permitted the establishment of a tavern just outside Moscow where foreigners could drink to their heart's desire. The new district around it, which was also intended for foreigners, became known popularly as *Naleyka*, derived from *naley!* (pour!). Ordinary Russians are said to have looked askance at the whole business. Adam Olearius called the district *Saufstadt* ("Booze City").

By the time the Romanovs ascended to the throne in the early seventeenth century, the Russians had learned to drink vodka – to the benefit of the treasury, which grew steadily. Whenever a tsar did not think of his own purse, but instead put public health first, steps to curb alcohol consumption would fail as mere halfway measures, and a subsequent tsar would then repeal them.

Peter the Great did crack down on drunkenness. However, his own licentious drinking encouraged the ordinary people to follow his example, and they began drinking more. This in turn prompted coachmen to respond greedily to the increased demand by offering extremely cheap vodka. Peter put an end to this in 1695; he thought that readily available alcohol impeded human functioning. Drinking was fine, as long as you could still do your job. Drunks who squandered their possessions were given a cast-iron medallion weighing seven kilograms to wear around their neck, together with a sign that read "because of drunkenness," and they had to walk to the Kremlin that way. Peter also created the first sobering-up station (*vytrezvitel*), near the soldiers' barracks.

It was not until the second half of the nineteenth century that popular initiatives arose against alcohol abuse. The first sobriety associations were founded in the western part of the empire in 1859. Others soon arose and quickly spread east. The initiators were often priests acting on their own. Which is not to say that there was no resistance to them, because the financial interests were enormous.

20-го октября [1859]. Бешеная весть! Газеты сообщают, что в июле сего года откупщики жаловались министру внутренних дел на православных священников, удерживающих народ от пьянства, и господин министр передал эту жалобу обер-прокурору святейшего синода, который отвечал, что "св. синод благословляет священнослужителей ревностно содействовать возникновению в некоторых городских и сельских сословиях благой решимости воздержания от употребления вина". Но откупщики не унялись и снова просили отменить указ святейшего синода, ибо, при содействии его, общества трезвости разведутся повсеместно. Тогда министр финансов сообщил будто бы обер-прокурору святейшего синода, что совершенное запрещение горячего вина, посредством сильно действующих на умы простого народа религиозных угроз и клятвенных обещаний, не должно быть допускаемо, как противное не только общему понятию о пользе умеренного употребления вина, но и тем постановлениям, на основании которых правительство отдало питейные сборы в откупное содержание. Затем, сказывают, сделано распоряжение, чтобы приговоры городских и сельских обществ о воздержании уничтожить и впредь городских собраний и сельских сходок для сей цели нигде не допускать. Пей, бедный народ, и распивайся!

October 20th [1859]. Insane tidings! The newspapers report that in July of this year the liquor-tax collectors lodged a complaint with the minister of internal affairs against Orthodox priests who restrain the people from drunkenness, and the esteemed minister transmitted their complaint to the chief procurator of the Holy Synod, who responded, that "servants of the church have the blessing of the Holy Synod zealously to support the worthy decision which has arisen in certain segments of urban and rural populations to abstain from the use of spirits." But the tax collectors would not give up and again requested that the Holy Synod's edict be rescinded, for with the Synod's support temperance societies would spring up everywhere. Then the minister of finance allegedly informed the head of the Holy Synod that a complete prohibition of spirits by dint of promises made under oath and religious threats, which have a powerful effect upon the minds of simple folk, cannot be permitted, as it is contrary not only to the general opinion that drinking in moderation is beneficial, but also to those decrees on the basis of which the government has given out concessions for the collection of liquor revenues. Then, I hear tell, a decree was issued annulling the resolutions of the urban and rural societies concerned with abstinence and banning henceforth all town meetings and rural gatherings devoted to that purpose. So drink up, you poor people – wallow in drunkenness![2]

Nikolai Leskov, *The Cathedral Clergy* (1872)

By 1900, there were dozens of associations dedicated to combating alcohol, both private and state-run. The private ones regarded official efforts with skepticism, since the government made money from its monopoly and had no interest in getting people to give up drinking entirely. It only wanted to encourage them to use alcohol in moderation. Most of the private associations promoted complete abstinence.

Each of the various government associations had its own approach. The one in St. Petersburg was completely different from the one in Moscow. Indeed, Petersburgers generally consider Muscovites barbarians. This divide has existed ever since St. Petersburg was founded in 1703. Petersburg is the city of intellect, of Western customs, and of civilization, whereas Moscow is Asiatic, savage, and impulsive. The association in St. Petersburg emphasized cultural activities, in the belief that the principal cause of alcohol abuse was boredom and underdevelopment. It established the Nicholas II People's House, with a concert hall, a theater, and a restaurant; it opened tea houses and libraries; and it organized activities for children. Lectures were everyday fare, and visitors were attracted with presentations using the *laterna magica* (projection lamp). The People's House also included a temperance museum where images illustrated the devastating effects of alcohol. In order to keep people out of taverns, public canteens offering inexpensive meals were opened, and periodicals such as *Vestnik trezvosti* (*The Sobriety Herald*) and *Trezvoe slovo* (*The Sober Word*) were published for their general refinement.

The Muscovites were more interested in treating symptoms. The focus was on the consequences of alcohol abuse and the well-being of the drunkards; efforts were made to educate and find housing and jobs for the "unfortunates." Under the leadership of the famous psychiatrist Vladimir Bekhterev, an institution was established for combating drunkenness among the masses – a novelty in Europe at the time.

The first modern sobering-up station opened its doors in Tula in 1904. This was a place where police could drop off drunks that they had picked up on the streets. The boozer was registered, stripped to his underwear, and sent to the detox chamber, where he remained for a few hours or several days. The conditions were abominable. The small rooms held between 30 and 70 people who lay shoulder to shoulder, vomiting and defecating in a stupefying cacophony. Staff would vigorously rub the drunk's ears and force him to smell a few drops of ammonia, which he then had to drink. They poured cold water on his head, and he received cold compresses and, if necessary, artificial respiration. If these steps did not bring the severely inebriated person to his senses, he was referred to a hospital. Psychotic drunks were referred to a psychiatric hospital. The sobering-up station still evokes strong fear on the part of alcoholics.

In 1907, the Duma set up a commission to combat the alcohol problem. One of the most fanatical members was Mikhail Chelyshev: "Vodka is a horrible, accursed drink that kills everything good and pure in man. If we do not turn our attention to this [problem] and if the government remains silent, destruction and impoverishment await us and we will not be able to exist as a powerful state."[3] The commission drafted a law to regulate alcohol use, under which alcohol sales near train stations and ferry wharves were prohibited and a customer could buy no more than one half-liter bottle. Labels were to include messages such as "Drinking is a sin," "Don't get drunk," and "Vodka = poison." The hours during which alcohol could be sold were restricted, local governments were to gain greater authorities to close taverns, the illegal trade was to be curtailed, and temperance was to be taught in the schools. However, the manufacturers of alcoholic beverages did all they could to stop the law. This resistance led to a compromise through which the measures were introduced in only one district, and there only on a trial basis. For lack of alternatives, the people in that district began to drink surrogates en masse, resulting in many deaths. A huge number of arrests were made on charges of bootlegging *samogon*. In the end, the law was not enacted.

For the first time, doctors too spoke out not as representatives of the bureaucracy, but as medical practitioners with their own voice. Up to that point, most publications about alcoholism had been religious in nature, and sometimes the matter was addressed in novels and short stories. In May 1895, the Commission for the Alcoholism Question was established, the first medical initiative in this area. In 1909, it held the First All-Russian Congress on Combating Drunkenness. One of the speakers was the well-known activist Dmitry Borodin:

Our people are underfed; they become accustomed to heavy drinking over the years. Drinking has become the national characteristic of the Russian people. From the bottom up, the country is being thoroughly brutalized. Violence, stabbings, robberies and murder are endemic. Russia is flooded with a half-crazy army of vagrants and hooligans, and the sober elements of the population, dying out in the general conflagration of drunkenness, can hardly repulse the drunken brotherhood. Drunkenness eats up not only the peasant's household and income; it eats up his body and soul, it tortures a thousand-year-old tribe, cutting off the root of the race, its health and fertility. Under our very eyes, a great tragedy of life, a tragedy of the people and country, is taking place; social cruelty is growing, impoverishment of the country is growing; general dissatisfaction is growing.[4]

The temperance activists were divided over the question of what caused alcoholism. One camp believed that with improved living conditions, the urge to drink would disappear. All it took was enough diversion and alternatives to alcohol, and thus there was no need to tinker with human nature.

The other camp believed in the theory of "the bears and the bees." Those animals have a natural, instinctive proclivity for alcohol, so why should humans be any different? Individuals must shoulder the responsibility for their own drinking and must learn to steer themselves in the right direction.

Around 1890, specialized clinics came into being, the first in Kazan, which had once been the location of Russia's first taverns. Doctors administered injections of strychnine, but that didn't keep patients from quickly reverting to their old habits. Hypnosis was used, especially by psychiatrists who regarded alcoholism as a mental illness, and medical practitioners argued over whether treatment should be voluntary or administered under duress. Others contended that a course of treatment should be coupled with the patient's pledge never to drink again.

The physician Livery Darkshevich was the founder of the first clinic for alcoholics in Russia. He believed that alcoholism was the result of bad habits – people acquire a taste for it and are then unable to stop. In order to combat drunkenness, priests, teachers, and employers should remain sober. The practice of paying with vodka should end, as should the custom of celebrating holidays and important events with much drinking. People had to realize that vodka is not medicine, and bars and distilleries needed to be shut down. Even drinking in moderation was totally wrong, because every alcoholic begins with one glass.

АКТЕР. Раньше, когда мой организм не был отравлен алкоголем, у меня, старик, была хорошая память... А теперь вот... кончено, брат! Все кончено для меня! Я всегда читал это стихотворение с большим успехом... гром аплодисментов! Ты... не знаешь, что такое аплодисменты... это, брат, как... водка!.. Бывало, выйду, встану вот так... (Становится в позу.) Встану... и... (Молчит.) Ничего не помню... ни слова... не помню! Любимое стихотворение... плохо это, старик?

ЛУКА. Да уж чего хорошего, коли любимое забыл? В любимом – вся душа...

АКТЕР. Пропил я душу, старик... я, брат, погиб... А почему – погиб? Веры у меня не было... Кончен я...

ЛУКА. Ну, чего? Ты... лечись! От пьянства нынче лечат, слышь! Бесплатно, браток, лечат... такая уж лечебница устроена для пьяниц... чтобы, значит, даром их лечить... Признали, видишь, что пьяница – тоже человек... и даже – рады, когда он лечиться желает! Ну-ка вот, валяй! Иди...

THE ACTOR Formerly, before my organism was poisoned with alcohol, old man, I had a good memory. But now it's all over with me, brother. I used to declaim these verses with tremendous success – thunders of applause... you have no idea what applause means... it goes to your head like vodka! I'd step out on the stage – stand this way – [*Strikes a pose*] – I'd stand there and ... [*Pause*] I can't remember a word – I can't remember! My favorite verses – isn't it ghastly, old man?

LUKA Yes – is there anything worse than forgetting what you loved? Your very soul is in the thing you love.

THE ACTOR I've drunk my soul away, old man – brother, I'm lost... and why? Because I had no faith... I'm done with...

LUKA Well – then – cure yourself! Nowadays they have a cure for drunkards. They treat you free of charge, brother. There's a hospital for drunkards – where they're treated for nothing. They've owned up, you see, that even a drunkard is a human being, and they're only too glad to help him get well. Well – then – go to it![5]

Maxim Gorky, *The Lower Depths* (1902)

Herbalists in the countryside brewed all sorts of potions against the "devil's blood" that had a nauseating effect when combined with vodka. For example, drunks who were trying to kick the habit were told to drink vodka mixed with mice, fish, the sweat of a white horse, the placenta of a black pig, vomit, snakes and worms, grease, maggots, urine, and the water used to wash cadavers. Another course of treatment practiced by quacks involved locking the drunkard inside a shack and giving him nothing but food drenched in vodka. After about five days he would be so profoundly sick that he would have a lifelong aversion to alcohol.

Although the church warned about drinking to excess in sermons and literature, overall it had a tolerant attitude toward alcohol. Priest Dmitry Bulgakovsky published a book with Bible quotes about drinking. He explained in the preface: "Never despair of reforming an alcoholic, and do not pronounce accusatory verdicts in a definite fashion upon him. It is better to warm him with your love, forget everything even to the point of forgiving his scandalous behavior as the consequences of a weakening mind and failure of the will."

It could be that this charitable attitude was partly attributable to the use of alcohol among the clergy itself, whereby monks were usually judged more harshly than priests, who had to work for a living. They worked their own land, for which they were dependent on help from the farmer-parishioners. If they did not offer alcohol before, during, and after the work, that help would not be forthcoming. And the priest's primary jobs – baptisms, marriages, and funerals – also entailed the consumption of vodka. He simply had to drink and willingly accept this occupational necessity. Some clergy advocated financial independence for priests so that there would be less need to pal around with the parishioners and they would have an easier time maintaining their moral authority.

There were certainly some priests in rural areas who resisted such mores and established abstinence groups. Others had peasants swear an oath of total abstinence under an icon. They were sometimes helped by employers who demanded that their staff take such an oath, or by wives who dragged their husbands to church for that purpose.

One original and certainly very nice institution was what was known as "registering." The drunk would go to the priest, take an oath not to drink any liquor for a certain time, and sign his name at the bottom of a document presented by the priest as additional confirmation. Many priests worked with all their might to combat drinking, thereby exercising a great deal of sensitivity for how sick their patients were. This pledge often began with one day, and the period was then extended gradually. This was a salutary function of the Russian church, and it certainly deserves gratitude and appreciation on that account. It helped many, many people to get back on their feet.[6]

Egbert Engberts, *Herinneringen aan Rusland* (1929)

The year 1911 saw the establishment of Temperance Day, observed on September 29. The holiday, which was established by the All-Russian Labor Union of Christian Abstainers, was celebrated with sermons, lectures, and processions throughout Russia. Streetcars bearing placards drove through the cities, and women sold brochures, pamphlets, and postcards. Something similar took place in 1914, but this time during the three days before Easter, when Russians traditionally live it up after the long period of fasting.

The temperance campaign set the clergy at odds with the authorities, who favored drinking in moderation, whereas the church aspired to complete abstinence. But by now even Tsar Nicholas II had become convinced that action was needed. During his travels around the country, he had observed that all segments of society were receptive to a strict temperance policy. People were fed up. Women would show up at the factory gate on payday to keep their husbands from going to the bar. In St. Petersburg, female workers broke their male colleagues' strike when they went to the bar on payday. Fifty women stormed into the bar, smashed the bottles, and forced the men outside. Other women besieged liquor stores.

In reaction, local governments were given the authority to impose prohibition on a city or district. The tsar contemplated additional measures. Alcohol "is ruining the spiritual and economic vigor of many of my subjects." However, no new measures or legislation were enacted, and the conflict with the church did not escalate either: The outbreak of World War I put an end to the discussion. Nicholas II ordered that vodka could not be sold anywhere during mobilization, with the exception of first-class restaurants. Many people were happy about this. During a demonstration in August 1914, they carried banners bearing slogans such as "Long live sobriety" and "Long live the great sower of sobriety – the tsar."

TOLSTOY

One of the most vehement opponents of alcohol and drunkenness was Count Lev Nikolayevich Tolstoy (1829-1910). The world-famous author of *Anna Karenina* and *War and Peace* saw the error of his ways around his fiftieth birthday.

Без ужаса, омерзения и боли сердечной не могу вспомнить об этих годах. Я убивал людей да войне, вызывал на дуэли, чтоб убить, проигрывал в карты, проедал труды мужиков, казнил их, блудил, обманывал. Ложь, воровство, любодеяния всех родов, пьянство, насилие, убийство... Не было преступления, которого бы я не совершал, и за все это меня хвалили, считали и считают мои сверстники сравнительно нравственным человеком. Так я жил десять лет.

I cannot think of those years without horror, loathing and heartache. I killed men in war and challenged men to duels in order to kill them. I lost at cards, consumed the labor of the peasants, sentenced them to punishments, lived loosely, and deceived people. Lying, robbery, adultery of all kinds, drunkenness, violence, murder – there was no crime I did not commit, and in spite of that people praised my conduct and my contemporaries considered and consider me to be a comparatively moral man.

So I lived for ten years.[7]

Lev Tolstoy, A Confession (1882)

Having arrived at this realization, Tolstoy was plunged into a deep spiritual crisis. He questioned everything: reason, the church, and faith. He became a vegetarian and swore off all means of pleasure. His quarrel with the church led to his excommunication. Tolstoy became the conscience of the nation, to whom enlightened souls such as Mahatma Gandhi paid close attention, while the common people regarded the writer as an oracle.

Lev Tolstoy (1910)

Tolstoy complained repeatedly about the intelligentsia, which was supposed to be a role model, but whose members were themselves often heavy drinkers. The demurral that there is no harm in having a single glass prompted this response: "You drink in moderation, but your younger brother, your wife and your children model themselves on you and may become drunkards. It is impossible to blame the environment for everything. Every individual must have the courage to overcome bad habits and serve God, not Mammon." [8]

He regarded drunkenness as the mother of all sins, because without drunkenness there would be no violence and no "sins of the flesh": "Drunkenness of any sort is a sin that makes it impossible to combat any other sin: a drunken man will not contend with either idleness, or lust, or lechery, or ambition. Therefore, in order to combat other sins, man must first and foremost free himself from the sin of drunkenness."[9] In his 1896 article *"Bogu ili Mamone?"* (God or Mammon?), Tolstoy wrote: "Enormous expanses of the best land, from which millions of now suffering families might have gained a sustenance, are covered with tobacco, grapes, barley, hops, and, above all else, rye and potatoes, which are used for the preparation of spirituous beverages, wine, beer, and, above all else, vodka. Millions of working people, who might have been producing useful things for men, are occupied in the manufacture of these articles."[10]

Ivan Bunin's 1950 work *Memoirs* suggests that Tolstoy was initially skeptical of abstinence associations:

Вспоминаю еще, как однажды я сказал ему, желая сказать приятное и даже слегка подольститься:

– Вот всюду возникают теперь эти общества трезвости...

Он сдвинул брови:

– Какие общества?

– Общества трезвости...

– То есть, это когда собираются, чтобы водки не пить? Вздор. Чтобы не пить, незачем собираться. А уж если собираться, то надо пить. Все вздор, ложь, подмена действия видимостью его...

I remember once saying to him, in an attempt to make myself agreeable and get into his good graces:

"Temperance societies are now springing up everywhere."

He frowned slightly. "What societies?"

"Temperance societies..."

"You mean, when people meet in order not to drink vodka? There is no need to meet in order not to drink. But if you have to meet, then you had better drink. What nonsense all this is, what a deceit, what substitution for action of the semblance of action..."[11]

In 1887, Tolstoy had a radical change of heart and organized his own association against drunkenness. The members included celebrities such as the painter Nikolai Ge, the explorer Nikolai Miklukho-Maklay, and the Czechoslovakian politician Tomáš G. Masaryk. The association reached its apex in 1891, with 1,100 members. The peasants in the village near Tolstoy's Yasnaya Polyana estate were also members, even though some of them had reservations. Had "their ancestors not always drunk vodka"? There were other members who had problems with complete abstinence. Bunin was not a member, but he was not unsympathetic to Tolstoy's ideas:

Вскоре вся "братия" смотрела на меня уже как на своего, и Волкенштейн – это было в самом конце девяносто третьего года – вдруг пригласил меня ехать с ним сперва к "братьям" в Харьковскую губернию, к мужикам села Хилково, – принадлежавшего известному толстовцу князю Хилкову, – а затем в Москву, к самому Толстому.

Трудно это было путешествие. Ехали мы в третьем классе, с пересадками, все норовя попадать в вагоны наиболее простонародные. Ели "безубойное", то есть чорт знает что, хотя Волкенштейн иногда и не выдерживал, вдруг бежал к буфету и с страшной жадностью глотал одну за другой две-три рюмки водки, закусывая и обжигаясь пирожками с мясом.

Soon after I had joined the Tolstoyans, all the "brethren" regarded me as one of their own; and Volkenshtein – all this happened at the very end of 1893 – suddenly invited me to go with him first to stop in at the "brothers" of Kharkov Province, to the peasants of the village of Khilkovo, which belonged to the well-known Tolstoyan Prince Khilkov, and then on to Moscow, to visit Tolstoy himself.

The journey was difficult. We went third class and had to change trains, always trying to get seats that were designated for the "common people." We ate things that "had not been killed," that is, God-knows-what, although Volkenshtein sometimes could not resist temptation and would suddenly run off to the buffet, where he would greedily gulp down two or three shots of vodka and snack on meat pies, which were so hot they burned his hands.[12]

Ivan Bunin, *The Liberation of Tolstoy* (1937)

Tolstoy devoted various essays, plays, and short stories to the anti-alcohol efforts. He was also asked to design a warning for vodka labels, resulting in an image of a skull and crossbones with the word "Poison." In the end, the proposal to print this image on labels was not adopted.

Beginning in 1926, the authorities organized campaigns to provide information about the harmful effects of alcohol, and they forced people to kick the habit.

Наконец-то вышло обязательное постановление насчет пьющих граждан. Немного им поубавили свободу действия.

Раньше, бывало, захочет, например, пьяненький покататься на трамвае – пожалуйста, выезжайте, милый человек, освежайтесь поездочкой. Не хочет на трамвае, хочет на поезде – можно и на поезде.

Одним словом, раньше к ихним услугам был любой транспорт. На чем хочешь, на том и дуй.

Ну а теперь прекратили это удовольствие. Вышло постановление. Расклеено по всем трамваям. Мол, не допущайте и так далее пьяному влезать на транспорт. А то, мол, он может с пьяных глаз сунуться под колесья. А управление после плати.

Finally they issued a mandatory decree about citizens who drink. They took away some of their freedom of action.

In the past, if a tippler wanted to take a little ride on the trolley, for instance, it was "please, be my guest, ride away, dear man, take in a bit of fresh air." If he preferred the train, he also had that option.

In short, in the past, any form of transportation was available to him. Whatever your riding pleasure, have a nice little outing.

But now they've put an end to that pleasure. A decree has been issued. It's been pasted up in all the trolleys. It says that we shouldn't let the drunk into transportation anymore. Otherwise, it says, in his tipsiness he might fall onto the tracks. And then the administration gets stuck with the bill.[13]

Mikhail Zoshchenko, "Pity the Man" (circa 1928)

In 1927, the government launched a far-ranging temperance campaign. Countless brochures and posters were generated and children received anti-alcohol instruction in the schools. A ban was imposed on giving alcohol to minors and to people who were already inebriated. Alcohol sales in theaters, parks, and movie houses were prohibited. The notorious sobering-up stations were reintroduced. An association to combat alcoholism was established in 1928, and Ukraine even had a temperance theater. The inaugural issue of the periodical *Trezvost i kultura* (*Sobriety and Culture*) was published. There were conferences and meetings devoted to combating alcohol and rallies specifically for children. They carried banners bearing slogans such as "We demand sober parents," "No *spirt* [alcohol], more sports," "Papa, don't go to the bar, bring the money home," and even "Execute the drunkards." According to reports in *Pravda*, in some cases thousands of children gathered at factory gates and in front of bars on paydays. There were reported cases of children smashing out the windows of distilleries.

A poster by the famous artist Deni, "Bring the hammer down!" with a poem by Demyan Bedny:

Drunkenness is not for joking
But for battering,
Civilly,
Roughly,

Passionately, angrily,
Hammering daily,
And each step of the way,
Never letting the enemy up for air.

"Every river begins with a stream. And drunkenness with a single glass."

However, history soon repeated itself, and in 1932 Stalin shut down all associations promoting sobriety, his motivation being, "What's better: the slavery of foreign capital or the introduction of vodka? It should be clear that we have opted for vodka, because we thought and still do think that if we have to wallow in the mud a bit for the sake of victory by the proletariat and peasants, we will do just that." In addition, he had absolutely no need for those associations. Alcohol consumption was already on the decline; huge grain shortages had arisen and the standard of living had dropped substantially, because of which people were distilling less *samogon*.

After this, there were no major temperance campaigns under Stalin. There was the occasional poster or pamphlet, such as the "moderation pamphlet" from the early 1940s that featured the slogan, "Drink, but not to recover from a hangover. Drink, but don't be a drunkard." (*Pey, da ne opokhmelyaysya. Pey, da ne upivaysya*). Khrushchev did not launch any major campaigns either.

Opportunism usually won out over ideology. Kingsley Amis, who wrote columns about all sorts of drinks and was interested in Russia, had a sharp eye, and thus the situation in 1983 did not escape his attention. "The Soviet government recently issued one of its condemnations of public drunkenness and the usual warning about stern countermeasures. This is partly routine, like official attacks on rock music, jeans and other signs of decadence, but it's also an indication that the legal booze supply is improving after a setback. Like every other industry in the USSR, the state liquor monopoly, Prodintorg, is appallingly inefficient, the constant victim of breakdowns and shortages. At such times the authorities' attitude to illicit distilling, normally harsh in the extreme, mellows wonderfully. The bootleg stills spring up in their tens of thousands and the police look the other way until Prodintorg recovers."[14] During the Brezhnev era, opportunism resulted in much play-acting. If people would pretend to work, the party leadership would suggest that the train of communism was hurtling at incredible speed toward the shining future. People looked the other way at all levels; the "black door" (the best goods were sold surreptitiously through the back door of shops and factories) became a standard concept, and drunkenness on the job was nothing special. While the propaganda machine complained about inhuman conditions in the West, it boasted towering feats of socialist construction. One such project was the Baikal-Amur Mainline (BAM). The route of this rail line was shorter than the Trans-Siberian line but an exceptional engineering challenge due to geographic obstacles such as mountains, marshes, and rivers. It was the biggest civil engineering project in history. But here too, the official motto from those years held true: "Wherever there is work, there is also drinking." Dutch journalist Willem Oltmans visited the Soviet Union and reported his impressions in the 1976 book *USSR 1976-*

1990: "In his comfortable Moscow apartment, I spoke with the famous director Vladlen Troshkin, who has done a series of superlative films – some of them for television – about the lives of students working their way through college in Siberia. I remembered one passage from a BAM film in which a young student was lectured by his comrades during a public gathering about his alcoholism, or at least about his excessive drinking."[15]

Under party leaders Yuri Andropov (a teetotaler) and Konstantin Chernenko (a serious drinker), the realization sunk in that alcohol abuse had assumed staggering proportions. In the early 1980s, 30 percent of the household budget in rural areas went to alcohol. Still, the government did not make truly serious attempts to address this. Then, on May 16, 1985, only two months after he took office, Gorbachev issued Edict No. 369 of the Presidium of the Supreme Soviet, also known as the "drunk edict," which announced an intensification of efforts to combat drunkenness. The opening salvo for the campaign was a public letter from a despairing housewife about her drunk husband. It elicited thousands of reactions, after which the Politburo took action.

Although Gorbachev had taken an interest in the alcohol problem at earlier points in his career, critics contended that it was mostly his wife Raisa who prompted him to seriously tackle the "socially dangerous problem." In Politburo member Yegor Ligachev, the party's chief ideologue, Gorbachev found an enthusiastic supporter of the campaign. Vodka became Public Enemy Number 1, and all energy had to be devoted to eliminating addiction to drink. The resolution "On Measures to Defeat Drunkenness and Alcoholism" adopted by the Central Committee of the Communist Party, and printed in *Pravda* on May 17, 1985, stated that "under current circumstances, in which the creative force of our socialist system and the advantages of our Soviet lifestyle are becoming increasingly evident, ever greater importance is attached to observance of the principle of communist morality and the vanquishing of harmful habits and remnants from an earlier time, specifically nasty phenomena such as drunkenness and the abuse of alcoholic beverages."

Gorbachev believed that the previous short-term campaigns had been halfhearted, and he demanded that party commissions, ministries, labor unions, managers, and local governments adopt measures to curb alcohol abuse. The use of alcohol during receptions and banquets was to be banned entirely, with harsh penalties for violations. Radio, television, and movie theaters were supposed to air anti-alcohol films or entertain their audiences with sports and examples of healthy living. Authors such as Valentin Rasputin described characters in their books who expressed regret over their addiction to drink. In Giuseppe Verdi's opera *La Traviata*, censors cut a scene showing binge drinking; two other operas were removed from the repertoire entirely because of their emphasis on drinking, and there were calls to edit the works of Alexander Pushkin and Omar Khayyam. A scene was cut from the 1959 Sergei Bondarchuk film *Sudba cheloveka* (*The Fate of a Man*), based on the novel of the same name by Mikhail Sholokhov, in which a Soviet soldier symbolically challenges advancing Germans by offering them a glass of vodka.

In September 1985, "volunteers" established the All-Union Association of Volunteers in the Struggle for Moderation, and in January 1986 they began publishing a periodical with the time-honored title *Trezvost i kultura* (*Sobriety and Culture*).

This time they did not stop at fine words, censorship, and declarations of intent. The price of vodka skyrocketed, the age at which young people could buy alcohol was raised from 18 to 21, liquor stores closed their doors, and the stores that were left could be open only five hours a day. In the city of Chelyabinsk in the Urals, 146 out of 150 distilleries shut down operations. Restaurants could serve alcohol only after two o'clock in the afternoon, and so at that time – the new "wolf's hour" – they were filled with men expectantly looking at their watches. People spoke of "mausoleums" (liquor stores, because of the long lines to get in), "Gorbachev's noose" (the queue in front of the liquor store itself), or "storming the fortress" (shoving matches in the queue).

> Joke: There's a long line in front of a liquor store. A drunk can't stand it any longer and walks away angrily to kill Gorbachev. He returns a little later. "Well, did you do it?" they ask him. "What do you mean?" the drunk grumbles. "That line was even longer..."

Vodka manufacturers produced soft drinks, and in some places stylish bus shelters were built using glass made from the millions of vodka bottles that had been destroyed. In fact, there were too few bottles left for the remaining vodka, so now it was marketed in beer, mineral water, or cola bottles. The production figures for spirits plunged, and the wine trade was also hard hit. The temperance ideal consumed entire vineyards; in four years' time, the country lost two-thirds of the land devoted to growing grapes, some of it dating back centuries.

Drunks disappeared from the street. In some rural districts – the Sobriety Zones – all liquor stores were closed, whereas in others vodka was rationed. Vodka became a favorite product for speculators, and a bottle could always be obtained from taxi drivers or waiters for a king's ransom. Moreover, vodka took the function of currency away from the ruble to an even greater extent. In the countryside especially, hardly anything got done unless you paid in vodka.

People were very skeptical toward Gorbachev's measures. One well-known story concerns a director of a watch factory in Uglich who wanted to finance an alcohol-free wedding but could not find a couple willing to take him up on his offer.

Nevertheless, most newspapers were full of praise for the campaign and applauded the results of the struggle against "the green serpent." The number of teetotalers is said to have increased 30 percent in two years; (legal) alcohol sales were down 40 percent, and a dramatic decrease was reported in occupational injuries, traffic accidents, and crimes of passion. In 1986 and 1987, 500,000 more children were born than in comparable periods over the previous 20 years, and 300,000 fewer people died. The life expectancy of Russian men increased from 63 to 65 years. Per capita alcohol consumption nearly bottomed out: from a consistently high ranking among European countries, the Soviets dropped to next-to-last place (according to official figures, that is). A Ukrainian minister even predicted that there would be no more drinking whatsoever by the year 2000.

Because of the anti-alcohol efforts, doorposts, lampposts, and notice boards were full of ads for courses of treatment in special clinics for kicking the habit. Hypnotists offered their services; you could get help from the church, and incurable alcoholics could have the Polish drug Esperal implanted subcutaneously, making you sick as a dog if you had even a sip of vodka. The famous singer Vladimir Vysotsky is said to have continued drinking even with Esperal, attempting to cut the implant out from his skin.

In C.S. Walton's *Ivan Petrov*, the alcoholic Vanya goes to the famous clinic run by Doctor Burenkov in Chelyabinsk.

At the clinic we joined 25 other men, each accompanied by his wife or mother. We introduced ourselves. I was surprised to see the alcoholics were not all ordinary working men like me. There was a surgeon who confessed he had once been so drunk that he had fallen on top of a patient on the operating table. Next to me sat a Hero of the Soviet Union, with medals on his jacket but no shirt under it; he had sold his clothes for a drink. Professor Burenkov said to him: "Well, you defeated the fascists but you allowed vodka to defeat you."

The Hero looked sheepish.

First Burenkov gave us each a bitter herb drink, then a massive dose of Antabuse. Next we had to down a glass of vodka. The Antabuse reacted badly with the vodka and soon we were vomiting and writhing in pain. It is hard to see two dozen men retch and groan all around you without feeling dreadful yourself. I thought I was going to die. Professor Burenkov strode around the group roaring: "Anyone want another drink?"

The relatives outside were excitedly watching the drama through a window, beating on the glass and cheering: "Give them more vodka!"

Burenkov injected us with camphor and made us lie on mattresses with our left arms above our heads in order not to strain our hearts. Later he took us all outside. We sat under trees, feeling life return. The doctor showed us slides of swollen livers and the abnormal brains of children of alcoholics. That night we took our trains home, clutching our supplies of Antabuse.

As Burenkov's popularity grew throughout the country he stopped practising. An unknown number of people died after anxious wives and mothers slipped Antabuse into food. It had no smell or taste so alcoholics consumed it unknowingly and then choked to death after they had had a few drinks. Women usually administered the Antabuse in good faith – they were simply desperate to keep their menfolk out of prison.[16]

C. S. Walton, *Ivan Petrov: Russia through a Shot Glass* (1999)

In September 1988, the authorities abandoned a number of the campaign's measures, and scarcely two years later the entire temperance law was declared a mistake and repealed. In his 2006 book *Ponyat perestroyku* (*Understanding Perestroika*), Gorbachev writes that the temperance campaign was a realistic and responsible decision, the failure of which was attributable most of all to its disastrous execution. Solid principles were betrayed by the "omnipotence of commando methods... But now the situation is the same again, if not worse." There is a good chance that the Russians will resume the struggle with the green serpent in the near future, especially in view of the fact that dollars from oil and natural gas are far outstripping excise revenues. On the other hand, Putin and company are pragmatic enough to weigh the fact that vodka does not require expensive pipelines.

Interregnum

WHAT TO DO BEFORE, DURING, AND AFTER A DRINKING BOUT

The top Russian culinary historian and absolute authority concerning vodka is William Pokhlyobkin (1923-2000). As an ardent champion of the right way to drink vodka, he considered it one of government's duties to teach Russians how to drink in a civilized manner, because over the centuries they had lost sight of that. In his view, vodka is a culinary product that is preeminently well-suited to accompany Russian meals – as long as it is used properly. The patriotic Pokhlyobkin wholeheartedly despised unbridled orgies of drinking. The following recommendations can be distilled from his writing.

- Vodka must be cooled to between 8-10° Celsius (46-50° F) before use.

- Like any noble beverage, vodka should be drunk slowly, in small sips, so that it can wash the entire mouth. Tossing down vodka in one swig is considered to be in bad taste.

- In Russia it is not customary to mix vodka with other alcoholic or nonalcoholic beverages.

- Vodka is drunk from vodka glasses with a volume of no greater than five centiliters.

- Vodka is a noble product, created for pleasure, informality, and the elimination of fatigue, stress, etc. It is completely wrong to equate vodka with harm or drunkenness. The roots of drunkenness lie not in wine or vodka, but rather in the human being himself. That is why it is important that the drinker maintain self-control, in order to account for the amount of alcohol consumed.

- The use of vodka is accompanied by a special Russian spread of food. These cold and warm snacks are obligatory whenever vodka is being consumed.

Nevertheless, even a civilized drinker can experience the intoxicating effects of vodka, to say nothing of the uncivilized drinker. If you add together those two categories in Russia, the result is a formidable number, and you can well imagine that the Russian people must have an abundant store of popular wisdom on how not to get drunk, or for how to slow down the process, or for how to recover after a serious binge.

BEFORE DRINKING

- Of course, you should drink in moderation. But if you know in advance that it's going to be a long and lavish dinner, then it is advisable to drink five centiliters of vodka two to three hours beforehand. This prepares your body for the heavy load.

- Eat something fatty or buttery before the drinking bout. You can also drink a raw egg or a tablespoon of vegetable oil. This inhibits the absorption of alcohol into the bloodstream.

- Never drink on an empty stomach. Author Vladimir Yozh quotes from an old medical reference book:

Силы вина состоят в следующем: оно стрекочет, возбуждает и натягивает гибкие части отверстия желудочного, следовательно производит оно сначала теплоту, бодрость и охоту к еде, или аппетит... Укрепляет оно и ободряет в единый миг человека, утрудившегося в дороге или от какой-нибудь тяжкой работы. Оно выгоняет в стужу урину, а в теплоте – пот. Оно разрушает гнезда глист, производит аппетит. Согретое на огне, в случае ушиба разгоняет скипевшуюся кровь, а холодное стягивает перерезанные сосудцы в ранах. Подкрепляет отнявшиеся места и члены, унимает в свежих ранах кровь. Но оно жидит и портит, питое натощак, желудочный сок. И потому надлежит принимать оное после кушания, когда желудок не пуст, а имеет в себе пищу...

Alcohol's potency consists in the following: it trills, stimulates, and stretches the elastic parts of the gastric aperture and thus produces at first, warmth, vigor, and desire for food, or appetite.... In an instant, it also fortifies and revitalizes anyone tired by travel or any sort of hard work. In cold weather, it flushes out urine, and when the weather is warm, perspiration. It destroys tapeworm nests and produces appetite. Heated over a fire, in case of injury, it removes congealed blood, and when cold, it heals severed blood vessels in a wound. It fortifies numb spots and limbs and stops the bleeding in fresh wounds. However, it dissolves and damages digestive juices when drunk on an empty stomach. It should therefore be consumed after eating, when the stomach is not empty, but rather contains food.[1]

Vladimir Yozh, *Notes from a Moonshiner* (2001)

WHILE DRINKING

- Try to limit yourself to one type of beverage for the occasion.

- Mixing light alcoholic drinks (beer, wine) and hard liquor (vodka, cognac) is strongly discouraged. If that proves to be unavoidable, then drink beverages with successively higher alcohol content. For example, begin with a light gin and tonic and end with vodka.

- Never mix wine and vodka.

Туман. Туман. Туман. Тонк-танк... тонк-танк... Уже водку пить немыслимо, уже вино пить немыслимо, идет в душу и обратно возвращается. В узком ущелье маленькой уборной, где лампа прыгала и плясала на потолке, как заколдованная, все мутилось и ходило ходуном. Бледного, замученного Мышлаевского тяжко рвало. Турбин, сам пьяный, страшный, с дергающейся щекой, со слипшимися на лбу волосами, поддерживал Мышлаевского. [...]

"Боже-е, боже-е, как тошно и противно. Не буду, клянусь, никогда мешать водку с вином". Никол... [...]

В кабинете у меня... на полке склянка, написано Liquor ammonii, а угол оборван к чертям, видишь ли... нашатырным спиртом пахнет.

– Сейчас... сейчас... Эх-эх.

– И ты, доктор, хорош...

– Ну, ладно, ладно.

– Что? Пульса нету?

– Нет, вздор, отойдет.

– Таз! Таз!

– Таз извольте.

– А-а-а...

– Эх вы!

Резко бьет нашатырный отчаянный спирт. Карась и Елена раскрывали рот Мышлаевскому. Николка поддерживал его, и два раза Турбин лил ему в рот помутившуюся белую воду.

– А... хрр... у-ух... Тьф... фэ...

– Снегу, снегу...

– Господи боже мой. Ведь это нужно ж так... Мокрая тряпка лежала на лбу, с нее стекали на простыни капли, под тряпкой виднелись закатившиеся под набрякшие веки воспаленные белки глаз, и синеватые тени лежали у обострившегося носа. С четверть часа, толкая друг друга локтями, суетясь, возились с побежденным офицером, пока он не открыл глаза и не прохрипел:

– Ах... пусти...

– Тэк-с, ну ладно, пусть здесь и спит.

Fog. Fog. Fog. *Tick tock... tick tock...* It made no sense to be drinking vodka, or wine either at this point, because it got inside you and came right back out. In the narrow ravine of the little W.C., where a lamp flickered and danced on the ceiling as if bewitched, everything was blurry and spinning. Pale Myshlayevsky was vomiting in agony. Turbin, himself drunk, and ghastly, his cheek twitching and his hair plastered to his brow, was holding Myshlayevsky up. [...]

"My God, my God, this is so disgusting, so awful. Never, I swear, never again am I going to mix vodka and wine. Nikol..." [...]

"In my study, on the shelf, there's a vial that says 'Liquor ammonii,' but the corner's torn off, damn it, see... it smells like methylated spirits."

"Right away. Oh my."

"And you, doctor, you're a fine one."

"All right, all right."

"What? No pulse?"

"No, this is nothing, it'll pass."

"A basin! A basin!"

"A basin, please."

"A-a-a-ah."

"Oh you!"

The awful liquid ammonia hit hard. Carp and Yelena opened Myshlayevsky's mouth. Nikolka supported him, and twice Turbin poured the cloudy white liquid into his mouth.

"Argh... ugh... bah..."

"Some snow, some snow."

"My God. You just had to go and..."

A wet washcloth lay on his forehead and dripped onto the sheets. Beneath the washcloth you could see the bloodshot whites of his eyes rolling under his swollen eyelids and the dark blue shadows beside his aquiline nose. For a quarter of an hour, elbowing each other, bustling about, they tended to the vanquished officer until he opened his eyes and rasped, "Oh, leave me be."

"All right, he can sleep here."[2]

Mikhail Bulgakov, *The White Guard* (1922-1924)

- Don't start out with a sweet wine, champagne, or cognac.

- You absolutely have to eat something after every glass; potatoes, bread, and sauerkraut in particular neutralize the effects of alcohol.

- Some people observe the Western fashion of mixing just about all beverages with cola or tonic. But bear in mind that those beverages are carbonated and thus promote the absorption of alcohol into the bloodstream.

- If you notice at the height of the festivities that you're overplaying your hand, then have a glass of cognac and don't drink anything for forty minutes.

- Have some saxaul root...

Little by little the party's spirit mellowed. The men's quick, guttural language was mysterious to me, but they translated their jokes into a babbling Russian, and finally Murad conjured up three bottles of vodka. "This is the whole point!" He slopped it into shallow glasses, and we flung them back in one gulp, Russian fashion, at every toast. Only the old Mongol refused to drink at first. It suborned his stomach, he said. "He's an *ishan,* a holy one!" roared the big man, mocking.

"They drink most of all!" retorted the Mongol, and they were rolling in the flowers with laughter.

Some charred pots of green tea created a moment's hiatus. Then the vodka-drinking went on. Sometimes, secretly, I spilled mine into the sand, but Murad replenished my glass at every toast, and fatally I lost count of them. Meanwhile they absolved themselves with blessings, and peppered their talk with "If God wills!" or "Thanks be to God!", while pouring out the forbidden spirit. Then they expatiated on remedies for hangover, and confided the medicinal properties of saxaul root or green tea (sovereign against headaches if you inhaled the aroma between cupped hands).

"Try it! Try it!" But it was too late. The vodka had already detached me, and I was seeing them all from far away. Sitting cross-legged on their carpet among the flowers, they seemed to have regressed into a Persian miniature.[3]

Colin Thubron, *The Lost Heart of Asia* (1994)

- If you're fairly drunk, don't go outside during cold weather, because then you will be totally smashed, and you could pass out.

- Smoke as little as possible: Smoking makes the effect of alcohol between one and a half and two times stronger.

Водочное опьянение приходит не сразу, не как пивное, а постепенно. От пива вы можете быть на грани падения лицом в салат, а через полчаса оказаться трезвее всех за столом, главное эти полчаса не курить. Человек, пьющий водку, понятен моментально. Вы забираетесь все выше, все ближе к небесам, а потом оказываетесь в самом низу. Можете дать в морду ближайшему другу или пописать посреди ресторана. Все равно с утра вспомнить удастся лишь испуганные глаза женщин и стыдное ощущение полета.

Vodka intoxication does not come immediately, not like with beer, but gradually. With beer, you might be on the verge of falling face-first into your salad, and a half hour later you could be the soberest one at the table. The most important thing is not to smoke during that half hour. A person drinking vodka is immediately recognizable. You are climbing higher and higher, closer and closer to the heavens, but later you wind up as low as it gets. You might punch your best friend in the face or take a leak in the middle of a restaurant. It doesn't matter – in the morning all you'll remember is the horrified eyes of the women and the shameful feeling of flight.[4]

Ilya Stogov, *Machos Don't Cry* (1999)

- Don't rely on your sense of "drinking in moderation," because liquor does not take full effect until an hour later. It is also useful to know that alcohol is metabolized at a rate of one gram of pure alcohol per 10 kilograms of body weight per hour. This means that a man weighing 70 kilograms needs around three hours to be rid of a five-centiliter glass of vodka.

- If you have assembled a rumbling mixture in your stomach that urgently wants out, you should not prevent that, and that should not be cause for shame.

AFTER DRINKING
- After the serious bout, it is beneficial to drink a cup of strong tea with peppermint or lemon or coffee with lemon. A light intoxication passes quickly.
- Drink soda water with lemon.

– Вот мои спасители! – закричал, увидав вошедших, Петрицкий, пред которым стоял денщик с водкой и соленым огурцом на подносе. – Вот Яшвин велит пить, чтоб освежиться.

– Ну, уж вы нам задали вчера, – сказал один из пришедших, – всю ночь не давали спать.

– Нет, каково мы окончили! – рассказывал Петрицкий, – Волков залез на крышу и говорит, что ему грустно. Я говорю: давай музыку, погребальный марш! Он так и заснул на крыше под погребальный марш.

– Выпей, выпей водки непременно, а потом сельтерской воды и много лимона, – говорил Яшвин, стоя над Петрицким, как мать, заставляющая ребенка принимать лекарство, – а потом уж шампанского немножечко, – так, бутылочку.

– Вот это умно. Постой, Вронский, выпьем.

– Нет, прощайте, господа, нынче я не пью.

– Что ж, потяжелеешь? Ну, так мы одни. Давай сельтерской воды и лимона.

"Here come my saviors!" cried Petritsky, seeing the men come in. His orderly was standing in front of him holding a tray with vodka and pickles. "Yashvin here tells me to drink so as to refresh myself."

"Well, you really gave it to us last evening," said one of the newcomers. "Wouldn't let us sleep all night."

"No, but how we finished!" Petritsky went on. "Volkov got up on the roof and said he was feeling sad. I said: 'Give us music, a funeral march!' He fell asleep on the roof to the funeral march."

"Drink, drink the vodka without fail, and then seltzer water with a lot of lemon," Yashvin said, standing over Petritsky like a mother making a child take its medicine, "and after that a bit of champagne – say, one little bottle."

"Now that's clever. Wait, Vronsky, let's have a drink."

"No, good-bye, gentlemen, today I don't drink."

"Why, so as not to gain weight? Well, then we'll drink alone. Bring on the seltzer water and lemon."[5]

Lev Tolstoy, *Anna Karenina* (1878)

- A glass of cold water with twenty drops of peppermint extract will help you sober up. Drink the water in one gulp.

- Slight inebriation can be helped by drinking a glass of cold water containing two drops of alcohol with sal ammoniac (a powder once used to treat sore throats). If you're very drunk, use five or six drops. And if your drunk partner can't get it down, you should open his or her mouth and pour the solution down the throat.

- In 1640, Adam Olearius discovered a Russian universal remedy: "The Russians prepare a special dish when they have a hangover or feel uncomfortable. They cut cold baked lamb into small pieces, like cubes, but thinner and broader, mix them with peppers and cucumbers similarly cut, and pour over them a mixture of equal parts of vinegar and cucumber juice. They eat this with a spoon, and afterwards a drink tastes good again."[6]

- If you're nauseous, drink a cup of hot coffee with salt.

- To bring a drunk around, rub his ears briskly and vigorously with the palms of your hands. The arrival of blood in his head will bring him to full consciousness.

- In order to sober up, drink a teaspoon of cognac, an egg yolk, two teaspoons of tomato puree, a teaspoon of sunflower oil, and a pinch of salt with red and black pepper. Add to this mixture a half a teaspoon of sharp (prepared) horseradish and drink in one gulp.

- Experienced drinkers (especially alcoholics) just have another glass...

– Нет ли у вас, голубушка... рюмочки водочки? Душа горит! Такие во рту после вчерашнего перепоя окиси, закиси и перекиси, что никакой химик не разберет! Верите ли? Душу воротит! Жить не могу!

"You wouldn't happen to have a glass of vodka would you, my good man? I'm in a state of torment. After last night's drinking I have such oxides, protoxides, and peroxides in my mouth that no chemist would be able to sort them out! Do you believe it? My stomach! I can't go on!"[7]

Anton Chekhov, "The Comedian" (1884)

- If you're extremely drunk, there's nothing better in the evening than to rinse the stomach with a soda solution (one tablespoon of baking soda in one liter of water). After that, take an aspirin and eight to ten tablets of activated charcoal. Instead of soda, drink a glass and a half of *kefir* (a fresh-fermented effervescent milk drink).

- Or you can drink a glass of pickle brine (in Russia there's even a powdered pickle juice concentrate called Guten Morgen that can be reconstituted in hangover emergencies when no pickle jars are available).

- In the morning, massage your face and neck. Take a cold and warm shower or, even better, a bath with sea salt, and then take a walk in the fresh air.

- Make a spicy infusion with four tablespoons of young rose hips, one tablespoon of St. John's wort, two tablespoons of motherwort, and three tablespoons of honey. Dilute this with boiling water and allow it to stand. Have a light breakfast – preferably with an omelet, buckwheat, vegetables, and dairy products.

- When drunk, have two doses of between 100 and 120 grams of honey – this helps you sober up (the fructose in the honey neutralizes the effects of alcohol).

Well, if you still don't feel better, you're a hopeless case. But you might wonder whether it's really so bad to have a hangover. It's simply part of the process. It's something that a drinker has to expect. In Abram Tertz's novel, the bicycle maker Lenny Makepeace has seized power in the city of Lyubimov. Through hypnosis, he makes his subjects believe that they are the chosen people. They can no longer distinguish reality from fantasy. Until they discover that there's something wrong with the vodka:

Леонид Иванович целыми днями пропадал на хозяйственном фронте. Либо сам следил за тишиной в городе и в сумрачном одиночестве делал обходы по улицам, истощенный, с провалившимся взглядом, с опухшими сосудами, оплетавшими его чело синим жгутом молнии. У него завелась привычка появляться в публичных местах, окутав свою персону покровом неузнаваемости. Под видом простого учетчика или колхозного бригадира, не внушавшего опасений, он заглядывал в пивные, где околачивался народ и выдавали по талонам дневную порцию водки. После печального эпизода с упившимся арестантом – ввели строгий лимит: 150 грамм на брата. Полностью упразднить эту моду – на такую затею даже Тихомиров не решался: попробуй отмени вино в России,– революция вспыхнет...

– Скажи-ка, братец, что ты думаешь о нашей внешней политике? – подсел Леонид Иванович к безногому инвалиду войны, который уже осушил свой законный стаканчик и прицеливался ко второму, добытому, видать, нелегально, по краденому талону.

– Чего о ней думать, добрый человек? Политика у нас прямая, справедливая. Миролюбивая, можно сказать, у нас политика... Будь здоров!

И, спровадив другой стаканчик, скроил вкусную рожу.

– Только винцо-то у нас, сам знаешь,– поддельное...

– Это почему же поддельное?! – изумился Леня столь откровенной наглости. Приняв двойную порцию, мерзавец раскраснелся, распарился, глаза у него тоже достаточно посоловели, язык заплетался – чего еще? Но, заплетаясь, настаивал, что винцо все равно поддельное, получаемое из обыкновенной воды – путем гипноза...

– Да откуда все это известно? Ведь ты же сейчас – пьян, ведь пьян ты, а? Ты же чувствуешь внутри физическое наслаждение?..

– Сейчас-то я чувствую, – отвечал инвалид, облизываясь, – но сам посуди: пьешь-пьешь эту фашистку, а голова с похмелья все равно не болит. Разве ж это винцо?

Калека всхлипнул. Непритворные, пьяные слезы градом покатились по промасленной гимнастерке. Напрасно Леонид Иванович пытался его ободрить:

– Ну чего ты, братец, плачешь? чего расстраиваешься?

Leonard vanished for days on end, working on the economic front or watching over law and order in the city. In gloomy solitude he patrolled the streets, gaunt and hollow-eyed, the dark veins knotted on his brow like a sheaf of forked lightning. He took to going about incognito. Disguised as some harmless character such as an accountant or a village foreman, he would drop into a pub crowded with people drawing their daily ration of vodka. Ever since the death of the drunken jailbird, consumption had been strictly limited to 150 grams a head. Not even Makepeace ventured to introduce total prohibition in a Russian city: try it and you'll get a revolution at once.

"Tell me, what d'you think of our foreign policy?" he asked a legless war veteran who had put away his legal portion and was addressing himself to one obtained on a stolen coupon.

"What's there to think about it, chum? It's straight and just. It's a peace-loving policy as you might say... Cheers!"

He drained his glass and smacked his lips.

"Our only trouble is this substitute vodka they give us, as you know."

"What d'you mean – substitute?" Lenny was staggered by the brazen insolence of the man. After his double portion he was red in the face and sweating like a pig, his eyes glazed and his speech slurred – what more did he want? But although he could hardly get his tongue round the words, he went on insisting that the vodka was a substitute, produced out of plain water by hypnosis.

"But how could you know such a thing even if it were true? Look at you at this very moment – you're drunk! Don't you feel drunk? Don't you experience all the pleasure of being drunk?"

"I do now, but judge for yourself – you could drink this Fascist brew all day and never get a hangover! Call that vodka?"

The cripple gave a sob and genuine drunken tears poured and dripped on to his greasy tunic.

"Cheer up, old man, don't take it so much to heart," Leonard tried to comfort him.[8]

Abram Tertz, *The Makepeace Experiment* (1963)

13

What to Eat?

Однако надо бы и закусить что-нибудь. Пьешь-пьешь, словно бочка
с изъяном, а закусить путем не закусишь. А доктора сказывают,
что питье тогда на пользу, когда при нем и закуска благопотребная
есть, как говорил преосвященный Смарагд, когда мы через Обоянь
проходили.

But I ought to have a bite of something. I soak up drink like a leaky tub,
and I never have a square meal. And doctors say liquor is only good for
you if there's appropriate nutriment to go with it, as Bishop Smaragd put it
when we were marching through Oboyan.[1]

Mikhail Saltykov-Shchedrin, *The Golovlyov Family* (1880)

FOR A WELL-MANNERED RUSSIAN, drinking vodka without eating
something at the same time is a cardinal sin. Only barbarians do that. The
culinary historian William Pokhlyobkin saw many barbarians around him in
Russia, and he considered it his personal mission to teach the people how to
drink. Which is to say that first you eat and then you drink; you regard vodka
as a pleasant accompaniment to the meal and not the main purpose; you drink
in moderation in order to promote digestion; and you know what foods go well
with vodka. If it is drunk in the correct volume, with the right dishes, and in

the proper order, then vodka is a superior beverage, according to Pokhlyobkin. But this knowledge and the art of drinking vodka have been lost; in earlier days, Russians were well aware that they should drink like the French, and they regarded vodka as a sort of table wine that accompanies the meal and makes the food taste better.

От водки пожжет, подерет тебе в горле, а как проглотишь устрицу, в горле чувствуешь сладострастие. Не правда ли?

The vodka burns and stings your throat and you have a voluptuous sensation in your throat when you swallow an oyster. Don't you?[2]

Anton Chekhov, "Drunk" (1887)

The common man often could not afford to eat well. Egbert Engberts had this to say: "The main reason that liquor had such an appalling effect on ordinary people is that they did not eat well along with it. The Russian always drinks in one gulp, and among the lower classes there would often be no food other than a pickle or a half a herring, which meant that the stomach and the entire body were systematically poisoned. Thus, tuberculosis was rampant."[3]

Of course, the practical advantage of eating while drinking is that the liver is not as stressed and the alcohol enters the bloodstream more gradually, which means that drunkenness sets in more slowly.

– Так что же, Веничка, что же ты, все-таки, купил? Нам страшно интересно!
Да ведь я понимаю, что интересно. Сейчас, сейчас перечислю: во-первых, две бутылки кубанской по два шестьдесят две каждая, итого пять двадцать четыре. Дальше: две четвертинки российской, по рупь шестьдесят четыре, итого пять двадцать четыре плюс три двадцать восемь. Восемь рублей пятьдесят две копейки. И еще какое-то красное. Сейчас вспомню. Да – розовое крепкое за рупь тридцать семь.
– Так-так-так, – говорите вы, – а общий итог? Ведь все это страшно интересно...
Сейчас я вам скажу общий итог.
– Общий итог – девять рублей восемьдесят девять копеек, – говорю я, вступив на перрон. – но ведь это не совсем общий итог. Я ведь купил еще два бутерброда, чтобы не сблевать.
– Ты хотел сказать, Веничка: «чтобы не стошнило?»
Нет, что я сказал, то сказал. Первую дозу я не могу без закуски, потому что могу сблевать. А вот уж вторую и третью могу пить всухую, потому что стошнить

может и стошнит, но уже ни за что не сблюю. И так вплоть до девятой. А там опять понадобится бутерброд.

– Зачем? Опять стошнит?

– Да нет, стошнить-то уже ни за что не стошнит, а вот сблевать – сблюю.

Вы все, конечно, на это качаете головами. Я даже вижу – отсюда, с мокрого перрона, – как все вы, рассеянные по моей земле, качаете головами и беретесь иронизировать:

– Как это сложно, Веничка, как это тонко!

"All the same, Venichka, so what did you buy? We're *terribly* interested."

"Yes, I can tell. Just a minute, I'll list it all: first, two bottles of Kubanskaya for two sixty-two each; total, five twenty-four. Next, two quarter bottles of Rossiiskaya at a ruble sixty-four; total, five twenty-four plus three twenty-eight, eight rubles fifty-two kopeks. And then some red. Just a moment. I'll remember. Yes, stout rosé for one ruble thirty-seven."

"So-oo," you say. "And the grand total? This is really terribly interesting."

"The grand total is nine rubles eighty-nine kopeks," I say, stepping onto the platform. "But that's not really the grand total. I also bought a couple of sandwiches so as not to puke."

"You mean 'so as not to throw up,' Venichka?"

"No, what I said I said. I can't take the first dose without a bit to eat, because I might puke otherwise. But the second and third now, I can drink straight, because it's OK to feel sick, but I won't start puking no matter what. Right up to number nine. And, there, I need another sandwich."

"How come? You'll throw up again?"

"Oh, no, I won't throw up for anything. But as for puking, I'll puke."

Of course, you all nod your heads at that. I even see from here, from the wet platform, how all of you scattered about my world are nodding your heads and getting ready to be ironic.

"How complicated that is, Venichka, how subtle!"[4]

Venedikt Erofeev, *Moscow to the End of the Line* (1970)

In earlier times, foreign travelers often complained about how the Russians ate, because the Russian table was often lacking essential things such as napkins and utensils, and the guest would be given only one plate, which was often filthy to boot. They did get plenty to eat: bread, salt, roasted pork, and big goblets of wine were available in abundance. Important guests of the tsar reported that there were no limits to the extravagance and that eating was followed by ceremonies in which gifts were exchanged. Each gift was accompanied by a complex ritual of standing, bowing, standing, bowing... After the reception, the hosts escorted the guest to his accommodations, where a bout of drinking would begin. A barrel of vodka was left in the courtyard for the lower-ranking staff.

Whatever else you might say about the Russians, hospitality is in their blood. The average Westerner could learn a lot from them on that score. An unexpected visitor around mealtime doesn't upset a Russian; on the contrary, it makes him happy as he dashes to the refrigerator, and if what he finds there is disappointing, then he checks with his upstairs, downstairs, or next-door neighbors. He couldn't care less about what he himself will eat the next day. This disposition is strikingly illustrated by the abundance mandated in the well-known cookbook *Podarok molodym khozyaykam* (*A Gift to Young Housewives*) by Yelena Molokhovets, first published in 1861. In it, she provides a number of nine-course menus, not including the appetizers. It is charming and liberally annotated, with lovely descriptions:

> Such meals began late and continued for hours. Anyone who was invited to 'evening tea' or a supper after the theater knew that he would not be going to bed until the early morning hours. The meal began around midnight. After the smoked salmon, herring, ham, pâté, the inevitable caviar, and other delicacies, there was dumpling soup, a fish course, a meat course (filet of wild boar with currant sauce, bear ham, partridge breast in cream), pancakes with cream and caviar, and ice cream and fruit to finish. After dinner, cards were played over coffee, cognac, liqueurs, and cake. In the morning hours, those who had made it through would have a second meal, a sort of repeat of the first one.[5]

Ever since the Russians have known vodka, bread has been the most important candidate to accompany it. In earlier times there was often nothing else on the table. Thus, there is also a typical Russian custom of smelling bread after having a swig (and if there is no bread, you smell your hands or sleeve). The spirit of the grain is said to help the drink slide comfortably down the gullet. However, others contend that the main reason that Russians smell bread is that they actually find vodka nasty and they want to avoid the strong odor.

Another simple accompaniment for vodka is a big lump of fatback (*salo*), often the only meat that the lower classes could afford. Cut into pieces, it is an excellent complement to vodka. And of course, there is herring. But nothing can beat a pickle. Delicious! And also useful.

> Вот и канун Ивана-Постного, – "усекновение Главы Предтечи и Крестителя Господня", – печальный день.
> Завтра пост строгий: будем вкушать только грибной пирог, и грибной суп с подрумяненными ушками, и рисовые котлетки с грибной подливкой; а сладкого не будет, и круглого ничего не будет, "из уважения": ни картошки, ни яблочка,

Tavern Keeper, Boris Kustodiev (1920)

ни арбуза, и даже нельзя орешков: напоминают "Главку". Горкин говорит, что
и огурчика лучше не вкушать, одно к одному уж пусть. Но огурчики длинные?..
Бывают и вовсе круглые, "кругляки", а лучше совсем не надо. Потому, пожалуй, в
канун огурцы и солят.

На нашем дворе всю неделю готовятся: парят кадки и кадочки, кипятят воду в чугунах, для заливки посола, что-бы отстоялась и простыла, режут укроп и хрен, остропахучий эстрагоник; готовят, для отборного засола, черносмородинный и дубовый лист, для крепкости и духа, – это веселая работа.

Выкатила кадушки скорнячиха; бараночник Муравлятников готовит целых четыре кадки; сапожник Сараев тоже большую кадку парит. А у нас – дым столбом, живое столпотворение. Как же можно: огурчика на целый год надо запасти, рабочего-то народу сколько! А рабочему человеку без огурчика уж никак нельзя: с огурчиком соленым и хлебца в охотку съешь, и поправиться когда нужно, опохмелиться, – первое средство для оттяжки.

And the day before St. John's Lent – "the Beheading of John the Forerunner and Baptist of the Lord" – is a sad day.

The next day is going to be a strict fast day: we'll eat nothing but mushroom pies and mushroom soup with browned dumplings, and rice cutlets with mushroom sauce. And there won't be anything sweet, or anything round "out of respect": no potatoes, no apples, no watermelon, and we can't even have nuts, since they look a bit like "the Head." Gorkin says that it's better not to eat cucumber. Fine, but cucumbers are long? Some are round, "roundies," so you'd better do without. That's probably why they're pickled the day before.

There's a whole week of hustle and bustle in our farmstead getting ready: they clean the barrels and tubs, boil water in iron pots to make brine, so it would have time to stand and cool, they chop dill and horseradish, pungent tarragon; to make the finest of brine, they prepare the leaves of the black currant bush and oak tree, for robustness and spirit – it's cheerful work.

The furrier woman rolled out some tubs; the sheep tender Muravlyatnikov got four whole barrels ready; the cobbler Sarayev also cleaned a big barrel. A thick column of smoke rises up, there's a great clamor of people. And why wouldn't there be: a year's supply has to be pickled, and there are so many hardworking mouths to feed! And working people can't get by without their pickles: with a pickled cucumber a slice of bread becomes a tasty treat, and when you start to get too thin or need to cure a hangover, it's the best way to set things right.[6]

Ivan Shmelyov, *Year of the Lord* (1944)

There are countless dishes that go well with vodka.

ЛЕБЕДЕВ. [...] Что ж, господа, Жомини да Жомини, а об водке ни полслова. Repetatur! (Наливает три рюмки.) Будемте здоровы... (Пьют и закусывают.)
Селедочка, матушка, всем закускам закуска.

ШАБЕЛЬСКИЙ. Ну, нет, огурец лучше... Ученые с сотворения мира думают и ничего умнее соленого огурца не придумали. (Петру.) Петр, поди-ка еще принеси огурцов да вели на кухне изжарить четыре пирожка с луком. Чтоб горячие были. (Петр уходит.)

ЛЕБЕДЕВ. Водку тоже хорошо икрой закусывать. Только как? С умом надо... Взять икры паюсной четверку, две луковочки зеленого лучку, прованского масла, смешать все это и, знаешь, этак... поверх всего лимончиком... Смерть! От одного аромата угоришь.

БОРКИН. После водки хорошо тоже закусывать жареными пескарями. Только их надо уметь жарить. Нужно почистить, потом обвалять в толченых сухарях и жарить досуха, чтобы на зубах хрустели... хру-хру-хру...

ШАБЕЛЬСКИЙ. Вчера у Бабакиной была хорошая закуска – белые грибы. Лебедев. А еще бы...

ШАБЕЛЬСКИЙ. Только как-то особенно приготовлены. Знаешь, с луком, с лавровым листом, со всякими специями. Как открыли кастрюлю, а из нее пар, запах... просто восторг!

ЛЕБЕДЕВ. А что ж? Repetatur, господа! (Выпивают.) Будемте здоровы...

LEBEDEV [...] I say, we've fought quite a few armchair battles, but no one's mentioned vodka. Another dose. [*Pours out three glasses.*] Our very good health! [*They drink and eat.*] There's nothing to touch a spot of herring, old boy.

SHABELSKY I don't know. Cucumber's better. Wise men have cogitated since the dawn of history without hitting on anything smarter than salted cucumber. [*To Peter.*] Peter, go and get more cucumber, and tell them to cook four onion pasties in the kitchen. Make sure they're hot. [*Peter goes out.*]

LEBEDEV Caviar isn't bad with vodka, but the thing is to serve it properly. You need a quarter of a pound of pressed caviar, two spring onions and some olive oil. Mix the lot together, and then, you know – add the odd drop of lemon. Hell's bells, the mere smell will make you swoon!

BORKIN Fried gudgeon also helps the vodka down – but fried properly. First clean. Then dip in toasted bread-crumbs and fry them so crisp, they crunch in your teeth. Crunch, crunch, crunch.

SHABELSKY There was something good at Martha Babakin's yesterday – mushrooms.

LEBEDEV Not half they were.

SHABELSKY Cooked in some special way – with onion, you know, bay leaves and spices. When they took the saucepan lid off and that steamy whiff came out – sheer ecstasy, it was.

LEBEDEV What do you say? Another dose, everyone. [*They drink.*] Our good health![7]

Anton Chekhov, *Ivanov* (1887)

The Russians are big on breakfast. Bread is part of it, of course, but they also prefer something warm, such as eggs with bacon or buckwheat (*kasha*) with a pat of butter. But they're also not afraid of something more substantial...

> The breakfast must be set down in detail because there has never been anything like it in the world. First came a water glass of vodka, then, for each person, four fried eggs, two huge fried fish, and three glasses of milk; then a dish of pickles, and a glass of homemade cherry wine, and black bread and butter; and then a full cup of honey, and two more glasses of milk, and we finished with another glass of vodka. It sounds incredible that we ate all that for breakfast, but we did, and it was all good, but we felt heavy and a little sick afterward.[8]
>
> John Steinbeck, *A Russian Journal* (1949)

The main meal is preceded by *zakuski* (hors d'oeuvres). There is often an entire table of them: smoked fish, calf's tongue, caviar, cheese, tomatoes, cucumbers, cabbage salad, pies (*pirogi*), marinated mushrooms, and much more. Vodka is essential. Non-Russians, being unaccustomed to such a large quantity of appetizers, tend to eat so much in appetizers that they have no room for the main course. Soup such as *borshch* (beet soup) or *shchi* (cabbage soup) is served between the *zakuski* and the main course.

Russians are masters of enjoyment. In a Chekhov story that takes place around the end of the nineteenth century, a panel of judges, while waiting for their chairman to write out his opinion, begin fantasizing...

> – Я раз дорогою закрыл глаза и вообразил себе поросеночка с хреном, так со мной от аппетита истерика сделалась. Ну-с, а когда вы въезжаете к себе во двор, то нужно, чтобы в это время из кухни пахло чем-нибудь этаким, знаете ли...
> – Жареные гуси мастера пахнуть, – сказал почетный мировой, тяжело дыша.
> – Не говорите, душа моя Григорий Саввич, утка или бекас могут гусю десять очков вперед дать. В гусином букете нет нежности и деликатности. Забористее всего пахнет молодой лук, когда, знаете ли, начинает поджариваться и, понимаете ли, шипит, подлец, на весь дом. Ну-с, когда вы входите в дом, то стол уже должен быть накрыт, а когда сядете, сейчас салфетку за галстук и не спеша тянетесь к графинчику с водочкой. Да ее, мамочку, наливаете не в рюмку, а в какой-нибудь допотопный дедовский стаканчик из серебра или в этакий пузатенький с надписью «его же и монаси приемлют», и выпиваете не сразу, а сначала вздохнете, руки потрете, равнодушно на потолок поглядите, потом этак не спеша, поднесете ее, водочку-то, к губам и – тотчас же у вас из желудка по всему телу искры...
> Секретарь изобразил на своем сладком лице блаженство.

Искры... – повторил он, жмурясь. – Как только выпили, сейчас же закусить нужно.

"Once, while traveling, I closed my eyes and imagined a suckling pig with horseradish, and I had a fit of hysterics, it so excited my appetite. And when you arrive home, there should be a smell wafting from the kitchen into the yard, something of the sort, how to describe it?..."

"Roasted goose fits the bill," remarked the justice of the peace, breathing heavily.

"I beg to differ, my good man, Grigory Savvich. A duck or snipe will outsmell a goose ten times over. The goose's bouquet lacks tenderness, delicacy. Most pungent of all is the smell of a young onion, don't you know, when it just starts to be seared, and, don't you see, its sizzling fills the whole house, the little devil. And if I may say, when you enter the house, the table should be set, and once you take your seat, first thing a napkin into the collar, and, without hurrying, you reach for the vodka decanter. And you pour it – ah, mama – not into a shot glass, but into some antediluvian tumbler that belonged to grandpa, made of silver, or into a pot-bellied vessel with the old inscription "wine fit for a monk," and you don't throw it down right away, but first take a deep breath, rub your hands together, take an unhurried look at the ceiling, and then, without haste, bring it, the vodka, to your lips and then, instantly, sparks will radiate from your stomach throughout your entire body..."

The secretary simulated a look of bliss on his sugary face.

"Sparks..." he repeated, screwing up his eyes. "And as soon as you've had your drink, you must immediately eat something."[9]

Anton Chekhov, "The Siren" (1887)

One specialty of Russian cuisine is *pelmeni*, dumplings stuffed with meat, usually a blend of ground meats. When the first hard-freeze arrives, Siberians sit down with their entire family and spend a couple of days making *pelmeni*. One person kneads the dough and rolls it out, another makes the filling, and a third folds the tiny meat balls into little envelopes of dough. The *pelmeni* are then left out in the cold in burlap bags, after which they can be dumped into boiling water at any time, to be cooked for seven minutes. *Pelmeni* are delicious with sour cream, pepper, dill, vinegar, and a glass of vodka. *Pelmeni* were – and still are – considered food for the common people; the upper class turns its nose up at them...

Ровно в семь часов вечера я уже был у Маслобоева. Он встретил меня с громкими криками и с распростертыми объятиями. Само собою разумеется, он был вполпьяна. Но более всего меня удивили чрезвычайные приготовления к моей встрече. Видно было, что меня ожидали.

Хорошенький томпаковый самовар кипел на круглом столике, накрытом прекрасною и дорогою скатертью. Чайный прибор блистал хрусталем, серебром и фарфором. На другом столе, покрытом другого рода, но не менее богатой скатертью, стояли на тарелках конфеты, очень хорошие, варенья киевские, жидкие и сухие, мармелад, пастила, желе, французские варенья, апельсины, яблоки и трех или четырех сортов орехи, – одним словом, целая фруктовая лавка. На третьем столе, покрытом белоснежною скатертью, стояли разнообразнейшие закуски: икра, сыр, пастет, колбасы, копченый окорок, рыба и строй превосходных хрустальных графинов с водками многочисленных сортов и прелестнейших цветов – зеленых, рубиновых, коричневых, золотых. Наконец, на маленьком столике, в стороне, тоже накрытом белою скатертью, стояли две вазы с шампанским. На столе перед диваном красовались три бутылки: сотерн, лафит и коньяк, – бутылки елисеевские и предорогие.

At seven o'clock on the dot I was at Masloboyev's. He greeted me with loud exclamations and open arms. He was, of course, half drunk. But what struck me most was the extraordinary preparation that had been made for my visit. It was evident that I was expected.

A pretty brass samovar was boiling on a little round table covered with a handsome and expensive tablecloth. The tea table glittered with crystal, silver and china. On another table, which was covered with a tablecloth of a different kind, but no less gorgeous, stood plates of excellent sweets, Kiev preserves both dried and liquid, fruit paste, jelly, French preserves, oranges, apples, and three or four sorts of nuts; in fact, a regular fruit-shop. On a third table, covered with a snow-white cloth, there were savories of different sorts – caviar, cheese, a pie, sausage, smoked ham, fish and a row of fine glass decanters containing spirits of many sorts, and of the most attractive colors – green, ruby, brown and gold. Finally, on a little table on one side – also covered with a white cloth – there were two bottles of champagne. On a table before the sofa there were three bottles containing Sauterne, Lafitte, and Cognac, very expensive brands from Eliseyev's.[10]

Fyodor Dostoyevsky, *The Insulted and Injured* (1861)

After the October Revolution, few people ate like this. And maybe that was a good thing. After all, such exquisite food makes other demands of the human body. Russian food is hearty and solid. During the 1880s, agricultural scientist and commentator Alexander Engelhardt wrote about a birthday visit to an aristocratic family member:

В час пополудни завтрак – дома я в это время уже пообедал и спать лег – разумеется, прежде всего водка и разный гордевр. Выпили и закусили. Завтракать стали: паштет с трюфелями съели, бургонское, да настоящее, не то, что в

уездных городах продают с надписью: "Нуй бургунский", выпили. Цыплята потом
с финзербом каким-то. Съели. Еще что-то. Ели и пили часа два. Выспался потом.
Вечером в седьмом часу – обед. Тут уж – ели-ели, пили-пили, даже тошно стало.
На другой день у меня такое расстройство желудка сделалось, что страх. Им всем,
как они привыкли к господскому харчу, нипочем, а мне беда. Доктор случился,
достали где-то Tinctura opii, уж я ее пил-пил – не помогает. Ну, думаю, – умирать,
так уж лучше дома, и уехал на другой день домой. Приезжаю на постоялый двор,
вхожу и вижу: сидит знакомый дворник Гаврила, толстый, румяный, и уписывает
ботвинью с луком и селедкой-ратником.

– Хлеб-соль!

– Милости просим.

– Благодарим.

– Садитесь! Петровна, принеси-ка водочки!

– Охотно бы поел, да боюсь.

– А что?

Я рассказал Гавриле о своей болезни.

– Это у вас от легкой пищи, у вашего родственника пища немецкая, легкая
– вот и все. Выпейте-ка водочки, да поешьте нашей русской прочной пищи,
и выздоровеете. Эй, Петровна! неси барину водки, да ботвиньица подбавь,
селедочки подкроши.

Я выпил стакан водки, подъел ботвиньи, выпил еще стакан, поел чего-то
крутого, густого, прочного, кажется, каши, выспался отлично – и как рукой сняло.
С тех пор вот уже четыре года у меня никогда не было расстройства желудка.

At one in the afternoon we had breakfast (at home by this time I would have had my
dinner and been taking a nap already). Of course, there was vodka, first and foremost,
and various hors d'œuvres. We had a round of drinks and then began our breakfast: we
ate truffle pâté, with Burgundy, the real thing, not the stuff labeled "New Burgundy" that
was sold in provincial shops, and then we had another round. After that, we ate chicken
with some sort of *herbes fines.* We finished with that and then had something else. We
ate and drank for about two hours. I then had a good nap. In the evening, around six,
we had dinner. Now we really got down to eating: we ate and drank and drank and ate;
it was starting to get a bit nauseating. The next day my stomach was so upset, it was
awful. They had already grown accustomed to this lordly grub, but for me it was terrible.
A doctor turned up, they managed to get their hands on some *Tinctura opii*, which I took
over and over again, but it didn't help. "Well," I thought. "if I'm going to die, better to do it
at home, and I left the next day. I arrived at the inn, walked inside, and immediately saw
my acquaintance Gavrila, the yardman, sitting there, fat, red-faced, and putting away a
botvinia with onions and herring.

"Bon appetit!"

"Be my guest."

"You're very kind."

"Have a seat! Petrovna, bring some vodka!"

"I'd be happy to join you, but I'd better not."

"What's the matter?"

I told Gavrila about my illness.

"You got that from eating too lightly. Your relative's diet is too light, that's all there is to it. Drink some vodka and have some of our hearty Russian food, and soon you'll recover. Hey, Petrovna! Bring the gentleman some vodka, and botvinia too, and sprinkle in some herring.

I drank a glass of vodka, had some botvinia with it, drank another glass, ate something dense, thick, and hearty (I think it was *kasha*), had an excellent night's sleep, and I was good as new. It's been four years now since I've had a stomach ache.[11]

Alexander Engelhardt, *Letters from the Countryside* (1883-1885)

POLAND AND VODKA

Besides Russia, there is another country that considers itself the cradle of vodka: Poland. Vodka means "little water" in both Russian and Polish (*wódka*, pronounced "vudka"), and etymologically there is no basis for ascribing the word exclusively to either of the two languages. The American historian Edward Keenan argues – not very convincingly – that the word vodka comes from Polish, because Russian has a different way of forming diminutives. Whatever the case, the word was first used in an official document in Russia in 1533, even though in this case it referred to alcohol for cleaning a wound, not to the delightful beverage.

Meanwhile, there is a Polish book from 1534 in which the botanist Stefan Falimirz describes how vodka is distilled on a large scale: "Vodka can be cooked or distilled, and herbs and aromatics can be added to it, or herbs only, or herbs and flowers, or flowers and no herbs, or any number of mixed ingredients." The Poles sometimes flavored it with fruit, berries, pears, juniper, and laurel. However, those beverages contained very little alcohol. They called strong distilled beverages *gorzalka*. The word vodka as a social drink – not as a medicine – did not appear until 1600, and in Russia, not until the eighteenth century.

The question of vodka's provenance has simmered for centuries, and in 1982 it led to an international lawsuit, brought by the Russians. They claimed the right to declare vodka an exclusively Russian drink. The judgment that was reached was an un-Slavic compromise: "Only vodka from Russia is genuine Russian vodka." The Russians now often say derisively that the Poles distill their vodka from potatoes. That is only partly true, because Poles also make grain vodka; in addition, with the modern distillery and filtering techniques it is less important what the underlying ingredient is. After all, the end product is pure. And lastly, the Poles have developed varieties of potatoes intended specifically for vodka, containing twice as much starch as ordinary potatoes.

Vodka plays a major role in Polish society. Poland's relationship to vodka may not be as all-encompassing or as well documented as Russia's, but it is an integral part of the culture. In Poland too, it has occasionally been rationed, the Poles too like to drink a lot of it, and the Poles too recognize its therapeutic effect. For example, they have an effective means of avoiding stomach problems: vodka with flakes of gold. The recipe, which dates back to the sixteenth century, has a salutary effect on digestion. This vodka is called Złota Woda (Gold Water) and is made in Gdansk. The gold is said to be imported from Switzerland. Not everyone agrees that this Gold Water is vodka, as opposed to a cordial. Moreover, Złota Woda is not unique: Attila vodka from Mongolia also contains gold flakes. And the Amsterdam distillery A. van Wees says in its brochure that its "Guldenwater" ("drunk by stock traders and businessmen to treat headache") is based on those golden beverages.

14

Making Vodka

Things are different in Russia, where they don't only drink to get drunk, they drink to stay drunk too. The demand for vodka is so enormous that any and every form of vegetable protein gets shoved into the distiller's pan, from potatoes and mangelwurzels to the nuts and dried fruit that a delinquent female keeper should have fed to the monkeys in the Moscow zoo, as in a famous case reported in *Pravda*.[1]

Kingsley Amis, *Every Day Drinking* (1983)

MASH

The first thing you need to make vodka is the mash, which goes into the distilling pot or vessel. Grains can serve as the raw material for the mash, but so can potatoes, beets, onions, carrots, apples, corn, pumpkin, bread, chocolate, or whey. Even oil can be used as a base, or wood if you can get it to ferment. And these days grapes are also used in southern Europe. Wheat, rye, and potatoes are the most commonly used bases. The Russians typically use rye, whereas wheat is mostly preferred in the West. The base ingredient is crushed and water is added. Sometimes people add other types of grain to the mash. Whatever the case, the essential element of the mash is starch, which can be converted to sugar.

Алкоголизм распространяется в геометрической прогрессии, и государство справедливо видит в нем угрозу: экономический ущерб от него огромен. Для алкоголиков построены тысячи резерваций, где режим почти что равен лагерному – принудительный труд, наказание голодом и прочие атрибуты «воспитания» – да плюс принудительное лечение. Естественно, в этих «профилакториях» любыми средствами добывается спиртное – и подкупом охраны, и «химией». В сущности, разве что из кирпича нельзя выгнать самогонку.

Alcoholism is growing geometrically, and the state is justified in seeing a threat in this: the economic losses from it are huge. Thousands of reservations have been built for alcoholics, where the regime is almost like that in camps: forced labor, hunger as punishment and similar attributes of "character building," plus of course compulsory treatment. Naturally, in these "profilactories," spirits are obtained by any means necessary, be it through bribing guards or "chemistry." In essence, about the only thing you can't make homebrew from is a brick.[2]

Vladimir Bukovsky, *To Build a Castle: My Life as a Dissenter* (1978)

YEAST

Yeast is a fungus that is capable of breaking down sugar. Grapes contain yeast cells in their skin, which means that eventually grape juice ferments on its own. Because that's not the case with grains, malt must be added to the mash for beer or distilled beverages. Malt contains enzymes that convert starches into sugars. The sugars ferment to yield an alcohol content up to approximately eight percent.

DISTILLING

The principle of distilling is based on the simple fact that alcohol boils at a lower temperature than water. You put a suitable mash in a pot, bring it to a boil, catch the alcohol vapor, and then cool it. Repeated distillation means repeated heating. The malt spirit that results from "pot-boiling" is usually distilled three times, the result being around 50 percent alcohol. This method is known as pot distillation (using a "pot still") and is used for cognac, malt whiskey, and some vodkas.

The other distilling method involves continuous heating, whereby steam is forced through the mash in column-shaped boilers. The steam takes the alcohol with it to higher levels. After that, it passes to a second column (rectifier), which also has several chambers stacked on top of each other, and so on. The more intensive the rectification, the purer the alcohol. Specifically, rectification eliminates impurities. This is how most distilled beverages are produced, including vodka. The continuous still was not invented until the mid-nineteenth century.

– Теперь еще, слава богу, винниц развелось немного. А вот в старое время, когда провожал я царицу по Переяславской дороге, еще покойный Безбородько...

– Ну, сват, вспомнил время! Тогда от Кременчуга до самых Домен не насчитывали и двух винниц. А теперь... Слышал ли ты, что повыдумали проклятые немцы? Скоро, говорят, будут курить не дровами, как все честные христиане, а каким-то чертовским паром. - Говоря эти слова, винокур в размышлении глядел на стол и на расставленные на нем руки свои. - Как это паром - ей-богу, не знаю!

– Что за дурни, прости господи, эти немцы! - сказал голова. - Я бы батогом их, собачьих детей! Слышанное ли дело, чтобы паром можно было кипятить что!

"Now, thank God, distilleries are doing better. But years ago, when I was guiding the Tsarina by the Pereyaslav Road, Bezborodko, now deceased..."

"Well, old friend, that was a time! In those days there were only two distilleries all the way from Kremenchug to Romny. But now... have you heard what the damn Germans are going to do? They say that instead of burning wood in distilleries like all decent Christians, they are soon going to use some kind of devilish steam..." As he said this the distiller looked thoughtfully at the table and at his hands lying on it. "How is it done with steam – I swear I don't know!"

"What fools they are, those Germans, God forgive me!" said the mayor. "I'd give them hell, the bunch of bastards! Did anyone ever hear the like of boiling anything by steam?"[3]

Nikolai Gogol, "A May Night" (1829-1830)

FILTERING

There are various filtering techniques for eliminating unpleasant flavors. Originally, vegetative fiber, sand, or even felt was used for filtering. In the nineteenth century, Russians discovered filtering through charcoal, which absorbs much better than other materials and thus removes more impurities from the alcohol. Some types of wood are better than others for making charcoal. Russians usually prefer birch wood, which is, after all, readily available. Beech, linden, oak, or alder are better, but more expensive. Types that are not as good as birch, but are nevertheless usable, include pine, spruce, aspen, and poplar. In any event, the bark and any knots must be removed, together with the core, especially if it's darker than the surrounding wood. Preferably trees used to make charcoal should be older than roughly 40 years.

After being filtered through several yards of charcoal clippings, British vodka is a very pure spirit. What has been taken out of it is those substances which impart flavour and also give you hangovers. So the tastelessness of vodka is connected with its harmlessness. At the opposite extreme are impure drinks like cognac and malt whisky.[4]

Kingsley Amis, *Everyday Drinking* (1983)

Vodka distillers are still trying to improve filtration. One particularly trendy method at present is filtering through milk.

WATER

Vodka is renowned for its purity. Everything has been distilled, rectified, and filtered out of it, and so you shouldn't be able to tell what base was used to make the mash (although many Russians think differently). But if that's the case, how do you differentiate yourself as a vodka maker? By adding minimal amounts of flavors? That's blasphemy to purists like Russian culinary historian Pokhlyobkin. You might put your vodka in a stylishly shaped bottle, or emphasize the water used to dilute the distilled alcohol. Glacier water, water from Lake Baikal, spring water – these are some of the ways that producers try to gain a marketing advantage. The general rule is that soft water makes the best vodka. The quality of the water that is added to the mash earlier in the process is less important.

Vodka is not aged. An exception is *Starka* (see page 308).

FLAVORING

Another method for eliminating bad tastes in vodka, or rather masking them, is flavoring. In the nineteenth century, as it was not yet possible to achieve a high degree of purity through distillation and filtering, various fruit vodkas were in vogue. Herbs and other plants were also used to add aroma – always after the distilling process. Steeping (maceration) was (and still is) used to impart flavor: The aromatic ingredients are placed in the vodka for a few weeks. You can also run the alcohol through a flavored filter a couple of times, which is more efficient and cheaper. An alternative method is to add a flavored oil to the vodka.

ГУРЕВИЧ (с трудом улыбается). Ну, ладно. (С тревогой взглядывает в сторону Вити, потом наблюдает, как сосед адмирал делает вздорные попытки вырваться из пут.) А этого за что?

ПРОХОРОВ. Делириум тременс. Изменил Родине и помыслом и намерением. Короче, не пьет и не курит. Все бы ничего, но мы тут как-то стояли в туалете, зашла речь о спирте, о его жуткой калорийности, – так этот вот говноед ляпнул примерно такое: из всех поглощаемых нами продуктов спирт, при всей его высокой калорийности, – весьма примитивного химического строения и очень беден структурной информацией. Он еще и тогда поплатился за свои хамские эрудиции: я открыл форточку, втиснул его туда и свесил за ногу вниз – а этаж все-таки четвертый – и так держал, пока он не отрекся от своих еретических доктрин... Сегодня он, решением Бога и Народа, приговорен к вышке... Я не очень верю, что вначале было Слово, но хоть какое-то задрипанное - оно должно быть в конце, так что пусть этот пиздобол лежит и размышляет...

GUREVICH (*Smiles with difficulty.*) Right. (*Glances at Vitya anxiously, then notices his neighbor the admiral making useless efforts to free himself from his shackles.*) And what's with this one?

PROKHOROV *Delirium tremens*. He betrayed the Motherland in thought and intention. In short, he doesn't drink or smoke. That would be fine, but once we were all standing around in the bathroom, talking about alcohol, about its tremendous number of calories. So this shit-eater blurts out: of all the stuff we gulp, alcohol, with all of its calories, has a really primitive chemical composition and very poor structural information. He paid for his insolent erudition right then: I opened the window, jammed him in there and hung him by an ankle – and it was the fourth floor, too – and held him there until he renounced his heretic doctrines... Today, by the will of God and the people, he is sentenced to the gallows... I don't really believe that in the beginning was the Word – it must be at the end, even if it's only a shabby one, so let this motherfucker lie there and think it over... [5]

Venedikt Erofeev, *Walpurgis Night, or "The Steps of the Commander"* (1985)

15

Varieties of Vodka

Сон и водка – вот истинные друзья человечества. Но водка
необходима такая, чтобы сразу забирала, покоряла себе всего
человека; что называется вор-водка, такая, чтобы сначала все
вообще твои суставчики словно перешибло, а потом изныл бы
каждый из них в особенности. Такая именно водка подается у моего
доброго знакомого, председателя.

Sleep and vodka – these are mankind's true friends. But the kind of vodka
that's needed is the kind that immediately takes total hold, subjugates the
entire person, the sort that might be called thief-vodka, the sort that would
start by breaking every last one of your joints so that each of them aches
individually. That is the sort of vodka that is served by my good friend the
chairman.[1]

Mikhail Saltykov-Shchedrin, "Boredom" (1857)

VODKAS COME IN ALL varieties and sizes. As long as you're not a purist, that
is. If you are, all sorts of cordials and liqueurs that are made by steeping fruit,
berries, herbs, or grasses in vodka do not deserve the name. In the eighteenth
century, the Russian nobility was granted the privilege of distilling vodka for its
own use, and because the distillation techniques were not yet perfect, they tried

to disguise impurities with flavoring. For the blue-blooded distillers, making a product that was as pure as possible was not the only point of honor. They also tried to outdo each other with the number of varieties. Some noblemen tried to come up with a different vodka for each letter of the alphabet.

Anise vodka, apple vodka, apricot vodka

Berry vodka, bird cherry vodka, buckthorn vodka

Cherry vodka, chicory vodka, citrus vodka, cumin vodka

Dill vodka

Elderberry vodka

Fig vodka

Grape vodka

Hemp vodka, honey vodka, horseradish vodka

Juniper berry vodka

Kiwi vodka

Lemon vodka

Marigold vodka, mint vodka

Nut vodka

Orange vodka

Pear vodka, pistachio vodka, plum vodka

Quinine vodka

Raspberry vodka, rose vodka, rowan vodka

Sage vodka, sorrel vodka

Tarragon vodka, tea vodka

Vanilla vodka

Watermelon vodka

Становой положил перо и, потирая руки, сказал, прихорашиваясь:

– У нас, кажись, отец-то Иоанн взалкал; дело доброе-с, коли хозяин не прогневается, можно-с.

Человек принес холодную закуску, сладкой водки, настойки и хересу.

– Благословите-ка, батюшка, яко пастырь, и покажите пример, а мы, грешные, за вами,– заметил становой.

Поп с поспешностию и с какой-то чрезвычайно сжатой молитвой хватил винную рюмку сладкой водки, взял крошечный верешок хлеба в рот, погрыз его и в ту же минуту выпил другую и потом уже тихо и продолжительно занялся ветчиной. Становой – и это мне особенно врезалось в память, – повторяя тоже сладкую водку, был ею доволен и, обращаясь ко мне с видом знатока, заметил:

– Полагаю-с, что доппель-кюммель 60 у вас от вдовы Руже-с?

Я не имел понятия, где покупали водку, и велел подать полуштоф, действительно, водка была от вдовы Руже. Какую практику надобно было иметь, чтоб различить по букету водки – имя заводчика!

The police officer put down his pen and, rubbing his hands together said, in an elevated tone:

"It would seem that Father Ioann is in need of sustinence. It's perfectly fine if our host will not be annoyed, it's permissible."

A servant brought some cold refreshment along with some sweetened vodka, a liqueur, and some sherry.

"Give your blessing, father, as pastor, and lead by example. We, poor sinners, will follow," the police officer said.

The priest hurriedly and with an extremely succinct prayer grabbed one of the glasses of sweetened vodka, put a tiny piece of bread into his mouth, chewed it, and immediately took another drink, after which he gave his prolonged attention to the ham. The police officer – and this particularly etched itself onto my memory – after taking a second helping of the sweetened vodka and being extremely satisfied with it, turned to me with the look of an expert and remarked:

"Doppelkümmel 60, I presume, from the widow Rouget?"

I had no idea where the vodka had been purchased and ordered that a bottle be brought. Indeed, the vodka was from widow Rouget. How practiced he must have been to be able to distinguish the manufacturer by the vodka's bouquet![2]

Alexander Herzen, *My Past and Thoughts* (1855)

ANNIVERSARY VODKA

Yubileynaya. Usually grain vodka of forty percent, produced for a special anniversary or commemoration, such as an anniversary of World War II.

Да, да. Теперь уже пора бы менять этикетки. А то ну, что это за преснятина? «Юбилейная», «Стрелецкая», «Столичная»… Когда я это вижу, у меня с души воротит. Водяра должна быть, как слеза, и все ее подвиды должны называться слезно. Допустим так: «Девичья Горючая», пять рублей двадцать копеек, «Мужская Скупая» – семь рублей. «Беспризорная Мутная» – четыре семьдесят. «Преступная Ненатуральная» – четыре двадцать. «Вдовья Безутешная» тоже не очень дорого: четыре сорок. «Сиротская Горькая» – шесть рублей. Ну и так далее. Но только прежде чем ломать Россию на глазах изумленного человечества, надо бы вначале ее просветить…

Oh yes. Now it's time to remodel these cages. Just listen how bland these names sound: Jubilee Vodka, Warrior's Vodka, Stolichnaya … When I see this, I want to puke. Vodka should be pure as tears, and all of its subspecies should have tearful names too. Like this: Maiden Bitter Tears Vodka – 5 rubles, 20 kopeks. Boys Don't Cry Vodka – 7 rubles. Homeless Cloudy Tear Vodka – 4.20. Widow Disconsolate's Tears Vodka – also not expensive: 4.40. Wretched Orphan's Tears Vodka – 6 rubles. Crocodile Tears Imported Vodka – 10 rubles. And so on... Only, before demolishing Russia, in front of astonished humanity, you need to enlighten her...[3]

Venedikt Erofeev, *Walpurgis Night, or "The Steps of the Commander"* (1985)

BALTIC TEA

Vodka with Cocaine

Жербунов открыл банку, взял со скатерти нож, зачерпнул им чудовищное количество порошка и быстро размешал его в водке. То же сделал и Барболин – сначала со своим стаканом, а потом с моим.

– Вот теперь и за мировую революцию не стыдно, – сказал он.

Видимо, на моем лице отразилось сомнение, потому что Жербунов ухмыльнулся и сказал:

– Это, браток, с «Авроры» пошло, от истоков. Называется «балтийский чай».

Они подняли стаканы, залпом выпили их содержимое, и мне ничего не оставалось, кроме как последовать их примеру. Почти сразу же горло у меня онемело.

Zherbunov opened the tin, picked up a knife from the table, scooped up a monstrous amount of the white powder and rapidly stirred it into his vodka. Barbolin did the same, first with his own glass, and then with mine.

"Now we can do the world revolution justice," he said.

My face must have betrayed an element of doubt, because Zherbunov chuckled and said: "This goes right back to the Aurora, brother, back to the very beginning. It's called 'Baltic tea.'"

They raised their glasses and drained them at a gulp, and there was nothing left for me but to follow their example. Almost immediately my throat became numb.[4]

Viktor Pelevin, *Buddha's Little Finger* (1996)

BIRCH VODKA

Beryozovka. Vodka in which birch buds or leaves have been steeped. Used as a cholagogue or a diuretic, it is smeared on wounds, sores, and eczema. Also good for stomach aches, colds, fever, and gastrointestinal problems.

– Предупрежу, помещение приличное, а водка, и не говори! Из Киева пешком пришла! Пил, многократно пил, знаю; а мне худого здесь и не смеют подать. Знают

Филиппа Филиппыча. Я ведь Филипп Филиппыч. Что? Гримасничаешь? Нет, ты дай мне договорить. Теперь четверть двенадцатого, сейчас смотрел; ну, так ровно в тридцать пять минут двенадцатого я тебя и отпущу. А тем временем муху задавим. Двадцать минут на старого друга, – идет?

– Если только двадцать минут, то идет; потому, душа моя, ей-богу, дело...

– А идет, так идет. Только вот что, два слова прежде всего: лицо у тебя нехорошее, точно сейчас тебе чем надосадили, правда?

– Правда.

– То-то я и угадал. Я, брат, теперь в физиономистику пустился, тоже занятие! Ну, так пойдем, поговорим. В двадцать минут, во-первых, успею вздушить адмирала Чаинского и пропущу березовки, потом зорной, потом померанцевой, потом parfait amour, а потом еще что-нибудь изобрету. Пью, брат! Только по праздникам перед обедней и хорош. А ты хоть и не пей. Мне просто тебя одного надо. А выпьешь, особенное благородство души докажешь. Пойдем! Сболтнем слова два, да и опять лет на десять врозь. Я, брат, тебе, Ваня, не пара!

– Ну, да ты не болтай, а поскорей пойдем. Двадцать минут твои, а там и пусти.

"I tell you it's a decent place, and the vodka – there's no word for it! It's come all the way from Kiev on foot. I've tasted it, many a time I've tasted it, I know; and they wouldn't dare offer me poor stuff here. They know Filip Filippich. I'm Filip Filippich, you know. Eh? You make a face? No, let me have my say. Now it's a quarter past eleven; I've just looked. Well, at twenty-five to twelve exactly I'll let you go. And in the meantime we'll drain the flowing bowl. Twenty minutes for an old friend. Is that right?"

"If it will really be twenty minutes, all right; because, my dear chap, I really am busy...."

"Well, that's a bargain. But I tell you what. Two words to begin with: you don't look cheerful ... as though you were put out about something, is that so?"

"Yes."

"I guessed it. I am going in for the study of physiognomy, you know; it's an occupation, too. So, come along, we'll have a talk. In twenty minutes I shall have time in the first place to sip the cup that cheers and to toss off a glass of birch wine, and another of orange bitters, then a *parfait amour*, and anything else I can think of. I drink, old man! I'm good for nothing except on a holiday before service. But don't you drink. I want you just as you are. Though if you did drink you'd betray a peculiar nobility of soul. Come along! We'll have a little chat and then part for another ten years. I'm not fit company for you, friend Vanya!"

"Don't chatter so much, but come along. You shall have twenty minutes and then let me go."[5]

Fyodor Dostoyevsky, *The Insulted and Injured* (1861)

BLACK VODKA

A relatively new vodka making a big splash in the Western markets, to which the extract of a rare root – the catechu (cachou) – has been added. This root accounts for the beverage's black color and also has a darkening effect on one's stools if consumed in excess. The best-known brand is Great Britain's Blavod.

CENTAURY VODKA

Под другим деревом кучер вечно перегонял в медном лембике водку на персиковые листья, на черемуховый цвет, на золототысячник, на вишневые косточки, и к концу этого процесса совершенно не был в состоянии поворотить языком, болтал такой вздор, что Пульхерия Ивановна ничего не могла понять, и отправлялся на кухню спать.

Under another tree the coachman was forever distilling in a copper retort vodka with peach leaves, or bird-cherry flowers or centaury or cherry stones, and at the end of the process was utterly unable to control his tongue, jabbered such nonsense that Pulkheriya Ivanovna could make nothing of it, and had to go away to sleep it off in the kitchen.[6]

Nikolai Gogol, *Mirgorod*: "Old-World Landowners" (1835)

COCKTAILS

"What'll it be, folks? Tears of Margarita, Hiroshima mon amour, Cherchez la femme Cuban-style, or C'est la via Hawaiian-style?"

"What's in a Cherchez la femme Cuban-style?" the young classicist asked.

"One-third Cuban rum, one-third vodka, one-third cherry syrup, and a slice of Cuban orange. A real man's drink, I can assure you. And you, ladies? Tears of Margarita? I thought so; I mean, what can be sweeter than the tears of a beautiful woman... one-third champagne, one-third cognac, one-third lemonade with extra carbonation, and a few drops of the purest, crystal-clear Russian vodka.[7]

Sana Valiulina, *Het Kruis* (2000)

FOURTEENTH-RATE FRENCH VODKA

The name given to inferior vodka that was served in state-run bars, alluding to the rankings of soldiers and civil servants in which the fourteenth rank was the lowest. Without the modifier, the term "French vodka" referred to cognac, which in Russia was also usually of mediocre quality.

GORBACHEVKA

Derisive name for vodka of poor quality. There is also the Gorbatschow brand, which became popular after Mikhail Sergeyevich became party leader in 1985, but that has been made in Germany since 1921 by Russian emigrants who had fled the October Revolution. These days, it is said that whoever drinks this vodka talks a lot of nonsense about *perestroika* and *glasnost.*

GRASOVKA

Also known as Zubrovka (or Żubrówka in Polish) and, to a lesser extent, as bison vodka. Famous for the aroma of buffalo grass that grows only in eastern Poland, where wild buffaloes still graze in the primeval forests of Białowieża. The Poles put a blade of buffalo grass in the bottle. Somerset Maugham described Zubrovka in 1944: "It smells of freshly mown hay and spring flowers, of thyme and lavender, and it's soft on the palate and so comfortable, it's like listening to music by moonlight."[8]

KHANZHA

Khanzha is Chinese vodka made of sorghum and foxtail millet. It is drunk warm.

Не менее интересна и китайская водка, которая называется ханжа. По-русский это название означает притворщицу или лицемера: но от китайской водки не заханжишь, а скорее полезешь на стену: вкус "ханжи" напоминает сиволдай, смешанный с рыбьим жиром и вскипяченный на стручковом перце.

Of no less interest is Chinese vodka, known as *khanzha.* In Russian this name suggests an impostor or hypocrite, but you won't be playing the hypocrite under the influence of Chinese vodka. You are more likely to be climbing the walls. The taste of *khanzha* is reminiscent of *sivolday* [raw or poorly purified vodka] mixed with fish oil and boiled with hot peppers.[9]

Vladimir Prygalovich-Skachenko, published in the journal *Strekoza* (1904)

У него [молодого вина] есть и еще одно удивительное свойство, какое присуще и китайской водке ханджин: если на другой день после попойки выпить поутру стакан простой холодной воды, то молодое вино опять начинает бродить, бурлить и играть в желудке и в крови, а сумасбродное его действие возобновляется с прежней силой.

[This young wine] has yet another amazing property that is also characteristic of Chinese vodka, *khandzhin*: if the morning after a drinking bout you consume a simple glass of cold water, the young wine again begins to ferment, to play inside the stomach and in the blood, and its tempestuous effect will be renewed with the same force as earlier.[10]

Alexander Kuprin, *The Laestrygonians* (1907-1911)

LENTEN VODKA

Postnaya vodka. Vodka that can also be drunk during fasting.

Алкоголя публика во время поста отнюдь не избегала. И сами церковные первоиерархи на сей счет особых запретов не давали. Мол, поскольку вино-водка – продукт "не животного происхождения", то пить "горячительное" вполне можно. Однако желательно "в меру". (Как будто на Руси когда-нибудь эту самую меру знали.)

The public by no means steered clear of alcohol during Lent. And the church fathers did not place particular prohibitions against it, feeling that insofar as liquor and vodka were not of "animal origin," drinking a little "warm-me-up" was perfectly permissible. But "moderation" was advised. (As if this moderation was ever a familiar concept in Rus.)[11]

Alexander Dobrovolsky, published in the newspaper *Moskovsky Komsomolets*

LOVAGE VODKA (LAVAS)

Он разлегся на диване, закурив одну из прекрасных сигар, которые я выписывал для себя из Петербурга, и ораторствовал. Перед диваном, на круглом столе, стояла закуска, херес и водка, и надо отдать справедливость Горехвастову, он не оставлял без внимания ни того, ни другого, ни третьего, и хотя хвалил преимущественно херес, но в действительности оказывал предпочтение зорной горькой водке. Рогожкин, с своей стороны, не столько пил, сколько, как выражаются, "потюкивал" водку.

– А скажите, пожалуйста, Николай Иваныч, – сказал мне Горехвастов, – откуда у вас берутся все эти милые вещи: копченые стерляди, индеечья ветчина, оленьи языки... и эта бесценная водка! – водка, от которой, я вам доложу, даже слеза прошибает! Да вы Сарданапал, Николай Иваныч!.. нет, вы просто Сарданапал!

Я сообщил ему, как умел, требуемые сведения.

– А что ни говорите, – продолжал он, – жизнь – отличная вещь, особливо если есть человек, который тебя понимает, с кем можешь сказать слово по душе!

He stretched out on the couch, lit one of the marvelous cigars I ordered for myself from Petersburg, and orated at length. In front of the couch stood a round table on which appetizers, sherry, and vodka had been placed, and I must give Gorekhvastov his due: he did not neglect any of them, and although he primarily praised the sherry, in actuality he showed a preference for the bitter root vodka. Rogozhin, for his part, did not so much drink as "chip away at it," so to speak.

"Tell me please, Nikolai Ivanych," Gorekhvastov said to me. "Where did you get all these lovely things: smoked sterlet, turkey ham, deer tongue…and this priceless vodka! The vodka – I'm telling you – even brings a tear to my eye! You're a real Sardanapalus, Nikolai Ivanych!...no, you really are simply a Sardanapalus!"

I did the best I could to provide him the information he had requested.

"Whatever you may say," he continued, "life is an excellent thing, especially when you have someone who understands you, with whom you can talk from the heart!"[12]

Mikhail Saltykov-Shchedrin, "Gorekhvastov" (1856)

MILK VODKA

The milk vodka (*kumyshka, arak, arkhi*) made by Turkic herdsmen dates back much earlier than Western liquors. They make it out of *prostokvasha* (condensed sour milk) that contains little alcohol. After the first distillation, the *arak* contains between six and ten percent alcohol. The Russians were not very interested in this, since *braga* or strong beer had an equivalent amount of alcohol. But the *arak* is often distilled repeatedly, as many as four times, which achieves an alcohol content of 20 to 35 percent.

In contrast, twice-distilled *kumyshka* (usually made from mare's milk) was originally much stronger than the traditional Russian drinks. It is entirely possible that the Russians had contact with distilled beverages before the arrival of the delegation from Kaffa in 1386.

Next we were offered fermented mares' milk, but this time I was more cautious, and after passing it across my firmly closed mouth, murmuring appreciation to please my host, I placed my glass on the ground and took the first opportunity of upsetting it.[13]

Alexandre Dumas, *Adventures in Tsarist Russia* (1860)

NEMTSOVKA

In Nizhny Novgorod, a vodka factory was constructed in a former nuclear reactor. The vodka is distilled in converted water filters. This vodka is known as Nemtsovka, after Boris Nemtsov, a good friend of the late president Boris Yeltsin, who was governor of the province at the time.

NEWLY BLESSED

Novoblagoslovennaya. After a period of prohibition, in 1924 vodka production and sales were again permitted in the Soviet Union. Initially, however, it could not contain more than thirty percent alcohol. One of the nicknames for the new vodka was *novoblagoslovennaya.*

In Mikhail Bulgakov's *The Heart of a Dog*, the doctor Filipp Filippovich operates on the dog Sharik, after which it begins to exhibit human traits. One of them is a thirst for vodka. It's a Russian dog, after all. One evening, Filipp Filippovich has visitors and allows his guests to sample a vodka made by the housekeeper.

– Доктор Борменталь, умоляю вас, оставьте икру в покое. И если хотите послушаться доброго совета: налейте не английской, а обыкновенной русской водки.

Красавец тяпнутый – он был уже без халата в приличном черном костюме – передернул широкими плечами, вежливо ухмыльнулся и налил прозрачной.

– Ново-благословенная? – Осведомился он.

– Бог с вами, голубчик, – отозвался хозяин. – Это спирт. Дарья Петровна сама отлично готовит водку.

– Не скажите, Филипп Филиппович, все утверждают, что очень приличная – 30 градусов.

– А водка должна быть в 40 градусов, а не в 30, это, во-первых, – а во-вторых, – бог их знает, чего они туда плеснули. Вы можете сказать – что им придет в голову? – Все, что угодно, – уверенно молвил тяпнутый.

– И я того же мнения, – добавил Филипп Филиппович и вышвырнул одним комком содержимое рюмки себе в горло, – ...Мм... Доктор Борменталь, умоляю вас, мгновенно эту штучку, и если вы скажете, что это... Я ваш кровный враг на всю жизнь.

"I beg you, Doctor Bormenthal, leave the caviar alone. And if you want a piece of good advice, don't touch the English vodka but drink the ordinary Russian stuff."

The handsome Bormenthal – who had taken off his white coat and was wearing a smart black suit – shrugged his broad shoulders, smirked politely and poured out a glass of clear vodka.

"Newly Blessed?" he enquired.

"Heavens no, my dear fellow," replied his host, "it's pure alcohol. Darya Petrovna makes the most excellent homemade vodka."

"But surely, Filipp Filippovich, everybody says that 30 percent vodka is quite good enough."

"Vodka should be at least 40 percent, not 30 – that's firstly," Filipp Filippovich interrupted him didactically, "and secondly – God knows what muck they make into vodka nowadays. What do you think they use?"

"Anything they like," said the other doctor firmly.

"I quite agree," said Filipp Filippovich and hurled the contents of his glass down his throat in one gulp. "Ah... m'm... Doctor Bormenthal – please drink that at once and if you ask me what it is, I'm your enemy for life."[14]

Mikhail Bulgakov, *The Heart of a Dog* (1925)

OIL VODKA

It is alleged that party leader Nikita Khrushchev ordered that grain should be saved and vodka should be made from petroleum and corn. The efforts were discontinued because the first samples smelled like gasoline.

PEPPER VODKA

Milovan Djilas was a member of the Yugoslav delegation that negotiated with the Soviets following World War II about what attitude the communist world should take toward America's Marshall Plan.

The evening could not go by without vulgarity, to be sure, Beria's. They forced me to drink a small glass of *pertsovka* – strong vodka with pepper (in Russian, *perets* means pepper, hence the name for this drink). Sniggering, Beria explained that this liquor had a bad effect on the sex glands, and he used the most vulgar expressions in so doing. Stalin gazed intently at me as Beria spoke, ready to burst into laughter, but he remained serious on noticing how sour I was.[15]

Milovan Djilas, *Conversations with Stalin* (1962)

There is a well-known brand made by Nemiroff in Ukraine featuring several red peppers in each bottle. Stolichnaya's Pertsovka flavor was popular in the West before it was discontinued. Recently the brand has come out with a jalapeno-flavored vodka.

PESACH VODKA

Peysakhovskaya vodka. Vodka made specially for Pesach, the Jewish Passover, and containing honey and milk thistle. There is also vodka that has been blessed by a rabbi: *koshernaya*. Israel and Poland in particular have many kosher vodkas. Russia's Putinka has also been awarded this mark of quality.

PRIEST'S VODKA

Popovskaya. High-quality vodka, worthy of a priest (*pop*).

Редкостная птица, про которую так далеко расхаживали добрые слухи, сейчас же показывалась, вследствие чего приезжий человек, имея в виду самому выпить с дорожки махонькую и попотчевать таковою же обязательно хозяина, посылал за полуштофом дворянской или поповской, так как важное дело осмотра такой удивительной птицы, какою слыл скворец пономаря Григорья, решительно исключала употребление простой водки, называемой в просторечии "сиволдаем"...

This rare bird, about which enchanting rumors were traveling far and wide, had just been sighted, prompting the visitor – who himself was inclined to take a little drink for the road and, of course, treat his host to the same – to send for a bottle of noble or priest's vodka, insofar as the important matter of examining a bird as wondrous as sexton Grigory's starlet was reputed to be most decidedly precluded the consumption of ordinary vodka, the sort the simple folk called *sivolday*.[16]

Alexander Levitov, "Rural Teaching" (1872)

QUININE VODKA

The teacher Turbin has not lived in the village for long when the local notables send him an invitation. He's not quite sure how to behave. And the drinks are a bit strange, too...

Но тут позвали к столу. Турбин настроил себя чинно и шел медленнее всех.

Хозяин особенно хвалил и предлагал селедку. Член суда, с видом знатока, попробовал ее и нашел "гениальной".

– Николай Нилыч! Водки? – сказал хозяин.

– Можно! – ответил Турбин.

– Хинной или простой?

– Хинной так хинной.

– Так будьте добры – распоряжайтесь сами.

– Не беспокойтесь, не беспокойтесь, пожалуйста!

Около стола теснились, оживленно переговаривались. С тарелкой в руках Турбин долго стоял в конце всех. Он не обедал и с особенным удовольствием выпил рюмку водки, погонялся вилкой за ускользающим грибком и ограничился на первое время пирогом. После первой же рюмки он почувствовал легкий хмель, очень захотел есть и долго, поглядывая искоса и стараясь не торопиться, ел одних омаров. Член суда уже дружески предлагал ему выпить с ним, и Турбин выпил еще рюмку простой водки. И водка и дружеский тон члена суда совсем размягчили его.

Первые минуты опьянения он чувствовал себя так же, как в самом начале вечера: как сквозь воду видел блеск огней и посуды, лица гостей, слышал говор и смех, чувствовал, что теряет способность управлять своими словами и движениями, хотя сознавал еще все ясно. Раскрасневшееся, потное лицо затягивало паутиной; в голове слегка шумело. Но все-таки он старался оглядываться смело и весело своими томными глазами. Ему было жарко. Когда же Линтварев (Турбину казалось, что и Линтварев запьянел) взял его под руку и повел к столу ужинать, он почувствовал себя очень большим и неловким.

– Не выпьем ли еще по одной? – сказал член суда.

– Блаженный Теодорит велит повторить, – отвечал Турбин со смехом.

– Repetito est mater studiorum. Не так ли? – промолвил с другого конца флотский офицер, явно подделываясь под семинарскую речь.

Турбин понял это и вызывающе поглядел на офицера. "Ну, и черт с тобой!" – подумал он и, усмехаясь, крикнул:

– Optime!

Член суда поспешил налить. Хозяйка как будто вскользь, но значительно поглядела на него. И это Турбин заметил, но никак не мог обидеться: так просто и тепло стало у него на душе.

– Да и последняя! – сказал он, выпивая и махая рукой, – Я и так мокрый, как мышь. ...

But then they were called to the table. Turbin assumed a dignified manner and walked slowest of all.

The host was particularly pleased with the herring and recommended that he try it.

One of the guests, a court justice, took a bite of the herring with the air of a connoisseur and declared it to be "genius."

"Nikolai Nilych – vodka?" asked the host.

"Don't mind if I do!" answered Turbin.

"Quinine or regular?"

"Quinine it is."

"Then, please, help yourself."

"Don't worry, don't worry, I beg of you!"

The table was surrounded by a flurry of lively conversation. Turbin waited his turn near the back, plate in hand. He had not had any dinner, so he drank a shot of vodka with particular relish and used his fork to chase after a slippery little mushroom. For the time being, he limited himself to one mince-pie. After the very first shot, he felt a slight intoxication and became extremely hungry; but he decided to eat only the lobster, throwing furtive side-glances as he tried not to hurry. The court justice was already inviting him to have another drink, so Turbin took a second shot of plain vodka. The combination of the vodka and the friendly air of the court justice loosened him up completely.

The first few minutes of inebriation made Turbin feel the same way that he had felt during the very start of the evening: it was as though he were looking through water at the glint of candles and tableware, at the faces of the guests, and hearing their chatter and laughter while feeling that he was losing all ability to control his own movements and words, despite still comprehending everything perfectly clearly. His flushed, sweaty face felt as taut as a web and his head filled with a soft din, but he tried to gaze cheerfully and confidently out of his languid eyes. He was growing very hot. When at last Lintarev – who, it seemed, was also drunk – grabbed him under the arm and led him toward the dinner table, he suddenly felt big and clumsy.

"Why don't we each have another one?" the court justice asked.

"Saint Theodore bids us to drink one more," Turbin replied with a laugh.

"Repetito est mater studiorum – isn't that right?" said a naval officer from the other side of the room, in an obvious attempt to sound like a seminarian.

Turbin picked up on the mockery and gave the officer a reproachful look.

"Oh, to hell with you!" he thought at last, and shouted with a smirk: "Optime!"

The court justice hurried to fill their glasses. The hostess gave Turbin a fleeting but meaningful glare. Turbin noticed this too, but he couldn't bring himself to feel angry: his soul had filled with such stillness and warmth.

"And one last one!" he yelled, waving his hand after he downed the first glass. "I'm already soused anyway..."[17]

Ivan Bunin, "Teacher" (1894)

RUFFE (YORSH)

Слепушкин служил на заводе подкурщиком; лицо у него было толстое, обрюзглое и темное, как у заправского алкоголика, голос тяжелый, фигура медведя. Пил Слепушкин водку, смешанную с пивом: такой состав назывался "ершом", по трудности проглотить его сразу. В гостях у Турбина он засиживался до трех часов ночи и часто просил писать к лавочнику записки, чтобы тот прислал "дюжинку".

Slepushkin worked as a distiller's assistant at the factory. He had a face that was bloated, saggy and dark, like that of a veteran alcoholic, a heavy voice and the build of a bear. Slepushkin liked to drink vodka mixed with beer. This combination was dubbed the "*yorsh*" on account of it being difficult to swallow on the first try. Stepushkin would linger at Turbin's until three o'clock in the morning and would often ask him to write a note to the shopkeeper with a request to send up "a little dozen."[18]

Ivan Bunin, "Teacher" (1894)

SAFFRON BRANDY

– К водке был подан балык, единственный! Да, не нашего балыка, которым, – при этом судья сделал языком и улыбнулся, причем нос понюхал свою всегдашнюю табакерку, – которым угощает наша бакалейная миргородская лавка. Селедки я не ел, потому что, как вы сами знаете, у меня от нее делается изжога под ложечкою. Но икры отведал; прекрасная икра! нечего сказать, отличная! Потом выпил я водки персиковой, настоянной на золототысячник. Была и шафранная; но шафранной, как вы сами знаете, я не употребляю. Оно, видите, очень хорошо: наперед, как говорят, раззадорить аппетит, а потом уже завершить...

"There was vodka, and dried sturgeon, excellent! Yes, not our sturgeon," there the judge smacked his tongue and smiled, upon which his nose took a sniff at its usual snuff box, "such as our Mirgorod shops sell us. I ate no herrings, for, as you know, they give me heartburn; but I tasted the caviar – very fine caviar, too! There's no doubt it, excellent! Then I drank some peach brandy, real gentian. There was saffron brandy also; but, as you know, I never take that. You see, it was all very good. In the first place, to whet your appetite, as they say, and then to satisfy it."[19]

Nikolai Gogol, *Mirgorod*: 'How the Two Ivans Quarrelled' (1835)

SEVEN-DAY VODKA

Semidennaya. Made from an extract of fly agaric, the aim being to prolong the high. The accompanying motto is "drunk on Monday, intoxicated until Sunday."

SNAKE VODKA

Zmiyovska. Vitali Vitaliev, a Russian who emigrated to England, traveled to Eastern Europe in the 1990s in search of the old drinking culture there. When he arrived in Poland, he found a young market economy where the craziest recipes were being concocted in order to compete with vodkas from the West.

"How about Zmiyovska, the snake vodka?" I enquired with hope. "Some people say they saw it but never tried it, others that they have tried it but never saw it, and so on. Does it exist?"

"We first thought of making Zmiyovska after a visit of Korean vodka-makers, who brought us a similar drink as a gift. We analyzed it and replaced the Korean snake with our Polish black adder. The brand became so popular that soon we ran out of snakes and had to wrap up its production."[20]

Vitali Vitaliev, *Borders Up! Eastern Europe through the Bottom af a Glass* (1999)

Recently, two vodkas have come onto the market that show similarities to Zmiyovska: Villa Lobos Vodka from Mexico, to which the producers have – extremely originally – added a worm, and the English Skorppio Vodka. You can guess what's in the bottom of that bottle.

STARKA

Vodka is not aged. An exception is *starka* (*stary* means "old"), although the wood in the barrel must not impart any flavor. *Starkas* are sweet because sweet fortified wines (e.g., Malaga) are added to it, and they are also savory because various plants are added. The aging process can go on for as long as ten years, which helps with the aromas. Formally speaking, of course, it is not vodka.

The only vodka available was a half-Polish rye vodka, Wodka Starka, which no one could have been happy about. [...] Did that rye vodka, with its dark brown tint caused by aging in wine casks, leave just as little stench on your breath as the colorless varieties? Ernst was not entirely convinced. He removed the tin cap from the bottle and took a whiff. An unpleasant, ripe odor, hard to identify, shot through his nose. He filled a shot glass and sampled it... He couldn't escape the thought that he was conducting an experiment, satisfying an almost scientific curiosity. He was in his laboratory.

In fact, there was a musty cardboard aftertaste of moist black rye bread, whereas vodka is usually characterized by the absence of taste. No, he was not convinced. After a few more test sips, he held his hand right in front of his mouth and breathed hard into his palm. Stench or not? Hard to say. But it was in him now. He accepted the risk.[21]

A.F.Th. van der Heijden, *Advocaat van de hanen* (1990)

STOLICHNAYA

Much about this famous vodka is shrouded in mystery. Even the year in which this "Capital" vodka was born is uncertain; in any event, it was right before the war, in 1939 or 1941. According to Stolichnaya's own sources, Viktor Svirida formulated its recipe in 1938. It is certain that Stolichnaya was served at the big banquet in the Kremlin celebrating the victory over Nazi Germany on May 24, 1945, and that it was initially vodka for the elite.

The label showing the famous and since demolished Hotel Moskva was designed by Andrei Johanson, who is said to have come up with it while sitting in a café across from the hotel (see also Chapter 8). Johanson was taking part in a competition to design the label. Why was that label chosen? One explanation is that the Soviets wanted to promote the hotel and name one of Russia's most well-known products after it. It is more likely that the Capital vodka needed a prestigious Moscow building from the Soviet era for its label. And at that point there were not that many of them in the city.

An early Stolichnaya label, from when vodka was R2.95

In 1975, Stolichnaya underwent its baptism in space. To celebrate the joint Apollo/Soyuz flight, cosmonaut Aleksei Leonov brought along a cylinder bearing a Stolichnaya label. Never mind that the cylinder contained borshch, not vodka.

SULI
Korean vodka made of barley or sorghum.

Утренняя еда продолжается около часа; манзы едят непомерно много и притом пьют из маленьких чашечек, величиной немного более наперстка, нагретую водку (сули), которую приготовляют сами из ячменя. [...] В то же время мне предложили самого лакомого напитка – нагретой водки с медом; я нарочно попробовал один глоток – мерзость ужасная.

The morning meal lasts approximately an hour; the Manzi are prodigious eaters and furthermore drink – from tiny cups, slightly larger than a thimble – heated vodka (*suli*) that they themselves make out of barley. [...] At the same time they offered me the greatest treat – warmed vodka with honey. I made a point of trying one swallow – a vile abomination.[22]

Nikolai Przhevalsky, *Travels in the Ussuri Region* (1870)

TRUE VODKA

Полно, полно выть, старуха! Козак не на то, чтобы возиться с бабами. Ты бы спрятала их обоих себе под юбку, да и сидела бы на них, как на куриных яйцах. Ступай, ступай, да ставь нам скорее на стол все, что есть. Не нужно пампушек, медовиков, маковников и других пундиков; тащи нам всего барана, козу давай, меды сорокалетние! Да горелки побольше, не с выдумками горелки, не с изюмом и всякими вытребеньками, а чистой, пенной горелки, чтобы играла и шипела как бешеная.

Enough, you've howled quite enough, old woman! A Cossack is not born to run around after women. You would like to hide them both under your petticoat, and sit upon them as a hen sits on eggs. Go, go, and let us have everything there is on the table in a trice. We don't want any dumplings, honey-cakes, poppy-cakes, or any other such messes: give us a whole sheep, a goat, mead forty years old, and as much corn-brandy [*gorelka*] as possible, not with raisins and all sorts of stuff, but plain scorching corn-brandy, which foams and hisses like mad.[23]

Nikolai Gogol, *Mirgorod*: "Taras Bulba" (1839-1842)

WHITE TOP

Between the 1950s and the 1970s, bottles were topped by a white metal cap. For lower-quality vodkas, the cap was made with dark red resin. This gave rise to nicknames such as white top, red top, red cap, etc. The cap was not attached very firmly, so one could open the bottle by slapping the bottom with the palm of your hand. Bottles with a "tab" on the metal cap were called "U Nu" ("Oops, what now," apparently a reference to the headgear worn by the first prime minister of Burma, U Nu); bottles without a tab were nicknamed seaman, sailor, or beret. Those with screw tops were called screw, gun, screw thread, and so on. During the 1920s, there were 0.25-centiliter bottles with a red cap called "Pioneers," a reference to the communist organization for children.

WORMWOOD VODKA

Polynnaya vodka enjoyed renown as a means for curbing the libido. In old texts, it is strongly recommended for "priests, monks, and nuns, because it frees them of physical desire and defilement."

YEROFEYICH

Herbal vodka from 1768. When Count Grigory Orlov, Catherine the Great's right-hand man, was declared incurably ill by all manner of physicians from Russia and abroad, the herbalist Yerofeyich was finally summoned to court. Known as a charlatan, Yerofeyich gave the count an herbal potion, and Orlov was miraculously cured. The original recipe of the still-famous herbal drink is lost to history, but it probably contained ginseng. The historical record does contain the herbalist's full name: Vasily Yerofeyich Voronov. These days, Yerofeyich contains mint, anise, and bitter orange. In a tale by the fabulist Ivan Krylov, it cures a giant.

Notes

Front Matter (pages 3-4)

1. Babel, Isaac. *The Collected Stories:* "How It Was Done in Odessa." Edited and translated by Walter Morison. London: Methuen and Co. LTD, 1957.

2. Терц, Абрам. «Любимов». Abram Tertz is the pen name of Andrei Donatovich Sinyavsky. *Lyubimov* is the original Russian title of the novel published in English as *The Makepeace Experiment.* Excerpt translated by Nora Seligman Favorov (2012).

3. Chekhov, Anton. *The Horse Stealers and Other Stories:* "In Trouble." Translated by Constance Garnett. New York: Willey Book Company, 1921.

Preface

1. Dostoyevsky, Fyodor. *Demons.* Translated with an introduction by David Magarshack. London: Penguin Books, 1971.

What is Vodka?

1. A Dutch encyclopedia, founded by the Dutch poet and clergyman Anthony Winkler Prins (1817-1908). Its final edition (1990-1993) is one of the most comprehensive works of its kind published in any country, containing more than 200,000 articles and references.

2. ATF Ruling 97-1. http://www.ttb.gov/rulings/97-1.htm

3. Blosfeld, G. A. «О пьянстве в судебно-медицинском и медико-политическим отношениях». Quoted in: Christian, David. *Living Water: Vodka and Russian Society on the Eve of Emancipation.* Oxford: Oxford University Press, 1990, p. 2.

4. Excerpt translated by Nora Seligman Favorov (2012).

Chapter 1: Vodka on Life's Journey

1. Gogol, Nikolai. *The Inspector-General.* Translated by Thomas Seltzer. Digireads.com, 2009. Translation slightly edited.

2. Segal, Boris Moiseevich. *Russian Drinking: Use and Abuse of Alcohol in Pre-Revolutionary Russia.* New Brunswick: Monographs of the Rutgers Center of Alcohol Studies, No. 15, Publication Division, Rutgers Center of Alcohol Studies, 1987.

3. Excerpt translated by Nora Seligman Favorov (2012).

4. Babel, Isaac. *The Collected Stories:* "Karl-Yankel." Edited and translated by Walter Morison. London: Methuen and Co. LTD, 1957.

5. Excerpt translated by Olga Kuzmina (2012).

6. Gogol, Nikolai. *The Complete Tales of Nikolai Gogol:* "St. John's Eve." Translated by Constance Garnett (translation edited and updated).

7. Pushkin, Alexander. *Tales of Belkin and Other Prose Writings:* "The History of the Village of Goryukhino." Translated by Ronald Wilks. London: Penguin Books, 1998.

8. Excerpt translated by Nora Seligman Favorov (2012).

9. Excerpt translated by Nora Seligman Favorov (2012).

10. Каледин, Сергей. «Смиренное кладбище». "The Humble Cemetery" was Sergei Kaledin's first short story. It was written in 1979 as his graduation project but was not published until 1987. Excerpt translated by Nora Seligman Favorov (2012).

11. Montefiore, Simon Sebag. *Stalin: The Court of the Red Tsar.* London: Weidenfeld and Nicholson, 2003.

12. Limonov, Edward. *It's Me, Eddie.* Translated by S. L. Campbell. New York: Random House, 1983.

13. Chekhov, Anton, *The Wife and Other Stories*: "Gooseberries." Translated by Constance Garnett. New York: The Macmillan Company, 1918.

14. Korb, Johann Georg. *Diary of an Austrian Secretary of Legation at the Court of Tsar Peter the Great.* Translated from the Latin and edited by Count Mac Donnell. London: Bradbury & Evans, 1863.

15. Olearius, Adam. *The Travels of Olearius in Seventeenth-Century Russia.* Palo Alto: Stanford University Press, 1967.

16. Christian, David. *Living Water: Vodka and Russian Society on the Eve of Emancipation.* Oxford: Oxford University Press, 1990.

17. Herzen, Alexander. *My Past and Thoughts.* Translated by Constance Garnett. Berkeley: University of California Press, 1973.

18. Солоухин, Владимир. «Олепинские пруды» [The Ponds of Olepino]. Excerpt translated by Nora Seligman Favorov (2012).

19. Excerpt translated by Nora Seligman Favorov (2012).

20. "Вот мы говорим, что народ пьет; не знаю, кто больше пьет, народ или наше сословие; народ хоть в праздник, но..." Tolstoy, Lev. *Anna Karenina.* Translated by Richard Pevear and Larissa Volokhonsky. New York: Viking Press, 2001.

21. Tolstoy, Lev. *The Complete Works of Count Tolstoy*, Volume 17. "The Holiday of Enlightenment of the 12th of January." Translated by Leo Wiener. Boston: Dana Estes & Company, 1904 (back then, lobsters were known as "sea crabs").

Chapter 2: Everybody Drinks

1. Excerpt translated by Olga Kuzmina (2012).

2. "Присутствует неотлучно на всех черных лестницах петербургских домов." Gogol, Nikolai. *The Collected Tales of Nikolai Gogol.* www.digireads.com, 2009, p. 67. Translation has been slightly edited.

3. Dostoyevsky, Fyodor. *Demons*. Translated by Constance Garnett, 1916.

4. Saltykov-Shchedrin, Mikhail. *Tchinovnicks: Sketches of Provincial Life*: "Times of Yore: The Underling's Story." Translated by Frederic Aston. London: L. Booth, 1861. (Edited and updated.)

5. Gorky, Maxim. *My Childhood*. Translated by Ronald Wilks. New York: The Century Co., 1915.

6. Chekhov, Anton. *Ivanov*. Translated by Ronald Hingley. London: Oxford University Press, 1967.

7. Chekhov, Anton. *The Seagull*. Translated by Laurence Senelick. New York: W.W. Norton & Company, 2006.

8. Excerpt translated by Nora Seligman Favorov (2012).

9. Dovlatov, Sergei. "Driving Gloves." Translated by Antonina W. Bouis. *The New Yorker*, May 8, 1989.

10. Broekmeyer, Marius. *Het verdriet van Rusland* [Russia's Sorrow]. Amsterdam: Jan Mets, 1995. Excerpts translated from the Dutch by David Stephenson (2012).

11. Engel, Barbara Alpern. *Women in Russia, 1700-2000* New York: Cambridge University Press, 2003.

12. Sholokhov, Mikhail. *The Fate of a Man*. Translated by Robert Daglish. Moscow: Progress, 1971.

13. Segal, Boris. *The Drunken Society: Alcohol Abuse and Alcoholism in the Soviet Union: A Comparative Study*. New York: Hippocrene Books, 1990, p. 95.

14. Крылов, Алексей. «Мои воспоминания» [My Memoirs]. Leningrad: Sudostroenie, 1979. Excerpt translated by Nora Seligman Favorov (2012).

15. This menu was published in the humorous magazine *Budilnik* (Alarm Clock) in March 1882.

16. Chekhov, Anton. *The Cook's Wedding and Other Stories*: "The Cook's Wedding." Translated by Constance Garnett. New York: The Macmillan Company, 1922.

17. Excerpt translated by Nora Seligman Favorov (2012).

18. Ерофеев, Венедикт. «Москва-Петушки». The Russian title "Moskva-Petushki," based on the two ends of a commuter train line, has been rendered "Moscow to the End of the Line" in English translation. Excerpt translated by Nora Seligman Favorov (2012).

19. Gogol, Nikolai. *Taras Bulba and Other Tales*: "Taras Bulba." Translated by C. J. Hogarth. London: J. M. Dent & Sons, 1918.

20. Ibid.

21. As the Russian text explains, "Allah birdi" and "saul bul" mean "God has given" and "to your health" respectively.

22. A strong Caucasian wine.

23. Tolstoy, Lev. *The Cossacks*. Translated by Peter Constantine. New York: The Modern Library, 2006.

24. Sholokhov, Mikhail. "The Birthmark." Translated by Robert Daglish. Moscow: Progress, 1966.

Chapter 3: Rituals

1. Pushkin, Alexander. *Tales of Belkin and Other Prose Writings*: "The Shot." Translated by Ronald Wilks. London: Penguin Books, 1998.

2. Фохт, Николай. «Похмельная книга» [The Hangover Book]. Excerpt translated by Nora Seligman Favorov (2012).

3. Excerpt translated by Nora Seligman Favorov (2012).

4. Маканин, Владимир. «Андеграунд, или Герой нашего времени» [The Underground, or a Hero of Our Time]. Excerpt translated by Nora Seligman Favorov (2012).

5. Woensel, Pieter van. *Russland beschouwt met betrekking tot l. zijn aardrijkskundige en natuurlijke ligging, grond en luchtsgesteldheid* [...] [Russia Considered With Regard to l. Its Geographic and Natural Position, Land, and Air Quality]. Haarlem: François Bohn, 1804. Excerpt translated from the Dutch by David Stephenson (2012).

6. Vitaliev, Vitali. *Borders Up!: Eastern Europe through the Bottom of a Glass*. New York: Scribner, 1999.

7. Erofeyev, Victor. "The Russian God." *The New Yorker*, December 16, 2002. Translated by Andrew Bromfield.

8. Amis, Kingsley. *Everyday Drinking*. London: Hutchinson & Co., 1983.

9. Excerpt translated by Nora Seligman Favorov (2012).

10. Агеев, Михаил. «Роман с кокаином» [Novel with Cocaine]. Published in English translation as Novel with Cocaine. Translated by Michael Henry Heim. Evanston, Ill.: Northwestern University Press, 1998.

11. Olearius, Adam. *The Travels of Olearius in Seventeenth-Century Russia*. Palo Alto: Stanford University Press 1967, p. 143.

12. Leskov, Nikolai, *The Cathedral Clergy: A Chronicle*. Translated by Margaret Winchell. Bloomington, Ind.: Slavica, 2010, pp. 271-272.

13. Dostoyevsky, Fyodor, *The Eternal Husband and Other Stories*. Translated by Richard Pevear and Larissa Volokhonsky. New York: Bantam Classics, 2000.

14. Segal, Boris. *The Drunken Society: Alcohol Abuse and Alcoholism in the Soviet Union: A Comparative Study*. New York: Hippocrene Books, 1990, p. 119.

15. Olearius, Adam. *The Travels of Olearius*, pp. 144-145.

16. Erofeev, Venedikt. *Moscow to the End of the Line*. Translated by H. William Tjalsma. Evanston, Ill.: Northwestern University Press, 1992.

17. Walton, C.S. *Ivan Petrov: Russia Through a Shot Glass*. New Orleans: Garrett County Press, 1999.

18. Bulgakov, Mikhail. *The Master and Margarita*. Translated by Mirra Ginsburg. New York: Grove Press, 1967.

19. Roosevelt, Elliott. *As He Saw It*. New York: Duell, Sloan and Pearce, 1946.

20. Scott, Mark, and Semyon Krasilshchik. *Yanks Meet Reds*. Santa Barbara: Capra Press, 1988.

21. Ibid.

22. Excerpt translated by Nora Seligman Favorov (2012).

23. Dovlatov, Sergei. *The Suitcase*. Translated by Antonina W. Bouis. Berkeley: Counterpoint, 2011.

24. Bunin, Ivan. *Ivan Bunin: Collected Stories*. Translated by Graham Hettlinger. Chicago: Ivan R. Dee, 2007.

25. Писемский, Алексей. «Тысяча душ» [One Thousand Souls]. Excerpt translated by Nora Seligman Favorov (2012).

26. Djilas, Milovan. *Conversations with Stalin*. Translated from the Serbian by Michael B. Petrovich. New York: Harcourt Brace & Company, 1962.

27. Солоухин, Владимир. «Поминки» [Funeral Banquet]. Excerpt translated by Nora Seligman Favorov (2012).

28. Erofeev, Venedikt. *Walpurgis Night, or "The Steps of the Commander."* Translated by Alexander Burry and Tatiana Tulchinsky (with minor edits). *Toronto Slavic Quarterly* online. http://bit.ly/walpurgisnight

Chapter 4: Vodka in Russia (988-1800)

1. Gogol, Nikolai, *Dead Souls*. Translated by Robert A. Maguire. London: Penguin Books, 2004.

2. Barbaro, Josafa, and Ambrogio Contarini. *Travels to Tana and Persia*. Translated from the Italian by William Thomas and S.A. Roy, Esq. New York: Burt Franklin, 1963.

3. Pouncy, Carolyn (editor and translator). *The "Domostroi": Rules for Russian Households in the Time of Ivan the Terrible*. Ithaca, N.Y.: Cornell University Press, 1994, pp. 82-83.

4. Tolstoy, Aleksei. *Peter the First*. Translated by Edith Bones and Emile Burns. London: Victor Gollancz Ltd., 1936, pp. 28-29.

5. Voinovich, Vladimir. *Moscow 2042*. Translated by Richard Lourie. New York: Harcourt, Brace, Jovanovich, 1990.

Chapter 5: Religion

1. Leskov, Nikolai. *The Cathedral Clergy: A Chronicle*. Translated by Margaret Winchell. Bloomington, Ind.: Slavica, 2010, pp. 271-272.

2. Прыжов И.В. «История кабаков в России в связи с историей русского народа». St. Petersburg: Avalon, 2009. http://lib.rus.ec/b/304160/read. Retranslated from the Dutch by David Stephenson (2012).

3. Olearius, Adam. *The Travels of Olearius in Seventeenth-Century Russia*. Palo Alto: Stanford University Press 1967, p. 146.

4. Christian, David. *Living Water: Vodka and Russian Society on the Eve of Emancipation*. Oxford: Oxford University Press, 1990, p. 81.

5. "Он встал и, шатаясь, подошел к огромному, жарко натопленному камельку, чтобы закурить у огня трубку. Он был слишком уж пьян, покачнулся и упал в огонь. Когда пришли домочадцы, от попа остались лишь ноги." Korolenko, Vladimir. *Makar's Dream and Other Stories*. Translated by Marian Fell. New York: Duffield and Company, 1916.

6. Помяловский, Николай. «Очерки бурсы» [Seminary Sketches]. Excerpt translated by Nora Seligman Favorov (2012).

7. Герцен, Александр. «Былое и думы» [My Past and Thoughts]. Excerpt translated by Nora Seligman Favorov (2012).

8. Segal, Boris Moiseevich. *Russian Drinking: Use and Abuse of Alcohol in Pre-Revolutionary Russia*. New Brunswick: Monographs of the Rutgers Center of Alcohol Studies, No. 15, Publication Division, Rutgers Center of Alcohol Studies, 1987.

9. Бунин, Иван. «Жизнь Арсеньева» [The Life of Arseniev]. Excerpt translated by Olga Kuzmina (2012).

10. Dumas, Alexandre. *Adventures in Tsarist Russia*. Translated from the French and edited by Alma Elizabeth Murch. London: P. Owen, 1960.

11. Olearius, Adam. *The Travels of Olearius*, pp. 142-143.

12. Leskov, Nikolai, *The Cathedral Clergy,* p. 154.

13. Шмелев, Иван. «Неупиваемая чаша» [The Inexhaustible Cup]. Excerpt translated by Nora Seligman Favorov (2012).

14. Olearius, Adam. *The Travels of Olearius*, pp. 162.

15. Чернышевский, Николай. «Откупная система» [The Concession System]. Excerpt translated by Nora Seligman Favorov (2012).

16. Letter dated June 20, 1834. "Прости, женка. Благодарю тебя за то, что ты обещаешься не кокетничать: хоть это я тебе и позволил, но все-таки лучше моим позволением тебе не пользоваться. Радуюсь, что

Сашку от груди отняли, давно бы пора. А что кормилица пьянствовала, отходя ко сну, то это еще не беда; мальчик привыкнет к вину и будет молодец, во Льва Сергеевича." http://bit.ly/pushkinletter. Excerpt translated by Nora Seligman Favorov (2012).

17. Montefiore, Simon Sebag. *Stalin: The Court of the Red Tsar*. London: Weidenfeld and Nicholson, 2003, p. 70.

18. Chekhov, Anton. *The Party and Other Stories*: "My Life." Translated by Ronald Wilks. Penguin Classics, 1995, p. 136.

19. "Инбиря 2 золотника, калгана 1 1/2 зол., острой водки 1 зол., семибратней крови 5 зол.; все смешав, настоять на штофе водки и принимать от катара натощак по рюмке." Excerpt translated by Nora Seligman Favorov (2012).

20. Quoted in Christian, David. *Living Water.*

21. Gogol, Nikolai. *The Complete Tales of Nikolai Gogol*: Mirgorod: "Old-World Landowners." Translated by Constance Garnett. Chicago: University of Chicago Press, 1985.

22. "Универсальное средство от всех болезней; придает силу и храбрость, возбуждает фантазию и валит с ног; с ее помощью можно видеть зеленого змия и даже белых слоников. [...] Пьют из рюмашечек, стаканчиков и из горлышка, ее – душат, губят, опрокидывают, но погубить не могут." Excerpt translated by Nora Seligman Favorov (2012).

23. Excerpt translated by Nora Seligman Favorov (2012).

24. Gogol, Nikolai. *Taras Bulba and Other Tales*: "Taras Bulba." Translated by C. J. Hogarth. London: J. M. Dent & Sons, 1918.

25. Dostoyevsky, Fyodor. *The Brothers Karamazov*. Translated by Constance Garnett. New York: Modern Library, 1977 (text lightly edited).

26. Merridale, Catherine. *Night of Stone*. London: Granta Books, 2000.

27. Excerpt translated by Nora Seligman Favorov (2012).

28. Chekhov, Anton. *Uncle Vanya*. Translated by Marian Fell. New York: Charles Scribner's & Sons, 1916.

Chapter 6: Why?

1. Tolstoy, Lev. *The First Distiller*. Translated by Louise and Aylmer Maude. London: Grant Richards, 1903.

2. Segal, Boris Moiseevich. *Russian Drinking: Use and Abuse of Alcohol in Pre-Revolutionary Russia*. New Brunswick: Monographs of the Rutgers Center of Alcohol Studies, No. 15, Publication Division, Rutgers Center of Alcohol Studies, 1987, p. 37.

3. Ibid, p. 42.

4. Dostoyevsky, Fyodor. *Crime and Punishment*. Translated by Constance Garnett. New York: Bantam Classic, 1981.

5. Herzen, Alexander. *My Past and Thoughts*. Translated by Constance Garnett. Berkeley: University of California Press, 1973.

6. Excerpt translated by Olga Kuzmina (2012).

7. Segal, Boris Moiseevich. *Russian Drinking*, p. 37.

8. Erofeev, Venedikt, *Moscow to the End of the Line*. Translated by H. William Tjalsma. Evanston, Ill.: Northwestern University Press, 1992.

9. Segal, Boris Moiseevich. *Russian Drinking,* preface.

10. Kaminer, Wladimir. *Die Reise nach Trulala* [The Voyage to Trulala]. Munich: Manhattan Verlag, 2002. Excerpt translated from the German by David Stephenson (2012).

11. Excerpt translated by Nora Seligman Favorov (2012).

12. Chekhov, Anton. *Selected Stories*: "At Sea – A Sailor's Story." Translated by Ann Dunnigan. New York: Signet Classic, 1960. Translation has been edited and updated.

13. Tolstoy, Lev. *The Living Corpse*. Translated by Louise and Aylmer Maude. 1900. (The Maudes titled the work *The Live Corpse*.) http://bit.ly/livingcorpse

14. "– А что вы пьете? – спросил он. – Панацею, – сказала Тамила и выпила еще. – Лекарство от всех зол и страданий, земных и небесных, от вечернего сомнения, от ночного врага." Tolstaya, Tatyana. *White Walls: Collected Stories*: "Date with a Bird." Translated by Antonina W. Bouis and Jamey Gambrell. New York: New York Review of Books, 2007.

15. Dostoyevsky, Fyodor. *The Brothers Karamazov*. Translated by Constance Garnett. New York: Modern Library, 1977.

16. Bunin, Ivan. *The Life of Arseniev: Youth*. Translated by Gleb Struve and Hamish Miles. Evanston, Ill.: Northwestern University Press, 1994.

17. Christian, David. *Living Water: Vodka and Russian Society on the Eve of Emancipation*. Oxford: Oxford University Press, 1990.

18. Horn, Walter. *Wodka & Kaviar* [Vodka & Caviar]. Frankfurt am Main: Lorch-Verlag, 1977. Excerpt translated from the German by David Stephenson (2012).

19. Чехов, Антон. «Драма на охоте» [A Hunting Drama]. Excerpt translated by Nora Seligman Favorov (2012).

20. Olearius, Adam. *The Travels of Olearius in Seventeenth-Century Russia*. Palo Alto: Stanford University Press, 1967, p. 46.

21. Ibid, p. 42.

22. Стогов, Илья. «Мачо не плачут» [Machos Don't Cry]. http://bit.ly/stogoffmacho. Excerpt translated by Nora Seligman Favorov (2012).

23. Engberts, Egbert. *Herinneringen aan Rusland* [Memories of Russia]. Amsterdam: Athenaeum-Polak & Van Gennep, 2004. Excerpt translated from the Dutch by David Stephenson (2012).

24. Чехов, Антон. «Беда» [The Mishap]. This story has also been published in English under the title of "The Accident." Excerpt translated by Nora Seligman Favorov (2012).

25. "Этот психоз такой же, как морфинизм, онанизм, нимфомания и проч." Chekhov, Anton. *A Life in Letters*. Translated by Rosamund Bartlett and Anthony Phillips. London: Penguin Books, 2004, p. 161.

26. Ibid, p. 163.

27. Fletcher, Giles, and Jerome Horsey. *Russia at the Close of the Sixteenth Century*. Edited by Edward Augustus Bond. Cambridge: Cambridge University Press, 2010.

28. Olearius, Adam. *The Travels of Olearius*, p. 144.

29. Olearius, Adam. *The Travels of Olearius*, p. 212

30. Turgenev, Ivan. *Sketches from a Hunter's Album*: "Singers." Translated by Richard Freeborn. London: Penguin Books, 1990.

31. Engberts, Egbert. *Herinneringen aan Rusland*.

32. Гиляровский, Владимир. «Козел и «чайка» [The Goat and *The Seagull*]. Gilyarovsky (1855-1935) is best known for his chronicle of life in prerevolutionary Moscow, *Moscow and Muscovites*, which was published in 1926 (English translation forthcoming from Russian Life Books, 2013). Excerpt translated by Nora Seligman Favorov (2012).

33. "Где напиться чаю?" [Where can you get a good drink of tea?] *Pravda*, 30 July 1940, no. 21- (8258), p. 2. Excerpt translated by Olga Kuzmina (2012).

34. Excerpt translated from the Dutch by David Stephenson.

Chapter 7: Vodka in Russia (1800-1917)

1. Chekhov, Anton. *The Schoolmaster and Other Stories*: "Drunk." Translated by Constance Garnett.

2. Gogol, Nikolai. *Dead Souls*. Translated by Robert A. Maguire. London: Penguin Books, 2004.

3. Герцен, Александр. «Колокол» [The Bell]. Excerpt translated by Nora Seligman Favorov (2012).

4. Leskov, Nikolai, *The Cathedral Clergy: A Chronicle*. Translated by Margaret Winchell. Bloomington, Ind.: Slavica, 2010, p. 200.

5. Chekhov, Anton. *The Cherry Orchard*. Translated by Julian West. New York: Scribner's, 1917.

6. Маршак, Самуил. «В начале жизни» [At Life's Beginning]. Excerpt translated by Nora Seligman Favorov (2012).

7. Segal, Boris Moiseevich. *Russian Drinking: Use and Abuse of Alcohol in Pre-Revolutionary Russia*. New Brunswick: Monographs of the Rutgers Center of Alcohol Studies, No. 15, Publication Division, Rutgers Center of Alcohol Studies, 1987, p. 96.

8. Бунин, Иван. «Деревня». Excerpt translated by Olga Kuzmina (2012).

9. Turgenev, Ivan. *Sketches from a Hunter's Album*: "Bailiff." Translated by Richard Freeborn. London: Hutchinson & Co., 1946.

10. Turgenev, Ivan. *Fathers and Children*. Translated by Richard Hare. London: Penguin Books, 1990.

11. Dostoyevsky, Fyodor. *The Village of Stepanchikovo*. Translated by Ignat Avsey. London: Penguin Books, 1983.

12. Tolstoy, Lev. *Anna Karenina*. Translated by Richard Pevear and Larissa Volokhonsky. New York: Viking Press, 2001.

13. Krukones, James H. "Satan's Blood, Tsar's Ink: Rural Alcoholism in an Official 'Publication for the People,' 1881-1917." *Russian History/Histoire Russe*, 18, No. 4 (1991), p. 435-56, The College of Humanities, University of Utah, citing *Selsky vestnik* (SPb), 27-10-1881, 73.

14. Shlapentokh, Dmitry. "Drunkenness and Anarchy in Russia: A Case of Political Culture." *Russian History/Histoire Russe*, 18, No. 4 (1991), 457-500, The College of Humanities, University of Utah, citing Vandervelde, Emile, *Three Aspects of the Russian Revolution*, G. Allen & Unwin Ltd., London, 1918.

15. Chekhov, Anton. *The Lady and the Little Dog and Other Stories*: "My Life." Translated by Ronald Wilks. New York: Penguin, 2002. p. 197.

Chapter 8: Vodka and Power

1. Djilas, Milovan. *Conversations with Stalin*. Translated from the Serbian by Michael B. Petrovich. New York: Harcourt Brace & Company, 1962.

2. Herberstein, Baron Sigismund von. *Notes Upon Russia*. Translated from the Latin and edited by Richard Henry Major. London: The Hakluyt Society, 1851.

3. Dumas, Alexandre. *Adventures in Tsarist Russia*. Translated from the French and edited by Alma Elizabeth Murch. London: P. Owen, 1960.

4. Montefiore, Simon Sebag. *Stalin: The Court of the Red Tsar*. London: Weidenfeld and Nicholson, 2003.

5. Ibid.

6. Ibid.

7. Ribbentrop, Joachim von. *Zwischen London und Moskau. Erinnerungen und letzte Aufzeichnungen* [Between London and Moscow: Remembrances and Final Notes]. Leoni am Starnberger See: Druffel-Verlag, 1954. Excerpt translated from the German by David Stephenson (2012).

8. Hilger, Gustav, and Alfred G. Meyer. *The Incompatible Allies*. New York: The Macmillan Company, 1953.

9. Голованов, Александр. «Дальняя бомбардировочная» [Long-Distance Bombing]. Moscow: Tsentropoligraf, 2007. Excerpt translated by Nora Seligman Favorov (2012).

10. Excerpt translated by Nora Seligman Favorov (2012).

11. Toonen, Elbert. *De glorietijd van de Russen onder L.I. Brezjnev* [The Russians' Glory Days Under L.I. Brezhnev]. Haarlem: Personalia, 2001. Excerpt translated from the Dutch by David Stephenson (2012).

12. Ibid.

13. Excerpt translated by Nora Seligman Favorov (2012)

14. Yeltsin, Boris. *Midnight Diaries*. Translated by Catherine A. Fitzpatrick. New York: PublicAffairs, 2000.

15. Ibid. (Translation has been slightly edited.)

16. Ibid.

17. Voinovich, Vladimir. *Monumental Propaganda.* Translated by Andrew Bromfield. New York: Knopf, 2006. (Translation has been slightly edited).

Chapter 9: Army and Prison

1. Gogol, Nikolai. *Taras Bulba and Other Tales*: "Taras Bulba." Translated by C. J. Hogarth. London: J. M. Dent & Sons, 1918.

2. Bruijn, Cornelis de. *Reizen over Moskovie* [Travels Into Muscovy]. Amsterdam: Terra Incognita, 1996. Excerpt translated from the Dutch by David Stephenson (2012).

3. Lermontov, Mikhail. *A Hero of Our Time*. Translated by Paul Foote. London: Penguin Books, 1966.

4. Tolstoy, Lev. *War and Peace*. Translated by Richard Pevear and Larissa Volokhonsky. New York: Borzoi Books, 2007.

5. Herlihy, Patricia, *The Alcoholic Empire. Vodka and Politics in the Late Imperial Russia*, New York: Oxford University Press, 2002. Page 54, citing the Moscow newspaper *Golos*.

6. "У огромной спиртовой бочки с выбитым дном стоял интендантский зауряд-чиновник и черпаком наливал спирту всем желающим. [...] Кругом толпились солдаты с запыленными, измученными лицами. Они подставляли папахи, чиновник доверху наливал папаху спиртом, и солдат отходил, бережно держа ее за края. Тут же он припадал губами к папахе, жадно, не отрываясь, пил, отряхивал папаху и весело шел дальше. [...] И во все последующие дни, во все время тяжелого отступления, армия наша кишела пьяными. Как будто праздновался какой-то радостный, всеобщий праздник." Segal, Boris Moiseevich. *Russian Drinking: Use and Abuse of Alcohol in Pre-Revolutionary Russia*. New Brunswick: Monographs of the Rutgers Center of Alcohol Studies, No. 15, Publication Division, Rutgers Center of Alcohol Studies, 1987.

7. Politovsky, Yevgeny Sigizmondovich. *From Libau to Tsushima*. Translated by F. R. Godfrey. New York: E. P. Dutton and Company, 1908.

8. Excerpt translated by Nora Seligman Favorov (2012).

9. Grossman, Vasily. *Life and Fate*. Translated by Robert Chandler. New York: Harper & Row, 1985.

10. Seekel, Friedrich. *Die Sowjetunion und ihr Wodka* [The Soviet Union and Its Vodka]. Berlin: Neuland-Verlagsgesellschaft, 1941. Excerpt translated from the German by David Stephenson (2012).

11. "Красноармейцы! Как долго желаете вы еще так страдать? Освобождайтесь от этих извергов! У нас вы будете обеспечены едой и питьем!" Excerpt translated by Nora Seligman Favorov (2012).

12. "Жены и матери командиров и бойцов Красной Армии! Не подлость ли напоить человека водкой, чтобы он, одурманенный ею, не отдавая себе ни в чем отчета, лез в бой, в котором ему предстоит верная смерть. Так поступает командование Красной Армии с вашими мужьями и сыновьями на передовых позициях. Прочтите приказ [...] и вы поймете весь ужас его действия. Внушите вашим близким, чтобы они не верили лжи сталинской пропаганды, чтобы не исполняли приказаний, толкающих их на неизбежную гибель. Мы уже близко! Мы несем вам освобождение от сталинского гнета, террора и лжи!" Excerpt translated by Nora Seligman Favorov (2012).

13. Broekmeyer, Marius. *Stalin, de Russen en hun oorlog* [Stalin, the Russians, and Their War]. Amsterdam: Jan Mets, 1999. Excerpt translated from the Dutch by David Stephenson (2012).

14. Grossman, Vasily. *A Writer at War: A Soviet Journalist with the Red Army, 1941-1945*. Edited and Translated by Antony Beevor and Luba Vinogradova. New York: Vintage Books, 2007.

15. Merridale, Catherine. *Ivan's War: Life and Death in the Red Army, 1939-1945*. New York: Metropolitan Books, 2006.

16. Sholokhov, Mikhail, *Fate of Man*. The Netherlands: Fedonia Books, 2003.

17. Rasputin, Valentin. *Live and Remember*. Translated by Antonina W. Bouis. Evanston, Ill.: Northwestern University Press, 1992.

18. «Дружба народов», Moscow: 1995. 272c, Nr. 3, Page. 14-16

19. Kaminer, Wladimir. *Militarmusik* [Military Music]. Munich: Wilhelm Goldmann Verlag, 2001. Excerpt translated from the German by David Stephenson (2012).

20. Segal, Boris. *The Drunken Society: Alcohol Abuse and Alcoholism in the Soviet Union: A Comparative Study*. New York: Hippocrene Books, 1990, citing Suvorov, 1984.

21. Dostoyevsky, Fyodor. *Memoirs from the House of the Dead*. Translated by Ronald Hingley. Oxford: Oxford University Press, 1965.

22. Excerpt translated by Nora Seligman Favorov (2012).

23. Hochschild, Adam. *The Unquiet Ghost: Russians Remember Stalin*. New York: Mariner Books, 2003.

24. Applebaum, Anne, *Gulag: A History*. New York: Doubleday, 2003.

25. Shalamov, Varlam. *Graphite*: "Committees for the Poor." Translated by John Glad. New York: W. W. Norton & Company, 1981.

26. Shalamov, Varlam. *Graphite*: "Descendant of a Decembrist." Translated by John Glad. New York: W. W. Norton & Company, 1981.

27. Solzhenitsyn, Aleksandr. *The Gulag Archipelago Three (1918-1956: An Experiment in Literary Investigation V-VII)*. Translated by Harry Willetts. New York: Harper & Row, 1978.

28. Ратушинская, Ирина. «Серый – цвет надежды» [Gray is the Color of Hope]. London: Overseas Publications Interchange, 1989. Excerpt translated by Nora Seligman Favorov (2012).

29. Solzhenitsyn, Aleksandr. *The Gulag Archipelago Two (1918-1956: An Experiment in Literary Investigation III-IV)*. Translated by Thomas P. Whitney. New York: Harper & Row, 1975.

30. Dostoyevsky, Fyodor. *Memoirs from the House of the Dead*. Translated by Ronald Hingley. Oxford: Oxford University Press, 1965.

31. "Спирт привозили и в жестянках, имевших форму сахарной головы, и в самоварах, и чуть ли не в поясах, а чаще всего просто в бочках и в обыкновенной посуде, так как мелкое начальство было подкуплено, а крупное смотрело сквозь пальцы." Excerpt translated by Nora Seligman Favorov (2012).

32. Solzhenitsyn, Aleksandr. *The Gulag Archipelago Two*.

33. Ратушинская, Ирина. «Серый – цвет надежды».

34. Walton, C. S. *Ivan Petrov: Russia through a Shot Glass*. New Orleans: Garrett County Press, 1999.

35. Turgenev, Ivan. *Knock, Knock, Knock and Other Stories*: "Lieutenant Yergunov's Story." Translated by Constance Garnett. New York: The Macmillan Company, 1921.

36. Игнатьев, Алексей. «Пятдесять лет в строю» [Fifty Years in the Ranks]. Moscow: Voenizdat, 1986. Excerpt translated by Nora Seligman Favorov (2012).

37. Астафьев, Виктор. «Веселый солдат» [The Jolly Soldier]. http://bit.ly/astafievsoldat Originally published in *Novy Mir*, Nos. 5, 6, 1998. Excerpt translated by Nora Seligman Favorov (2012).

38. Merridale, Catherine. *Ivan's War*.

Chapter 10: *Samogon* and Surrogates

1. Приставкин, Анатолий Игнатьевич. «Долина смертной тени», http://lib.rus.ec/b/143533. Excerpt translated by Nora Seligman Favorov (2012).

2. Чехов, Антон. «Сирена» [The Siren]. http://bit.ly/chekhovsiren Excerpt translated by Nora Seligman Favorov (2012).

3. Астафьев, Виктор. «Веселый солдат» [The Jolly Soldier]. http://bit.ly/astafievsoldat Originally published in *Novy Mir*, Nos. 5, 6, 1998. Excerpt translated by Nora Seligman Favorov (2012).

4. Excerpt translated by Olga Kuzmina (2012).

5. Voinovich, Vladimir. *The Life and Extraordinary Adventures of Private Ivan Chonkin*. Translated by Richard Lourie. New York: Farrar, Straus and Giroux, 1977.

6. Translated by Nora Seligman Favorov (2012). Demyan Bedny (real name Yefim Alekseevich Pridvorov) was a Soviet poet, satirist, and Bolshevik who lived from 1883-1945.

7. Ilf, Ilya and Evgeny Petrov. *The Little Golden Calf*. Translated by Anne O. Fisher. Montpelier, Vt.: Russian Life Books, 2009, pp. 110-111.

8. Segal, Boris. *The Drunken Society: Alcohol Abuse and Alcoholism in the Soviet Union: A Comparative Study*. New York: Hippocrene Books, 1990, p. 104.

9. Walton, C. S. *Ivan Petrov: Russia through a Shot Glass*. New Orleans: Garrett County Press, 1999.

10. Excerpt translated by Nora Seligman Favorov (2012).

11. Heijden, Reinout van der. *De vloek van Oesovo* [The Curse of Usovo]. Amsterdam/Antwerp: Contact, 1998. Excerpt translated from the Dutch by David Stephenson (2012).

12. Erofeev, Venedikt. *Moscow to the End of the Line.* Translated by H. William Tjalsma. Evanston, Ill.: Northwestern University Press, 1992.

13. Valiulina, Sana. *Het Kruis* [The Cross]. Amsterdam: De Geus, 2000. Excerpt translated from the Dutch by David Stephenson (2012).

14. Лейкин, Николай. «Первые шаги» [First Steps]. Excerpt translated by Nora Seligman Favorov (2012).

15. Erofeev, Venedikt. *Moscow to the End of the Line.*

16. Excerpt translated by Nora Seligman Favorov (2012).

17. Bunin, Ivan. *Night of Denial: Stories and Novellas:* "Zakhar Vorobyov." Translated by Robert Bowie. Evanston, Ill.: Northwestern University Press, 2006.

18. Nabokov, Vladimir. *Mary.* Translated by Michael Glenny in collaboration with the author. New York: McGraw-Hill Book Co., 1970.

19. Горин, Григорий. «О семейном бюджете» ["On the Family Budget"]. http://bit.ly/gorinbudget Excerpt translated by Nora Seligman Favorov (2012).

20. Gogol, Nikolai. *Plays and Petersburg Tales:* "The Portrait." Translated by Christopher English. New York: Oxford University Press, 1995.

21. Chekhov, Anton. *Stories of Russian Life:* "Murder Will Out." Translated by Marian Fell. New York: Charles Scribner's Sons, 1914.

Chapter 11: Vodka in Russia (1917-Present)

1. Tertz, Abram. *The Makepeace Experiment.* Translated and with an introduction by Manya Harari. New York: Pantheon Books, 1965.

2. Bunin, Ivan. *Cursed Days, Diary of a Revolution*. Translated by Thomas Gaiton Marullo. Chicago: Ivan Dee Publisher, 1998, p. 185.

3. Segal, Boris. *The Drunken Society: Alcohol Abuse and Alcoholism in the Soviet Union: A Comparative Study*. New York: Hippocrene Books, 1990.

4. Паустовский, Константин Георгиевич. «Начало неведомого века (Повесть о жизни-3)» [The Story of a Life: "Beginning of an Unknown Age"]. Excerpt translated by Nora Seligman Favorov (2012).

5. Segal, Boris. *The Drunken Society.*

6. Excerpt translated by Nora Seligman Favorov (2012).

7. Pilnyak, Boris, *The Naked Year.* Translated by Alexander R. Tulloch. Ann Arbor, Mich.: Ardis, 1975.

8. "К сожалению, украинская деревня осталась такой же, какой ее описывал Гоголь – невежественной, антисемитской, безграмотной... Среди комиссаров взяточничество, поборы, пьянство, нарушение на каждом шагу всех основ права... Советские работники выигрывают и проигрывают в карты тысячи, пьянством поддерживают винокурение..." Excerpt translated by Nora Seligman Favorov (2012).

9. Паустовский, Константин Георгиевич. «Время больших ожиданий» [A Time of Great Expectations]. Excerpt translated by Nora Seligman Favorov (2012).

10. Grossman, Vasily. *Life and Fate.* Translated by Robert Chandler. New York: Harper & Row, 1985.

11. Hochschild, Adam. *The Unquiet Ghost: Russians Remember Stalin.* New York: Mariner Books, 2003.

12. Broekmeyer, Marius. *Het verdriet van Rusland* [Russia's Sorrow]. Amsterdam: Jan Mets, 1995. Excerpt translated from the Dutch by David Stephenson (2012).

13. Заиграев, Г.Г. «Конкретное социологическое исследование пережитков прошлого» [A Specific Sociological Study of the Vestiges of the Past]. Moscow: 1966.

14. Рожнов, В. Е. «По следам зеленого змия» [In the Wake of the Green Serpent]. Moscow: Voenizdat, 1969, p. 160.

15. Sorokin, Vladimir. *The Queue.* Translated by Sally Laird. New York: Readers International Inc., 1988.

16. Neidhart, Christoph. *Russia's Carnival: The Smells, Sights, and Sounds of Transition.* Boston: Rowman & Littlefield Publishers, 2003.

17. Voinovich, Vladimir. *The Life and Extraordinary Adventures of Private Ivan Chonkin.* Translated by Richard Lourie. New York: Farrar, Straus and Giroux, 1977.

18. Tolstoy, Lev. *The Death of Ivan Ilyich and Other Stories:* "Three Deaths." Translated by Anthony Briggs. London: Penguin Classics, 2008.

19. Горин, Григорий. «О семейном бюджете» [On the Family Budget]. http://bit.ly/gorinbudget Excerpt translated by Nora Seligman Favorov (2012).

20. Broekmeyer, Marius. *Het verdriet van Rusland.*

21. Heijden, Reinout van der. *De vloek van Oesovo* [The Curse of Usovo]. Amsterdam/Antwerp: Contact, 1998. Excerpt translated from the Dutch by David Stephenson (2012).

22. Ibid.

Chapter 12: Temperance

1. Erofeyev, Victor. "The Russian God." *The New Yorker*, December 16, 2002. Translated by Andrew Bromfield.

2. Leskov, Nikolai, *The Cathedral Clergy: A Chronicle.* Translated by Margaret Winchell. Bloomington, Ind.: Slavica, 2010, p. 64.

3. Segal, Boris. *The Drunken Society: Alcohol Abuse and Alcoholism in the Soviet Union: A Comparative Study.* New York: Hippocrene Books, 1990, p. 329, citing M. D. Chelyshev, «Речи М. Д. Челышова. произнесенные в Третьей Государетвенной Думе о необходимости борьбы с пьянством и по другим вопросам». St. Petersburg, 1912.

4. Ibid., citing Бородин Д.Н. «Кабак и его прошлое». St. Petersburg: Vilenchik, 1910.

5. Gorky, Maxim. *The Lower Depths.* Translated by Jenny Covan. New York: Brentanos Publishers, 1922.

6. Engberts, Egbert. *Herinneringen aan Rusland* [Memories of Russia]. Amsterdam: Athenaeum-Polak & Van Gennep, 2004. Excerpt translated from the Dutch by David Stephenson (2012).

7. Tolstoy, Lev. *A Confession and What I Believe.* Translated by Louise and Aylmer Maude. London/New York: Oxford University Press, 1921.

8. Segal, Boris. *The Drunken Society*, p. 101.

9. "Грех, предаваясь которому невозможна борьба ни с каким из грехов, есть опьянение, какое бы то ни было: опьяненный человек не поборется ни с праздностью, ни с похотью, ни с блудом, ни с властолюбием. И потому для того, чтобы бороться с другими грехами, человек должен прежде всего освободиться от греха опьянения." Tolstoy, Lev, *Христианское учение.* (from Полное собрание сочинений в 90 томах, академическое юбилейное издание, том 39, Государственное Издательство Художественной Литературы, Moscow, 1956. Excerpt translated by Nora Seligman Favorov (2012).

10. Tolstoy, Lev. *The Complete Works of Count Tolstoy: Miscellaneous Letters and Essays.* "God or Mammon?" Translated by Leo Wiener. London: J.M. Dent & Co., 1905.

11. Bunin, Ivan. "Tolstoy." Memories and Portraits. Translated by Vera Traill and Robin Chancellor. New York: Doubleday & Company, Inc: 1951, p. 28.

12. Bunin, Ivan. *The Liberation of Tolstoy: A Tale of Two Writers.* Translated by Thomas Gaiton Marullo and Vladimir T. Khmelkov. Evanston, Ill.: Northwestern University Press, 2001.

13. Зощенко, Михаил Михайлович. «Человека жалко» http://bit.ly/zoshchenkozhalko Excerpt translated by Nora Seligman Favorov (2012).

14. Amis, Kingsley. *Everyday Drinking.* London: Hutchinson & Co., 1983.

15. Oltmans, Willem L. *USSR 1976-1990.* Baarn: In den Toren, 1976. Excerpt translated from the Dutch by David Stephenson (2012).

16. Walton, C. S. *Ivan Petrov: Russia through a Shot Glass.* New Orleans: Garrett County Press, 1999.

Interregnum: What to Do Before, During, and After a Drinking Bout

1. Еж, Владимир. «Записки самогонщика» [Notes of a Moonshiner]. Rostov-na-Donu: Feniks, 2001. Excerpt translated by Nora Seligman Favorov (2012).

2. Bulgakov, Mikhail. *The White Guard.* Translated by Marian Schwartz. New Haven, Conn.: Yale University Press, 2008.

3. Thubron, Colin. The Lost Heart of Asia. New York: HarperCollins Publishers, 1994.

4. Стогов, Илья. «Мачо не плачут» [Machos Don't Cry]. http://bit.ly/stogoffmacho. Excerpt translated by Nora Seligman Favorov (2012).

5. Tolstoy, Lev. *Anna Karenina.* Translated by Richard Pevear and Larissa Volokhonsky. New York: Viking Press, 2001.

6. Olearius, Adam. *The Travels of Olearius in Seventeenth-Century Russia.* Palo Alto: Stanford University Press, 1967, p. 156.

7. Чехов, Антон. «Комик» ["The Comedian"]. http://bit.ly/chekhovcomic Excerpt translated by Nora Seligman Favorov (2012).

8. Tertz, Abram. *The Makepeace Experiment.* Translated from the Russian and with an introduction by Manya Harari. New York: Pantheon Books, 1965.

Chapter 13: What to Eat?

1. Saltykov-Shchedrin, Mikhail. *The Golovlyov Family.* Translated by Natalie Duddington. New York: New York Review Books, 2001.

2. Chekhov, Anton. *The Schoolmaster and Other Stories:* "Drunk." Translated by Constance Garnett. MobileReference.

3. Engberts, Egbert. *Herinneringen aan Rusland* [Memories of Russia]. Amsterdam: Athenaeum-Polak & Van Gennep, 2004. Excerpt translated from the Dutch by David Stephenson (2012).

4. Erofeev Venedikt. *Moscow to the End of the Line.* Translated by H. William Tjalsma. Evanston, Ill.: Northwestern University Press, 1992.

5. Molokhovets, Jelena. *Een geschenk voor de jonge huisvrouw. Het klassieke Russische kookboek* [A Gift to Young Housewives: The Classic Russian Cookbook]. Amsterdam: Jan Mets, 1995/1996. Excerpt translated from the Dutch by David Stephenson (2012).

6. Шмелев, Иван Сергеевич. «Лето Господне» [Year of the Lord]. http://bit.ly/shmelevleto Excerpt translated by Nora Seligman Favorov (2012).

7. Chekhov, Anton. *Five Plays:* "Ivanov." Translated by Ronald Hingley. Oxford: Oxford University Press, 1998.

8. Steinbeck, John. *A Russian Journal.* New York: Viking Press, 1948.

9. Чехов, Антон. «Сирена» ["The Siren"]. http://bit.ly/chekhovsiren Excerpt translated by Nora Seligman Favorov (2012).

10. Dostoyevsky, Fyodor. *The Insulted and Injured.* Translated by Constance Garnett. New York: The Macmillan Co., 1914.

11. Энгельгардт, Александр Николаевич. «Из деревни» [From the Countryside]. Excerpt translated by Nora Seligman Favorov (2012).

Chapter 14: Making Vodka

1. Amis, Kingsley. *Everyday Drinking.* London: Hutchison & Co., 1983, page 23.

2. Буковский, Владимир. «И возвращается ветер» (1978) Published in English by Viking, 1979, as *To Build a Castle: My Life as a Dissenter.* Excerpt translated by Paul E. Richardson (2012).

3. Gogol, Nikolai. *The Complete Tales of Nikolai Gogol:* "A May Night." Translated by Constance Garnett, edited by Leonard J. Kent. Chicago: University of Chicago Press, 1985. Vol I, page 61-2.

4. Amis, Kingsley. *Everyday Drinking.*

5. Erofeev, Venedikt. *Walpurgis Night, or "The Steps of the Commander."* Translated by Alexander Burry and Tatiana Tulchinsky (with minor edits). Toronto Slavic Quarterly online. http://bit.ly/walpurgisnight

Chapter 15: Varieties of Vodka

1. Салтыков-Щедрин, Михаил Евграфович. «Скука» [Boredom]. Excerpt translated by Nora Seligman Favorov (2012).

2. Herzen, Alexander. *My Past and Thoughts*. Excerpt translated by Nora Seligman Favorov (2012).

3. Erofeev, Venedikt. *Walpurgis Night, or "The Steps of the Commander."* Translated by Alexander Burry and Tatiana Tulchinsky. Toronto Slavic Quarterly online. http://bit.ly/walpurgisnight

4. Pelevin, Viktor. *Buddha's Little Finger*. Translated by Andrew Bromfield. New York: Penguin Books, 2001.

5. Dostoyevsky, Fyodor. *The Insulted and Injured*. Translated by Constance Garnett. New York: The Macmillan Co., 1914.

6. Gogol, Nikolai. *The Complete Tales of Nikolai Gogol: Mirgorod*: "Old-World Landowners." Translated by Constance Garnett. Chicago: University of Chicago Press, 1985.

7. Valiulina, Sana. *Het Kruis* [The Cross]. Amsterdam: De Geus, 2000. Excerpt translated from the Dutch by David Stephenson (2012).

8. Excerpt translated by Nora Seligman Favorov (2012).

9. Excerpt translated by Nora Seligman Favorov (2012).

10. Excerpt translated by Nora Seligman Favorov (2012).

11. Maugham, W. Somerset. *The Razor's Edge*. New York: Doubleday, Doran & Company, 1944.

12. Sardanapalus was an Assyrian king known for decadence. Excerpt translated by Nora Seligman Favorov (2012).

13. Dumas, Alexandre. *Adventures in Tsarist Russia*. Translated from the French and edited by Alma Elizabeth Murch. London: P. Owen, 1960.

14. Bulgakov, Mikhail. *The Heart of a Dog*. Translated by Mirra Ginsburg. New York: Grove Press, 1968. (Translation has been slightly edited.)

15. Djilas, Milovan. *Conversations with Stalin*. Translated from the Serbian by Michael B. Petrovich. New York: Harcourt Brace & Company, 1962.

16. Левитов, Александр Иванович. «Сельское учение» [Rural Teaching]. Excerpt translated by Nora Seligman Favorov (2012).

17. Бунин, Иван. «Учитель» [The Teacher]. Excerpt translated by Olga Kuzmina (2012).

18. Ibid. The *yorsh,* or ruffe, is a small species of fish related to the perch that lives in parts of Eurasia and has a large, spiny fin that makes it unpalateable to predators.

19. Gogol, Nikolai. *Taras Bulba and Other Tales*: "How the Two Ivans Quarrelled." Translated by C. J. Hogarth. London: J. M. Dent & Sons, 1918. Excerpt translated by Nora Seligman Favorov (2012).

20. Vitaliev, Vitali. *Borders Up!: Eastern Europe through the Bottom of a Glass*. New York: Scribner, 1999.

21. Heijden, A.F.Th. van der. *Advocaat van de hanen* [Lawyer of the Cocks]. Amsterdam: Querido, 1992. Excerpt translated from the Dutch by David Stephenson (2012).

22. Пржевальский, Николай Михайлович «Путешествие в Уссурийский край» [Travels in the Ussuri Region]. Excerpt translated by Nora Seligman Favorov (2012).

23. Gogol, Nikolai. *Taras Bulba and Other Tales*: "Taras Bulba." Translated by C. J. Hogarth. London: J. M. Dent & Sons, 1918.

Index

AUTHOR'S ACKNOWLEDGMENTS

Many people assisted me in the writing of this book. Some read sections of it, others gave me tips, and others still brought me bottles from distant locations. Still others listened patiently to my complaining. I would like to acknowledge the following people by name: Otto Boele, Esther Brandt, Vittorio Busato, Paul Enkelaar, Sigrid van Essel, Andrei Goncharov, Wilhelmina E. Jansen Fonds, Sergei Karnet, Jan Mets, Aleksandr Nikishin, Sjeng Scheijen, Katherine Sims, Marcel Verweij, Gert Jan de Vries, Greetje van der Werf and Harry van der Woud.

I realize that the translators of *Davai* had to plumb many unfathomable depths when working on *Davai*, because there are so many different writers, spanning centuries and genres. So my heartfelt compliments to the translators of the Russian fragments, Nora Seligman Favorov and Olga Kuzmina. Good work! The same applies to David Stephenson, with whom I enjoyed working throughout the process. I many times imagined him sweating and cursing at his computer while translating fragments from old Dutch or digging up an obscure Russian source. Yet I also know that he saw those moments as a challenge! Thanks David.

And, obviously, my thanks to Paul Richardson, who showed courage for publishing this book in the United States. Although we have never met face to face, it seems to me that we have known each other for a long time, and I look forward to continuing to work together!

TRANSLATOR'S ACKNOWLEDGMENTS

Preparing a U.S. edition of Edwin Trommelen's *Davaj! De Russen en hun wodka* proved to be more complicated than simply translating the original Dutch text into English. The presence of dozens of Russian literary quotes meant that many hours had to be spent on related research and editing (locating and attributing existing translations, preparing new translations, locating and proofing the Russian source texts). Because of the limits to my Russian skills, I relied on the contributions of several persons in addressing this key aspect of the project. I am grateful to Nora Seligman Favorov, who furnished new translations from Russian and also functioned as editor extraordinaire; to Olga Kuzmina, for her translation and proofreading services; and to the book's publisher, Paul Richardson. I am especially grateful to the author, Edwin Trommelen, not only for writing such a fascinating and engaging work, but also for his gracious assistance and advice at various steps of the process. I also thank Rob Croese, Ilja Isani, and Marianne van der Lubbe-van Gogh for their generous help with the niceties of the Dutch language. Finally, I am grateful to Steve Jones, Boris Silversteyn, and Jim Walker for their perspectives on contemporary Russia.

ABOUT THE AUTHOR

After high school, Edwin Trommelen began studying Russian language and literature, first at the University of Utrecht and later at the University of Amsterdam. In 1986, he spent a half a year in Moscow as part of his studies, before completing his studies in Amsterdam, with minors in Czech and Film Studies. After college, he worked at various jobs: as an intpreter and translator, as a tour guide, and as an editor for the Dutch television company AVRO. In 1989, he translated the novella *Street of Freedom* and poems by Nizametdin Akhmetov into Dutch.

Russia is a common thread in most all of Trommelen's work. In the late 1990s, he decided to concentrate on documentaries, with a good part of his work focused on Russia or the former Soviet Union. He worked on John Appel's *Ilya Repin, Painter of the Russian Soul,* Marjoleine Boonstra's *Bela Bela – What Keeps Mankind Alive*, and Jan Bosdriesz's *Black Eyes.* As director, his credits include *Back to the Camp* (about an Amsterdam woman who was imprisoned in Russia) and *Behind the Black Mountains* (about the Amsterdam Jewish boy Anton Devier, who traveled to Russia with Peter the Great and became the first Police Chief of St. Petersburg).

After publishing *Davai! The Russians and Their Vodka* in Dutch, Trommelen began work on a book about Russia's BAM (Baikal Amur Magistral) railroad. It is a travelogue about life along the railroad that will incorporate accounts by travelers in Russia from earlier centuries. He is also working on a documentary about Ilf and Petrov and another about the nearly extinct Tundra-Yukagir people in Yakutia (Sakha).

ABOUT THE TRANSLATOR

David Stephenson is an independent translator in Durham, North Carolina. His previous book-length works include *An Interview with Desi Bouterse* by Willem Oltmans (Dutch to English) and *The Last Days of the Socialist Federal Republic of Yugoslavia* by Borisav Jović (Serbian to English). He studied at the Heinrich Heine University in Düsseldorf, Germany, is a graduate of the University of North Carolina at Chapel Hill, and is certified by the American Translators Association for translation from Dutch, German, and Croatian into English.